Talking
with
Harry

Books by
Ralph E. Weber

Notre Dame's John Zahm (1961)

Admission to College (1964)

As Others See Us (1972)

Voices of Revolution (1972)

*United States Diplomatic Codes and Ciphers,
1775–1938* (1979)

From the Foreign Press (1980)

*American Dissent from Thomas Jefferson
to Caesar Chavez* (1981)

Awakening of a Sleeping Giant (1981)

The Final Memoranda (1988)

Masked Dispatches (1993)

Spymasters (1999)

Talking
with
Harry

Candid

Conversations

with

President

HARRY S.

TRUMAN

Edited and with Commentary by

RALPH E. WEBER

A Scholarly Resources Inc. Imprint
Wilmington, Delaware

© 2001 by Scholarly Resources Inc.
All rights reserved
First published 2001
Printed and bound in the United States of America

Scholarly Resources Inc.
104 Greenhill Avenue
Wilmington, DE 19805-1897
www.scholarly.com

Library of Congress Cataloging-in-Publication Data

Truman, Harry S., 1884–1972.
    Talking with Harry : candid conversations with President Harry S.
    Truman / edited and with commentary by Ralph E. Weber.
        p.   cm.
    Includes bibliographical references (p.   ) and index.
    ISBN 0-8420-2920-6 (alk. paper) — ISBN 0-8420-2921-4 (pbk. :
alk. paper)
    1. Truman, Harry S., 1884–1972—Interviews. 2. Presidents—
United States—Interviews. 3. United States—Politics and government—1945–1953. 4. United States—Politics and government—
1953–1961. 5. Truman, Harry S., 1884–1972—Social and political
views. I. Weber, Ralph Edward. II. Title.

E814 .A3 2001
973.918'092–dc21
[B]   00-066110

For Rosemarie

About the Editor

RALPH E. WEBER was born in St. Cloud, Minnesota, and educated there before joining the U.S. Naval Air Corps in World War II. After graduate studies and teaching at the University of Notre Dame, he joined the faculty of Marquette University in 1954. As professor of history, he teaches several courses on American foreign intelligence as well as American foreign relations. Several of his earlier books focus on American codes and ciphers in addition to military and central intelligence history. He and his wife, Rosemarie, who were blessed with nine children, live in Brookfield, Wisconsin.

The doings of men, their prayers, fears,
Wrath, pleasure, delight, and
Recreations, are the subject of this book

—Juvenal, *Satires,* I.I.85

Contents

Acknowledgments   *xi*

Editor's Note   *xv*

Prologue: The Atom Bomb   *1*

Session One   *13*

Session Two   *21*

Session Three   *31*

Session Four   *43*

Session Five   *57*

Session Six   *65*

Session Seven   *85*

Session Eight   *103*

Session Nine   *117*

Session Ten   *127*

Session Eleven   *141*

Session Twelve   *151*

Session Thirteen   *163*

Photographs follow page 183

Session Fourteen   *193*

Session Fifteen   *217*

Session Sixteen   *239*

Session Seventeen   *265*

Session Eighteen   *283*

Session Nineteen   *305*

Session Twenty   *323*

Biographical Directory   *341*

Bibliography   *367*

Index   *373*

Acknowledgments

THIS BOOK BEGAN on a beautiful spring morning in late April 1996 at the Truman Library in Independence, Missouri, when a gracious archival staff introduced me to books, multiple finding aids, oral histories, and correspondence in a sunny research room. This was the third of my visits to six Presidential libraries and the National Archives, I and II, scheduled for my sabbatical year from the History Department at Marquette University. My project covered the relationships between directors of the Central Intelligence Agency since its founding in 1947 and the Presidents, beginning with President Harry S. Truman. A search for primary source documents that described Truman's relations with his CIA directors brought me to Missouri from the Kennedy Library in Boston and the Johnson Library in Austin, Texas. In the days and weeks that followed in Independence, skilled librarians and staff archivists—along with many finding aids—took me down more and more research paths.

While searching for Truman's reasons and explanations for establishing an intelligence agency after he had quickly closed an earlier one, the World War II Office of Strategic Services in September 1945, I found numerous documents, some still classified, that traced CIA plans. In one extensive file, I also came upon hundreds of typed pages stapled into fascinating transcripts of conversations that recorded selected highlights in Truman's career. Several pages described in his own words the reasons for starting the CIA: a dire necessity, he explained, to provide the President with significant analyses and summaries compiled from hundreds of foreign-affairs reports prepared by dozens of American military and civilian officials. Increasingly after 1945, Cold War threats and intricate diplomacy sharpened Truman's focus on reliable and evaluated information.

As I read through the transcript pages of these conversations, I became convinced that they revealed a vivid personal portrait of President Harry S. Truman—frequently, "warts and all." Thoughtful and detailed questions from his ghostwriters William Hillman and David Noyes elicited frank, and sometimes caustic, replies. Threads of Truman's political loyalty, bluntness, frustration, family pride, decency, thrift, humanity, and humor became a tapestry of his Presidential character. These conversations—along with other primary sources in the Truman Library, such as the President's correspondence and documents and transcripts of oral-history interviews with cabinet members and advisers such as Sidney Souers, first director of the Central Intelligence Group, which was established in early 1946—proved insightful. Brilliant secondary accounts of Truman by Robert J. Donovan, Robert Ferrell, Alonzo L. Hamby, David McCullough, and Margaret Truman provided perspectives that added significance and edge to these conversations.

However, before I could turn to editing the conversations, it was necessary to sketch the early years of American foreign-intelligence efforts, which date back to 1775, and present the first three decades of the CIA through the eyes and words of its first directors and deputy directors. This research, based on data from six Presidential libraries and the National Archives, became the book *Spymasters,* which was published in 1999. With its completion, I could return to the conversations book.

Through the kind assistance of Ray Geselbracht at the Truman Library, I learned about William Hillman's daughter, Alessandra Hillman Devine, and David M. Noyes's son, David. Both gave me permission to edit and publish their fathers' questions and comments in the conversations.

The historian Robert Ferrell's enthusiasm for research on President Truman proved contagious, and I am grateful for this, as well as for his friendship. Researchers at the Truman Library are blessed to have the always knowledgeable and patient assistance of Elizabeth Safly, Dennis E. Bilger, Carol A. Briley, Jan Davis, Philip D. Lagerquist, Scott Roley, Anita Smith, Randy Sowell, and Pauline Testerman. Sabbatical and financial support from Marquette University, the Bradley Institute for Democracy and Public Values of Marquette University, and the Harry S. Truman Library Institute permitted me to carry out the research. Despite stringent budget considerations, Dean Thomas E. Hachey, a truly wise academic administrator, and Father William Leahy, S.J., now the president of Boston College, proved especially supportive of these foreign-intelligence and Truman projects. Dr. David Buckholdt, academic vice president at Marquette University, continued to encourage my research and writing by granting an academic leave. And time after time, Mary Dunnwald took me through the budgetary paper jungle. I am also indebted to Dr. L. A. Anderson and his wife, Carlotta, in Pahrump, Nevada, who provided a welcome place to stay during a special period of research and editing.

Marquette University faculty and staff are so fortunate to have an intelligent and considerate library staff under the astute guidance of Dr. Nicholas Burckel. Notable, too, are the reference staff members Rose Trupiano, Valerie Beech, Mary Frenn, Susan Hopwood, John Jentz, Molly Larkin, Ramon Luzarraga, Julie O'Keeffe, Anne Reuland, Nia Schudson, and Suzy Weisman. I also appreciated careful reference assistance from the Marquette graduate students Douglas Charles, Stephanie Bauer Ferguson, Steve Richards, and

Julie Tatlock. My granddaughter Meghan Jung added biographical data with expert efficiency. And Linda Vincent at the Milwaukee Public Library's Periodical Desk graciously researched and provided archival data.

Once again, I am deeply grateful to Richard M. Hopper, vice president of Scholarly Resources, whose enthusiasm for this perspective on President Truman guided the manuscript, as it did two earlier manuscripts, through publication. His efficient and pleasant editorial staff, guided by Linda Musumeci, and Susan Maier of Berliner, Inc., provided skilled and very competent assistance.

My wife, Rosemarie, to whom this book is dedicated, joined me on the research trips to the Presidential libraries. No one can match her efficiency at the photocopying machines. More than this, her gentle kindness and her enthusiasm for exploring Presidential papers lessened the rigors of modest motels and restaurant food during months and months away from home. In addition, her suggestions and insights during the research and writing phases enhanced this manuscript. Our son Ralph A. was a notable source of wisdom for this project and for earlier publications. And I thank our other children—Mary, Elizabeth, Anne, Catherine, Neil, Therese, Thomas, and Andrew—together with their husbands, wives, and children, for tolerating the demands of research and writing.

Editor's Note

WHEN HARRY S. TRUMAN left the Presidency in 1953 at age sixty-eight, he was also leaving a salary of $100,000, plus $50,000 in tax-free expenses. According to the November 7, 1952, *New York Times,* after leaving the White House, he would receive a military pension of $95.66 a month, because he had more than twenty years of active and inactive service and held the rank of colonel. Not until 1958 would Congress provide the Former Presidents' Act granting former Presidents (Herbert Hoover and Truman) a pension of $25,000 and staff, which would be revised upward in future decades. Thus, for financial and educational reasons, and perhaps because he was uncertain in 1951 about whether to run for reelection, Truman authorized a picture book about his life while he was still in the White House. It would focus on his Presidential years before 1950 but include some material up to 1952, and it would be entitled *Mr. President.* Indeed, of all American Presidents to that time, only one other, Herbert Hoover, had written about his own career in his lifetime.

For assistance, Truman turned to a close friend and literary agent, William Hillman, whom he termed an "objective reporter and penetrating interviewer," and provided private notes, memos, papers, personal diaries, private letters, and photographs from his office files. He also gave interviews to Hillman so that the reading public would have a better comprehension of the Presidency and the thirty-second President. For this novel project, Hillman sought his astute friend from California, David Noyes, former newspaper editor, advertising executive, and consultant to Hollywood actors, to provide guidance and counsel. Moreover, Noyes, who had served as one of Truman's speechwriters and consultants, especially during the Whistle Stop Campaign in 1948, greatly respected Truman, as did Hillman.*

---

*Oral-history interviews with John Franklin Carter; Clark M. Clifford; Matthew J. Connelly; Tom L. Evans; Edwin A. Locke, Jr.; and Robert G. Nixon at the Truman Library provide partial profiles of both Hillman and Noyes. In a ceremony honoring Truman in Jerusalem, the President was unable to attend, and he chose his loyal associate Noyes to deliver his speech on June 11, 1966: Papers of David M. Noyes, Box 1, President Harry S. Truman Library (hereafter, Truman Library).

It was during the research for *Mr. President* that Truman told the "Alexander the Great" story: In talking about Hitler's invasion of Russia, Truman explained that Alexander had made the same mistake of conquering and expanding. Alexander was so successful at conquering peoples, Truman recounted, that his associates convinced him he was immortal. However, during one victory celebration, and after thirty-three quarts of wine, Alexander died in Babylon. Hillman, eager to make sure that the President's answers and historical vignettes were accurate, had made an arrangement with the Library of Congress to check the historical accuracy of the events recounted by the President; thus, each week, Hillman sent over copies of the interviews for double-checking. One day, a library assistant phoned Hillman and told him he had checked every biographical account of Alexander the Great in the library and still could not confirm the strange story. Reluctant and protective, Hillman delayed telling the President that the library's reference assistants could not confirm the account. Several days later, the staff member called back in nervous excitement and said he hoped Hillman had not told the President he was wrong because an assistant had just found a monograph that the Library of Congress had acquired in 1867. It had been checked out only three times—once to Senator Harry S. Truman. Hillman recalled this incident as the only time there had been a bit of confusion during all of the interviews.*

As Truman predicted, reporters and reviewers greeted the coffee-table book *Mr. President,* published in 1952, as a shrewd political act—and, they judged, as the opening salvo in the battle for reelection.† However, in March, soon after the book's publication and after considerable soul-searching and consultation with wise advisers, Truman announced he would not run for reelection. Thus, this beautifully designed book threatened no potential Presidential contenders. A two-hundred-page volume, with numerous color and black-and-white photographs combining elements of Presidential history, Truman's heritage and family, and the President's foreign and domestic challenges, *Mr. President* delighted an admiring audience of loyal Democrats, especially during a hopeful Presidential election year. Actually, what began as a picture book became, under Hillman and Noyes, a special collection of brief chapters highlighting significant personal events since Truman's birth in 1884, often in his own words. Especially insightful and interesting were snippets of his military exploits under fire in World War I, his farm and business ventures, and his executive decisions relating to Cold War anxieties. The book's final chapter told of the future as seen through Truman's eyes: strengthening the United Nations; warring against hunger, pestilence, and disease; and harnessing atomic energy for the benefit of civilization.

*Oral-history interview with Mrs. Joseph H. Short, February 16, 1971, Truman Library.

†William Hillman, *Mr. President* (New York: Farrar, Straus and Young, 1952).

An honest and decent person, Truman wrote to Noyes four months before leaving the Presidency: "I want to be exceedingly careful that nothing I do after leaving Office can in any way be considered a reflection on that Office. If I were a rich man I would consider nothing that had any financial connection but since I am not I'll have to do something to maintain the position which an Ex-President has to occupy but it must not be any sort of promotion scheme for any interest or any other outfit."*

Truman's next venture in publishing, which became a distressing one, began shortly after he left the Presidency. Explaining "I'm not a writer," he approached Hillman and Noyes again in 1953 to assist in preparing his memoirs for publication in installments in *Life* magazine, as well as in book form for Doubleday. These very loyal advisers would alternate full-time and part-time research, flying into Kansas City from each coast. The trio was joined in Kansas City at various brief times by a covey of several professors (at least two of them incompetent), research assistants, a doctoral candidate, an additional *Life* writer, and a Doubleday editor. Former cabinet members, including Dean Acheson and General George Marshall, came to the project office to add their recollections and review the manuscript. During those hectic months of tight schedules, chapters were enlarged, cut, stylistically modified, or rejected as author after author revolved in and out of the research rooms. Then, in the middle of 1954, emergency gallbladder surgery left Truman deathly ill. His gradual recovery further slowed publication.

By May 1955, a much stronger President, pleased and excited with the revised manuscript, broke ground for his Presidential library in Independence, Missouri. September would witness the first installment of the memoirs in *Life* magazine and, soon thereafter, volume one of the book, *Year of Decision*, which opened on April 12, 1945, the first day of Truman's Presidency. Volume two, *Years of Trial and Hope*, would be published by Doubleday in 1946. Although Truman would receive $670,000 for the publications, he netted only $37,000 after paying income tax and salaries for his staff.† Although this autobiography had been initiated as a profitable and educational venture, it turned out to be a very modest financial success, even in 1955 dollars.

A new publishing opportunity came to the President in August 1959, when it was announced that he had signed a contract for a forthcoming book, *Mr. Citizen*, which would recount his views and experiences after leaving the Presidency. Publication was promised for the following March.‡ Once again, Truman turned to Hillman and Noyes for guidance, interviews, and

---

*Truman to Noyes, September 10, 1952, Papers of David M. Noyes, Box 1, Chronological File, 1947–52, Truman Library.

†Robert H. Ferrell, *Harry S. Truman: A Life* (Columbia, Mo., and London: University of Missouri Press, 1994), 387. Also, cf. Margaret Truman, *Bess W. Truman* (New York: Macmillan, 1986), 411, who notes the 67.5 percent income tax.

‡Press release for Sunday morning papers, Post-Presidential Files (hereafter, PPF), Box 616, Truman Library.

new material. On September 8, 1959, a muggy Independence, Missouri, day with temperatures reaching the low nineties, and two weeks after the book contract had been signed, the Truman trio began an interview process. Using thoughtful questions prepared by Hillman and Noyes, Truman dictated insightful and sometimes hesitant answers and comments. His office at the Library became a manuscript center.

This team, especially Noyes, had worked with Truman part time during most of the Presidential years; thus, the questions probed the President's memory from personal as well as research data. Frequently, the Hillman–Noyes queries were polite and brought forth fresh information on Truman's religious views and political opinions, personal likes and irritations. Hostile questions, which are popular with certain recent media reporters (especially since the Watergate days), were not asked. Moreover, Hillman and Noyes made wise follow-up queries. Truman's answers, comments, and insights promised a first-rate study by the time the interviews ended on November 17, 1959, a cold day with temperatures well below freezing. Truman's secretarial office produced legal-size transcripts, numbering 568 pages, from audio recordings (no longer available). Reviewed by Truman, these transcripts contain his handwritten corrections and clarifications about several complex answers.

Strangely, however, most of Truman's answers and reflections from the transcripts were not incorporated into the book *Mr. Citizen,* which was published in 1960. Probably because of a tight publication schedule, this volume was based primarily on five articles that were first published in the *American Weekly* in 1953, and on other articles from the North American Newspaper Alliance that were printed in 1957 and 1958. Only two brief middle chapters contain some of the questions and answers from the Truman conversations. This pair of chapters fails to convey Truman's sometimes caustic and quick thinking processes as he targeted a topic and searched his memory. Unfortunately, the President's sharp answers during the interviews were homogenized and smoothed over in the editing of *Mr. Citizen.*

As might be expected from a Republican newspaper, on June 12, 1960, the *Chicago Sunday Tribune* called *Mr. Citizen* a product of "Sassy Harry," a book that displayed Truman's bitterness toward Dwight D. Eisenhower and his scorn for Adlai Stevenson. The unsympathetic *Tribune* reviewer, Willard Edwards, concluded that the book "fizzles after a spectacular launching." Curiously, Edwards and other reviewers during this political season failed to report that large sections of the book had been published earlier.

Truman, of modest formal education but always sensitive to history, hoped for perfection in these writing projects. In a letter to Noyes, Truman urged special care. A stickler for accuracy, he wanted careful proofreading of the manuscript pages: As he explained, "In the White House we'd go over them sometimes as many as twelve or 15 times. From our experience I'd judge half a dozen would be about right. All I want to impress—lets [*sic*] not hurry. . . . Dave, you and Bill are so damned good and patient with me, I don't want to let you down. My think tank works slower than most—but give it time and something comes out."*

His "think tank" conversations, significantly more so than the book *Mr. Citizen*, bring out Truman's intense pride and manner, especially as he explains bitter political and domestic controversies and foreign-policy decisions. Evident as well is his firm loyalty to the United States, to his family and friends, and to the Democratic Party. These interviews also emphasize certain of his personal dislikes—particularly for political opponents such as Richard M. Nixon; for Dwight D. Eisenhower for more than a decade after 1952; and for New York City bankers for decades. His personal resentments, however, are more than matched by his fair-minded judgments of former President Herbert Hoover, American farmers, laborers, and racial groups.

Unfortunately missing from these conversations are elements of Truman's early national career, including a Washington-style political baptism by the *New York Times* on December 19, 1934. Eastern establishment bias among the editors surfaced in an editorial entitled "Just a Farmer Boy," which scolded the recently elected but not yet inaugurated, thus "sub-freshman," Senator Truman for a "highly indecorous" speech in Kansas City in which he had labeled Senators who paid $1,500 for their Washington, D.C., apartments "sapheads!" (Truman paid $150 for his first apartment.) One year later, the *Times*† reported that Senator Truman had argued against a proposed Democratic Jackson Day $10 Dinner recommended by the master politician and Postmaster General James Farley. The Senator had said that Andrew Jackson would "turn over in his grave" if this expensive fund-raiser were held. Nor do the transcripts record the death-threat letter that targeted Truman in April 1937,‡ or Truman's suggestion after Nazi Germany invaded Russia in June 1941 that the United States should help whichever nation seemed to be losing the war and "that way let them kill as many as possible, although I don't want to see Hitler victorious under any circumstances." He argued that neither nation thought anything of its "pledged word."§ Nevertheless, the conversations convey many other fascinating facets of Truman's career.

As historical sources, these oral-history transcripts have a notable advantage over earlier published Truman memoirs because significance is conveyed not only through language but also through form: Truman gives both partial and complete answers in a dictation format. Hillman and Noyes's follow-up queries enliven the lengthy interviews and add flavor to these data. Fortunately, these 1959 conversations, conducted in twenty sessions, escaped being heavily

---

*Truman to Noyes, March 11, 1957, Papers of David M. Noyes, Box 1, Truman Library.
†December 22, 1935.
‡*New York Times*, April 23, 1937.
§Ibid., June 24, 1941.

processed or turned into book sentences and paragraphs, as had happened to interviews with Truman that were published in several earlier autobiographical books. The 1959 questions and answers undoubtedly were edited lightly for accuracy by the President, as well as by Hillman and Noyes. However, the basic verbal rhythm and flow of an ambitious Midwestern drugstore clerk, railroad timekeeper, bank clerk, farmer, army captain, merchant, county judge, U.S. Senator, Vice President, and President remain to delight the casual reader as well as the Truman scholar.

Except for the prologue, these conversations appear in the same order as the typed transcripts, thus revealing the ebb and flow of the questioning and, especially, Truman's answers, which occasionally lead into different topics. His answers describe decision-making; pressures upon himself, particularly in foreign affairs; and his intense loyalty to family, friends, and the Democratic Party. For ease of reading and out of respect for the integrity of the interviews, spelling and typographical errors have been emended. Very little of the original transcripts has been omitted; exceptions to this rule are cases of duplication of information. I have added first names and, in a few instances, corrected basic historical data in footnotes.

Prologue

The Atom Bomb

FOURTEEN YEARS after he had made his crucial decision to use the atom bomb in August 1945 against military targets in Japan, President Harry S. Truman recalled his late July 1945 discussions about this "high explosive" with Winston Churchill and Joseph Stalin at the Potsdam Conference. Thrust into the Presidency three months earlier, this World War I army captain who had fought in France remembered the ugliness, bloody brutality, and anxiety of war.

Truman's decision, which became increasingly controversial for scholars and journalists, brought forth a large volume of books and critical articles regarding the President's motives. Writers focused on making scholarly estimates of the staggering number of casualties—military and noncombatant, Allied and Japanese—that would have occurred during projected invasions of the Japanese homeland. Also calculated were the number of deaths, military and civilian, that would have resulted from more bombing of major Japanese cities, as compared with Manila, Hamburg, and Dresden. Writers debated whether Japan had been close to surrender before the atom bomb was delivered, whether the bomb should be used against noncombatants, and whether the bomb raised grave new dimensions about the morality of warfare. Some who opposed using the bomb would have been willing to trade the lives of hundreds of thousands of Americans and Japanese during an invasion for some perceived reduction in fear of nuclear war—a reduction in fear that is hypothetical, at best, given that the weapon had been tested, whereas loss of lives during an invasion is a certainty. In 1959, Truman would call certain of these questioning opponents "synthetic liberals."

Some revisionist American historians argue that the bomb was used primarily to intimidate the Soviets rather than simply to end the war with far fewer Allied and Japanese casualties. Others estimate that Japan would have surrendered before an invasion commenced. In "Truman and the A-Bomb: Targeting Noncombatants, Using the Bomb, and His Defending the 'Decision,'" published in the July 1998 issue of the *Journal of Military History,* Barton Bernstein continues to probe the issue of casualties estimated by Allied war planners had invasions of Japan been required. He also surveys published literature and archival documents, some written many months or years after Hiroshima, concerning use of the bomb, and he is often critical of Truman's decision and motives.

Other dedicated authors have gathered documentary information provided to and by Truman and published significant and insightful volumes. The best of these books is Robert Ferrell's *Harry S. Truman and the Bomb: A Documentary History.* The most recent interpretative—indeed, brilliant—book, *Downfall: The End of the Imperial Japanese Empire,* by Richard Frank, provides a stunning display of fresh research and careful analysis based on crucial information, especially from newly declassified top-secret Magic and Ultra decrypts from enemy radio intelligence and diplomatic intercepts. These messages were available to American military and civilian leaders during the spring and summer months of 1945, and helped to shape the recommendations and final decision to use the atom bomb. Frank concludes, as did President Truman, that the bomb saved not only American and Japanese lives but also Chinese and other nationalities, as well as prisoners of war.

Interviewed on October 23 and November 17, 1959, at the newly opened Truman Library in Independence, Missouri, about the bomb by his close associates and writers William Hillman and David Noyes, the President explained his determination to bring about the end of the brutal war with Japan. Moreover, he elaborated on his analysis of war and human nature and his optimism for the peaceful development of atomic energy. His comments follow.

Mr. President, I'd like to start with the atomic bomb. I'd like to go back to a question which I still think ought to get a little more clarification. Bill Laurence in his book* says that Truman first told [Joseph] Stalin about the atomic bomb on July 24th during the Potsdam Conference, which had opened the day after the test in New Mexico, about which Truman had been informed at once. On the advice of his chief advisers, he told Stalin "casually" that the Americans had "a new weapon of unusual destructive force." Stalin, Truman recalled—and [Laurence] quotes from the Memoirs—*"showed no special interest." All [Stalin] said was that he was glad to hear it and hoped that we would make "good use of it against the Japanese." Then [Laurence] goes on to say, "As we learned about five years later, Stalin had known all about it even before Truman did." Now, Mr. President, what [Laurence] says is that you discussed this thing first with [Winston] Churchill before you approached Stalin.*

---

*William L. Laurence, *Men and Atoms: The Discovery, the Uses and the Future of Atomic Energy* (New York: Simon and Schuster, 1959), 144–45. Laurence's chapters trace in vivid fashion the scientists and their achievements in the United States as they probed the mysteries of atomic energy. His powerful descriptions even included his eye-witnessing of the second atomic-bomb mission—that is, over Nagasaki.

That isn't true. Well, when I received the two-page telegram, on this long paper, I immediately gave it to Churchill and to [Henry L.] Stimson and to all the rest of the people engaged in the thing. When [Laurence] says that Stalin knew, he did not. He knew nothing whatever about it until it happened. That's the answer to that part of the thing, because we had been anticipating such an explosion from the time that I became President. I'd been going into this Manhattan Project and had learned all about it that I possibly could because when I was making investigations in the Senate, I went to Pasco, Washington, and into the Tennessee setup, and the Secretary of War, Mr. Stimson, came down and asked me not to go any further with it because it was a very secret project. . . . I told him that I would not, but after I became President, then they began to brief me on the whole thing. When the explosion came about, a great many of the people around me didn't think it would be a success. No one ever had any idea that the discovery was as great as it was. Well, after the explosion took place, I talked to Churchill and all of our friends over there, and at one of the meetings of the Potsdam Conference, as soon as it was over, I went over and told Stalin about the explosion and that it would turn out, I thought, to be one of the most powerful weapons in the history of the world. Stalin said that he was very glad to hear about it and he hoped we would make good use of it against Japan. He knew no more about it than the man in the moon.

Despite the fact that later history shows that [Klaus] Fuchs, the British scientist, had transmitted the secret even before the bomb was exploded in the . . .

Well I don't think the Russians thought very much of it. I don't think it had any connection with Fuchs.* And I don't think Stalin was interested in this situation, because he didn't think what I was telling him was the truth.

Then you don't think even if some of the Russian scientists or Russian intelligence was informed that he [Stalin] actually was informed himself?

He may have been informed, but he didn't believe it any more than my people did.

I see. When you discussed this matter with Mr. Churchill, or when you showed him the telegram which you had received that the first test bomb had been fired, did he make any comment or say anything?

*Fuchs, a German-born physicist, left Nazi Germany in 1933 for France and later settled in England. He swore allegiance to Great Britain in 1942. As a member of the British atomic-research team—first at Howell, and later at Oak Ridge and Los Alamos—he provided his Soviet spymasters with vital atomic-bomb information. This brilliant spy returned to the British Atomic Center at Howell and continued to pass highly sensitive scientific data to the Soviets. In 1950, Fuchs was convicted and imprisoned for espionage. A year earlier, and ahead of U.S. estimates, the Soviets exploded their first atomic bomb.

Well, he was highly pleased, of course, because he and I both were of the opinion that that would be the end of the Japanese war when we used that weapon.

But at no time did he recommend or did you discuss with him the possibility of informing Stalin about it?

Yes, we did. We discussed it, and I told Churchill I thought Stalin ought to be informed, and he was. And Churchill agreed with that.

May I get a little more specific? Did you say to Churchill that you thought he [Stalin] ought to be informed about the atomic bomb or that he ought to be informed about the high explosive?

The high explosive was the word used.

And that was your . . .

We didn't know that it was an atomic bomb at the time. We just called it the most powerful explosive that had yet been discovered.

Are you frequently asked about the atomic bomb?

No, not frequently. Once in a while. I am asked by one of these synthetic liberals why the atomic bomb had to be dropped, and then I give him the information of Stimson and [Robert P.] Patterson, who were the Secretaries of War when I was President, and also the ideas of all the people who worked on the situation, and that the idea was to end the war and save lives.*

How did you go about the business of making a decision? What did you do? Did you depend upon your own judgment most of the time, or did you combine your judgment with the advice that you got from experts?

I listened to all the information I could get—the background of every question, how it originated, what it meant, and what the ideas were in the future—and talked with the people I thought were most interested in the welfare of the country and who would give me their viewpoint exactly as they thought, which is hard to get. Most of them tried to find out what you wanted to hear and then give it to you, but the ones I had around me didn't do that,

---

*During the years after 1959, hostile criticism of Truman's decision and his motivation for using the bomb increased and troubled the former President. As the historian Robert Ferrell noted in his essay "A 50th Anniversary Commemoration of His Presidency," when Truman was dying in a Kansas City hospital on December 26, 1972, former Supreme Court Justice Tom Clark came to visit. Truman's doctor told Clark to stay only five minutes; however, he stayed forty-five minutes because Truman wanted to talk about, and defend, his decision to use the atomic bomb: Robert H. Ferrell, "Harry S. Truman: A 50th Anniversary Commemoration of His Presidency," Truman Election Anniversary Project, Missouri State Government Web site, http://mosl.sos.state.mo.us/ofman/truman.html.

and when I got all the information I could get, I studied it and then made the decision. That was it.

During what part of the day did you do this reflective business when you came to those major decisions you made? Was it during your working hours or during your walks or when you got home?

It was during all of them. I was always thinking about what was pending and hoping that the final decision would be correct. I thought about them on my walks. I thought about them in the morning and the afternoon and thought about them after I went to bed and then did a lot of reading to see if I could find some background of history which would affect what had to be done. . . .

I understand. Now further along that line, Mr. President, this goes into the period since you left the White House: Laurence says that "in those three fateful years between August 1953, and May 1956, the Soviet Union was the only power in the world possessing a stockpile of hydrogen bombs. During those three years, we did not have even one weapon in the megaton range." Then he goes on to say, "Those who demanded in 1956 that we call a halt to our testing of hydrogen bombs were unaware of the fact—kept secret from our people and from the world—that the Russians had had three years in which to accumulate a multi-megaton stockpile of intermediate ballistic missiles with thermonuclear warheads whereas at that time we had just begun to build up such a stockpile, and it is well to keep in mind that even as late as 1958, they had had five years in which to design and test improved thermonuclear weapons for both offense and defense as against only two years on our side."

I don't believe that, for I authorized the thing in 1946.

Well, he says that, Mr. President. He says that late in January 1950, President Truman issued his historic order to the Atomic Energy Commission to continue with the development of the so-called hydrogen or super bomb, and that date [came about] because on September 23, 1949, President Truman announced [to the White House Press] that the Russians had exploded an atomic bomb.* It soon became evident that we were in the race for our very . . .

The atomic bomb that the Russians exploded was the same sort of a bomb as was exploded in New Mexico on July 16th. They didn't have the hydrogen bomb.

*On January 31, 1950, Truman issued a historic and public order to the Atomic Energy Commission to continue development of a hydrogen bomb, but it would be May 1956 before the United States tested a hydrogen bomb dropped from a B-52 bomber. In November 1952, the United States set off the world's first thermonuclear explosion; however, the weapon was much too large to be carried by a bomber.

*He says that between August 1953 and May 1956, they [the Russians] were piling up a stockpile of hydrogen bombs.**

I don't think that's true at all.

He says, "As we learned three and a half years later"—after you had issued your historic order to continue with the development of the so-called hydrogen or super bomb— "Russia was already well ahead of us in the development of the hydrogen bomb."†

I can't believe that at all.

Well, what is interesting along here is that you had opposed any ban on or any cessation of experimentation on bombs.

That's correct. I wanted the scientists to go ahead and develop the thing for whatever it was worth to the nth degree. That was the order, and the order was made way back, long before 1950.

He says that in January 1950 you issued this historic order.

Well, that order was a formal one, but the order had been issued to the Atomic Energy Commission long before that.‡

Yes. You had discussed the matter, as you said in the Memoirs, *both with [Lewis] Strauss, who had come to see you, and with [J. Robert] Oppenheimer, who also had come to talk to you about not going ahead with it.*

That's right, and I ordered them to go ahead at that time.

Well then, may I ask this question? Looking back on this whole thing, do you think you would have done anything differently?

---

*Laurence stated that the Soviet Union was "the only power in the world processing a stockpile of hydrogen bombs" and that, during those years, the United States did not have even one weapon in the megaton range: Cf. Laurence, *Men and Atoms,* 181. The Soviets' startling success with an atomic bomb in 1949 prompted numerous secret meetings of the Atomic Energy Commission to discuss development of a hydrogen or thermonuclear bomb. Lewis Strauss and Edward Teller provided significant support; J. Robert Oppenheimer, James Conant, Enrico Fermi, and David Lilienthal sat in opposition. When the commission voted against developing this weapon, Truman named Dean Acheson, Louis Johnson, and Lilienthal to serve as a special committee to the National Security Council. After sessions in December 1949 and late January 1950, this group, with Acheson's pleading, supported further development: David McCullough, *Truman* (New York: Simon and Schuster, 1992), 756 ff.

†In the summer of 1953, the Soviets tested their first airborne thermonuclear (hydrogen-fusion) bomb.

‡In September 1949, Truman approved the transfer of $300 million to the Atomic Energy Commission for fissionable material. However, as Ferrell has noted, it is arguable whether this order was the decision to proceed with the hydrogen bomb: Ferrell, *Truman: A Life,* 349.

I couldn't. I was trying to keep the United States in the lead as the leader of a free world. I couldn't do anything else.

Well, Mr. President, what is important in this book of Laurence's, as I see it, is that he outlines historically all the steps which had led to the making of the atomic bomb, and at no stage anywhere was anybody concerned except to produce a weapon of war, because the fear was that the Germans were going to produce one.

That's right. There were two Danes who had been working for the Germans who came to this country along with [Albert] Einstein, and that's how the thing originated.* Then Roosevelt was a gambler enough to go ahead with it and spend $2.6 billion to get the first bomb off . . .

And you've also said that the Presidency is the most powerful single office in the world. Now, supposing that we have a President in there who has a power complex, or where something goes a little bit haywire with him: What is there in the Constitution that would protect a nation against a willful President who might in this atomic age undertake an adventure?

In extreme cases, the right of impeachment. But the best asset is the right to kick him out when the next election comes along.

Can we wait in this period when annihilation can occur practically in seconds?

I don't think we'd have to wait. The facts of the case are that I'm not a pessimist. I don't think we'll ever have a President of that kind, but if we do, we've always got the power of impeachment in the Congress, and we've always got coming along—sometimes within a year or two—an election that would get rid of him. I don't worry about that part of the thing. We've got a three-power government that keeps the man on horseback off the horse.

Yes. There's a question I'd like to ask you now in that connection, because it comes up more and more: There's always the dread that the atomic bomb, the hydrogen bomb, may be willy-nilly set into motion and thrown without the proper authority of the President. What do you feel about that?

I don't think that can happen. I don't think it will happen for the very simple reason that once started, a thing of that kind would eliminate the population of almost the whole world, and we can't afford to do that, and I don't think anybody wants to. I don't think anybody'd have the nerve to start a thing of that kind.

---

*Niels Bohr (1885–1962), a Danish scientist, was awarded the Nobel Prize in Physics in 1922 for his quantum theory to explain the internal structure of the atom. A year earlier, Albert Einstein had won the Nobel Prize for his experiments on the photoelectric effects whereby light caused emission of electrons by a metal.

Do you think the controls we now have around the thing are sufficient to prevent that?

I do.

You don't think that any general or any Secretary of Defense could willy-nilly set off the thing without consulting the President?

No. You know, it's easy enough to relieve generals when you want to do it.

You had to do it with one of the most arrogant ones.

So did Lincoln. So did Lincoln. No, [Abraham] Lincoln had the most arrogant one.

Do you consider ... That's a good point. Do you consider [George B.] McClellan even more arrogant than [Douglas] MacArthur?

Oh, yes, I do! He [McClellan] was exceedingly disrespectful to the President. MacArthur never was disrespectful to the President; [he was disrespectful] only by implication. . . .

Do you consider [Henry L. Stimson] to be the mastermind behind the development of the atomic bomb more so than anyone else in the Roosevelt administration?

I can't answer that, because I was not familiar with the development of the atomic bomb until after I became President and Einstein and half a dozen other of the great scientists were mixed up in it. Of course, the program had to be carried on under the direction of the Secretary of War, because it was a military project. But all these people were equally informed on the subject and on the inside, and I didn't know anything about it until after I had become President of the United States. They had a committee on the atomic-energy program. That's what they called it. And Secretary Stimson, of course, being the Secretary of War, and Secretary Patterson, who was the Undersecretary of War, were those most intimately connected with it from the viewpoint of decision-making. But there were a great many scientists who were brought over here from England, from Denmark, from France, who worked on the development of the breaking of the atom. I don't think that you can justly say that any single one of them was the man who really did the job. It took the combination of all of them.

Nevertheless, looking back at it now, as you have done frequently, do you think this was one of the greatest gambles and one of the most courageous gambles of Mr. [Franklin D.] Roosevelt?

Yes, that's undoubtedly true. Mr. Roosevelt, of course, as the President of the United States was the one who put the energy into all these people I've been naming, and there was the expenditure of $2.6 billion before the first bomb went off. Had it not been that we were in the midst of a tremendous emergency, it never could have been done. There's no private enterprise or individual that could have brought about the development of the breaking of the atom but the government of the United States under a President who was willing to take the chance and get it done.

Do you think that the government should continue—as it does in the TWA—to develop . . . atomic energy?

The TVA [Tennessee Valley Authority, a plan drafted by President Franklin Roosevelt and passed by Congress in 1933 to have the federal government provide regional planning and development of dams in order to provide hydroelectric power, flood control, and soil conservation]. Oh, yes, of course. I've said in an article which we've just had published in the North American Newspaper Alliance that the experiments ought to continue, because unless those experiments continue, how in the world are we ever going to come to a position where we can make use of this tremendous source of power for peacetime purposes? It can be done, I'm sure of that.

I would like to direct your thoughts in another direction for a second. You were an officer in the First World War, so you directly engaged personally in the combat. You were involved in the conclusion of the Second World War, the end of the European war. And in the final conclusion in the Pacific, you had to direct the use . . . the historic use of the dropping of the atomic bomb. You've had to re-engage in a protective operation in Korea. You've been through a lot of war, and you've also been very closely and intimately identified with the instruments of peace—the United Nations, the Marshall Plan, the Truman [Doctrine]. You've been on both sides of the fence. How do you reflect upon civilization's constant resorting to war, desperately crying for peace, never quite getting it, and now we find that as we wage a battle for the atom, we do it out of a military necessity—out of a war necessity? We're having a little difficulty keeping it going in peacetime. Are we so organized—and this is the heart of the question—that we can only make important progress directly related to war and as a consequence of war?

I think that's a necessity and has always been the case. If you remember, this great Swedish foundation was [based] on the discovery of dynamite: The old man who set up that foundation thought he'd brought forth something that would absolutely ruin the world, but it has been used more often and more thoroughly for the welfare and benefit of the people as a peacetime instrument.* The same thing will happen to this. But emergencies bring forth these things, and if you have a man at the controls who understands the things with

*Alfred Bernhard Nobel (1833–96) became so appalled by the use of dynamite in war that he established the Nobel Foundation, which began awarding annual Peace Prizes in 1901. Today, these awards recognize great achievements in physics, literature, medicine, chemistry, and the promotion of peace.

which we are faced, then he'll go ahead and get the job done, just as Roosevelt did in the discovery of how to break the atom. Now, eventually, we're going to have to use that great source of power just as we use dynamite for the benefit and welfare of peacetime. You know, the first time that artillery was ever used in a battle was down in Italy between some of those counts down there who were always fighting with each other to see who could control Italy, and they hanged the artillerymen the first time they used the guns for the simple reason that it was unethical to have a weapon that could shoot the armor off a knight.

(Laughter)

Do you think, Mr. President, that abolition of weapons could lead to an abolition of war?

No. I do not. I do not for the simple reason that if you're going to have a premise like that, why don't you fire all the police and take the guns away from them?

In other words, wars grow out of the inability of people to resolve their differences?

That's right. And that's the only reason for them at all.

Is this part of nature? What is it? Is the human element, the human animal, incapable of ever adopting peaceful ways that are . . .

We are always hopeful that that will come about, but I don't think we've reached that millennium yet. I'm sincerely hoping that sometime or other, it will be reached. But it's a difficult program with which we are always faced, because there have always been two forces in the world—what we call good and evil. You'll find that all the great philosophies in the world are founded on the premise that the good will finally prevail. Generally, it does. Sometimes it doesn't. But you've got to be in the position to meet these evil forces like [Adolf] Hitler and [Benito] Mussolini and [Francisco] Franco and this old man down here in Santo Domingo.* There isn't any difference between those people. They don't care what they do to people as long as they can maintain the power with which to run things to suit themselves, not for the welfare and benefit of their inhabitants.

What do you think, Mr. President, of this continuous exposure of mankind to the horrors of war [and the fact] that they don't seem to learn about these horrors from one generation to another?

No. No, they don't, and that brings me to one thing that I've always been thinking about. If the things that are of the most good could be carried through

---

*General Rafael Leónidas Trujillo Molina, a ruthless dictator of the Dominican Republic from 1930 until his assassination in May 1961.

from the experience of the previous generation, we'd eventually approach a millennium. The main difficulty is that the youngsters always think that the old folks didn't know what they were doing anyhow, and they have to go through the same experience. That's the reason we have, every once in a while, a debacle in the world in the form of a war. Now we've reached the point where if we have any such a program, there won't be anybody left to carry on what comes later. . . .

Session One

I always thought it would have been a good thing if the former Presidents of the United States had access to the floors of Congress for the purpose of discussion without a vote, and ... I was one of those who tried to get that done long before I was in the White House.

One of the first things we wanted to ask was this: You have had great political power. Now you have been out of office for a number of years. Can you give us your feeling about what it means to go from that great political position to what you have at the present?

It's a most satisfactory situation and one that I like. When you have statements to make, people still pay attention ...

Then you still feel you are being listened to, and most respectfully so, but you don't have the same political leverage on the party that you had while you were in the White House?

No. That's true, and that's the way it ought to be. When a man serves his term in a place of importance, he ought to be willing to leave that place of importance and let the next man take charge. But people are always willing to listen to what he has to say, and he has to be very careful what he says, because it does have influence even when they don't carry out what he suggests.

Does the next man [Democratic Party Presidential nominees]* exist, Mr. President?

Interview at the newly opened Truman Library in Independence, Missouri, on Tuesday morning, September 8, 1959, with William Hillman and David Noyes posing the questions to President Harry S. Truman. This transcript and the ones that follow are in the Post-Presidential Files, Box 617, Truman Library.

*This speculation about the next Presidential nominee of the Democratic Party continued until John F. Kennedy defeated Lyndon Johnson's bid in the first ballot, 806 to 409, at the convention in Los Angeles and won the nomination. Truman did not become an early supporter of Kennedy but would campaign modestly for him.

Yes, there's always a next man.

Is he here now?

I don't know. We'll try to find him.

Has the next man since you left the White House, whoever he was, correlated with you to have continuity of policy?

No. That hasn't been done, I'm sorry to say, because there was a very vicious campaign in 1952 and in 1956 in which the effort was made to make it appear as if the administrations before—that is, Franklin Roosevelt's and mine—had been all wrong. They've discovered by experience that they were all right, and they wish now, I think, that they'd taken the advice.

Well, let me ask you Mr. President: Have you ever felt that all the experience you had has been wasted since you left the White House and that it might have been used in some way?

Well I don't know that it's been wasted, but it hasn't been used. It would have been much better if the people in charge of the [Dwight D. Eisenhower] administration, instead of devoting their time to . . . discrediting the administrations before, had taken the good things of the previous administration and gone ahead with them, and then made such revisions as they thought were necessary, and that would have been better for the country and for the world. But that wasn't the idea. The idea was to completely discredit the administrations before. They haven't succeeded in doing that, and they haven't done themselves any good by that policy.

Personally, have you felt that you could have served in some way, perhaps as the former President of the United States John Quincy Adams served in Congress? Do you think that you could have served, or . . .

Yes. I always thought it would have been a good thing if the former Presidents of the United States had access to the floors of Congress for the purpose of discussion without a vote, and . . . I was one of those who tried to get that done long before I was in the White House. I think that the experience and advice of a former President is well worthwhile; in fact, I showed that I felt that way, because Mr. Herbert Hoover was with me on several occasions, and he did a wonderful job.*

Then it isn't wise for a new administration, regardless of political affiliation, to cut completely loose and abruptly off from a preceding administration?

---

*Critics of this idea complain that former Presidents on the floors of Congress would be the only members without an electorate to answer to; moreover, their advice might split the particular political party to which they belong.

No, I don't think so, because government is a continuing thing, and policies that have been inaugurated have to be carried out, as has been amply demonstrated in this administration which followed the one that I was in.

As for example, Mr. President?

Foreign policy and the internal policy of the United States and the domestic policy, especially the financial policy of the United States, has been rather garbled by this administration, and someday I'll discuss that in full.

Now, you feel that in certain respects there is essential and needed continuity regardless of what party is in charge at the moment.

There isn't any question about that. It must be followed through, and the policies, if they're wrong, should be considered carefully, and if they have to be changed, it ought to be done gradually, and then there would be no upset. You know one of the greatest things and one of the causes of our two-party system as a success is the fact that there are people in both parties who have all shades of opinion, and when one party takes charge in succession to another one, the changeover is not a revolution, and it is not done as it is after dictators. Sometimes it is for the best interests of the country that the policies of the previous administration be worked out and followed through to their conclusive end. It hasn't been done in this administration, I'm sorry to say.

Now we have a Republican administration and a Democratic Congress. To whom should a Democratic Congress look for some guidance, with a surviving former President around to do some coaching?

Well, it would be a good thing once in a while if they'd consult him, because, while the members of Congress were there—a great many of them [were there] while I was President of the United States—there are a great many things with which the present members on my side of that House and Senate are not familiar. A little instruction and advice might be well from the old man who was there during eight terrible years.

Do you feel, then, that some of the members and leaders of Congress today should have consulted you more than they have?

Well, I wouldn't say that they should have consulted me, but, then, it might have been to their welfare and benefit if they had.

Let me say this, Mr. President: What we're recording here can all be wiped out. What we're trying to do is get a ...

I understand that.

On the other hand, it's staying put. . . . May I ask you what your relations with Mr. [Sam] Rayburn, Speaker Rayburn, have been?

They've always been the friendliest possible. I have always been a great admirer of Sam Rayburn. He's been one of the greatest Speakers of the House of Representatives that the country ever had, and he and I have always been exceedingly friendly. Of course, on a great many things we haven't agreed, but that didn't mean there were any personal differences between us. He may not like some of the things I did as President. I may not like some of the things he did as Speaker of the House, but fundamentally the policies which we pursued were the same. . . .

He had the viewpoint that when there was no leadership in the White House of the party to which he belonged, the leadership of the party in control of Congress should not be mixed up politically with the Democratic Party Committee on its policies. I did not agree with that, but that was one of the matters to which I referred a while ago that Sam and I didn't agree on. There was no harm in that, because the Advisory Committee, I think, has done a right good job for the welfare and benefit of the Democratic Party. I think Sam Rayburn has done a wonderful job as leader of the House of Representatives and Speaker, the second most powerful man in the government, and I wouldn't say anything that would reflect on Sam Rayburn, although he and I didn't agree on this Advisory Committee business.

What is your feeling about Senator [Lyndon B.] Johnson as the leader, Mr. President?

I am very fond of Senator Johnson personally. I have known him a long time, politically and otherwise, and I think very well of Senator Johnson. Senator Johnson, of course, as the leader of the Senate, is in a peculiar position. His idea is to get legislation through, and he has to make some compromises with the opposition sometimes that I don't agree with, but that doesn't mean that he's right and I'm wrong. I'm on the outside looking in, and he's in control of affairs in the Senate. He's doing a very good job. Some of the things he's done I wouldn't agree with.

What about the role of the former Presidential candidate [Adlai E.] Stevenson? What role do you think he should play?

Well, I think as the Democratic nominee he should be in the position of the leader of the party. It's been a very difficult matter to get Governor Stevenson to understand that as the nominee of the Democratic Party, he becomes the leader of the Democratic Party, whether they win or not, and it's been very difficult to get him to undertake that leadership.

Do you think he had any reluctance because of the fact that there was a living ex-President?

Well, I don't think so. I don't think there was any necessity for him to have any reluctance on that basis, because there would have been no difficulty on consultation between him and the former President.

Then you think that the Democratic candidate, whether he won or lost, should be the leader of the party, even when there is an ex-President?

Yes, I do feel that way, for the simple reason that he's the nominee of the party convention. The party convention is the Democratic Party when it meets, and when they nominate a man as the leader, he ought to continue to be the leader as long as another one has not been nominated or another President hasn't been elected. The former President can act in an advisory capacity, but his leadership ceases when he leaves the White House.

His leadership, after all, is expressed in terms of certain policies which are in continuity, especially now that foreign policy has become a major factor in the conduct of our government. Now, supposing the nominee does not quite agree with the former President as to the foreign policy of the United States?

Well, it's necessary that the nominee of the Democratic Party should thoroughly understand the policies of the President of his party, who has been in power [and] has been responsible for the foreign policy, and unless there is something radically wrong with it, he ought to go along with that policy.

If he fails to do it, or if he fails to coordinate with him, what does a former President do about it?

Not very much he can do except talk about it.

You have played an important role in that respect by having seized the opportunity of writing your views about the situation.

I have always made it perfectly plain as to what I felt and what I believe, and I shall continue to do that as long as I live. I sincerely hope that it will be constructive and for the welfare and benefit of the country.

But you strongly feel that a former President should definitely go into partial retirement or withdraw from the conduct or the leadership of the party?

If another leader succeeds him who can carry on, that's true. If the succeeding leader doesn't do it, then he has to do the best he can to keep the thing in shape . . . with the hope that the next leader will be able to do the job.

What is your feeling at the present moment on the leadership of the Democratic Party, Mr. President?

The Democratic Party is in somewhat of a chaos. The national chairman [Paul Butler] and the leadership in the House and the Senate are at loggerheads. The national chairman and the general run of the party membership are not exactly in complete harmony, but in a . . . little over a year, we'll have another Democratic convention which will set the policy of the party, and then I'm sincerely hoping that we'll nominate somebody who has the nerve and the ability to lead the party to victory and to set up and to continue the Democratic principles which were inaugurated by Franklin Roosevelt and myself.

May I ask this? You made an important statement before touching on the policies of your administration and the necessity of the new administration coming in to change [them], if necessary, but in a constructive way. Mr. President, don't you think that you can't go on forever having a status quo about anything?

No. That's true. No, there's a change comes along as conditions to be met come up; they must be met by the leadership of the party in the interest of all the people, and it doesn't make any difference what those changes amount to. They have to be met. You mustn't sit still and live in 1880 when 1960 is here.

Well, now, you have a situation for almost two terms of a Republican administration and a Democratic Congress. This is a new experience in our history as a people, is it not?

No, it isn't. It isn't new. It's happened time and again before. In 1946 and '47, I had an opposition Congress* while I was President of the United States. It happened in Woodrow Wilson's . . .

Last term?

Last term. I think in 1916 they elected a . . . or in 1918, they elected an opposition Congress, and he lived through it, although they caused his downfall with his United Nations [League of Nations] program, but you go back through the history, you'll find it's been true in a great many instances since the War Between the States. In 1882, there was a Democratic Congress nominated, and after that we elected a Democratic President in 1884. I think if you go back and look through the situation, you'll find that's not at all unusual. Since the time of Rutherford B. Hayes [1877–81] there have been several times when the Congress has been of one party and the President of another.

That's on a midterm basis, but this is the first time that the people have deliberately voted for a Republican President and a Democratic Congress twice . . .

Not since the [1848] election of the old . . . Rough and Ready [Zachary Taylor], who was a general in the Mexican war, has a President of one party been elected and Congress of another. I think there are 104 years between those two instances, and the election of the Democratic Congress and a Republican President was supposed to show that the people were for certain things,

*There was a Democratic Congress in 1945–47 and a Republican Congress in 1947–49.

but the Democratic Congress didn't work out in quite that way, and that was true also with old General Taylor.

Well, now, here we have a President who was supposed to be a moderate for a conservative party, and here we have a Congress that's supposed to be liberal for a country that was preferring to be liberal. What is your judgment of what the result of that kind of a lineup is?

Well, it's ended up with the leadership that we have in the Congress as a compromise situation. But, of course, . . . there has been some anxiety to get legislation passed whether the President likes it or not, and there has been more anxiety to be sure that the legislation offered to the President will be signed. Well, it's my opinion that when the Congress by a vast majority which is there now on the Democratic side decides on a policy, they ought to put it through, veto or no veto, and if the President vetoes it, they have something to go to the country with in the next go-round and see what result . . . it is that the people want.

During your administration, you had problems with the conservative South and the conservative North Republicans forming coalitions all the time to prevent the carrying out of the will of the people. That's even more acute now. Isn't that why the vetoes are not being overridden?

That's correct. The vetoes are not being overridden for the simple reason that there's a collision of views between the so-called Democrats of the South—the Dixiecrats, if you want to call them, or Shivercrats—and the progressive people who make up the majority of the Democratic Party of the country, and it's too bad, because the legislation which has been passed by this Congress by a majority—by vast majorities, in most instances—has been for the welfare and benefit of the people. There's collusion between the Dixie–Shivercrats element of the Democratic Party and the Republican minority. It makes just a vote or two over one-third. The vetoes have been for the special interests. Never a single veto message that's been written lately has been for anything but the special interests in the country, and then there have been enough of the Dixiecrats and the Shivercrats in the South to go along with the Republican minority so act as to discount the will of the people, which is shown by the majority in the Congress. If the majority had its way, I know we'd have progressive legislation. It hasn't had that.

Mr. President, you have been undoubtedly restless about it, haven't you?

I've been stirred up about it and have been on the point of explosion on two or three occasions, but I didn't because I didn't think in the present foreign situation it would do the country any good.

In other words, you held back because of the foreign situation?

That's correct.

But, in effect, with this veto business—assuming that the President is not abusing his power of veto—isn't the result that a minority of the Congress of the United States is legislating whatever has to be legislated?

That's absolutely true. In fact, it is no legislation, because the policies of the Democratic majority are killed by a minority. It's legislation or no legislation by a minority with the assistance of the opposition President in the White House, and that shouldn't happen, especially with the overwhelming majority of Democrats that are in the Congress. They ought to pass the legislation, and they ought to stick to it, and if they can't override the veto, they ought to stick to it anyway.

So what we have now is a unique situation where an opposition President has mustered by himself more power than the total membership of the Congress in a legislative sense for nullification purposes.

It is negative in every sense. And that's the fault of the Democratic majority so far as the public is concerned, because it does not understand the procedure. The purveyors of information are in control, and they are and always have been against the Democrats.

How can that be cured, sir?

It can be cured only by an election, and we're going to have that in 1960.

Can I get back to your personal role throughout this year? How have you felt personally about what you would have liked to do?

Well, I was always very anxious to make any contribution I could for the welfare and benefit of the country, and I haven't done that by demagoguery or exploitation of any kind. I have tried to make it perfectly plain in the articles which we have been putting together to let people know just exactly what I thought the outcome ought to be, both foreign and domestic, without in any way interfering with the foreign policy, which is the problem of the President himself, and at the same time to inform the majority in the House and the Senate of what I thought their duties ought to be.

Haven't you wished during these periods, when you were feeling frustration that things weren't getting done, that you . . . were in the White House calling the turn on things?

Well, sometimes I did, but I've never had any yen to really go back to the White House, although there are times when I wish I had been there for purposes of the welfare of the country.

Session Two

Well, he [IBM's President Thomas Watson] was interested in the welfare of the country and anxious for me to understand that he was just like every other citizen who wanted to see the country prosper. And naturally, he wanted his own outfit to prosper, too—maybe a little more than he did the country.

You have a lot of mail, and you answer a lot of letters. What is your average mail?

Oh, I'd say that we answer anywhere from fifty to one hundred fifty [letters] a day.

People write to you about everything, don't they?

Everything under the sun.

Can you name some of the things?

Well, yes. There are a great number of people who want me to help them get certain days and weeks set aside for use, and some of them, to me, are ludicrous, but they're not to the people who ask for them. Someday I'll publish a list of all the days and weeks I have been asked to take a hand in, particularly since I have been out of the White House. They think I could have more influence than I have now. And then they want to know about things in the government. A great many of them want jobs, which I am in no position to give them now, though I always give them a courteous answer and tell them the person I think can be of help to them. And we have questions about various phases of the government, and wherever I can give them an answer that I think will do them any good, I try to do it. If I can't give them the answer, I tell them where they can go to get the information. . . .

You have also been in close touch with minority groups since you left the White House.

Transcript, Tuesday afternoon, September 8, and Wednesday morning, September 9, 1959, part one.

That's true. I am going to address the Negro Baptist Convention this evening.

Do these people continually petition you for your support and guidance?

Well, not so much the guidance, as they like to have a conversation with me to get me on a platform.

Are there any special minority groups that seek you out, or are they all represented?

Nearly everyone you can name is represented, as well as majority groups. I talk to more Democrats than any other organization.

But you also hear occasionally from Republicans, do you not?

Yes. I have some very cordial letters from Republicans. I had one just the other day stating the fact that he'd been here and seen what we had to offer and that he was sorry he was not acquainted with me in 1948. He might have voted for me.

Now, isn't it a fact that a great many businessmen and heads of industry, since your retirement, have been expressing themselves to you in a cordial and appreciative manner?

Yes. That's true. It doesn't make any difference which side of the fence they're on—Republican or Democrat, labor, or the head of a department in a great organization. They all understand that all in the world I have ever tried to do is to work for the benefit of all the people in the country, and they're beginning to find that out now at this late date.

How many Presidents, Mr. President, who have lived on after their terms have seen their course better understood since they left office? Have there been any?

I think most of them who lived after they had been in the White House and had been responsible as the Chief Executive of the nation found that to be true. Very few of them did live very long afterward—Grover Cleveland, Calvin Coolidge. President Hoover has lived longer than any of them, and I am hoping that I will top him when the time comes, because he's ten years older than I am.

The president of IBM [Thomas Watson] made a special call on you?

Yes, that's right.

What'd he say to you?

Well, he was interested in the welfare of the country and anxious for me to understand that he was just like every other citizen who wanted to see the country prosper. And naturally, he wanted his own outfit to prosper, too— maybe a little more than he did the country.

As an internationalist, didn't he go to particular lengths to express his appreciation of how you managed the world order of free nations?

Yes, he did, but I didn't want to bring that up. That would be bragging on myself, which I am not good at.

Mr. President, have you kept in touch with men like [Winston] Churchill and other international figures with whom you had had dealings when you were President?

Yes, I have had a great deal of correspondence with Prime Minister Churchill and President [Charles] de Gaulle of France, with Mr. [Paul-Henri] Spaak, who's the head of NATO and who was Prime Minister of Belgium . . . while I was in the White House. I have been in constant touch with those people all the time since I left the White House.

And [British Prime Minister Clement] Attlee came here to visit you.

Attlee came to the United States and paid me a visit. We had a very pleasant time.

But didn't you miss the enormous resource of information that you had at the White House at your disposal and what came later?

Oh, yes. You see, the Central Intelligence Agency was organized at my direction by Admiral [William] Leahy and Admiral [Sidney W.] Souers, who is now the head of the General American Insurance Company in St. Louis, and two or three other very able and distinguished men like that.* We finally

---

*In a handwritten letter to David Noyes on December 1, 1963, more than two years after the failure of the CIA-sponsored Bay of Pigs invasion, Truman wrote that he had not intended the agency to be a "Cloak & Dagger Outfit." Rather, it was intended to be a centralized reporting agency, not to act as a spy organization. On December 22, 1963, Truman's views were published in the *Washington Post*. This publicity prompted former CIA Director Allen Dulles to visit Truman on April 17, 1964, and review, or remind him of, CIA actions for supplementing the Truman Doctrine in Greece and Turkey; covert steps under Truman's authority to suppress the Huk Rebellion in the Philippines; and the adding of Radio Free Europe. Dulles also pointed out National Security Actions 4 and 10-2 dealing with covert CIA operations: "He studied attentively the *Post* story and seemed astounded at it. In fact he said that this was all wrong." However, six weeks after the Dulles visit, Truman wrote to William B. Arthur of *Look* magazine regarding its article on the CIA, and repeated that the sole purpose of the agency was to gather all available information for the President. He concluded with, "It was not intended to operate as an international agency engaged in strange activities": Truman to Noyes, December 1, 1963, CIA Box 24, Truman Library; Dulles to Lawrence Houston, CIA legal counsel, April 21, 1964, CIA Box 24, Truman Library; Truman to Arthur, June 10, 1964, PPF, Box 12, Truman Library. The answer to Truman's *Washington Post* article and to the author of the *Look* article is most probably found in a *New York Times* article dated June 7, 1960. In this two-column front-page account, Truman said that as President he had rejected aerial espionage: "Espionage is a dirty deal . . . I didn't want to be part of it." In discussing the downing of a CIA U-2 American reconnaisance plane piloted by Francis Gary Powers over the Soviet Union the previous month, he related that aircraft could

wound up by having Allen Dulles, who was the brother of [John] Foster Dulles, in charge of it, and he is a very able public servant and has been in touch with me since then. Of course, he can't furnish me with reports, because it's his business to keep the President informed, but that's one of the greatest services that's possible. You know, we have four or five departments—State, every branch of Defense, Agriculture, and Commerce—all with foreign connections. They used to get stacks of messages three feet high, and the President had no way of finding out what was in those messages unless he read them all. That couldn't be done, so the Central Intelligence Agency coordinates the information that comes to every department, as well as to the President and to the State Department, and that way the President has a viewpoint that no other man in the world has, or can get.

How do you form your opinions about issues and things now, in the absence of that kind of information?

Well, I read a great many newspapers, in which I had very little confidence when I had a Central Intelligence Agency, and I talk to everybody I have an opportunity to. When I really get to the point that I want some honest-to-goodness information, I write to Representatives in Congress and to representatives that I know in the State Department, and they give me the information.

This is information that is available to them but not necessarily the kind of information that was available to you as President?

No, no. No, no. And I don't want that sort of information. I have had it offered to me, and I didn't want to make use of it, because it's best to have the information that's available to the whole public, and then you can say what you please and do what you please. When you have confidential information, you have to keep your mouth shut, and I don't like to do that.

Well, at any rate, because of your past experience, you are better able to judge those events which are going on.

Oh, yes. Yes, indeed. Whenever, I see an article in some of the great newspapers—and I read three or four of them—on some subject, for instance, in Asia or Africa or South America, I can evaluate that better than the person who hasn't had the Central Intelligence information.

In other words, you keep yourself informed, but you have a built-in guard against being misinformed?

---

reach an altitude of 75,000 to 90,000 feet in 1949 or 1950. When the reporter asked him whether such spy flights might have been made without his knowledge, he replied, "Not with my permission." When pressed as to whether there was espionage during his administration, he replied that he had preferred to be ignorant—but then added, "I suppose so." In this *Times* edition, Dean Acheson said that he advised against spy flights over China or the Soviet Union in 1952.

That's the point, exactly. We don't want to be misinformed.

Do you depend upon any special occupation groups for constant contact?

No. I talk to all of them. I talk to labor and management and every other section of the population, and they all have information that's interesting, but you have to be very careful to coordinate the whole thing and see what the balance is.

Could we talk now a bit about your European trip? Just a very quick sketch of some of the talks that you had with some of the people over there . . . during your first trip to Europe.

The trip in 1956?*

That's right.

Well, I had a very, very pleasant time. Mrs. Truman and I had luncheon with the Queen of England [Elizabeth II] and the Duke of Edinburgh [Philip Mountbatten] at Buckingham Palace. We had a very pleasant conversation about our relationship with the British people. And I had lunch with Sir Winston Churchill at his country place and spent quite a bit of time there, and Lord Beaverbrook [William Aitken] was present, and we discussed all the angles of the situation at that time. Then over in France. I had dinner with the Prime Minister of France [Guy Mollet] at that time. With the Foreign Minister [Christian Paul Pineau]. I had a chance to talk very frankly, because he spoke better English than I do, and we got along in fine shape. He sat by me at the dinner. And then in Italy, I called on the President of Italy [Giovanni Gronchi], and the Prime Minister of Italy [Antonio Segni] came to see me, and we had an argument about whether there were 21 or 22 Amendments to the Constitution of the United States, and then I had a . . .

That was with the Chief Justice?

That's right. I also saw the Chief Justice [Aldo Moro], and he is the one with whom I had the argument about how many Amendments there were to the Constitution of the United States. It was all friendly. Then we had a very pleasant visit with Pope Pius XII. I went there for a fifteen-minute interview and stayed almost an hour and discussed all the angles of the situation as he could see them from his position. He has the best arrangement to hear things all around the world and anybody in the world, I judge, except the President of the United States and the heads of France and Great Britain. Then I went to Belgium and had a very pleasant dinner with Spaak, who at that time I think was Foreign Minister. I'm not sure, but I think he was Foreign Minister at the time I was there. Then we went to call on the Queen of the Netherlands

---

*This was Truman's third trip to Europe. However, it was his first as a private citizen, and the first time he needed a passport for the trip. Earlier, his army service had taken him to France in World War I, and then as President he cleared customs easily.

[Queen Juliana], and she had us at her country place for luncheon, and we spent a most pleasant time with her and discussed all the things that you'd think about in that part of Europe. And then went on to Germany and had . . . In fact, we went to Germany first, and I had luncheon with the President of Germany [Theodor Heuss] and dinner with Chancellor [Konrad] Adenauer, who . . . Both of those men struck me as being very able persons, and we discussed the German situation from start to finish. I haven't talked about those things, because most of the information I received was in confidence. I haven't used it in public and don't intend to.

Could you tell us what transpired when you visited the Queen and the Duke.

We had a luncheon around a table in their private apartments and present were the Queen and the Duke, and Mrs. Truman and myself, and Ambassador [Stanley] Woodward and Mrs. [Sara] Woodward, and we discussed things around the table just like you would at any other luncheon. . . .

Looking back now at your visit with [Konrad] Adenauer, what was your feeling about the man and his role in . . .

Oh, he impressed me as one of the ablest persons I had ever met. He knew the score from every angle, and we talked on every subject nearly, as it affected Germany, and the Berlin Airlift and things of that sort. When we went to leave that evening—we caught a train about dark—he came down to the station with us, and I was told by the head of the Associated Press service there that that was the first time that Adenauer had ever escorted anybody to the station.

Do you believe that he truly spoke for Germany?

I don't think there's any doubt about it. I think if there ever was an honest man, he's it. He knows what the score is, and his interest is the peace of the world and the welfare of his own country.

Did you feel that there was a new Germany in the making?

I did. I did. I was satisfied when I left there that with Adenauer at the head of the government, there was no danger to the world as far as Germany was concerned. Except to cooperate . . .

And that it was a one-man performance, or was he representing the intent and the feeling of a new Germany?

I think that's what it was, because the [German] President made the same impression on me: the then-President of Germany and nearly all the Germans I met—all the officials impressed me the same way. But Adenauer was the top one because he seemed to know more about it than all the rest of them put together. I think he did.

On your second trip to Europe, at the time when de Gaulle was about to move into power and then did move into power, you were invited, I understand, by him to go up to see him, but . . .

Yes, I was, but I told him—I got to talk to him personally—that I was only over there just for a few days and a few weeks' rest and that I was not making any public appearances, and that I didn't want to do anything that would in any way embarrass him in what he was trying to do. He said he understood, and that's all there was to it.

What was your feeling about de Gaulle?

I think de Gaulle has made a wonderful impression on the French, and I think he is doing his level best to pull the government into the position where it will make France a great power once more. If he can carry out his program, I am sure that will happen.

How did you talk to de Gaulle? Personally? Did he telephone you, or did he send . . .

He sent a messenger to see me, and then I talked to him over the telephone. He speaks fairly good English, as good English as I do French, and I don't speak any French.

But you understood each other? He understood what you wanted to say to him?

Yes, he understood it. We had interpreters at each end so there was no doubt about the understanding.

Did you want to avoid association or involvement with de Gaulle at a critical time, or did he?

Oh, no. I didn't want to do anything to embarrass him, and I wasn't going to go there for anything but to sit down and rest. If I had had any public appearances whatever in any one of the countries, I would have had to go to all of them, and I didn't want to do that. We were just going to be a short time in France, and that we did. We had no public appearances whatever of any kind.

And, of course, you were very meticulous not to make any speeches or do anything at all which might be interpreted either as trying to undermine or criticize [Dwight D.] Eisenhower.

No, no. I made no public statements whatever that would in any way reflect on the government of the United States or any other government in the world.

Did any of the heads of state that you saw express to you any deep concern about the survival of Western civilization?

They were all worried about it, and I guess they still are. The object of NATO was to prevent the subversion of the governments of the free world, and I think they are in just as much danger now as they were then.

What did the Pope [Pius XII] primarily find himself concerned with?

He was very much concerned, of course, about the Catholic prelates that were being mistreated by the communists, particularly in Yugoslavia and Poland.*

Did he feel that the Catholic church was not getting enough support from the Western governments?

We didn't get into that phase of the thing. What I was trying to find out was what he could hear that was taking place behind the Iron Curtain and his statement on the prelates who were in trouble. The result of that questioning was that he was not in a position then to get the information that he formerly had had in those countries.

He did not know what went on in Russia, Poland, Hungary?

Not as he had before, but he said the information that came was not as reliable as it had been when their people were allowed to send messages from behind the Iron Curtain. They couldn't do it at that time. I don't suppose they can now.

Did he touch upon South America at all? On what was going on down there?

No. He didn't discuss South America at all.

In any of your talks with statesmen on this, was any question raised about the atomic bomb? Or about nuclear warfare?

No, we didn't discuss that. We didn't discuss that at all. At that time, 1956, we were far superior to any other country in the control of that situation. We didn't talk about it at all. I didn't think it was the proper thing for me to discuss, because I was just a private citizen—or a retired farmer, in fact—taking a trip.

What were the opinions expressed about the government of the United States—it's important to have it in the record—since your leaving the White House? Were they feeling less secure? More trouble?

Well, that would be a political question, but they were, and I'm sorry to say it.

---

*Truman considered Pope Pius XII the "greatest statesman in the papacy in two hundred years": Harry S. Truman, *Mr. Citizen* (New York: Bernard Geis Associates, 1960), 41. This is a significant appraisal in view of certain recent books that are hostile to Pius XII on issues relating to the Holocaust.

Now, you ran into [Jawaharlal] Nehru* in London, and something happened in your discussions with him during the visit in 1956.

I had a very pleasant visit with Nehru. In fact, we went out to call on him at the Indian Embassy, and we had a very, very pleasant visit. And he then indicated to me that his viewpoint on the communist situation was changing. He didn't have the same peace-at-any-price attitude at that time, and I think it's been very well brought home to him now that he was on the right road, because now he's in trouble, sure enough, with the commies in China and Russia both.

Did he tell you why he was undergoing this change?

Oh, no. He didn't get into the details of the thing. I just judged that from the conversations I had with him how things were in India. He indicated to me that he was very much worried about the northern border. This was long before the Tibet thing [the Chinese invasion in 1951]. And [he indicated] that he didn't know exactly what the outcome was going to be, but he hoped for peace. So did I, and I told him there was one way to get peace with the Russians, and that's to be stronger than they are.

But he didn't subscribe to that?

He didn't say a word to that.

The feeling toward the United States was warm and cordial all through that period?

Just as cordial as it could be. I had the same sort of reception in every one of those places where we went. In fact, they mobbed us in Paris. It took a half a dozen *gendarmes* [French military guards] and police to get us through the crowds, and the same thing would have happened in Rome, only they were more careful there. In Belgium, going through Brussels, it was just as it was when I was on the way to Potsdam—the same sort of reception. The same thing was true in Bonn and everywhere else we stopped. In Munich also. We went to the birthplace of [Ludwig von] Beethoven and had to have a police guard to get in and out of the place.

Did any of them want to talk to you about FDR [Franklin Delano Roosevelt] at all?

All of them mentioned FDR, and they all expressed a very strong fondness for him, everywhere I went.

---

*Nehru was the first Prime Minister of India, from 1947 until his death in 1964. Nehru opposed alliances and served as a spokesman for nonaligned nations in Africa and Asia. In addition, he urged admission of communist China to the United Nations until Chinese forces attacked the Indian border in 1962.

What in particular did they remember about FDR's relationship to them?

Well, of course, the fact that he had come to the relief of Europe at the time when they needed it most, and they talked about the Atlantic Charter and the preliminaries to the United Nations, and they were very happy that it had worked out as it had. The preliminary arrangements, the forming of the United Nations, and the feeding and rehabilitation of Europe and the countries which had been devastated—enemy and the other kind—made them feel very friendly toward the United States.

Session Three

And on those two campaigns in '52 and '56.... The only time the President [Truman] was ever discourteously treated was during those two campaigns, and that was brought about by the fact the Republicans paid the youngsters fifty cents apiece to go down to the train and be disrespectful to the President.

What happens to the leadership of the party when you have a surviving former President and a newly nominated candidate for the Presidency by the convention.... Don't we have a unique situation in '52? In '52 in November (sic), the Democrats nominated a man [Adlai Stevenson]* you wanted nominated for the Presidency, you see?

That's right.

You continued in office for some time after that. Now we had a kind of peculiar period when you were President of the United States, a Democrat, leader of the party, and yet had a nominee. What happened during that period?

Well, every effort was made during that period to get the nominee elected as President of the United States. It failed principally because the nominee didn't have his whole heart in the support of the Democratic principles. He had listened to the advertising propaganda which had been put out by BBD&O [the Batten, Barton, Durstine & Osborne advertising agency] and was the man who started the rumor of the "mess in Washington" in a speech out in Oregon. Then, of course, the Republicans took that and made everything they could out of it, and we could never in the world get that nominee to understand that when he runs on the Democratic ticket, after a Democratic administration, it's his business to see that the Democratic administration has been endorsed and that the people understand what it's all about. That's what caused

Transcript, Wednesday morning, September 9, 1959, part two.

*Stevenson, then fifty-one, had became governor of Illinois in 1948 with a large vote margin in his first campaign for an electoral office. Truman thought this impressive.

all the trouble, and in 1956, long before the nominating convention came up, I was anxious that he should come out and assert his leadership. He didn't do it. He still was coy and wanted to be forced to run at that time, and there wasn't anything I could do about it. Only when I went to Chicago and I heard that he thought I was an albatross around his neck, I tried to take that albatross off, but it didn't do any good. He was still defeated. But I supported him both times when he ran.

Well, Mr. President, can you be a little bit more specific? Did you have a conversation with him in which you indicated that you would step out of his way if he thought . . .

Why, sure. Yes, I did. That happened at the convention in Chicago.

In '56?

In '56. But it didn't do any good. He was nominated all right, and I got out and tore my shirt for him, and on those two campaigns in '52* and '56 the only time that the President was ever discourteously treated was during those two campaigns, and that was brought about by the fact that the Republicans paid the youngsters fifty cents apiece to go down to the train and be disrespectful to the President. And I met a Catholic priest over in the middle of Ohio who ran these fifty-cent kids off the platform because they were disrespectful to the President—and he was for Eisenhower.

Well, Mr. President, may I ask you, did you have a conversation or a breakfast with Stevenson in Chicago in which you told him that you felt that he had a wrong impression of you?

Yes. That meeting took place—whether it was a breakfast or not, I can't remember—and I told him that if I was in any way a detriment to him, I would get out of the way, because I wanted a Democratic President of the United States.

I think you have in mind the meeting . . . at the Blackstone Hotel after you came back from Europe [July 1956], and the purpose of the meeting was not only that but to fill him in on what you had observed in Europe and what you thought were to be the big coming issues.

---

*On July 12, 1952, Stevenson issued a press release stating he was a candidate for reelection as governor of Illinois and no other office. Moreover, he requested that Illinois Democratic Party delegates respect these wishes. That same day, a draft Stevenson group, the Stevenson for President National Committee, urged every delegate to draft Stevenson; however, when the convention opened on July 21, Stevenson's fifteen-minute speech of welcome won new delegates, and on the third ballot, on July 26, he was drafted. Walter Lippman wrote that Stevenson drew his strength from the party mass rather than from the outgoing President and thus on his own right: cf. *Sun Times* (Chicago), July 24, 1952, as quoted in Walter Johnson, ed., *The Papers of Adlai E. Stevenson,* 8 vols. (Boston: Little, Brown, 1972–76), 4:6.

That's correct.

Will you tell tell about that, sir?

Well, I told him everything I had learned on the trip and told him that the United States was still considered the savior of the free world. I don't know whether it had any impression or not.

But you also indicated to him—I recall your talking about it—that the coming issue for the United States or the party was the peace issue and that he had to identify himself with the peace issue.

That's correct. But instead of that, he made statements that no further experiments should be made with the hydrogen or atomic bomb,* and I didn't fall in with that because I think the only way in the world that the Russians can understand an approach is when you're stronger than they are, and the reason for the development of the hydrogen bomb was to put us in a position where we were ahead of the Russians.

Mr. President, . . . there has been some consideration given to the fact that Eisenhower, being a popular war hero, did have an advantage when he ran in '52.

Of course, a war veteran who runs for President—Taylor and [Ulysses S.] Grant and Eisenhower are shining examples—always has the inside track. They wear a golden halo until they turn it into brass.

But nevertheless, you feel that if Stevenson hadn't messed up the approach . . .

If Stevenson had been willing to endorse the policies of Franklin Roosevelt and myself, regardless of what the advertising people had to say, I think he possibly might not have been elected, but he would have got at least 3 [million] or 4 million more votes than he did in 1952, and the same is true in '56.†

To get more personal, if I may, in terms of your impressions of Stevenson, you were not for him in '52. You saw him in action, and then you developed a reluctance about him in '56. What caused you to have that reluctance?

Because he would not say what he wanted to do. He didn't accept the leadership of the Democratic Party. Had he accepted the leadership of the Democratic Party long before the convention of 1956, it would have been no trouble to build him up, just as it would have been no trouble to build him up

*See Session Seventeen.
†In his letter of January 10, 1956, Stevenson argued he could not accept Truman's proposal in 1952 to run for the nomination in good faith because he had already asked Illinois voters to reelect him governor and it was too late to withdraw his request: Stevenson to Truman, January 10, 1956, PPF, Box 109, Truman Library.

if he had been willing to start in January 1952, instead of two or three days before the convention. You couldn't get him to do it. You didn't know whether he was going to run or not. He wasn't in complete sympathy with what the Democrats stand for, and that's what caused the trouble.

Did you get the feeling that he justifiably had the reputation of being an expert in foreign affairs?

Well, I didn't know about that. It wasn't necessary for a man to be an expert in foreign affairs to be President of the United States. The way to be elected President of the United States is to be an expert in domestic affairs, and then he can take the foreign situation and work it out, because he's the man who makes the foreign policy, and when he has all the information, he can do it without any trouble.

Do you mean, any person, even lacking an understanding of foreign policy, could become an able administrator of our foreign affairs after he became President?

I think I'm a shining example of it.

Well, we challenge that. You were a student of history. . . . You knew what was going on, and you certainly had a . . .

Well, I kept up with it, of course, and everybody . . . anyone who is interested in being a candidate for President ought to know exactly what's going on around the world, from start to finish. And most of them do.

To get more specific about Stevenson, did you have any serious misgivings about his grasp of domestic affairs?

Yes, I did. I didn't find that out until the campaign started. He was a wonderful governor of Illinois and the only prospect in sight when I decided not to run for reelection.* And we had no idea then that the Republicans would nominate a soldier. We thought they would nominate [Robert] Taft or someone like that, and that it would be not too hard to elect a Democratic President, but conditions changed, and we didn't get that done.

Now, just to throw you back a little to those moments in Key West [November 1951] when you were meditating to yourself, mostly, about your own plans, whether you were going to stand for reelection in '52 and whom you were going to try to persuade to run if you elected not to run: What was going through your mind at that time?

---

*Earlier, Truman had concluded that Chief Justice Fred Vinson would be the best Democratic candidate; however, Vinson declined. Reportedly, Truman spoke to General Eisenhower in November 1951 about running on the Democratic ticket although later, Truman and Eisenhower denied this offer. In early January 1952, Eisenhower from his NATO post in Paris stated he would accept a nomination from the Republican Party. Vice President Alben Barkley also had Truman's support early in the convention.

Well, I was thinking about the thirty years I had put in in public service, and I wanted to quit while I was physically able to go ahead and do some things I wanted to do in private life, and I studied the situation and considered all the Democrats in sight. After much consultation, I decided that Stevenson was the man. Then I asked him to come to see me, which he did—at the Blair House, I think, on January 28 or 29 [January 20, 1952]—and we discussed the thing for an hour and a half. And he refused. He said he had to run for governor Illinois again. Well, thirty days after that, on February 28, I think, he came back to see me. We had another discussion at the same place, same time. He had to slip in the back door so nobody would see what was going on. The same answer. Then in March, I got the national Democratic chairman, Frank McKinney, to go and see him, and he gave McKinney the same answer that he would not, under any circumstances, run.* Well, on Thursday, when the Democratic convention was in session, after Senator Barkley had withdrawn, he called me up at the White House and told me that his friends wanted to nominate him for President. Would I object to it? Well, I blew up and talked to him in a language I think he'd never heard before, told him that since January 28 [20], 1952, I had tried to get him to be the candidate for the Democratic Party, and that of course I'd support him. Then the convention got tied up, and we had to get on the plane, and that's the first time that a picture of a plane taking off was seen on the plane itself, and flew to Chicago, got all the people involved into conference, and he was nominated.† Then he went out and made a campaign that was not in support of the Democratic program that had been carried out by Roosevelt and myself but was based on the advertising in the Republican propaganda in which he thought that everything in Washington was crooked. Well, it wasn't. It's been conclusively proved. You take the time when [Herbert] Brownell made his terrible speech in Chicago, and this fellow [Harold] Velde in Illinois tried to upset the applecart—they both got their ears knocked down. And later on it was asserted by the Republican propagandists that George C. Marshall and myself were traitors, and I made the statement after that that if George Marshall and myself were traitors, the country was in a helluva fix. And it would have been, if that were the case. It was offered by the Republican national chairman, who thought he'd run for governor of New York at one time, that he'd give a thousand dollars if it could be proved that [Richard M.] Nixon had called me a traitor. It was proved, and I told him to send the thousand dollars to the Red Cross in Korea. It was never paid.

---

*In late March, Truman announced that he would not stand for reelection.

†In late August, Truman wrote to Stevenson in anger: "Had I not come to Chicago when I did the squirrel headed coonskin cap man from old man Crumps [sic] State, who has no sense of honor would have been the nominee." Truman distrusted that man, Senator Estes Kefauver of Tennessee: Handwritten letter (not sent), President's Secretary File, Box 334, Truman Library.

You once said about Governor Warren, Earl Warren, that he was a Democrat but didn't know it. Do you feel the same way about Governor Stevenson?

Well, I'd say he's a Republican and doesn't know it. Because he's been raised in that atmosphere. He's not the successor of Adlai Stevenson [his grandfather], to begin with, who was Vice President [under] Grover Cleveland. He's lived in—He owns a newspaper that's not ever been in the Democratic column, and I suppose that's what his trouble is, and I hate to say that because I was very highly impressed with him, but he didn't understand the maneuvers that go to make a leader of a party. My admiration for the Chief Justice started when he was governor of California. I stopped in Sacramento, California, about seven-thirty in the morning. There were about ten thousand people behind the train at that time—this was on the famous Whistle Stop Campaign [1948]—and the governor got on the train up in front and came back, and we sat and talked a while. I said, "Well, Governor, I'll be glad to go back to the front of the train so you won't be embarrassed at these people behind the train here." He said to me, "Mr. President, you're President of the United States; I'm the Governor of California, and I'm going out there on that back platform and introduce you." He did, and I never forgot it. Then when he was Chief Justice [1953–69], after he had been appointed Chief Justice and the Republicans wanted to get him out of the way. He's made a great Chief Justice. He came out here and dedicated this Library of mine with President Hoover and Sam Rayburn and all the leaders of the Republicans and the Democrats. Even [Charles] Halleck [the conservative Republican House majority leader in the Eightieth and Eighty-third Congresses] was here. And I want to say to you that there isn't a finer man in the United States than the Chief Justice. His name's Warren.

Mr. President, at one time you had thought of Vinson, Chief Justice Vinson, as a possible candidate.

That's right. I talked to Vinson about it, and he told me that his ambition had been achieved when he became Chief Justice of the United States; that it was the greatest honor that could come to any man, especially a lawyer, and that's what he was. And he made a great Chief Justice, and he told me he didn't think he ought to be considered in that line. He was right, of course. I was for him. We only had one Chief Justice who ran for President, and he was defeated. His name was [Charles Evans] Hughes.

Did Chief Justice Vinson give you any political reasons for not wanting to risk it?

No, no. He just was of the opinion that as head of the Judiciary of the United States he shouldn't get into the political . . .

Did he make any suggestions to you about whom else he would recommend to you?

No, he didn't. He didn't recommend anybody. At that time there was nobody in sight, and we had to figure this thing out and finally came to the conclusion that the governor of Illinois was the best man in sight, because of his name and his background and the fact that he had been elected governor in a Republican state by 500,000 [votes].

Mr. President, about 1956, at the time when there was still some controversial discussion about your picking Governor [W. Averell] Harriman at the last stage, can you give us a little bit of the background of your thinking which led up to that?

Well, the thing that really caused it was the fact that I had been informed that I was an albatross around the neck of a man [Adlai Stevenson] who would ordinarily be renominated, as Bryan was in 1900 at Kansas City. So I got to thinking about the situation, and I thought I'd be able to help both Harriman and Stevenson by saying that I thought Harriman would make a good President, and I thought he would.* But I wanted to get myself in a position where I would not be a handicap to Stevenson, because I knew he was going to be nominated.

In what way can you be a little more specific, Mr. President, about how you felt you could help by that maneuver? In other words, you would disassociate yourself from—

Why sure. If I was an albatross, I wanted to take it off his neck. That's all.

In other words, you deliberately took a public position which was unpopular and hurtful to you in order to remove yourself from Stevenson?

Yes. What I was interested in was to get a Democratic President in the White House. And I thought maybe that might help to do it. That's all there was to it. It didn't make any difference what happened to me personally. My reputation was either made or unmade long before that.

Didn't you feel, Mr. President, that the managers of the Democratic Committee had maneuvered the convention in a way as to embarrass you needlessly?

No, I didn't think so. If I was embarrassed, I embarrassed myself, and I didn't mind it.

---

*Three days after Stevenson was nominated on August 16, Truman sent a letter to Stevenson and explained he had tried to wake up the Democratic Party at the convention, and he believed Stevenson did not understand this action. Moreover, he wrote that the Democratic Party must embrace all the people, rich and poor, and that the President must fight for the needs of modest Americans. Concluding on a humble note, Truman wrote, "I wouldn't blame you if you'd never speak to me again—but let's win this campaign and think of that afterwards if it is even necessary to be thought about": Truman to Stevenson, August 19, 1956, in Johnson, ed., *Papers of Adlai Stevenson*, 6:191–92. Stevenson replied to Truman's "kind" letter and appreciated the "high motives" behind Truman's actions at the convention: ibid., 6:192.

No, but didn't they try to discount your position in the party to the point where they practically ignored it in connection with Stevenson?

No, I don't think so, because they didn't have chance enough to think about it. You see, when they got into trouble on the platform, I made a statement on the platform, and then there wasn't a fight, so they agreed with what I had to say. But when it came time for me to make the announcement, the presiding officer, who was my good friend Sam Rayburn, begged me not to make it. I said, "Sam, this is my personal affair. You don't have to get mixed up in it." And the motion was then put by Sam as to whether the former President of the United States could address the convention. It takes unanimous consent if you're not a delegate. And Sam put the motion in this way. He said, "The former President of the United States would like to address the convention. It requires unanimous consent. Is there an objection, I hear none. Mr. President you're recognized."

And that statement was to say . . .

That I was for Harriman.* And Sam knew that's what it was and he didn't think it ought to be done, because he was afraid it would embarrass me. Well, it didn't ever embarrass me. I got out then and worked for the committee and the party, and that's all there was to it.

May I ask you, . . . was Harriman aware of what was in your mind? And what was his feeling about it? Did he think he might have a chance?†

Yes, I think he did. I think he did, and he had a right to. He thought I had more influence with the Democratic Convention than I had. I knew I didn't have it.

Wasn't it a fact that it was not your influence, but that you put your influence on the auction block in order to open the convention, which had been closed for any competition or any further nominations?

Well, of course, that helped—but then, as I say, their objective was to take Stevenson off the spot, because I knew he was going to be nominated.

But even in '48, sir, you had the inside track, as a President always does—and yet, you encouraged an open convention.

That's right. It always ought to be an open convention.

---

*At a press conference on August 11, 1956, Truman announced his backing of W. Averell Harriman for the nomination and added that Stevenson lacked experience to be President. Franklin D. Roosevelt's wife, Eleanor Roosevelt, scolded Truman and argued that Governor Harriman had less experience than Stevenson: Johnson, ed., *Papers of Adlai Stevenson,* 6:180.

†Harriman had won a narrow victory for governor of New York in 1954; despite his notable qualifications, however, he lacked popular support: Alonzo L. Hamby, *Man of the People* (New York: Oxford University Press, 1995), 622.

But you found in '52 that it was not an open convention; that it was pre-set and prejudged, and Stevenson had it made.

No, he didn't have it made. If I hadn't taken a plane and flown from Washington to Chicago, he wouldn't have been nominated.

That's in '52.

Yes, '52.

In '56, sir.

Oh, in '56, he had the convention in control, which was all right. I didn't care. As I told you, the nominee of the party is the leader of the party, and that's what he ought to be, and he ought not to be coy or hesitant about accepting that leadership. And that's what we had in 1956. We had a helluva time getting Stevenson even to say he was going to run.

In '56, you said, he was running in states. He was in a good many primaries.

He didn't tell any of us that he was going to run. We could have done something for him.

But you said in a press conference in Chicago that in your judgment, Stevenson could not be elected. Now, what was your judgment based on, sir?

On the fact that he had lost by such a tremendous majority in the 1952 campaign and that he had not made an approach to the thing in the complete endorsement of the Democratic Party and its principles. That's what the trouble was, and I was satisfied that, if he were nominated again without having assumed the leadership of the Democratic Party, as he should have done after 1952, he couldn't be elected. But I was perfectly willing to try to help elect him, which I did.

But in disassociating yourself from Stevenson, you also made a public statement that a lot of people—columnists, particularly—criticized: You said he could not be elected when you knew he had to be nominated.

Yes. I said he couldn't be elected, basing it on the same statement I've just now made, and I also, if you remember, had a phrase attached to that that he couldn't possibly be elected without the support of the old man who was talking at the press conference, and that was myself.

You made that statement, and you also said he would not carry as many states in '56 as he did in '52. Now, what was that based on?

On a survey of the situation, because I knew the halo was still working [for Eisenhower] as far the military was concerned, just like it did for Grant.

In fact, Grant was almost nominated in 1880 for a third term after they had found out what a terrible administration he had had.

Then you felt that you saw no change at all in Stevenson in the way he would conduct his campaign?

No. I didn't, and I was sorry. But I got out and did everything I could. As I say, I got more disrespect in that '56 campaign than I had ever seen from the time I started in politics. I was perfectly willing to accept it—oh, the people in front of the cars from which I was speaking. It was a terrible thing.

Well, I was there on several of the tours, Mr. President, and I don't recall any of that.

If you remember, right north of New York one night—I forget the name of the town—they had brought out a whole string of schoolchildren, college kids, with instructions to go ahead and do what they could to break up the meeting. Well, they were having a game—a football game or something—that night, and I saw them fill up the whole space behind the train. I told them that I was very much interested in what they were trying to do. I knew that they wanted to be discourteous to the President, which was not very nice to do, but I was very much interested in who was going to win this game and was also interested in where they ought to be howling for their teams, and if they would get out of the way and let me finish my speech, I'd come up there and see if I couldn't help them to win. I never got a single boo.

Yes, the thing I am trying to emphasize, Mr. President, is from what I have seen on those trips, you have been glowing in the admiration of the public.

Well, I know that's true, but then the Republicans were hiring these kids at fifty cents apiece to come and be discourteous to the President, and that's absolutely wrong. I wouldn't allow it. If I were in charge of the Democratic Party, I wouldn't allow that to happen.

Now, in 1952, as the campaign progressed, the Democrats were gaining—the Democratic ticket was gaining—and it was a period when the Republicans were seriously worried until the thing came along: "If elected, I [Eisenhower] will go to Korea."

That's right.

Now, what happened in '56 that made it even easier for the Republican President to gain reelection?

I don't know. I don't know what really happened. There was no Korea at that time. . . . The surrender in Korea had already been made after '52, and they couldn't make another . . . surrender like that, but I don't understand, except that people are inclined to be very friendly to a military hero. President Roosevelt and I set [Eisenhower] up as a hero and made him, but he doesn't remember that.

Why is it that President Roosevelt and yourself, in all the time you had, couldn't find among the Democratic eligibles anybody who was an up ... an obvious front-runner entitled to succeed to the Presidency on the Democratic ticket?

I don't know. That's the thing I can't understand. One of the difficulties was always that a man at the top, when he's popular, has difficulty finding a successor, and that's true in any history of the country that you want to read. [Andrew] Jackson had difficulty. The man he did select [Martin Van Buren] didn't make good: Although he was a good President, he didn't make good as a successor to Jackson. That's been true of Grant and all the rest of the men who have been elected on popularity contests. Of course, Woodrow Wilson was ruined by the Irreconcilables [certain Republican Senators who were bitterly opposed to Wilson's League of Nations, 1919–20] and the lies they told on him, and I don't know what would have happened to Franklin Roosevelt had he lived and been able to finish his fourth term. He probably would have had the same trouble that the rest of them did. But as his successor, when he died a short time after he was elected to the fourth term, it was possible for me to build up a situation which finally ended up with a reelection in 1948. I don't know what would have happened after that, because I had no intention of trying to serve more than two terms in the White House. It's a backbreaking proposition, and it's terrible on your family, and that's what I was thinking about. I thought I had accomplished the things I had set out to accomplish, and I think I did, and then I had hoped that a successor would carry on from that point, but we couldn't find him. Now, where the hell he was, I don't know.

Mr. President, I want to ask you a sort of freakish question: Every President from 1840, taking every twenty years, 1860 and '80, and down to 1940 who had been elected President died in office, through death or assassination. Do you think 1960 holds any foreboding for anybody that way?

I hope not. I hope not. Those things were happenstance, of course, and I sincerely hope that nothing of the kind will happen. One of the most disastrous things that ever happened to the country was the assassination of Lincoln.

Session Four

Woodrow Wilson was a war casualty just the same as any man who got shot on the front.

We were discussing the fact of the great Presidents and how they had been talked about and treated, and I made the statement that I felt that if Lincoln had lived, he undoubtedly would have been impeached by the House, as was Andrew Johnson. [Lincoln's] idea was a settlement of the Southern situation, so it would be considered that the states had never been out of the Union and there wasn't any necessity for Reconstruction if the inhabitants of those states were loyal. But the old man from Pennsylvania, Thad Stevens, who was one of the worst old crooks who ever was in the Congress, insisted on the Reconstruction program, which caused all the bitterness between the North and the South. There wasn't any necessity for it at all, but you can't tell how those things are going to turn out. It doesn't make any difference how great the man is who's in the White House; if time continues, eventually they'll find some reason why they ought to be against him. You take every great President we've ever had and that's happened.

What is the biggest problem a President has in protecting himself against abuses that are deliberately directed against him for political purposes?

There isn't any defense against it when it's happening. The only thing that will satisfy the arrangement is for the President to leave a record of the facts as they were and let the liars go ahead and have their day, because eventually they'll be caught up with, just as they were after the Reconstruction period.

How do you account for the fact that you have undergone perhaps the most sustained abuse that any President has had during a critical period to find that, after your term of office, the abuses had ceased and you, during your lifetime, had uniquely achieved greater popularity out of office?*

Transcript, Wednesday morning, September 9, 1959, part three.

*A November 1951 Gallup poll registered only 23 percent approval of his Presidency. President Richard Nixon's rating shortly before leaving office in August 1974 was 24 percent: cf. Ferrell, *Truman: A Life,* 358.

Well, I lived long enough to tell the truth and the facts about what the conversations had been on the liar basis. I think that had some effect on it. You take the most abused President—people don't know that it was George Washington. He was roundly abused for everything he did when he was trying to set up the government, because the Colonies had been independent and they wanted to be still independent. Washington wanted to make a nation out of [them], and he did, but he was roundly abused, and that's one of the reasons he quit when he did. He could have had a third term or a fourth, if he'd wanted it, but he decided he'd quit. He wanted to quit after the first term, and the people in charge persuaded him to stay for another round.

Every President who has ever done anything has had that same experience. You take [Thomas] Jefferson and Jackson, and Lincoln, I guess, was as roundly abused as President as anybody, . . . but I think Washington was the worst abused. And then you come along with Grover Cleveland. The first term was one of his great periods in life, and yet he was so roundly abused that the next President [Benjamin Harrison] was elected on a minority popular vote. The same thing happened to Woodrow Wilson. They caused his death as a casualty of the First World War when he was trying to get a League of Nations established. Some of these old birds that didn't understand that the world was moving wanted to keep things like they were in 1896, and it didn't work. Woodrow Wilson was a war casualty just the same as any man who got shot on the front. And he was right, because it brought on a second world war, what they did.

And then, look what they've done to Franklin Roosevelt. They've misrepresented him, mistreated him in every way that's possible, and I also have been rather misrepresented, but I lived long enough to prove that the facts were as they should be and that the liars got caught up with. I don't know how long that's going to last, but it's one of the great things in a republic—the misrepresentation of their rulers. Of course, when they misrepresent the rulers in Russia or any absolute monarchy or dictatorship, they get shot for doing it, and they can't very well leave a record. Well, in a republic, they can leave a record, but the man who has been abused, if he's been right, can very well erase that record and tell the truth, and that's what we're trying to do now.

Mr. President, you have said one of your ambitions is to write about the twelve willful men who did so much to destroy Wilson's approach to the League of Nations, and in that you said you wished to point out the background of these men.

I think that ought to be done. I think that the Irreconcilables—there were more than twelve—but those twelve were the most prominent ones. The Irreconcilables ought to have their biographies stated from the viewpoint of what caused them to bring about the Second World War. Somebody ought to do it. I don't know whether I can or not.

Well, can you give us some indication of just what you mean by their background being responsible?

Well, they were . . . well, I can only give you an illustration of one man. He was the United States Senator from Missouri, and his name was James A. Reed. He was against everything. He never . . . his name's not on any single piece of progressive legislation. He helped to put the Federal Reserve in operation, true, for President Wilson, but there wasn't any origin on his part. He was against everything and against everybody, and that's how he got elected. He had a most bitter tongue, and it appealed to the country boys in Missouri, and they elected him.* He was one of the great Irreconcilables, along with Henry Cabot Lodge,† whose jealousy of Woodrow Wilson was something terrific because he thought he was an intellectual, and he knew that Wilson was smarter than he was and he didn't like it. I think that's one of the reasons he led the Irreconcilables, because he was chairman of the Foreign Relations Committee in the Senate, and that's what caused the . . .

[Hillman:] Mr. President, I think we can start now where we wanted to start—that is, about the Federal Reserve system. Dave, you wanted to start that. [Noyes:] The Federal Reserve system that you just referred to had its origin during the Woodrow Wilson administration. What was the purpose behind the enactment of the Federal Reserve?

The purpose of this Federal Reserve Act was to put the control of the finances of the country in the government of the United States, where it belongs. What Wilson was trying to do was to set up an organization that would control the finances of the country in such a way that it wouldn't be necessary, as was necessary in Theodore Roosevelt's administration, to go to J. P. Morgan to keep the country from going to pot.

The act itself transferred control of currency and monetary policies to the government of the United States?‡

To the government of the United States, where it belongs. No money or policy of any kind is worth anything financially unless the backing of the government of the United States is with it. Every law that has to do with the lending

---

*Reed complained the League of Nations would force the United States to submit substantial questions "to a tribunal on which a nigger from Liberia, a nigger from Honduras, a nigger from India . . . each would have votes equal to the great United States": as quoted in Ralph Stone, *The Irreconcilables* (Lexington: University Press of Kentucky, 1970), 88.

†Massachusetts Republican Senator who ridiculed Wilson's League of Nations.

‡President Wilson signed legislation creating the Federal Reserve System on December 23, 1913, which provided for elastic credit and currency. The Owen–Glass Act, the first complete reorganization of national banking, resulted in twelve district banks spread out from New York and Chicago to San Francisco.

and collecting of money originates under the government. It wouldn't be any good if it didn't.

For instance, which laws had been in existence before that?

The Bankruptcy Law is about the only thing that was for the benefit of the fellow who couldn't pay. Woodrow Wilson's objective was to set up a financial program that would put the control of the money power in the hands of the people and not have it in the hands ... the concentration of it in one city, which is New York.

Did the act do it?

Yes, it did, up to a certain period. It's gone back now to New York.

Didn't it go back to New York during the period of ...

After Wilson was out of office, the New York Federal Reserve Bank got absolute control, just like they tried to do while I was President of the United States and didn't have a chance to do. Now they've got control again, and somebody's got to wake up to the fact that the control of the finances of the country must be in the hands of the people and the Congress of the United States, and the President, if he wants to exercise that control.

You had occasion to exercise that control in a critical period when it involved the interest rate and the parity of bonds in the market.

Time and again. I was very particular to have the Secretary of the Treasury see to it that the financing of the government was on the best terms that could possibly be had, and those terms ran from about five-eighths of 1 percent to 1.5 percent for the financing of the obligations of the government. The record will show that. I also issued orders to the Federal Reserve Board. I had them come in to tell them exactly that I did not want under any circumstances to see the bonds of the United States sell below par, for the simple reason that many of those bonds had been bought on time by people who had to pay for them by the month or the year as they went along, and they should not be put in a position of doing what happened under old [Andrew] Mellon, who was Secretary of the Treasury under [Warren G.] Harding, when they did just exactly what the Secretary of the Treasury [Robert B. Anderson] has been doing here lately. They pushed the price of those bonds down to 80.* They are 4¼ bonds.

They were Liberty Bonds?

Liberty Bonds, 4¼, which had been bought on time, just like these other bonds had been bought, and as soon as they had control of things, they gath-

---

*Truman, needing cash, had to sell his Liberty Bonds at a loss after they depreciated from 100 to 80.

ered up all of those bonds after they pushed the price down to 80 from people who paid for them on time and they went to 125 between 1920 and 1930 and never went below that price. Well, that's just exactly what the present Secretary of the Treasury and the Secretary of the Treasury before him [George M. Humphrey] have been trying to do, following the example of old Mellon. They've now got the 2¹/₂ bonds, some of them down to 89. They're due in '61 and '62, which makes the interest income about 4.72 or 4.82 or whatever it is—you have to figure it—they've got the 3s down to 81, just like they had the 4¹/₄s way back yonder in the 1920s. They are just doing the same thing they've always done when you let the New York bankers take control. The Federal Reserve Bank in New York put every pressure on me possible to do just exactly what's been done by the last two Secretaries of the Treasury.

How did they pressure you?

They came to see me and told me the country was going to pot if we didn't raise the interest rate. I said if it goes to pot, you won't be the losers, and if it goes to pot, you'll go along with it. We're not going to let these people be trimmed, as they have been in the past. The reason for the setting up of the Federal Housing Administration, the Reconstruction Finance Corporation, and all of these things was to prevent the little fellow from being gypped. Now they've got the little fellow over a barrel, and they're gypping him. The interest rate on the $800 billion the people owe has been increased by $16 billion.* Now, that $16 billion might just as well have been applied [to] the reduction of the national debt—and that's what I was trying to do and did. I cut the national debt about $26 billion [1947–48], which has never been done since and won't be done under this present policy.†

And then they wonder why the government goes into debt. The operation and the cost of the handling of the national debt has been increasing at the rate of $500 million dollars a year. When John Snyder and I were operating the control of the finances of the U.S. government, the cost of the servicing of the national debt was about $5.2 billion. I think you'll find, if you look very carefully, that it's gone up about $4 billion, nearly $500 million a year since this outfit's been in control. With that in view, they cut the taxes of the rich people by $2.5 billion a year, and then they wonder why the hell they can't balance the budget. That's the reason. They don't know what the finances of the world mean or what the finances of the government of the United States mean. There isn't any reason in the world why the government of the United States should pay more than 1.5 or 2 percent for loans on short-time paper. The national debt all ought to be financed for about 2.6 percent, which is enough.

*The national debt in 1959 was $287 billion; in 1945, $261 billion. Truman was referring to private debt.
†Deficits of $1.8 billion in 1949; $3.1 billion in 1950; and $4 billion in 1952.

How can you compel the Federal Reserve to do the bidding of the President or the Secretary of the Treasury when under the law it is an independent and autonomous agent?

They have to work with the President, and when the President makes up his mind that something ought to be done, they'll do it. If they don't, why, when their terms expire, [replace them] or fire them and get somebody who will do the job. That's what I did.

You had some experience with [Thomas] McCabe.* Can you tell us about that before you appointed [William McChesney] Martin to succeed him?

Well, I had some difficulty with McCabe, but he went along eventually. The thing worked out in very good shape. We never did get out of line on the handling and the operation of the finances of the country, which are entirely in the hands of the government of the United States, and when they turn it over to the Federal Reserve Bank in New York, the bankers in New York get exactly what they're getting now. And when you raise the price of the service of the national debt of the United States and not reduce it any, which hasn't been done since I left the office, then you've got just exactly what we're faced with now, and every little borrower is the man who pays the bill. They raised the prime interest rate in New York 5 percent—5 percent—it ought to be about 3 [percent]. And the Federal Reserve Board's gone along with them. They were raised one-half of 1 percent, and that gives the bankers a chance to raise it 1.5 percent. What the Federal Reserve Board ought to do is, whenever bonds of a certain issue go below the 100 percent on which they were sold and which they'll pay when they're due, they ought to take control of the market buy these 81 percent bonds and retire them, then issue more at 2.5 percent. There wouldn't be any trouble about it if they wanted to do it.

They could do that?

Why, of course they could.

Now, when McCabe at the final session was pressured into requesting a higher interest rate and the abandonment of the protection of the bonds at par, John Snyder had difficulty making your instructions carry with the [Federal Reserve] Board. Then you sent for the chairman, who was then McCabe, and you had a showdown with him, didn't you?

---

*McCabe, who was president of the Scott Paper Company from 1927 to 1962, became director, and later chairman, of the Federal Reserve Board of Philadelphia. Recommended by Secretary of the Treasury John Snyder, McCabe was named by Truman as chairman of the board of governors of the Federal Reserve System in 1948. However, McCabe failed to maintain a financial policy of low interest rates, despite pressure from Truman and Snyder. In anger and frustration, McCabe resigned in March 1951. Martin would be appointed to succeed him and would serve for the next twenty years: *American National Biography,* 24 vols. (New York: Oxford University Press, 1999), 14:832–33.

That's correct. I told him that if he was going to carry on on this basis, we would withdraw every deposit the government had in the New York banks, and that cured him. That's all we had to do. Old Jackson did that to the Bank of the United States.

Didn't you give McCabe, at that time, three choices . . . you said you had three choices? One was because you couldn't fire him until his term expired.

No. I didn't want to.

That you had a choice of going before the Congress to ask for an amendment to the legislation; or go to the American people, who were the final judges of everything; or ask him to resign, if it would be easier for him to resign.

That's correct. That's exactly what I told him, and I also told him that the finances of the great banks in New York were based on these very things that they were trying to manipulate, and that the President of the United States was in a position to remedy that, and I had an example of that in old Jackson when he took care of the United States Bank, and if that's what he wanted, that's what they'd get. That stopped the whole thing. There isn't any sense in the world for any institution or any set of bankers or anybody else controlling the financial policy of the U.S. government. It ought to be controlled right in Washington with the President and the Secretary of the Treasury, and it can be.*

Why doesn't the Democratic side of the Congress, since the Federal Reserve is a creature of Congress, rise up and do something?

They can whenever they want to. . . . Senator [Albert] Gore of Tennessee [recently] made one of the great speeches on that very subject. That can be handled if the Congress itself wants to handle it; they could repeal the whole Federal Reserve laws and start anew. Maybe that's what ought to be done. I don't know.

Go on with that, Mr. President.

If the Congress sets these things up, they can take them down whenever they feel like it, and if this outfit's not performing the way it ought to, they can repeal the Federal Reserve Law and pass another one and put in another board that will carry out the objective, which is that the control of the finances of the government of the United States ought to be with the people and not with the Federal Reserve Bank in New York, [which is] made up of all the bankers of New York.

---

*Under William Martin, the chairman of the Federal Reserve became more powerful than the Secretary of the Treasury.

You appointed William McChesney Martin as the Chairman of the Federal Reserve.

Yes. . . . When I appointed him, I thought he was a liberal. He turned out not to be. He's in the control of the bankers in New York. That's what the trouble is.

What did you instruct Martin [to do] when you appointed him?

I told him to keep this policy going, for the control of the short-time loans of the United States should be in the hands of the government, and the control of the bonds should stay in such a position that they'd always be at par. The Federal Reserve Board—the head of the Federal Reserve outfit of the Federal Reserve Board in Washington—could prevent these bonds from going below par any time they want to.

All you had to do was buy them at par.

No. All they had to do was buy them up below par, and pretty soon they're all gone, and then they go to par. It's just a plain business transaction. . . .

What if you have a large issue of a federal loan—say, one that runs into billions—and the banks don't subscribe to it, and you have a large block of it left over. What do you do?

Offer them to the public in the first place, and they'll be oversubscribed every time. When 1958 was here, and there were all the appearances of a depression coming on, they didn't have any trouble reducing the interest rate, and every bond issue that they offered at any price that they wanted to offer it was oversubscribed.

What do they do differently now?

After these bond issues are out of the way, they let the New York bankers raise the interest rate on loans to 5 percent, and that cuts the 2.5 percents down to 80 or 81, or whatever it is they're selling for now.

What about the claim, Mr. President, that by reducing the interest rates you encourage inflation?

You encourage inflation by raising the interest rates. It was conclusively proved when they raised the cost of the national debt about $4 billion in four years. That's inflation, private inflation.

Just to wrap up, you feel that the Federal Reserve Act, as it stands, is amply armed with the necessary . . .

Why sure. The Federal Reserve Act is adequate to take care of the situation, if you have a board that's working in the interests of the people of the United States instead of the bankers.

And you feel that the President and the Secretary of the Treasury ought to be in a position, a better position, to interpret what is in the interest of the people?

Why, of course, and that's what he ought to do. That's exactly what he ought to do. He still thinks he's working for the Wagner outfit in Texas, the present Secretary of the Treasury.

Well, then, do you think that the Treasury—and the President, if necessary—should determine what the rate of interest should be on government obligations?

There isn't any question about it. It can be done, because it was done. During the seven years I was in there, we set the rate on which we'd make these loans, these short-time loans. It just saves money, just saves money. You take these 2½ bonds that are down to 89 and that are due in '60 and '61—anybody that buys those 2½ bonds at 89 has [to pay] a capital-gains tax when those bonds are due, because they'll get them at par. The government pays them at par. That's all there is to it.

Mr. President, have you any general reflection or thought about the condition of the banks today? You talked about the banks at the time of President Jackson. What do you feel is the position of the banks? Are they getting a little bit too strong?

The banks in the country are as solid as they can be on account of the . . . Federal Deposit Insurance Corporation, which protects the depositor and gives everybody confidence: Instead of putting money in a sock, they put it in the bank, because it's safe, up to $10,000. They are guaranteed on whatever they have, and the vast majority of the deposits are way below $10,000. Then the banks take that money and lend it to people who want to start a little business or build a house or something of the kind, and they've got the thing right now back where the hawks are on the roof watching every maneuver that's made. And the first thing you know, the Federal Housing Administration was set up to keep people from being trimmed on loans for homes. They've gone right back to the old situation where they charge them a commission every time the loan comes due, raise the commission every time the loan comes due, instead of making it 4 percent or 4.25 percent as was set out in the law, they now charge them 5 and 6 percent for these loans and charge them the commission in addition to that, which makes it 7 or 8 [percent] before they get through. It's an outrage, just an outrage. It's going right back to the situation we were in in the 1920s, and if they keep this thing up, they're going to have a settlement one of these days that will make 1929 look like a picnic.

What you're saying is that . . . interpreting the same acts of legislation that were put in there for the protection of the people is a difference between the occupants of the White House?

That's right. A difference in the administration. You can take a bad law with a good administrator and make it work. You can take a good law with the present sort of administration that we have now and make a debauch out of it, which has been done for the downfall of the common, everyday, little man who has only a little money, who lives on credit, and who's depending on his job to pay these things off....

You mean this is a question of interpreting the laws with sympathy for ... the little people?

That's right, and the laws were passed for that purpose. That's the reason we have to have laws. If it weren't for that, it wouldn't be necessary to have laws, if everybody would try to do the right thing to his fellow men. There wouldn't be any necessity for laws. The only reason we have these laws is on account of the cutthroats who take charge of the money power of the country.

In the same sense, there were, prior to the advent of FDR, problems with management abuses of labor, and labor had been on the defensive during that period ... and FDR got a lot of legislation on the books to protect labor.

That's correct.

Now what has happened since then? During your administration, the Taft–Hartley thing* came on the statute books. How did that happen to develop at that time, and what was the cause of it?

One of the causes of these things is, in my opinion, that you help the underdog all you can ... and when he gets to be the top dog, he's meaner than the top dog was before. What I tried to do with the Taft–Hartley bill at the time it was up was to make suggestions that the finances of these great unions ought to be reported, just as the order which made the stock exchange—the Securities and Exchange Commission—take care of the blue sky and things of that kind and ...

The privately owned companies ...

That's right, and these people couldn't understand that. When the unions got to be international in scope, then they [became] a part of the financial setup and the welfare of the country. Therefore, the federal government has a right to know what they're doing and why they're doing it. I tried to get these union leaders to understand that when a bank puts a teller in a cage with a million dollars every day and does not bond him and does not check him, he finally gets to the point that that's just so much paper, he might as well help himself. That's exactly what's happened to the treasurers of the unions. They've gone south with the money, and now they're reaping the rewards. There's no sense

*Regulation in 1947 to restrict union activities.

in it, because there are just as many decent, honorable men in the unions as there are in the banks. In fact, I'd rather trust them further than a banker, because when we were having trouble with the collection of taxes, we had 117 people that we had to send to jail because they went south with government money, and at the same time six hundred bankers went to jail for stealing the depositors' money. Under this deposit guarantee, they caught up with them. What I'm getting at is that the human animal's about the same, no matter how you have him, and if you trust him too far where money's concerned—it's been said, and I think it's in the Bible somewhere, that money is the root of all evil, and it is. But if it is properly guarded and properly taken care of by honest men, it doesn't happen. That's what the trouble is with these unions. They're reaping the reward. They wouldn't listen to me, and they're getting what's coming to them, and I don't feel sorry for them at all. . . .

You vetoed the Taft–Hartley bill.

Twice, on the grounds of the fact that it didn't contain things to carry out what the law should provide. That's the thing that counts. Now they're going to amend it, or have, I think . . . this labor law* that's just passed is an amendment to the Taft–Hartley Act.

So big labor did resist you in your campaign to . . .

Oh sure. They always do. They always do that. You know, money and power go together, and when these big unions get control of a whole pile of money, they think they're bigger than the government, just like the bank that gets so much money has the same feeling. When you get the two, you've got to have somebody in between them and the people, and that's the government of the United States to protect the fellow who's been ground between the two millstones. That's all there is to it.

You had labor in two important positions. It was important as an economic factor and also became important as a political factor, particularly to the Democratic Party.

That's right.

What was wrong with that?

Well, there wasn't anything wrong with it, and isn't as long as it's carried on honestly. Politics is government in a free country, and the man who understands the politics of government in a republic is one of the great leaders and always has been. But when . . . they get the thing in such a situation that money controls this situation, then you're going to pot. You'll finally end up a dictatorship, and what I was trying to do was to keep the control in such a way that there'd be a balance all the way through. I wanted the businessmen

---

*The Landrum–Griffin Act of 1959 set additional restrictions on unions.

to have a fair deal, and I wanted the labor to have a fair deal, but I wanted the government to be the one who made the controls and told them whether they were doing right or wrong. That's all there was to it. That's all there is to it. You just have to have a monitor to see that they carry out what is set out in the legislation, as I say. A proper administrator can make legislation work for the welfare and benefit of the country, and an improper one can't. That's all there is to it.

Now, this is a question that is a key and your claim to the issue of labor protection: Under President Roosevelt and yourself, a great many protective devices—economic devices, social devices—have been put on the statute books to guard the interest rates, to guard the mortgages, to do all kinds of things, [such as regulating] hours and child labor. Haven't you brought the right for labor to the point where labor doesn't need to exercise its enormous powers to strike and paralyze the economy at its will?

It shouldn't be done. I proved that conclusively in my fight with John Lewis and Alexander F. Whitney in the railroad and coal strike during the war, and, of course, I had even as high up as Senators come tell me to settle so they could save money. The objective wasn't to save them money; it was to save the country, because whenever any organization, whether it's bankers or labor or any other organization you want to name, gets to the point where they think they're bigger than a free government, then you haven't any government, and the thing for people who are responsible for these things, who have no personal interest in either banks or labor or anything else, they must sit as arbiters, and that's what the government's for. That's the only reason we have government: to see that the little fellow who has no representative gets a proper deal without exploitation . . . I've said time again that there are 15 [million] or 20 million people who have lobbies to take care of their interests at the source of government, both in states and nationally, but the 150 million people who don't have these representations have only one man to look after their interests, and that's the President. When he fails to do that, they're in a bad fix.

Now, labor is no longer worried about a minimum standard of living. That it has. It's now a drive for an ever growing standard of living. How do you feel about that particular drive?

I think that the proper balance between the profits of the investors who own these great organizations and employ the great labor unions ought to be in such a shape that the men who do the work ought to have a fair share of the income that goes to the stockholders, but neither one of them ought to penalized.

How is that balance to be determined?

It can be determined by the Federal Labor Relations Board. The board is constituted in such a manner that it is impartial between the two, and I am very much afraid that the present Labor Relations Board isn't. I think it has been padded, because this administration is anti-labor. They believe in the richer a man gets, the better it is. I don't believe in it. I think the richer he gets the greater citizen he ought to be.

Very interesting.

Do you feel that the particular leaders, like [Walter] Reuther and [George] Meany and [James B.] Carey and Phil Murray before them, were overactive politically? [Sidney] Hillman, for instance?

No, I never thought so. They had a perfect right to be politically interested, the same as anybody else has, and I was acquainted with all of them, every single one of them you've named. I found that the cross-section of the leaders from labor is just like the cross-section of any other organization in the country. [There are] good ones, and there are those who are radical, those who want too much, and those who do not want enough. When you get the whole thing balanced up, if you have a proper arbiter between them, which is the government of the United States, they'll come out all right.

Then the political activity of these people should not be legislated or abridged?

I don't think so. I think every man ought to have a perfect right to take his hand in the political setup of the country, because that's free government. When we get to the point where we can't trust the people in the government, as Jefferson said, then you've got a dictatorship or a monarchy, and they're both bad.

Well, you don't think that the right to assess upon membership political dues, as they have had in the past, should have been taken from these unions?

Yes, I do. I don't believe in the assessment of dues for political purposes. If the individual members voluntarily form a contribution to a political party, that's their privilege, but when somebody forces them to throw in a pot for the use of the leaders of the union, that's wrong. That's absolutely wrong. I don't believe in that, never have, and the less you have to do with political money, the better off you are. I never would handle it, and I got along all right. Most of the time I didn't have any.

Isn't it significant that men like [James R.] Hoffa and others who are alleged to be corrupt are in fact Republicans?

Hoffa and [William L.] Hutcheson, who's dead, were Republicans, and they had the idea that they should tell their constituents what to do. You know, one of the troubles with a fellow who has never been properly raised in the control of power of government, or the power to control a union, or a bank, or anything else, is that unless he has a public-interest complex to begin with, he usually succumbs and goes into the same class as dictators, like the old man down in Santo Domingo or any one of these other dictatorships. Franco* is another one whom I also like to name in a thing of this kind.

Do you see labor looming as a political third party in the United States?

No, I don't. Whenever they do that, they'll be out of business.

---

*Francisco Franco, who led the Spanish government from 1939 to 1975.

Session Five

Unless a man has an idea of public service and has the interest of most people at heart, there's no use putting him in a public place, because he is going to work for the people he thinks will do him the most good when he gets out.

When we ended up before, Mr. President, we were talking about the labor situation, and one thing that you mentioned suddenly occurred to us to ask you this: In connection with companies, you have the exchange, the Securities Exchange, and there are other ways in which the business is regulated by state control. Do you think it would be worthwhile to set up some sort of machinery like that to . . .

The only thing that should be done in the situation so far as labor is concerned is to see that the control of the finances and the honoring of contracts are carried out just like we have the machinery to make the people who are in business do the same thing. That's the only thing I'm interested in. I think it will be done eventually in spite of the fact that the thing had to go to a terrible place before the people who were interested agreed that that's what ought to be done. That's what I wanted to do when I was vetoing the Taft–Hartley bill.* If you read the veto message, you will find that that was the idea we had in mind. I had outlined the things I thought ought to be done.

We're going back to the labor thing and the possibility of setting up machinery. The President has said he thought eventually something would be set up, something to control monies which are paid in and also that labor lives up to its contracts.

To see that the people who pay the money in get what they are paying for and that it doesn't go into the pockets of some fellow like Hoffa or the old man in that Teamsters' union [David Beck] before him.

Transcript, Wednesday afternoon, September 9, 1959, part one.

*Legislation in 1947 to restrict union activities.

The other question we were going to ask was whether you thought that labor could eventually become more democratized in its setup and how it functions with respect to its members.

Of course, that's what has to be done, because you can't have a dictatorship in labor any more than you could have a dictatorship in industry, which we've been stopping, and we can't have a dictatorship in government. It's got to be arranged on a basis so that the ordinary fellow who supports the labor union has a voice in its operation.

But somewhere between organized labor and organized business there is the vast body of the unorganized consumer. What happens to him?

The unorganized consumer is in the hands of free government. He has a vote, and his influence is greater than both of them put together. When he exercises that vote, he should exercise it in such a way that he'll have people in control locally and in statewide government and in the national government who understand that the welfare of the country is in the fact that labor, management, and the people who pay the bills get the same sort of treatment.

Does the state come into this relationship? More and more states have been putting in more and more facilities for dealing with industry, labor, and consumers.

Well, some of the states have been fooled into passing a right-to-work law, and I went around over the country in the last campaign and did my best to make it clear that those right-to-work laws are right-to-wreck laws. That's not the way to meet the situation. The thing must be met by people who understand the situation of the consumer and the man who works—and he's a consumer, too—and the industry who controls business—and he's a consumer, too. All those three consumers must be looked after on an equitable basis, just as we look after the other two, labor and management. . . .

There is a growing feeling that the stock market is the dog that normally is being wagged by the tail now.

Well, that may be true, but the Securities and Exchange Commission was set up to prevent that, and if you have the right sort of man on that board, you won't have any trouble.

But the Securities and Exchange [Commission] has a limit in that it only begins to function when a stock issue is in an amount of several hundred thousand shares or thereabouts. Anything below a certain point they don't do anything with, and as a result, a number of small speculators and promoters have been hatched within the past few years to deal in uranium stocks, first. Then they got into these electronic stocks.

The blue sky is just like it always was in the old days, and the Federal Trade Commission is set up to meet that situation. If the Federal Trade Commission doesn't do it, there's no place else to go in the present form of things.

Where does the Federal Trade begin and where does the Securities and Exchange ...

The Federal Trade Commission can begin with a penny and run into millions of dollars if they want to look into things. They spend their time running down fake advertisements and things of that kind, but they've got a perfect right to look into the blue-sky thing, as it affects the little fellow, in the corporations that don't come under the Securities and Exchange Commission. That's the way to do it.

Does that apply to food products, too?

Yes.

And drugs?

Yes, all those things, and they've been ferreting out the fake advertisements of foods and drugs and tooth powder and toothpaste and things of that kind, but they could get after these fellows who are on a small scale disobeying the blue-sky laws that affect the Securities and Exchange Commission. They've got a perfect right to do that.

To whom do they report in the conduct of their various agencies? To the President?

Yes. They are supposed to report to the President, and to the country at the same time. They have a report, and it will be published in all the papers that are not working to prevent such a thing from being done, and there are a great many that are.

How are they agitated, or how are they stimulated to take a special interest in these?

Well, they ought to get after the members of Congress and the Senate and give them the information, and you'll find that there are a great many men in both those bodies who are anxious to do what's necessary to be done to prevent this from taking place, and it can be done.

But is it the administration in power that sets the climate to get these things done?

That's right. The administration in power can say to the attorney general, "Stop this stuff," and if he doesn't say it, they don't stop.

It's up to the Department of Justice, is it, to enforce these rules?

That's right.

Are these agencies, in themselves, in a position to enforce the regulations?

No. I think the thing would have to go through the attorney general.

All right.... We now have an unprecedented series of mergers taking place all over the country. What about those, Mr. President?

Well, the effect of that is to, as far as possible, get around the antitrust laws, and it keeps free enterprise—which these Republicans are always talking about—from actually working. They really don't want free enterprise. They'd like to have cartels in charge of everything, and unless the little business people are supported so that any fellow who wants to start in a little business—a grocery store or anything else like that—is protected and can get loans at a reasonable point so that he can carry an inventory, then we go into the very situation that the antitrust laws are set up to prevent, and that's what we're headed for, if we're not careful. It's one of the things that this [Eisenhower] administration is very much interested in. They think the bigger the man, the better he is, as far as finance is concerned. That doesn't mean he's big in mind or heart or anything of that kind. It means that he controls more money than anybody else.

Now we have the Defense Department, probably the largest single claimant on the American economy in these times.

That's correct.

These men place huge orders, and recently it's been proved that more and more of these go to the larger ones, and fewer and fewer go to the small ones.

That's true. We had a terrible time with that during World War II and set up an organization to be sure that the small business people, comparatively small—not small ordinarily but comparatively small—had a chance to get at it, these government contracts, and I think that nearly all have been abolished under this administration.

Do we need small business under present conditions?

We need small business all the time. That's really free enterprise. That's not what the trusts and the big organizations think. As you remember, the Standard Oil Company of New Jersey put all the little oil companies out of business, and that's one of the reasons for the institution of the antitrust laws, the Sherman Anti-Trust Act, under a Republican administration,* if you please, and it wasn't done willingly; it was done because it had to be done.

*In 1890 under President Benjamin Harrison.

Now, do these prosecutions get the ultimate relief that they were intended to get?

They're supposed to. When [in 1911] they broke up the Standard Oil Company of New Jersey into four or five companies—the Standard Oil of Indiana, the Standard Oil of California, the Standard Oil of Louisiana, and the Standard Oil of Kentucky—they thought they had broken it up, but the control was right where it always was. There wasn't any change.

And each of the components became bigger than the original company?

Each one of those. Of course they did, and they still control them all.

One of the factors in connection with the cost of living has to do with the cost of necessities in the open market.

That's right.

Now, we're seeing the growth of supermarkets all over the country, and we are seeing the gradual elimination of what they call the [Pa and Ma] stores. Is it good for the country?

I don't know whether it is or not. We'll have to wait and see. It's a change, and any change where small business get concentrated and centered for public convenience is a good thing. Now, let's wait and see what [effect] these business setups out in the country where the people can park will have on the retail market and what effect they may have on the small-business man.

One thing that has happened already is that the original purpose of these A&P [Atlantic and Pacific] stores—you will remember, they were being prosecuted during your administration—was that they were hurting the independent store because they were able to buy for less and sell for less, which they did.

That's true.

They controlled the market on coffee, for instance.

That's true.

Now you find that the prices in all of these supermarkets have gone up. The service has gone down. They used to have clerks, not all self-service. The consumer has to wait on himself, and yet the prices have continually gone up to the point where the independent fellow can match them and do well. Yet he is disappearing from the scene.

That's true, and the reason he can't match them and do well is because he can't buy in the same market that they do. In a great many instances, these great organizations like Safeway, A&P, and all those great drug combinations have access to the market just like Sears, Roebuck, and Montgomery Ward used to have. They'd set up people to make shoes or anything of that kind they wanted; then, when the time came that the shoe manufacturer was becoming independent, they'd break him, quit buying from him, and he was out of business. That's what these other people do with this market that we're talking about, and it's a dangerous thing. I don't know how we are going to get a free market unless we have somebody in control of affairs where they can be regulated, where the little fellow will have the same access to the prices that the big ones get, if he's going to be in any way able to compete with them.

What develops from your observation this morning is again to emphasize the importance of getting men into public life who have the welfare of the people in mind and in spirit. Otherwise, no matter what they are, they're going to miss the point.

That's true. That's absolutely the fundamental basis. Unless a man has an idea of public service and has the interest of most people at heart, there's no use putting him in a public place because he is going to work for the people he thinks will do him the most good when he gets out.

Therefore, the role of man in all this is very important.

That's right. That's the fundamental basis of it all.

But you cannot have any results favoring the public, the consumer, where you depend entirely on self regulation by either . . .

It can't be done. It can't be self-regulation. You've got to have a government that's standing there watching what goes on, with the ability to stop it when it's wrong and to help it when it's right.

Now, that's always being resisted by the organized chambers and so on, and as an intrusion and a control by government over free enterprise.

Well, they talk about free enterprise. If there's free enterprise, why, it's hard to find. Free enterprise is what the big boys think they can do without interference. That's what they call "free enterprise."

License to do whatever they want?

Right. Whatever they want, and the little man in the street's the man who pays the bill, and he pays through the nose.

Now, Mr. President, there's developing in this country, as all around the world, amazing leaps in population. There are two things that developed from that: [first], the . . . growing need for more housing, and second, the expansion of the economy. Now, about housing: What do you feel about housing?

Well, of course, you've got to have a housing program that will meet the expansion in population, and in meeting the expansion in population we must expand the industrial background so that it will grow along with the population. Now, it's been estimated that . . . The population, I think, is now about 2.3 billion or 2.4 billion [1960 estimate: 3 billion]—and in ten or fifteen years it will be 6 billion or 7 billion [1970 estimate: 3.7 billion]. You've got to meet that situation by the proper development of the resources so that they can be fed and clothed and have places to live and reproduce, if they want to, and the best way to do that is to try to find some way to increase the productive parts of the Earth that are not now in production. If they can get the program that's been worked on for quite some time to change sea water into fresh water, we can make a garden out of the Sahara Desert and the Gobi Desert and the Caspian Sea area, where there is no production now, and this soil is just as rich as it is anywhere else if you have the necessary water to make it work. Some time or other, we'll get that done. It'll have to be done, because the pressure of increased population will force it.

Do you think it has to be done on an international basis, or can we do this as a nation all by ourselves?

No, no. It has to be done on an international basis. These places that I've named are not under our control. The Sahara Desert is controlled by the Arabs on the east side and the French on the north and the increased number of independent countries in Africa on the south, and they'll have to agree on a way to handle things. In fact, I think Arabia could be made a garden if they get this water thing settled in a way so we can get the inexhaustible water sources of the great oceans made into fresh water as we go along. And I think that will come along some time or other. I don't know when it will be, but, then, I worked on it all the time while I was President. That was one of the projects I had in view—to find out a way to get salt water out of the sea made into fresh water so that it could be used for the development of the desert areas of the world for the production of foodstuffs and things of that sort. There are still immense areas in the world that have never been developed. You take in South America, in the Amazon basin, and in the southern part of Brazil, there are areas that would support a population of 300 million people, and there are only about 50 million people in Brazil. The same thing's true in Africa. There are parts of Africa that have never been properly developed that could support immense populations in luxury, if the development was made for the benefit of the people instead of exploited for the benefit of just a few, which is what's been done in times past.

But why, as President, with so many unfinished projects on the home front, did you find it necessary to concern yourself with problems of other nations—the problems of strange and remote people, in fact?

Because that would increase the welfare of our own country. The more they need, and ourselves being an industrial nation, the more market we'd have for the things we had to sell, and that was the idea entirely.

*Now, you don't mean to suggest, Mr. President, that the whole reason
for seeking out opportunities to improve the lot of these people was to find
new outlets for our own selfish purposes as a nation?*

That was one of the fundamental things, but when that was done, when
that could be done, you'll find that the improvement of the situation as it
affects all these other peoples would eventually result in their being just as
well off as we are. But you have to have somewhere to start, and when you
have a political situation to deal with, you have to talk to the people who have
selfish interests. Then, when you get them hooked so they'll go ahead, the
first thing you know they're helping people and don't know what they're
doing.

Session Six

We murdered as many Indians as we could and took the land away from them, but I felt they could have been maintained on the land and improved in their position and eventually would have become exceedingly friendly to us.

The President was just commenting that the overall purpose of his program was to enable people to help themselves. By doing so, they can achieve a higher standard of living, and he was hoping that they would achieve a standard of living comparable to our own.

That's correct. That was one of the things that caused the start of Point IV, the so-called Point IV: to help people help themselves without too much monetary help, but to instruct them on how to use the opportunities which they had. By getting a small start with this so-called Point IV program, it was hoped that eventually we'd have education enough around the world so that people would be willing to develop the resources which are available all around the world in such a way that it would not only help their own standard of living, but it would make it much easier for all the rest of the world to get along together.*

It sounds altogether reasonable and practical, Mr. President, but did this idea come to you? Because this would appear to be the first time in history that a major power undertook such an ambitious program.

It was the first time that a major power helped the rehabilitation of the defeated governments in a war, and in doing that, they were doing the thing that would help the people who were being injured. Now, you take Genghis

Transcript, Wednesday afternoon, September 9, 1959, part two.

*In his Inaugural Address on January 20, 1949, Truman spoke exclusively about American foreign policies and world peace as necessary for world recovery. Support of the United Nations, the Marshall Plan, and a proposed North Atlantic defense arrangement were his first three proposals. The fourth called for bringing U.S. scientific and industrial talent to undeveloped nations.

Khan and Tamerlane and all the great emperors of times past: [They] eliminated the people that they conquered and used the land from which they were
eliminated to help their own people. That's what the Romans used to do—
settle their legions in places and start them up and do away with the population. Well, that's not what should be done. The population that's already there
ought to be helped to improve its own situation, and if that's done, that will
contribute to world peace more than any other one thing that can be done.
Most wars are started for economic purposes. Some great conqueror wants to
increase the power that he has by getting control of lands which he thinks are
fertile, and that's what's been done all through the history of the world. I had
come to the conclusion that the best way to prevent a thing of that kind from
taking place was to have the people on the land that's fertile—they could have
the necessary resources to make it produce—go ahead and learn how to make
it produce. Then, in the long run, they'd understand what the situation is, and
those countries that have been developed in that way—that's the United States
and Canada and part of the African continent and parts of South America . . .
and in the long run we'd get people to understand that they can get along
together, if they have the necessary goods and exchanges to keep the people
satisfied on both sides of the line.

*Now, in a way, that was basic American thinking, Mr. President, some-
thing that you had also seen and read in American history, as a result of the
Civil War, the aftermath, when there was . . .*

Yes, that's right, only we didn't follow through on the basis on which
I had. We murdered as many Indians as we could and took the land away from
them, but I felt they could have been maintained on the lands and improved
in their position and eventually would have become exceedingly friendly to
us. They have the same sort of brains and setup that we do, and they are brave
people. And that could be done, I figured, all around the world. We learned
by doing what we ought not to do after the Civil War that you talk about.

*Now, the example set by you, as spokesman for the West, apparently was
lost on some of the communist sympathizers, or the borderline nations, uncom-
mitted nations, who were watching this very enormous thing happening. Here
you were giving up and dedicating our might and our riches to rebuild nations,
and especially the conquered nations. And here was Russia on the other side,
one of the conquerors, helped by us, who was exploiting her neighbors and
apparently making those neighbors like her—or, at least, not resent her to the
point where it made for any help for us.*

I don't think any of them ever liked her. You know what they were doing?
You see, [Vladimir I.] Lenin and his cohorts were trying to make the Marxist program appear as if it would work. Well, the Marxist program is out of
date, and they couldn't do anything, but instead of taking the countries that
are the most advanced—which [Karl] Marx had an idea that the proletariat

could take over—they took a country that was as low in the economic scale and as low in liberty and freedom as was possible for an outfit to get and organized a totalitarian state under the firm force of using concentration camps and murder to get done what they wanted. That's [also] what they've done in China, and that's what they want to do all around the world. It is not the economic situation that Marx anticipated at all. It's a situation which Lenin worked out himself. This is Leninism, not Marxism at all—and they are both -isms, as far as that's concerned—and it seemed to me that the proper thing to do was to try to get these nations who had suffered from the war rehabilitated and to understand that their proper development would meet the so-called communist proposition head-on. There's no communism in the world. The only communism there ever was was set out in the acts of the Apostles. That's dead. This so-called communism that we have now is not anything in the world but a totalitarian state, and there's no difference in dictatorships, whether you call it communism or something else.

But here we have the example of you offering under the Marshall Plan to help rehabilitate Czechoslovakia, which was a free nation patterned after us and an industrial nation.

Well, they [the Russian communists] murdered the President of Czechoslovakia [Edvard Beneš]. They threw him out a window and made out like he committed suicide, which he didn't, and that gave them the same opportunity to take over as it did in Romania, Bulgaria, Poland, and Hungary by force, where they murdered the people who understand what freedom means and what we were trying to do.* Every one of those countries should have been free. It was agreed by the Russians that they should have free elections and set up their own governments, and they'd have set up free governments if they had had an opportunity, but they didn't.

Well this is a pretty well advanced democracy that was subjugated— a self-sustaining democracy in the case of Czechoslovakia. How do you account for their inability to throw it off or to indicate that they would like to throw it off?

Well, let's say, how can a hundred thousand people operate . . . in opposition to a hundred million? That's about the proportion. The Russians have 200 million, and I expect Czechoslovakia has 3 or 4 or 5 million. That's what the trouble was. It was a matter of force, a matter of power, and that's what I've always contended, but when mama and papa got to crying, and we had to discharge all our military people under a basis that was not for the welfare

*Truman is mistaken and is actually referring to Jan Masaryk, Foreign Minister and son of the first President of Czechoslovakia, who jumped, or was pushed, from a window to his death on March 10, 1948. The previous month, communists had seized control of the government in a coup d'état. President Beneš resigned from the Presidency in June 1948 and died of a paralytic stroke on September 3 of that year.

of the world, we had to accept it. There wasn't anything we could do, but Czechoslovakia, Romania, Bulgaria—Greece we did save—and Poland could have been saved in the same way if we had had the power and the ability to make the Russians stay inside their own borders. And that didn't happen.

Mr. President, what you are suggesting is that at a critical moment in history we should not have disbanded, because then we could really have talked more firmly to the Russians . . . regarding the satellite states.

There isn't any question about that, and that's what we should have done.

Now at this point, where we are talking about these nations that have come under the domination of these despots and exploiters . . .
And you have a very interesting reflection there that with the disbandment of our forces and the weakening of our power, we certainly were not in a position to do very much about keeping Poland and those other countries free.

That's true. One of the things that caused the most serious difficulty was the fact that agreements starting at Quebec and Casablanca and Cairo and Tehran and Yalta—in order to be sure that the Russians would stay put—was on a division of Germany in such a way that the Russians would have a slice and the French a slice and the Americans a slice and the British a slice. The contemplation of the breaking up of the balance of power in Europe I don't think was seriously considered, without any reflection on anybody. I afterward talked to Winston Churchill, who had been in this thing ever since the First World War when, he was in charge of the Navy that made the failure at Gallipoli, and he wanted me, after all these agreements had been made, to let the Americans hold the line 170 [miles] east of the point where the line had been set by agreement. We were in Prague and the outskirts of Berlin, and the agreement had been made at these other places, particularly at Yalta, to set it up in a certain way. Well, I inherited those agreements, and I carried them out. If I had been in touch with the whole situation at that time, I don't think I would have withdrawn the American Army from the eastern boundary in Germany, and then we wouldn't have had serious trouble, but I labored under the feeling, as did a great many other people, that the Russians would keep their agreements. If they had, there wouldn't have been any trouble. They didn't, so we found ourselves in a Cold War as a result of that, and there's nothing you can do about it. It's just like talking about winning a football game on Monday after it's been lost on Saturday, and the thing we've got to do now is to meet the situation head-on as best we can. What I'm arguing for now is strength enough to meet that situation with an outfit that has no sense of decency or honor, and in order to make them behave, you've got to have more strength than they have. We have it now if we can just keep it up.

Did the possession of ballistics [sic] *and the nuclear equipment that the Russians now have alter your position on how to deal with them?*

No. The only way in the world that you can deal with them is to be in a position . . . to be stronger than they are, and we are. There isn't any question about it, unless we just sit back on a basis of peace at any price, as Nehru has done in India, and you can see what it's cost him. They [the Russians] have no idea of decency or the welfare of the people as a whole. That totalitarian dictatorship is one of the worst the world has ever seen. Rome at the height of its powers, with all its great emperors, was never as mean to the people under them as the Russians are to those that they control now. That's Hungary, Romania, Yugoslavia, Czechoslovakia, and Poland.

That's not a peculiar characteristic of the Russians. They are not barbarians in that sense. Why do they have to impose this kind of sadistic control?

I think they're the worst barbarians the world has ever produced. They have a cross of the Tartar in them, and they haven't changed a bit—just the same as Genghis Khan and Tamerlane, only they're not as smart as Tamerlane and Genghis were.

What would have happened if you had had your way in keeping the country mobilized immediately after the war?

Well we would have been in a position to meet this situation. I can give an illustration of it. [Josip Broz] Tito sent me word that he was going to march into Trieste before we had finally decided how the division was going to be made between Yugoslavia and Italy. I called in the chiefs of staff—General Eisenhower was then commander of the European situation, and I talked with the Chief of Naval Operations [Ernest J. King], the Air Force Chief [Hoyt S. Vandenberg], and the Chief of Military Affairs [Omar Bradley], and asked them how long it would take to move three divisions to the Brenner Pass, and they told me. It was a very short time, and I asked King, who was Chief of Naval Operations, how quickly he could get the Mediterranean Fleet into the Adriatic Sea. He told me, and I sent Tito word that we were moving the Mediterranean Fleet into the Adriatic Sea and that we were moving three divisions down to the border of Italy at the end of the Brenner Pass and for him to come on. He didn't. That shows you what can be done if you have the ability to do it, but after that we didn't have the means to do things of that sort.

Supposing you had a lot of divisions. You could not have matched the total number of Russian divisions.

I know, but it doesn't take but one American division—at that time— it wouldn't have taken but one American division to wipe out three Russian divisions, because they had no transportation except what we'd given them. They transported their men where . . . what's the old man's name who was the commander of the Russian Army? They just fired him the other day.

Yes, [Georgi] Zhukov.

Zukov in the movement of his army used horses and wagons and people on foot to pull his equipment. Well, we wouldn't have had any trouble holding them off because our divisions were equipped, and we could have held the line anywhere we chose to hold it. It doesn't make any difference how many people they have. We had the wherewithal, the guns, and the ability, and the young men who were willing to hold the situation and transport that would have taken care of the situation. The Russians didn't have it. We just let them into Germany, because that was an agreement that had been made previous to that time. There wasn't anything I could do about it, unless I wanted to break the agreements, and I always had a notion that when an agreement's made, it ought to be kept, and I also felt that the Russians would be honorable in their settlement after the Potsdam Conference, which was to implement what had been done before, and it was implemented. They broke every one of those agreements.

You said Churchill was the first one to sound the warning that the Russians were not going to keep their agreements?

That's right. He was sure that they would not keep their agreements and that we ought to hold the line. Well, I couldn't do that by myself.

Yet he was a party to all the agreements?

He was a party to all the agreements. He was there when they were made, every one of them.

Did he tell you what had caused him to change his mind?

His experience in the Black Sea Straits in the First World War, I think, was the cause of it.

And yet, in spite of that, he made agreements with them that he expected them to keep, or . . .

Of course he did. We all expected them to keep their agreements. But, as I say, it's a Monday-morning quarterback thing. We can see what might have been done, and you know that [John Greenleaf] Whittier said that the saddest of all sad words are: "It might have been."

Of course, what is important, Mr. President, is the fact that we did, almost automatically, lose our great military strength by this pullback of our troops.

Well, you know, one of the reasons for the pullback of those troops was the idea that it would take a million and half men to make Japan stop, and a great many of those troops were being moved across the country into the Pacific for the purpose of an invasion of Japan. Well, when we dropped the atomic bombs on Hiroshima and Nagasaki, that stopped the Japanese war, and it stopped the Japanese war with a great many of our divisions in the country. Some of the men who had been in longtime service in the Pacific were very much put out, because these boys who hadn't seen much service were discharged first because they were here. That was one of the reasons that brought the thing about, but, of course, we didn't know that the Japanese were going to surrender. All of my military advisers said it would take a year or a year and a half to make Japan surrender. But when they found out what a destructive weapon we had, why, they surrendered right away. And it saved a lot of lives doing that. But that's what took a great many of our divisions out of Europe on the way to the Pacific, and they stopped in the middle of the country.

Along that same line, having taken care of the Japanese problem, you still had the Russian problem on your hands, and Russia was beginning to show more and more belligerency, [even though] we had exhibited the atomic-bomb possession, and you had a monopoly of the atomic bomb at that time. Could you have used the persuasive power of that bomb to make Russia roll back to her frontiers?

I think so, if we had had the necessary soldiers and sailors to back it up. But a great many of them had been discharged, so there you are. We didn't have them.

Had you wanted to have some kind of leverage at that time in order to compel the Russians to come to terms?

Well, at that time, we didn't know that they would have to be compelled. We thought they were going to keep their agreements. I thought so for a year—a year after Potsdam. It was 1946 before we were fully assured that they were not going to keep their agreements, when they started their propaganda against us, and we had furnished them the equipment which got them out of Stalingrad. Then they made the statement publicly: Stalin made a speech to the conference of the Soviet Republics in which he said they had done it all themselves and that the Americans were not their friends and never would be. Then we began to wake up to the fact that he didn't intend to keep his agreements, and he didn't.

And you found yourself helpless to do anything about it.

There wasn't anything to do about it at that time, because it was too late. We'd demobilized.

Anyway, you threw in your lot with the United Nations at that time, and you were hoping that the United Nations would be a platform from which some of these things could be resolved?

That's right. Stalin was very friendly to the United Nations, and I talked to him over the telephone through Harry Hopkins while he was in the Kremlin, and he said, Go ahead; we'll back it up. But he didn't mean it.

Did you talk . . . through an interpreter?

I talked to Harry Hopkins, and he talked to Stalin through an interpreter and then Stalin talked to Harry Hopkins through an interpreter, and he talked back to me. . . . Harry Hopkins was with Stalin when I talked to him.

What was the subject you were discussing with him?

The endorsement of the Russians for the United Nations. That's when I told [Vyacheslav M.] Molotov where to get off when he came by to see me. He was the Foreign Minister of Russia, and I just told him straight out that this was not a one-way street. If they wanted to do the right thing, they wouldn't have any trouble with us. . . . And that's when he said he'd never been talked to like that before, and I said, You'll be talked to like that unless you keep your agreements.

So this was while the United Nations was being organized?

That's right. When Molotov was on the way to San Francisco for the organization of the United Nations.

And there was some doubt as to whether Russia would join the United Nations?

That's right. After my conversation with Molotov, I sent Harry Hopkins to Russia, and while he was with Stalin, I talked to him on the telephone and told him that I wanted to get this thing set up, and I wanted Stalin to go along and get it done. Hopkins told him that, and he said, All right, I'll go along. What else could you ask?

Stalin did not get on the phone to talk?

Oh, no, he couldn't. It was English and Russian. I talked to Hopkins and he talked to Stalin and Stalin talked to Hopkins and Hopkins talked to me.

Then your feeling is that, having gone through this, you had no prospects about liberation of any of those so-called satellites.

Not unless I could send 2 million men over there and take them away from them. And you can't do that.

That would be a forced rollback. Failing in that, how do you see those people getting out from under the yoke?

Well, they have gotten out from under yokes before. Poland, if I remember correctly, was divided into three countries at one time and was set up again after the First World War with [Ignace Jan] Paderewski as Prime Minister, and the same thing was true of Czechoslovakia. Part of their troops, you remember, marched all the way across Siberia in the First World War, and we brought them home. And the same situation has developed time and again in the history of the world. Sweden once controlled Poland, if you remember. Charles XII fought the battle of [Poltava] and had to back up.

Then you are hoping, or expecting, that these people [will] live up to the historic precedent of coming into their own some day and getting out from under?

They haven't changed a bit. They're still the same people; they still believe in freedom. That's true in Hungary and Czechoslovakia and Poland and all those countries, including Romania, where I'm told they speak almost the original Latin language.

But at any rate then, history must now go through this long waiting period to adjust.

I'm sorry that's the case, but I think the more education the Russians get, the more they find out how the rest of the world lives, it's going to make it much harder on the dictatorship to beat them down. I have thought the Chinese, in their long background from Confucius to date, would be satisfied with the sort of dictatorship they have now.

Do you see any conflict as between Russia and China?

I think the Russians are very much afraid of China. I think they have built a Frankenstein in their backyard. That's what they call Siberia. I'm not saying it is a backyard, because it's a great country and could be developed just like our West was, but they are very much alarmed at what they have to contend with on their eastern border. Let's put it that way.

Then your suggestion for our own position is that we do what? For the time being?

Well the best thing that we can do is to keep up our strength in the way that we can meet any sort of an attack anywhere around the world that affects us as a nation and try our best to get the educational program into these countries that have been used to freedom in such a way that they'll awaken again. Then, when they get ready, maybe we'll be in a frame of mind to help them win their freedom. I think that's about the only thing we can do.

What happens to our enormous foreign-aid program. Are you still for its continuity?

I think we've got to continue the foreign-aid program as far as it's necessary. Of course, there's not as much necessity for tremendous appropriations for that purpose now as there was when we first started. After we've got them all, most of them, in a position where they're economically sound; on this side of the Iron Curtain, they're in a position to support themselves. And we don't want to just keep wasting our money by sending it over there when it's not needed. I don't think it's very long before they'll be able to support themselves. They used to support us—didn't you know that? Nearly all the development of the West came from Great Britain and Germany—funds that they furnished . . . to develop that part of the country. And then I think that the tremendous amount of the European loans was balanced after the First World War when they used everything they had as a backlog to get arms to carry on the First World War before we got into it. Of course, it was finished off in the Second World War, and now we've got that same situation reversed. We've done the same thing over there, and they still owe us the money, and sometime they'll pay it, maybe.

Could I then go to this subject? With the world's expanding population . . . the question arises, as it does in this country: What do you do about getting increased amounts of money that you need to build up industry, to build up housing, to build up an expanding economy?

Well, we have untold resources that have not been developed. You know, what saved the country after the War Between the States was the discovery of gold in California and Nevada and Colorado, and we've got this thing that makes bombs [uranium] discovered in the same places, and we've got a very rich neighbor to the north whose money is worth now 105 as far as ours is concerned, which makes some people stand back on their heels when they find out about it, and we've got a very rich country on the south of us, whose economy has been stabilized. With all these things in view, I don't see any reason in the world for us to worry about the development of our own country, because as these other countries develop, as I tried to say in the first place, it helps develop our own country. That's what makes peace in the world—where there's plenty of trade and plenty of resources on each side, where there's an equal exchange of the things that we need that they have and the things that we have that they need. I don't think there'll be any difficulty about that.

Then you think that our first job is to bring the level of the economies of our neighbors and friends up to ours in order to create a level position?

Yes. Just like that between the states when they organized the government of the United States and took down the barriers between the colonies. Everybody thought that the colonies would grow apart, but they didn't. They're all richer than they ever hoped to be under the circumstances. I think that if we can get the United Nations Organization in such shape [that it keeps] the grabbers from trying to take over the nations that are well fixed, in the long run we'll have the same thing around the world. Now, how long it will last, I don't know. It may be that the development of another race of people who are energetic and who want to do something for their own welfare and benefit may put us all out of business, but I don't want to see that happen for the next three hundred years, and I don't believe it will.

So our main task now is to keep strong, keep on developing, and keep on expanding?

That's right, and keep the rest of the world doing the same thing.

Now you spoke of our rich neighbor to the north, with a parity of 105* now. There's some conflicts between that neighbor to the north, for the first time, and the neighbor to the south. I think it's become our biggest problem now.

Well, I don't [think] that amounts to anything. It's been in conversation ever since I can remember, and I think those people have common sense. We speak a common language and we can understand each other, and that's one of the difficulties around the world. There are so many different languages spoken in so many different places, and when you translate an agreement from one language to another, it's never the same as it was in the original draft. And I rather think that if we can work things around to the point where we have a language that's understood all around the world—French used to be the diplomatic language; I think English is now . . . eventually we'll get people to understand what we're thinking about in ways that they can understand it. Then they'll be satisfied, because we have no ambition to take over any nation or any of its resources, as the Point IV pointed out. We wanted to develop those resources for the benefit of the people who own them, and not for our benefit, because they'll have to spend some of their money when it works.

General [George C.] Marshall, when you made him Secretary of State, came back with a rather disturbing report to you after his visit to Russia and some of the satellite countries. His refrain at that time was, "They won't believe me; they won't believe me." He was terribly upset. I remember having heard him say that.

Well, that's true, that's true.

How did he explain that problem to you when you were having your conferences with him?

Well, he told me the same thing: that these people east of the Iron Curtain heeded the propaganda with which they had been fed by the Russians and

---

*The Canadian dollar was valued at $0.95 American.

couldn't believe that there was a country in the world as rich as ours and as powerful as ours that wanted to help them help themselves. He just couldn't make them believe that we did it by example, though they may come to believe it eventually.

Well, that is not a question of misunderstanding. It was their failing to believe us.

They thought we were as crooked as they were. And that's too bad. We weren't.

About the whole business of the communications problem: You had no difficulty in communicating yourself to our allies and friends. There was no need for any special interpreters; even those who spoke the language needed interpreters sometimes.

Well, that's true, but one of the reasons for that was that the ones who were friendly to us, the ones we were trying to help, were willing to understand, even when the translation was poor. It's just like I was saying about the enforcement of a law: A good administrator can do it. A good translator can make people believe what you have to say when you're on the right track and unselfish about it, and the country that doesn't want to understand you will do just like Russia does—garble and lie about what you said. But that didn't happen with our friends.

I just wanted to cover the point of you being selfless and interested in the future and in the benefits not only to your own people, but to our friends and neighbors. They were being prematurely selfish and self-centered, and they had difficulty in believing us, even though we were giving by example all we could. Yet you had no difficulty with any of the allies—in the sense that we do now.

We had no trouble with our allies, and we didn't have any trouble with our neighbors to the south, because they believed that our interest had ceased to be one of occupation and force and that we wanted to help them develop as they should, because they all have unlimited resources. Our southern neighbors are the greatest asset we have in the world at the present time.

Are we an asset to them?

We want to be. I hope we are.

I just want to get to one last thing, Mr. President. This has been going quite long. I want to get back to a very quaint and antiquated subject—that is, gold used to be of great importance.

It is yet. . . .

What do you think is the solution to ... our constantly losing gold, and then, when the balance tips against Europe and our trade, the gold shifts back here? Are we in any danger from this constant shift?

I don't think so. I don't think so, for this reason: We discovered in this country when the Federal Reserve was set up that the fundamental basis for a currency or an exchange is resources that the country has, which is not necessarily gold. Of course, gold is a medium that everybody understands, and it has been the medium of exchange right straight along. The British, of course, have always tried to control the gold reserves of the world, but the thing that really counts in exchange between countries ... the resources of that country as they are represented by goods and services and things of that kind, and not gold, although gold is a medium through which we transact business. It's always a good thing to have plenty of backing for what we want to do. Now, we've always had gold enough to pay off the national debt if we want. Issue currency against it on the basis that it has always been issued. But I don't think that the gold furor that's going on now will have any serious effect on the economy of the world, because some of these countries—France and Britain, for instance—[still] have the fetish that gold's the only commodity that can meet the situation for resources in a country.

Now, old [William Jennings] Bryan wasn't as crazy as everybody thought he was when he was for 16-to-1 silver, and we've got to the point now where silver's only 72 cents an ounce, and the Nevada people, the mines, with the help of [Patrick] McCarran, are still selling silver to the government of the United States at $1.29, which is perfectly silly, perfectly silly. It's my opinion that the background and resources behind the economy of any country is what makes currency stable, and we came to that conclusion under Woodrow Wilson, and nobody else, ... when he organized the Federal Reserve Bank and took control of the monetary resources of the government away from the gold barons in Wall Street. You remember, the old man who owned the Missouri Pacific Railroad coined gold in 1873, and in 1907, when Theodore Roosevelt was having so much trouble, old Morgan had $300 million in gold, and they used that to balance the situation to keep away from a panic. Well, Wilson made the Federal Reserve Board the center for the resources of the country, and those resources are based on corn and wheat and oats and hogs and cattle and whatever is raised in the country—fruit and everything else. It's just as good and as stable a background as is this yellow metal that everybody's so fond of, although it's a nice thing to have plenty of that yellow metal. While I was President, we had $22 billion in reserve. Now we've got $19 billion. I don't think that $4 billion [*sic*] is going to have any effect on the ...

But it's more a symbol than a fact.

That's exactly what it is. You can't eat it or wear it or do anything. . . . It's only fit to create a situation where you can get something to eat and wear and build a house.

Can I come back just to two tiny personal things? . . . Do you still look at the daily report issued by the Treasury?

Oh yes. I get it every day. It's a day late, but that doesn't make it old.

And you like to read it and have read it ever since you left the White House?

I keep track of it all the time, and I've watched the gold reserve go down, and I've wondered what caused the gold reserve to go down when the budget's supposed to be balanced, and it goes out of balance further every year.

Now, you also get some other things from Washington. You get, of course, the Congressional Record.

I get the *Congressional Record* every day.

And you do like to look over it.

I look over it as nearly as I can. Sometimes I get a little behind, but whenever there's anything of vital interest going on in the Congress—like arguments on the monetary situation, which was going on not long ago, or whenever we have arguments about foreign exchange and things of that kind—I always look over the situation, because there are men in the Congress who are as well informed on these things as any people in the world. When they make statements in the *Record,* you can rely on it because that's the truth, but you've got to read the *Record* to get it. You can't get it out of the newspapers.

Now, Mr. President, you also send for . . . You do get a weather map, don't you?

Every day. I get that weather map every day by air mail.

What do you get out of that?

Well, sir, it's an interesting thing. For instance, we're sitting here this morning, and the weather map showed that there was a low-pressure area over northwest Canada that had created a situation that caused six inches of snow up there at this time of year, and then there was a lower-pressure area below us to the southeast. When I came over here this morning, there was a line across the northwest sky which showed that a cool wave is going to move in. It did. It's turned a lot cooler, and I think by tonight we may have some showers.

Is that a hobby or a point of interest?

It's not only a point of interest, there's this about it: When you're on the farm and you have to harvest wheat or sow wheat or plant corn or gather corn or decide on what you're going to do with the livestock to be sure they don't go to town when the weather's cold and lose a lot of weight, you watch the weather all the time, and it's the most interesting thing in the world. If you watch the birds and the pigs and the cows, you can tell more about what the weather's going to do than the weatherman himself, and when you have these pressure areas that cause these antics by the livestock, you get some satisfaction out of it. It's just a hobby with me.

Better than golf.

It's interesting, most interesting. If you notice, Washington . . . kept track of the temperature, direction of the wind, all the time in his diary, every day. Jefferson did the same thing. Jefferson had a patent weathervane on his house—where he lived—Monticello. Well, Virginians call it *Montisello;* I guess that's right. He had a weathervane up there, and he had a hand in the hallway that would show him the direction of the wind. Well, he kept track of that every day in his diary, and in those books that we have in yonder, you'll see that every day he set down what the temperature was, which way the wind was, how much it was blowing. He had a weather measure for the wind which was previous to the one we have nowadays, and all those things, especially where a man is getting his living out of the ground—that is, on a farm— he has to know something about the weather.

So the wind gauge was also a part of his agricultural . . .

That's right. He owned—oh, I don't know—he owned a thousand, thousands of acres back there in Virginia, and his friends ate it all up. He was broke when he died because he entertained so many people at his house, but he had to go down to a little farm way down in the southwest corner of Virginia so they'd let him alone.*

In terms of gold, just before we close, the Russians since their takeover have been accelerating their mining of gold and have been accumulating vast hoards of it. There's some talk about their letting that loose on the capitalist world in order to break the symbol and the gauge of gold on the economy.

I wish they would let it loose. We'd take it all over, and then where would they be? And it wouldn't cost us anything.

How would you take it over? They're just going to drop it all over the goldless countries to give them the gold so they can buy.

---

*Jefferson also owned Poplar Forest Plantation in Bedford County, Virginia, ninety miles southwest of Monticello. He would enjoy quiet days there when a large crowd of friends and relatives took over Monticello.

Well, that would be all right. They'd have to pay us in the gold, and we'd finally get it, just as we did in this last go-round. But their gold mines up in northern Siberia are just like those in California, on the same kind of situation. The Riga River is one source of their gold, and there are very rich mines in Siberia, but they have not been economically worked. They have been worked by slave labor. Of course, they [the Russians] don't pay anything for getting that gold out of the ground, and the Russian gold reserves are, I guess, immense now, in comparison with what they had before, when they didn't have any, and they can use it for any purpose they see fit. But I don't think it will affect us very much, because if they get funny, we'll just take it over.

They couldn't embarrass us?

Not at all.

All right. Now, just just one more point about our being able to issue money: Could we, against our present gold reserve and taking into account all these commodity things you mentioned, issue more currency without either creating inflation or cheapening the . . .

Well, of course. The Federal Reserve Board has the right to issue enough money to meet the situation, and how much money is in circulation, if you'll notice, is always in that Treasury report. It expands and contracts as is necessary in the transaction of business in the country. What they've done now [is] contracted the currency in circulation in such a way as to make a tight money market so that they can raise the interest rate. The cost and the interest, as I told you this morning, is now $16 billion for the little fellow; his $800 billion worth of loans take a 2 percent increase in the cost of money. That $16 billion goes to the people who have control of this contraction and expansion of the currency. I don't think it's ever been over about $21 billion, or maybe up to $28 billion. That's the currency in circulation against a $22 billion gold reserve. Now, against that $22 billion gold reserve you could issue $220 million in currency if you wanted to, and it would still be just as good as in the first place.

That would not be just cheap greenbacks?

No. It would be the authorization of the United States government to meet this situation with the expansion or contraction of that money volume, whenever it was necessary. Now, you get this last Treasury statement and see how much money's in circulation.

Could you reduce the national debt by just willy-nilly issuing a certain amount of money?

Well, no. That would be the old greenback proposition . . . tried in the Civil War, but the national debt could have been contracted immensely if, instead of making a tax reduction, they had been willing to make the tax cost in the operation of the government what it ought to have been. The national debt could have been reduced by the payment of the surpluses that would have been accumulated. As I told you, I paid a tremendous amount on the national debt, and when I left the White House, that national debt had only increased ... reduced to $252 billion, from $279 billion, and that national debt had only increased $5 billion when I left the White House ... with the Korean problem. If the Congress had been willing to make the necessary tax assessment and meet that as we went along, we could have reduced that debt to $200 billion. It doesn't make any difference how much that debt is, to tell you the honest truth, as long as you have the assets of the United States of America, which are hundreds of billions of dollars: three or four times—maybe ten times—what the national debt is. When you've got private loans of $800 billion—$800 *billion,* now, not million—you can see what the assets of the United States are. That $800 billion must be on a 50 percent basis. Think what that means: That puts the economy over a trillion, as I said it would be a long time ago, and there's no ... reason for being alarmed about what the national debt is. The thing to do is get the finances of the government in such shape that it is easy to meet the payments as they come due, and then gradually reduce it each year. If the people paid to reduce [the debt] instead of giving them a fake tax reduction, then, when the time comes, they've got the tax for whatever is necessary to run the government.

These are things that come within the jurisdiction of the government.

Within the jurisdiction of the Federal Reserve Board and the Secretary of the Treasury, and whenever they want to meet this thing on the same basis, it can be done. But when they're working for the bankers who've got $16 billion in interest for nothing by just raising the interest rate, well, there you are. And I'm no fascist or anything of the kind.

Mr. President, in looking at this daily Treasury sheet, what is it you look for?

I look at what the income and the outgo is and translate it. I want to see background for the currency in circulation is, and ... how much there is in circulation and look at the gold reserve, and then that's about all.

And that gives you a fairly good idea?

It's just like looking at a bank statement, and that's what it is, really— a bank statement.

And you did that every day you were in the White House?

All the time. I did it all the time I was in the Senate. I was on the Appropriations Committee, and I kept track of it in the Senate just like I would if I had been on the Finance Committee, which I wasn't. But on the Appropriations Committee, I knew exactly how the government stood every day.

And you don't think we're in any difficulty at all in terms of the national debt or in anything except how it is administered?

The management of the national debt is the most important thing, outside an agricultural policy and a foreign policy. Of course, the financial operation of the government is the basis on which the foreign policy and domestic policy are run. You've got to know about the foreign policy; you've got to know about the domestic policy, which includes agriculture, labor and management, and everything of the kind. And then you've got to understand the financial background of the government of the United States, which is the solidest background that there is in the history of the world.

You spoke of private debts, or other ...

$800 billion.

$800 billion.

That's right.

Now these are subordinate to the government debt?

Oh, yes. The government debt is the first obligation of the government of the United States, and everybody owes it, whatever his proportion.

On everything, isn't it?

On everything, that's true, and nobody gets in ahead of the federal debt when it comes time to pay it

When you're talking about a $290 billion ceiling, the total debt of the United States government is not a frightening figure then?

No, not at all, and that's a fake figure anyhow. It is nearer $390 [billion] than it is $290 [billion]. But all the obligations that the government is responsible for ... And if you look at the various things that the government guarantees, every single one of those is a part of the national debt—federal housing and everything else that goes.

Those are commitments?

Why, sure. They've always handled this thing on a fake basis.

Their liabilities are not reflected in ...

Not at all.

Now what gave you this enormous interest in the fiscal policies of the government?

Because that's what makes it run. That's the background that makes the government run. I got the idea right here in running the county, whose fiscal policy had been nothing, and I left it in a solid condition, with everything in shape, so in the expanded economy of the county it came out ahead—

all debts paid off. The value of the assessment list in the county when I was there was $200 million. It's about $1 billion now, ... $900 million something. That was due to the expansion of the facilities that created all these building programs that went on in the county as a result of a road plan and an operation of the public buildings and everything else that went to make the county solvent. I found [the county] hopelessly in debt and left it solvent, and I wanted to do that in the federal government, if they'd have helped me along. I would have done it, too.

You also had a hand in cutting the interest rates of the road bonds for the ...

Oh, yes, yes, and I think we issued most of the road bonds for 4 percent or something like that, and the thing that was really a burden and a headache was the protested warrants of the county that had been issued previous to the time that I went in there—about $2.4 million, which is a lot of money for a county. I got them all refinanced on a basis of 3.5 and 4 percent on the income-bonds basis, and the increase in the tax basis of the county paid them off.

Didn't you go personally to visit the underwriting bankers in Chicago on La Salle Street to negotiate a lower rate?

Well, you see, the county on its tax basis issues anticipation notes against its taxes to be collected, and we were paying the National Bank of Commerce and the Commerce Trust Company in Kansas City 6 percent. I went to Chicago to the Harris Trust Company and two or three of those big banks and got an offer of 4 [percent] and finally got the thing down to 3.5 and 2 percent, because it's as solid ... Well, it's just as good as a government loan, and, boy, how they did scream. You see what that saved the county.

Yes, indeed. Are there any other Presidents who have been as keenly interested in the fiscal policies of the government?

I think Grover Cleveland was, because he had a whale of a lot of trouble with it, and Teddy Roosevelt had to get interested because he had a panic on his hands in 1907.

And yet, Woodrow Wilson ..., who was the college president [and] only governor for a short period, was he not? Of New Jersey? He got to the heart of the problem by instituting the reform of the whole monetary system.

That's correct. He had the best advice in the world [from] that old Carter Glass of Virginia, who was an expert on it and was a Secretary of the Treasury ... What was the name of the fellow who was [Wilson's] first Secretary of the Treasury? He died.*

---

*Wilson's first Secretaries of the Treasury were Franklin MacVeagh, who served briefly, then William Gibbs McAdoo. Carter Glass served from 1918 to 1920. Woodin served as Secretary of the Treasury under Franklin Roosevelt in 1933.

Woodin.

Woodin. But it wasn't McKinley Woodin. I had a boy in my battery named McKinley Woodin. What was Woodin's name? [William H.] Whatever it was. Anyway, all those people together . . . And I think Wilson made a very close study of the thing before he got into it, and he came out with a financial policy that's kept the country running ever since. Old Mellon and this Secretary of the Treasury we've got and the one before him have tried their best to upset it, but it won't upset.

If you'd care to tell about it perhaps tomorrow, you keep referring to Mellon as one of the men who undertook to reverse the purposes of the Federal Reserve under the first Republican administration that had administered it. What did he really do?

Well, sir, he did just what this Secretary of the Treasury who succeeded him—this Humphrey, who is in his corner . . . He raised the interest rate, made the 4¼ [bonds] go down to 80, and all the bankers then bought them all up, and they finally sold for 125 and never went below that. The objective was to raise the interest rate, and they raised it and caused the Panic of 1929. That's what brought it about. And we'll be on that same road, if we're not careful.

Session Seven

I don't think anyone I have ever come in contact with read more or was more familiar with the history and background of the country than was Franklin Roosevelt.

Now, Mr. President, what is happening to the American farmer?

The American farmer is being exploited, as he was way back in the '20s, and he's being exploited for the welfare and benefit of those who make loans on farms and on the prices of his products in such a way that he'll be out of business before long.

Are we talking about the so-called family farm, or are we talking about all farms?

We're talking about all farms, but particularly the family farm.

Is that a disappearing feature of American life?

If this thing keeps up, we'll have the same situation that the Russians are working for: the consolidation of all the farms and [the institution of] wages for which farmers will work—not for themselves, but for somebody else.

So we have the equivalent of the communal farm developing over here, or corporate farm?

That's exactly right.

Isn't there some advantage in cooperatives, in that farmers will cooperate to hire machinery?

Our cooperatives are excellent, and they've made a great impression on the farmers, but the Russian plan of cooperatives is not our plan.

Isn't it possible, with the development of modern machinery, that it might be advisable not to have so many small farms but a sort of pooling of farm resources?

Transcript, Thursday morning, September 10, 1959, part one.

Well, the small farm, where the family is raised on the farm, is the best thing that ever happened to this country. That's what made us great.

You think it's an important ingredient in our balance of social elements in the country?

There isn't any question about it.

But the farmer has been notoriously conservative in his political position in the country.

Well, that's true. He thinks that if he has 180, 160, or 240 acres of land, he doesn't have to pay any attention to anybody. But I think that during the last period of ten or fifteen years, he's found out that he has to.

You had a great deal to do in pointing out to him the error of his ways in [the presidential campaign of] 1948.

I pointed out the error of his ways, but he still voted the Republican ticket.

Not in '48?

Yes, he did. Yes, he did. He voted the Republican ticket in '48 in the vast majority of the farm states, but he shouldn't have done it.

Has he ever come over to the Democratic side?

Well, I don't know. We'll have to find that out in the next election.

He seems to have come over on the legislative side to the Democrats.

Well, yes, that's right. But, then, you can't tell what they're going to do. They make up their minds Monday morning, and [by] Saturday night they have changed [them].

Mr. President, the farm question seems always to revolve around the overproduction of certain products in this country.

That is taking place, it's true.

What can be done about it? And can we really call it overproduction if there are so many areas in the world which could use it?

Henry Wallace wanted the ever-normal granary, and that's what we ought to have. Then we ought to take the surplus and see if we can't make [international] deals that will take care of that surplus.

Would you go beyond that and suggest that the surpluses of all of the farming countries be pooled into an international pot?

Eventually that's what I think will have to be done.

You were for the ever-normal granary, but you were also for the distribution of our surplus during your administration.

That's right. I was for the Brannan Plan.* That's what it does.

Mr. President, I note this morning a dispatch which says that Russian wheat is down because of a drought they had.

Yes.

Let's take a hypothetical case: We have so much surplus wheat, do you think it would be wise to give Russia wheat or that sort of thing?

If they can pay for it, I'm for it, but otherwise not. And they can pay for it, because they have plenty of gold to pay for it.

You think it's advisable, then, to help them?

Well, of course, in every way we can.

In the case of China, would you take the same position? Red China?

Yes. If they were starving, I'd help them.

But they can't pay for it. How would you handle Red China?

Well, if they can't pay for it, and their people are starving, we ought to keep that from happening, just as we have in times past.

Are you taking the position now that American agriculture should not restrict its production but go on producing all that it can and have enough for our own people, enough to put into the ever-normal granary, and enough of the surplus to make available to the countries that don't?

To countries that are starving. Let's put it that way.

Now, Mr. President, there's a dispatch from Boston in [the day before] yesterday's New York Times *that says a Jesuit priest described the condition of migrant farm labor in this country as an abomination.† Father Murphy says that half of the 1 million migrant workers in the country are contract laborers imported from Mexico, the British West Indies, Japan, and the Philippines. Isn't that an astounding development that we have to import a million . . .*

*A proposed revision of New Deal agricultural policy by Secretary of Agriculture Charles F. Brannan. He proposed to ration agricultural production by limiting all produce, by large and small farmers, with direct support payments to small farmers. Also, a lower cost of production means a larger profit for the family farms.

†In his Labor Day sermon in Boston, Fr. Paul J. Murphy, S.J., director of St. Joseph's Retreat League for Workingmen, called the status of migrant farm labor "an abomination." These laborers, he said, are "little removed from the slavery of labor camps of communism," and that miserable housing, pitiful wages, child labor, and inadequate sanitation facilities add up to incredible injustice: as quoted in *New York Times,* September 8, 1959.

While I was President, we tried to work that out and got it worked out. Then after I left, why, they changed it over to a situation which the able priest has talked about.

He talks about their living in terrible conditions.

Well, he's right, absolutely right. . . . California, Arizona, and New Mexico—that's where this thing happens.

I see a lot on Long Island and [in] New Jersey.

[It goes] on all over the country, but that's where [it starts], in those three states.

There's been some corruption. Some of the farmers made deals with the employment agency of the state—disreputable deals where they exploited these people—and that's all being attended to. But isn't it amazing that we have to import a million workers into a country?

They don't have to. You know what they do? They treat them in those states that I have named—Southern California, Arizona, and New Mexico—as peons, and that's wrong.

It's not as simple as hiring those people. The peach crop of California this year went to pot. [The peaches] dropped to the ground because [the farmers] couldn't get pickers. These people are getting better jobs, and [the farmers] couldn't afford the pickers at these prices.

And it served them right, because [the farmers] joined with the people who wanted to exploit these poor people who came from Mexico. . . . While I was President of the United States, the President of Mexico, [Miguel] Alemán, and I made an agreement on these migrant laborers for their welfare and benefit. Of course, as soon as I left office, that was thrown out. I don't know how they're getting along now.

It's a serious strain. Mexico is very unhappy with us, and we seem to have done the wrong thing, because Mexico is not sending labor up as fast as California can use it.

Well, the agreement that the President of Mexico and I made while I was President and he was President was for the benefit of the people who needed labor and for the benefit of the laborers, and that wasn't what the people in Southern California and Arizona and New Mexico wanted. They wanted to exploit [the laborers] and take everything they made away from them.

Do you think [these laborers] ought to get the prevailing wage?

I think they ought to get the prevailing wage.

There should be no double standard?

That's right.

What should our national position be? This is not a state matter. This is something that should be in the hands of the federal government, should it not?

The federal government ought to control it, and that's what I thought while I was President. That's what I tried to get done, and I thought we had gotten it done, but it seems to have gone out the window.

In other words, these laborers ought at least to get a decent wage, and not peonage?

Well, of course, and they ought not to be charged for transportation and food and things of that kind—where the fellow who has control of the situation makes them pay double what they ought to pay for food.

Yes, that has been a serious problem. Now, . . . what can the government do to put our whole agricultural picture on the same level with the rest of the country's development?

All they've got to do is make an arrangement with the government of Mexico that the Mexicans, when they come into the country, will be treated just the same as American labor under the same circumstances. That's all that's necessary.

Won't that then defeat what most of these fruit growers or farmers want? They want labor which is cheap enough so that they can . . .

They want to exploit labor, and they shouldn't be allowed to do it any more than any other outfit in this country.

Now we're getting to a very difficult position: The farmer is gradually being upgraded and also being subjected to heavier expenditure than he used to be, and labor is organized and commanding a higher price in the market. What happens to the consumer in that double squeeze, in your judgment? How do you protect the consumer?

Well, that's a thing that we've got to work out. The consumer is the market for the farmer and for labor and for everything else, and most of the laborers and farmers are consumers. When they squeeze themselves out, they get just exactly what they deserve.

Our distribution methods in agriculture are antiquated. Is there something we can do about bringing those up to date?

I don't know how you're going to handle that. Around most cities are market gardeners who raise things for the market. For instance, right here in our home county we have a market for the market gardener. He comes in every morning at 3 o'clock, after working the fingernails off his hands, and has things to offer. And the merchants—that is, the independent merchants; I don't think the chain-store merchants ever pay any attention to him—go down there and stock up in season on whatever's available, and then come back and offer it to the public. In old times, they had a chance to make a profit for the gardener and the retail merchant. I don't know how that thing's handled today, because I haven't gone into it. These market gardeners are still at work in New Jersey and Connecticut; outside of Chicago, Illinois, and in Wisconsin; and in St. Louis County in Missouri, and also around the two Kansas Cities. Some time or other, we're going to find a way to protect all of them, for the benefit of the consumer. He wants something to eat and wants to get it as cheap as he can.

But while this is going on, what do we do about making sure that the farm population isn't going to be eroded and diminished to the point where [the family farm] is threatening to disappear?

If they want to make this situation one of the farms like the communists have, that's what will happen in the long run, but I think the individual family farm is much better for the country and much better for the individual. Of course, we're not in the same fix we were in after the Civil War, where a man could come out and take up land, improve it, and make himself independent. We're now in a position where all the public land, nearly, has been taken up, and we've got to be in a position to protect the little farmer as well as the little business. Neither one of them is being protected at the present time.

Do you think that the little farmer is needed [above] and beyond the mere economic facts involved—that he's needed for social and political reasons?

There isn't any doubt about that. That's what he's needed for.

What does he provide? What is his value to the country?

Well, he's independent in his thinking. He's independent in his voting. And when he makes a living, he's perfectly happy. He sends his children to school. That's all that counts.

May I ask you about this controversial question of whether farmers should be paid money to prevent them from growing things? In other words, to let the land lie fallow?

In some instances, that has been necessary, but I don't think it's a very good thing for the farmer.

Can you elaborate on that?

Well, I think that the farmer . . . , all a farmer wants is a fair price for what he raises. He doesn't want any pay that he doesn't earn, and that's one of the things that's caused all the trouble in the country with the farmers—paying them for what they don't do. Then the big farmers get the benefit, not the little ones.

What we're talking about is that the farmer should go on producing, and we should try to find a market for what he produces?

That's correct. And not only that: We ought to be willing to help the small farmers, and not the fellow who's working toward the Russian consolidation of the farm program.

So you think that it's important for the political balance, that it's a kind of checks and balance in the economic sense and in a social sense, to have an independent farmer as one of our important components?

We must have independent farmers We must have laborers that get fair wages. We must have industry that is working for the welfare and benefit of the people of this country. And in the long run, they'll all get together, because it's for the welfare of all of them that we're working.

Mr. President, as you pointed out yesterday, what is necessary is to protect these small enterprises, because that is really the competitive enterprise under our system. So that should be extended into the agricultural area?

Yes, it ought to be in every area. It ought to be in every area—particularly agriculture.

You've always taken the position, have you not, sir, that you were not for one and against the other? You were for both big and little, and that you had to be little before you could get big?

The President of the United States must look after the people who can't look after themselves with pull. When the President of the United States doesn't look after . . . the little fellow in business, in farms, or in any other line, they don't have anyone to look after them.

You get a lot of letters from people who come in and visit and talk to you. . . . What is it they want to know about it?

Well, of course, they all want to know what caused the Cold War, and I try to tell them that the only cause of the Cold War was the fact that the Russians didn't keep their agreements. One of the principal questions I hear every day . . .

Mr. President, the present occupant of the White House is supposed to be interested, before he leaves [office] in sitting down and devising some scheme or outlining some plan by which the President of the United States and the top executive officers can have periods of contemplation. What do you think that means?

Presidents have always had periods of contemplation when they want to make them. [The President] doesn't have to see anybody unless he wants to. If he wants to think about a subject, he has plenty of time to do it, although he has six jobs and each one of them is a full-time job. He can, any time he feels like it, sit down and think through a problem. It's been done by every President of the United States, I think.

Don't Presidents have difficulty getting perspective on situations and issues, because they're so completely sheltered from the outside?

Well, yes, that's true, but then when the President wants to find out what's going on, he can find out. I spent a great deal of time going over all the newspapers, although I didn't believe half what I saw, and then I had people who made tours around the country, who made tours to Europe, and who made special reports to me. By comparing that with what the propaganda as put out in the papers was, I finally came to a conclusion which I thought was right.

Who were some of these men that you sent out to make a . . .

They were individuals which I had confidence in, and I don't want to name them because it would cause them embarrassment.

That's all right. But they were trusted.

You could trust them. They were honest and would give me a right report.

Every President has his men who are assigned to keeping liaison with the Congress, but you, more than anyone, kept direct touch with all of your former associates on the Hill, did you not?

Yes, I knew them all. . . . When I went to the White House, I knew every member of the Senate. I knew more than half the members of the House and was personally acquainted with the leaders on both sides of the aisle in both the House and the Senate. I could talk to them any time I wanted do, and I did. Those men, when they know they're not going to be quoted to their disadvantage, will tell you what they think is right, and that's what I went up there for.

Is it difficult for a former Senator to get his former associates to get out of one relationship and regard the President as a President?

Well, of course, it's difficult, but I never asked them to do that. I always associated with my friends in the Senate—and the House, too—on the same basis I did when I was in the Senate. I never had any trouble in that line at all.

Mr. President, since you left the White House, how have you been kept informed of things? For example, what do you read now? What newspapers do you read?

I read half a dozen newspapers, just like I always did, to try to get the information, and then I am in touch with a great many people in the Senate and the House who keep me informed on things, just as they always did, and sometimes I have a chance to talk with the people who receive confidential information, which I never use publicly.

What magazines, for example, do you read? Do you read just a special type of magazine, or do you try to get a cross-section?

Well, I read all the current magazines that are published: *Harper's Weekly* and . . .

Time *and* Newsweek?

Time and *Newsweek* and the . . .

U.S. News. . .

Saturday Review of Literature, and even after they became an advertising medium I read the *Reader's Digest.* I'm sorry they got in the advertising business, because they didn't need it, and I'm very much afraid that their attitude and position will be changed by what they get for advertising, which they didn't need at all.

What type of books, Mr. President? Do you continue to favor history?

History and biography, that's right. I read them all. I got a good one the other day on Alexander Hamilton,* and I've just been reading one of the nicest things I've ever seen on the Civil War, *Blockade Runners.*† I . . . try to keep up with all those things. There's too much of it, and I can't keep up with all of it, but I read as much of it as I can.

What about light reading from time to time?

Well I sometimes read a whodunnit. Erle Stanley Gardner always sends me his latest book, inscribed to me. He used to send two of them to Charlie Ross, and after Charlie died, [Gardner] kept sending me one. But after you read three or four pages [of a whodunnit], you can always tell what they're going to come out with. That's what Roosevelt used to do. He used to read them and wonder how they were going to come out, and when he'd get over— oh, I'd say, a dozen pages—he could always tell how they were going to come out, and he and I used to discuss that.

That's interesting. That was his feeling, too?

*Truman is probably referring to Nathan Schachner, *Alexander Hamilton* (New York: T. Yoseloff, 1957).

†Hamilton Cochran, *Blockade Runners of the Confederacy* (Indianapolis: Bobbs-Merrill, 1958).

That's right. I don't think anyone I have ever come in contact with read more or was more familiar with the history and background of the country than was Franklin Roosevelt.

That's very interesting. He was also a good deal interested, I suppose, in naval things, because he fancied himself . . .

Well, yes, he was a naval officer* in the beginning, but he was just as interested in all the rest of the functions of the government as he was in the naval affairs. I think the result showed in his approach to the United Nations and several other things. When he found out that I was more interested in helping him win the war than in making a headline for myself, I used to get in the back door once or twice a week. Nobody knew that.

Did you ever discuss particular historians, since you were both interested in history? Did you . . . ever take apart the Beards?†

Well, yes, we did discuss them, because [Charles and Mary] Beard went haywire. It was too bad, because old man Beard was a great historian, but he got a personal view on the subject, and that didn't work. But we did discuss the various historians of times past, historians of the War Between the States, and the historians of the Napoleonic era, and the historians of the previous time when the Islamite approach to the conquest of Europe was going on—Charles Martel at Tours [732] when he turned them back, with the fellow at Belgrade, [Janos Hunyadi] at Belgrade [1456], and the fact that the Sultan of Turkey was turned back at Vienna [1529], and the stopping of Genghis Khan before he got to Austria [1275], although he almost made it. Those things we used to discuss when we didn't have anything else to do, after we got through the real business, and [Roosevelt] was . . . much more interested than I was and knew more about them than I did. I learned a lot of things from him.

Very interesting, Mr. President. You have frequently said that some of the early American historians, having been New Englanders, were a little bit distorted in their views about American history.‡

They are, and that's coming out now. That's the reason for all these Civil War writings that are taking place now. They're trying to offset the New England writers who . . . you know, old Whittier wrote a poem about the lady . . . Barbara Frietchie—she never existed. And that was a propaganda problem

---

*Assistant Secretary of the Navy under President Woodrow Wilson, 1913–20.

†Charles and Mary Beard, conservative American historians and unsympathetic critics of President Franklin D. Roosevelt's foreign policies.

‡Truman was always proud of his profession, politics, and he would tell his friends that if he had to make a second career choice, it would be as a historian, a farmer, or an architect. The last profession had appealed to him ever since he joined the Masonic order with, its building-trade symbols, some forty years before entering the Presidency.

that's going on right now. That's . . . it's all right. It's a good poem, and everybody likes it, but it wasn't true.

Whipping up sentiment . . .

That's right.

Since that time, then, American historians have become much more balanced and more serious?

I think they have. All but [Allan] Nevins. He's still prejudiced.

*I was surprised to see Nevins's new book on the Civil War.**

So was I.

It talked about [Robert E.] Lee as being a parochial . . .

Yes, and that shows how they still try to discredit the people who had convictions of their own. The best thing on Lee, if you want to read it before you read Allan Nevins, is Douglas Freeman's *Life of Lee.*† That's the best history of the Civil War that's ever been written. Also *Lee's Lieutenants* [1940]— there are seven volumes of them, and I've got them all right here. Nevins, I think, is a kind of propagandist and always has been. . . . I just wanted to make that perfectly plain.‡

Why is it that historians are always touted as being the final authorities . . . and are so inaccurate and so subjective in what they say?

Well, you know, my experience with the modern historian makes me believe that you've got to hunt around to find out whether the ancient historians told the truth or not. The propagandists of the days past are exactly on the same par with the propagandists of today. Now, for instance, [Julius] Caesar wrote his own *Memoirs,* and they're historical and school books. [Marcus] Cicero wrote his *Orations,* and they're taught in schools and things of that kind. The people who really counted in those ancient times were Aristotle—he wasn't writing propaganda; he was writing what he thought—and

---

*Allan Nevins, *The War for the Union,* 4 vols. (New York: Scribner's, 1959–71).

†Truman was referring to Douglas Freeman's Pulitzer Prize-winning book *R. E. Lee, A Biography,* 4 vols. (New York and London: Scribner's, 1934–35). See also Freeman's *Lee's Lieutenants: A Study in Command,* 3 vols. (New York: Scribner's, 1942–44).

‡Nevins, a professor of American history at New York's Columbia University, briefly mentions Truman's new book, *Mr. President,* in his essay, "Why Public Men Keep Diaries"; he also describes diaries of the Fathers of the Republic in an article in the *New York Times* (March 23, 1952). In his 1955 review of the first volume of Truman's *Memoirs,* Nevins alternately praises and faults the volume. Terming the writing crisp, vigorous, and honest, as well as a bit oversimplified, he claims that the book does not earn a place among the best contemporary memoirs because it makes too copious use of public papers and speeches. Nevins concludes, "[I]t well expresses one of the most conscientious, dynamic, and (within his horizons) clear sighted Presidents we have ever had": *New York Times,* November 6, 1955.

the history of the time by Thucydides of Pericles and that period. Then you take the Egyptians, [who had everything] translated and set up in the Alexandria Library, [where it was] destroyed. It was a terrible thing when that happened.

And not so far back in history, it was the policy of the Catholic church to destroy everything that was not in line with what it wanted to do. There isn't a question of a doubt but that great historical documents were destroyed because it wasn't believed they conformed with what [the Catholic church] thought. Well, now, we can't have that in this day and age. We've got to take fellows like Nevins and all the rest of them and let those of us who are still alive understand that it's our duty to tell our viewpoint, and then let future generations decide what's right or wrong.

The problem is still with finding source material, trying to sort out fact from fancy.

That's right. That's right. That's the fundamental basis of the whole thing, and that's what I've been trying all my life to do.

How do you get source material when, as you say, some of it was destroyed and some of it is still inaccurate?

Well, you can't. You can't. You just have to take things as they come along. Now, once in a while they dig up a situation as they did those documents in Israel [the Dead Sea Scrolls], and a few have been dug up lately in Greece that will force the fact onto us that the fellow who wrote about it afterward didn't know what he was talking about. I think Plutarch in his *Lives*— they're very interesting—used a great many documents that were not really source material, and that's what all the rest of these fellows do. When they write a biography . . . for instance, I just got a new biography of William McKinley,* and the lady who wrote it is a wonderful person, but when you read it, you'd think he was the greatest President that ever lived. He was maybe a great President, but not the greatest one that ever lived.

There was always a Madison Avenue [famous center of the American advertising business] when it came to writing history?

That's the point exactly. The Madison Avenue boys are just following along the same line that the historians have. It's hard to tell what the truth is.

You're going to write a history of the American Revolution, written around your predecessors. What are you going to use for source material?

Everything I can get my hands on, and then I sincerely hope that the people, when they look at it, will point out any factual errors—I hope I won't

---

*Margaret Leech, *In the Days of McKinley* (New York: Harper, 1959).

make any factual errors—and argue with me about my viewpoint on the facts that I have to give to the people.

You don't mind the viewpoint from the historian, if he makes it clear that it's his view?

That's right, Bill [Hillman]. If he tells us that this is my view and shows that he's an editor, that's all right, but if he's trying to garble the facts, then's when I fall out with him.

Then you see that most of the time he's giving an opinion rather than a fact?

That's right. Take the history of these two great governments . . . south of us—the Aztec government and the Inca government in Peru. The records were willfully destroyed by people who should not have destroyed them, but there are one or two documents that have come to light recently which show that those governments were not uncivilized. The calendar stone of the Aztecs is just as accurate as those that the old Chaldeans used before Galileo, and down in South America, while they didn't have a written history, they had a way of keeping track of things with strings with knots in them. There was a Spaniard* who was along with [Francisco] Pizarro who wrote all about that, and his writings are just now coming to light, because the Catholic church had suppressed them. Now they're coming out, and that's the reason we have to be careful about how we evaluate the history of what's gone before. In those days, [history was written] by the people who knew how to write, and their prejudiced views are the ones we get, not the facts.

There are some parchments that have come to light that have been dug up in the Arabian desert [the Dead Sea Scrolls] . . .

That's the ones I was talking about. The preachings of Isaiah and two or three others are confirmed in the King James version's translation of the Scriptures, which were made in the fifteenth [or] sixteenth century on the basis of the original documents, as far as they were available at that time.

Therefore, what is essential is not so much the historian's skill in writing [as his skill] in the presentation of facts and whether or not he states a particular prejudice?

That's right. If he wants to be an editor, he ought to show it.

How about [Arnold J.] Toynbee?

---

*Truman is probably referring to Pedro de Creza de León, called the "Prince of Chroniclers," who wrote a sixteenth-century global history of the Andes. Part III was entitled *The Discovery and Conquest of Peru: Chronicle of the New World Encounter* and was most recently published by Duke University Press in 1998.

Well, I have been reading a great many of the things that Toynbee's put out, and he's tried his best, I think, to stick to facts instead of propaganda, although he himself is a good propagandist.*

So you think it's also subjective writing?

That's right. Well, yes. It's subjective writing if you can compare it with what other people have to say on the same subject.

They [historians] have two distinct fields in what they do. First they give what are purported to be the facts, and then they give conclusions that are based upon those facts.

That's right. Editorial opinions of their own.

You have no quarrel with some of the facts, but you do have a definite objection to some of their conclusions?

Some of the conclusions. That's correct. That's editorial writing just the same as it is in a newspaper, although our modern newspapers put their editorial opinions on the front page instead of in the editorial column.

All right. Let's jump to Mr. Churchill's version of the Second World War as he has written it in those volumes [The Second World War, 6 vols. (Boston: Houghton Mifflin, 1948–53)]. I am sure that you have an opinion about those.

I think Mr. Churchill has put those facts together as far as possible from the viewpoint of the British. I don't know whether that will be the viewpoint of history or not, but I will say to you that they are most interesting reading.

You say the "viewpoint of history." That's a very interesting thing that's used as a final judgment on all things. How accurate and how dependable is that?

Well, it's just like reading an editorial on a page of a newspaper and making your own conclusion after you get through with it. The thing that is most important is that history doesn't become a propaganda agent to misrepresent the facts of a previous generation to the youngsters that are coming on.

As far as you are concerned, in terms of your own decisions and the consequences of those decisions, have you always marked your own paper without regard to a historical evaluation of that act?

Yes, on the facts as they were taking place at the time. Anybody can figure out what ought to have been done, but the man who has to make the deci-

---

*A classical scholar educated at Oxford, Toynbee began his massive study on the rise and fall of civilizations in 1929. Twelve volumes and forty years later, he completed his *Study of History.* In comparing civilizations, he wrote that spiritual rather than material forces form history, and that the Kingdom of God is the end of history. Toynbee died on October 22, 1975.

sion has to make it with the facts that he has when he makes that decision. I have tried my best to make it appear that I didn't do maybe what was right all the time—no man can. But I did the best I could with the information that was available to me. That's all that counts.

And under the pressure of time?

Well, yes. When you have to make a decision, you can't wait for tomorrow to make it. You've got to make it now, and then if it's wrong, maybe tomorrow you can make a better one.

Well, now, making a decision—this is one of the most difficult and elusive of all things. Woodrow Wilson said it when he said to the Congress, "We had but one choice and we made it." But that's not a decision to make when you've got no choice; in many of the decisions you made, you had choices.

Yes, there were supposed to be choices.

Well, say, the Berlin Airlift: You had a choice of several other ways to go about it.

The only choice was to do it or not. The only way to save Berlin was to see that they got the material and the food that they needed to keep going, and the only decision I thought was right was to move in there with everything we had and get it done. Some of my advisers said it couldn't be done. Well, I told them it would be done, and then we went to work, and it was done.

You overruled most of your advisers most of the time on some things.

Well, not most of them most of the time, but some of them some of the time. Let's put it that way.

You always had a clear directional beam on which you had to go.

That's true. After I had studied all the facts and the background, I tried to make up my mind and then get the people who had to carry out the decision to go along with me on doing it. And most of the time, they did.

In Korea, for instance, you had some conflicting advice.

Yes, that's true, but there wasn't but one thing to do in Korea, and that was to support the republic which had been set up by the United Nations, and that's what we were doing.

In other words, what always happened was that you also had but one important choice to make when you made it? One was right, and the other was wrong?

Well, I thought so. Maybe someone else might not have agreed with me, but the decision I made I always thought was the right one at the time I made it, and I still think that. I haven't changed.

Looking back now from the point of view of your experience, don't you think that many men are faced with the question, unless they're strong, of "Is what I'm doing going to be popular?" Don't you think that's a great temptation?

There's no question about that, but the question is not whether it's popular at the time, but whether it's right, and if it's right, in the long run it will come out all right. But the man who keeps his ear to the ground—You know, it was said of one of the Presidents of the United States that he had his ears so close to the ground they were full of grasshoppers. That's the trouble with most people who put their ears to the ground: They're full of grasshoppers, and they can't themselves make up their minds between what's right and what's wrong. It's not necessarily a popular decision that you want to make; it's one that is for the welfare and benefit of future generations. If it's right, make it, and let the popular part take care of itself.

Which President was that, Mr. President?

I don't want to say that.... Mark Hanna said that about William McKinley and the grasshoppers.

How do you keep a clear head with all the things that are being beamed at you? FDR kept himself pretty well insulated from callers, because he talked the first fourteen minutes and the caller had one minute.

That's right.

But you were a very serious, interested, and concentrated listener to all the people that got in to see you.

I think that's the way to find out what's going on. Listen to the people that come to see you, and as a President you don't see only the people who ought to be seen and listen to what they have to say, catalog it in your mind, and then when you get it all concentrated, you have to make a decision, and it helps. I always talked to everybody that wanted to talk to me.

I know. But you have to have a screening device. How do you screen out some very persuasive people and some people who really work up a lot of passion?

The only people that were screened out while I was President were people who were nutty on one subject and people who had made themselves believe that what they wanted to do was right, whether it was or not. It's not hard to screen them. But people who had something to say, the ordinary run of people—that is the farmers and the merchants and the laboring men who wanted to see the President—most of them wanted to see him about something that individually affected them. Well, he had to listen to that, and if he could help him, he did. If he couldn't, he put that in the background of his memory for the welfare and benefit of the whole country.

It's no trouble to see people. I see just as many now as I did when I was President, and they all have something to say to me that's worth something. But you've got to make up your own mind on whether what they want is correct or not. And sometimes it's necessary to say, "No, you can't do that." Sometimes it's necessary to say, "I'll consider that." Sometimes it's necessary to say, "Yes, I'll do it." And that's all there is to it.

Mr. President, wasn't it a pretty hard adjustment for you internally [to go] from the Presidency back to private life, from having been occupied with so much to suddenly not being occupied with responsibility for major questions?

No, it wasn't, Bill. I had made up my mind, knowing how I was going to operate after I got out of the office, and what I had in view was to write a history of what had taken place while I was President. I went off to Hawaii and stayed a month, had a good rest, and came back and spent most of my time trying to get the facts together in such a way that people could understand what had taken place during the administration while I was President. Since that time I've been interested, after having accomplished that, in setting up an institution for the information of the youngsters that come along as to what the government of the United States means, what the office of the President means, what the office of the Chief Justice means, and what the office of the Speaker of the House means—the three most powerful men in the government. I have had a most entertaining and informative time in doing that, because I have learned a lot myself by going into it.

But actually, you've taken the position that you would prefer to be a private citizen and go about [your] peaceful ways, only to find out that you can never be quite private again.

That's true.

Don't you always feel a little different after having been President? Once you're conditioned by the Presidency, can you regain the composure and serenity that you would like to have in view of all that you see that disturbs you in terms of the events that take place?

Well of course, you can't. That's natural. But when you remember that the Presidency is a gift of the people when they elect you, and that you never change from the position which you had before, and that the best thing that could happen to you, as dozens of Presidents have done . . . I say a dozen, not dozens, of Presidents have done, is to go back and see what you can do to contribute to the welfare of the country for its continuation on the basis that the government of the United States is a government installed for the purpose of giving the people a chance to do what they think is right. It may not be right, but you can correct it as time goes on. . . . I always thought that when a fellow who had started on a farm and had gone through all the political setup that there is, from precinct to President, came to that point where it was time to quit, he ought to quit, then go back and see if he couldn't give people information on what causes the greatest government in the history of the world to run. I'm a nut on the subject, I guess.

But . . . you develop a feel and a kind of intuitive thing about what's right and what's wrong [when you're President]—what you ought to decide one way and what you ought to decide the other way. Suddenly, all that's taken away from you. This is big and very moving stuff. Then all you have to worry about is getting the paper and getting the milk and what happens on a very pedestrian household level. What's the readjustment there?

Here is the situation. If a fellow in any public position—it doesn't make any difference whether it's a county judge or a mayor or a governor of a state or a President of the United States—gets to the point where he thinks he's just what the people think he is, he's a gone-gosling. What he's got to remember is that he's a common man who has been promoted by the people of the country, and that the proper thing for him to do, when he gets through with that job, is to contribute to the continuation of the experience that he's had for the welfare and benefit of the people. He'll probably get the idea that he's bigger than anybody else, or that he knows more than anybody else. [But] he'll find out very shortly that he doesn't if he tries to do that.

You think it's a temporary elevation by the people, and the man who is accelerated should consider himself a temporary occu[pant] . . .

That's true, and Cato the Younger is the best example of that in Roman history. . . . Cato the Younger was the grandson or grandnephew of Cato the Elder, whose preaching was, *"Delenda est Carthago"* ["Carthage must be destroyed"], on which I won a dollar one time from the Chief Justice of the United States.* [Cato the Younger] had the idea that a public servant was one who worked for the welfare and benefit of the people, and he did that. When the end of his term came, he retired and continued to try to make the Romans understand what they had and what they had to do to keep it. Then the empire came along, and one of the emperors forced [Cato] to commit suicide. But he was one of the greats of the Roman Empire.

---

*Cato the Younger (95–46 B.C.) was the great-grandson of Cato the Elder and, as a conservative opponent of Julius Caesar, he supported Pompey against Caesar in the civil war (49–46 B.C.).

Session Eight

I told the National Baptist Convention just the other evening that if I were black, I'd be as proud as I could be of my color.

You were discussing the younger Cato.

Cato the Younger was one of the great public servants in the history of the world, and you'll find that his idea was honestly to administer the government where he was assigned in such a way that the treasury of the Roman Republic would receive the benefit. He was almost in a class by himself for that day, and eventually he was forced to commit suicide by one of the Roman emperors, which was entirely wrong, but he did that rather than stultify himself and his principles.

Was that the first major experiment in total democracy?

The Roman Republic, of course, was one of the great experiments in democracy when they threw the Tarquins out after six Tarquin kings had robbed the republic. The Republic of Rome continued as a very great institution, [although] it was not the sort of republic that we understand today. It had a special privileged class, which did the ruling, and eventually their financial situation developed to the point where, instead of supporting themselves, the Romans depended almost entirely on conquered countries for their support. Then the financial situation got to such a point that, in the long run, the thing was taken over by an emperor after Julius Caesar was assassinated, and a nephew, Augustus Caesar, took things over and made a very great head of the state, and for quite a long time the ideals of the Republic were continued, for the first six Roman emperors were all great men. It finally wound up with the Antonines; the greatest of the philosophers of that period was Marcus Aurelius Antoninus, and his brother Pius had been with him as his co-emperor, and he finally wrote some of the greatest essays on government and how it ought to be pursued. He was not only a philosopher;

Transcript, Thursday morning, September 10, 1959, part two.

he was also an administrator, and he was a soldier in the field that could win a battle, which is something very unusual in the history of the world.

The point that you were seeking to illustrate with Cato the Younger was that a man, whatever his station is elevated temporarily when he takes power, and then he has to step down . . .

Well, that's correct, but the thing I was trying to illustrate with Cato the Younger was that he was an honest administrator who sent public funds into the public treasury, as he should have done, which was unusual in his day.

Beyond that, what were his social principles with respect to the various levels of society in Rome?

In the Roman tradition, they had the idea that the patricians were the ones who ought to run the government, and they did. Cato, of course, being the great-grandson of the great old Cato, was naturally a part of the ruling class. Up to the time of the empire, the ruling classes were very careful to see that the people who were not patricians were properly taken care of in the government, and Cato the Younger is one of those who was a contributor to that program.

Wasn't that the feeling among some of the early members of the Continental Congress? They felt that there should be a sort of elite class, the leaders of the government?

That's right. That was Alexander Hamilton's theory of government, and the Jefferson theory was that the common people, if they'd be instructed, as they should be, could make just as good administrators and would help just as well for the welfare of the country as to have a patrician class. That was the difference between Hamilton and Jefferson.

Did we always live up to that tradition throughout our history?

No. We've tried to, and we're still working at it.

Well, essentially, what is the difference that happens when Republican administrations take control and when Democratic administrations follow them?

The Republicans think that there ought to be a ruling class, just as Hamilton thought, and those of us who believe in the Democratic idea think that the common people have just as much right to have a say in the government as have the very rich with the aristocratic backgrounds who originated in New England and Virginia.

In our situation, though, the privileges have not come necessarily to families with aristocratic backgrounds, as to owners of large estates and possessors of wealth.

Well, that's true. That situation arose after the War Between the States. Then the development of the great West produced a tremendous number of gold millionaires—the Comstock Lode—there were the great railroad developments; Collis P. Huntington and John D. Rockefeller came out of the oil setup. A great many of those families obtained wealth out of the ground. As the development of the country took place, they became what they thought were aristocrats, and it took Grover Cleveland and Woodrow Wilson and Franklin D. Roosevelt to let them know that the Jefferson ideal was still just as good as it ever was.

Are we in any position of having to improve on the Jefferson concept?

Well, I don't think it can be improved upon. His ideas are expressed in the Declaration of Independence, and I don't think there's ever been an article of any sort written that sets out the ideals of government as well as they are set out in that document. We have also the Bill of Rights, which was added to the Constitution at the suggestion of Jefferson and some of his people who believed as he did. When you take the Declaration of Independence and the first ten Amendments of the Constitution, you have the layout of a government that's by and for the people, as Lincoln said. He was a Jefferson Democrat and didn't know it.

Mr. President, in your observations as President and since you left office, looking around the world and all the developments of peoples everywhere, haven't you found that there are certain peoples who have found it difficult to develop the idea of a republic or a democracy?

Well, that's true. I am not for a democracy, Bill. I never have felt that a democracy would be a success in government. A republic is a government of elected officials with responsibility, and there's a difference between a democracy and a republic. The New England town meeting is the idea of a democracy, and all they do is talk. They hardly ever get anything accomplished. The republic is the idea that the men who wrote the Constitution had in view when they set up an elective Congress and a Chief Executive who was elected by the whole people through an Electoral College. The idea was to keep the thing in shape so those people could act without the fear of being thrown out while they were acting, but at the end of a certain term they could be thrown out.

There's a difference between a republic and a democracy. I'm for a republic. This great government of ours is a government of a republic. It's the most successful one in the history of the world, and I think it's going to continue to be that.

Essentially, what does a republic accomplish that a democracy cannot?

Well, a democracy is where the people meet in a sort of a town meeting. They can throw out their rulers whenever they feel like it. A republic is one that has checks and balances in it, as ours is set up for that purpose. The Congress is elected, the lower House of the Congress, the House of Representatives—I won't say it's the lower House, because they don't like to be called the lower House. The House of Representatives is elected every two years. They change that every two years, and the Senate is elected every six years, and a third of them are elected every two years. Those people cannot be thrown out of office except for malfeasance or treason or something of that sort. And the President is elected for four years. That means that there can be a continuing form of government carried out by men who are responsible to the people and yet who can't be thrown out every fifteen minutes if something goes wrong.

In other words, you protect the people and, at the same time, you protect the government from the people so that they have tenure.

That's the idea. You want to make it a continuing proposition, and the Senate is the best example of that. They elect a third of them every two years, and it's a continuing body, and the House is elected every two years.

You are vesting the authority of the people in the government, not subject to withdrawal on . . .

On whim. Or a demagogue, or something of that kind.

In other words, you elect what you hope are responsible men, and you hold them responsible for carrying out the mandate of the people. If the people don't wish the men . . . then they can change at election time.

That's right, and those men are elected under the theory that they have opinions which they expressed to the public when they were elected and that they have the backbone to stand by those opinions and do the things that they think are right, no matter what the popular situation may be. There may be a wave going through the country where everything would be upset, unless these men have the backbone to maintain their position as honorable men for the best government in the country . . . And most of them have done that all the way through, although we've had a few demagogues in Congress now. We've had some good demagogues in Congress, one while I was there.

Very recently some Congressman took umbrage and exception to the remarks by certain labor leaders that they would be cleaned out because they hadn't followed a certain course favorable to them.

It's perfectly all right for the labor leaders to say that, but if the Congressmen let that affect their viewpoint, they're wrong.

Now the Congress . . . achieves a certain amount of experience, and it's now expressed in seniority. Doesn't that wear a little thin? At this point we don't get the fresh point of view that we're supposed to get.

Well, you know, the main difficulty with the situation is that the chairmen of committees inherit those chairmanships by having been longer in the Senate or the House than their colleagues. It was tried, to begin with, that the chairman of these committees be elected, and there was so much confusion and so much bickering and things of that kind that you couldn't carry on the business of the Congress. After experience, it was decided that seniority would be the easiest way to approach the thing. The only difficulty with seniority is that in some districts in the country, that seniority is brought about by a minority group who elect the Congressmen and Senators. Now, if we could have a majority group to elect the Congressmen and Senators, you wouldn't have any trouble with seniority.

But we now have a situation where the purpose of the Congress is being thwarted by a few senior members of the party who are not permitting the will of the people to be expressed. What do you do about that?

Well, that can happen, but it won't last. That's happened time and again in the history of the country, but eventually the people who thwart the will of the people are finally kicked out. I can remember way back in the '90s when all the old economic royalists controlled the Senate. It was a rich man's club. It's no longer that. We've changed the manner of electing Senators. Now they are elected by the people, and that situation was cured then. You take these Southern Congressmen who are the chairmen of these committees who have been holding up legislation. Eventually, when we get full rights for people to vote, as we should, in the South and the North and everywhere else, we won't have that trouble. I'm not worried about it, because we'll overcome it, but unless you handle the Senate and the House in such a way that there's no bickering and no beating up of people who are interested in the chairmanships of these committees, you're going to have trouble, and I think seniority probably will come out as the very best way to do it. But in order to remedy the situation about which you're talking, we've got to have a full and complete vote of the people who are entitled to vote. Most of the people . . . or, a great many people are prevented from voting, which makes the seniority what it is.

Well, Mr. President, I believe it was the first Congress which attempted to elect the officers of the different committees, and I think it was abandoned in the second Congress, wasn't it?

Yes, it was abandoned in the second Congress, because it wouldn't work. They just couldn't get it done. Every Congressman and every Senator, when he goes there, knows he is the biggest man in his community, and he's not going to knuckle under to anybody. The only way to overcome that was seniority.

When you speak of creating a situation where all those who are entitled to vote get to vote, that brings up the obvious question of civil rights in the South. How is that going?

Well, I think I got out a booklet called *To Secure These Rights,* which covered the situation completely and thoroughly, and this last administration has had a commission working on the same subject. They have come up with exactly the same results and the same recommendations that were in the one that I set up. And that, of course, almost gave the Southerners hydrophobia, but it was the right thing.

You think that the Southerners, left to themselves, will eventually solve the problem, or does it need a certain amount of prodding from the man who occupies the White House?

There are an immense number of people in the South who believe that our system is the right system, and eventually I think they would settle it, but the more prodding they get, the quicker they'll settle it.

Then you feel that these problems as they have developed—let's say, in the notorious state of Arkansas at the moment—are partly the result of failure to prod at the right moment by the occupant of the White House?

Well, yes, but you'll find now that the Arkansas thing is working out,* just as it worked out in a number of other Southern states and would have worked out in the beginning when ... if it hadn't been for the fact that the Governor felt like he had to do a little demagoguing to keep himself before the people. He's changed his attitude now, and you'll see that things eventually will work out all right. Everybody has a system in his mind of fairness, and it generally comes to the top in the long run. Now, when they had this trouble in Little Rock, the governor called out the National Guard, and all the President of the United States had to do was to declare an emergency and call the National Guard into federal service, and there wouldn't have been any argument at all. Nobody would have been hurt, and the thing would have been finished. Well, now they've come at it in another way. They have decided that they'll take enough United States Marshals down there and enforce the law on the Supreme Court decision, which is the law, after they made the decision. They're not having any serious trouble, and eventually it will work out all right. It's worked out here in Missouri and it's worked out in Tennessee.

---

*In September 1957, Orval Faubus refused to comply with federal integration orders, so he sent state military troops to Little Rock, Arkansas, to prevent black students from entering a white high school. A federal district court directed the governor to comply, as did President Eisenhower, and federal troops finally secured admission of the students. One year later, a Little Rock school-board appeal was rejected by the Supreme Court, and in August 1959, nine black students entered Central High School under heavy guard. Faubus continued his loud condemnations.

It's worked out in Texas, and it will work out in any of these states where common sense and goodwill are used.

We're just having a meeting now in this big suburb of Independence, over in Kansas City, of the National Baptist Convention, and one of their leaders made a speech yesterday in which he said that he was very happy to see that common sense and goodwill were gradually working out things both in Arkansas and Oklahoma, and Tennessee, and has worked just the same in every other state. The people had that sort of approach to it. People have a wrong attitude on this thing. All citizens of the United States ought to have the same approach to an education and to the right to an economic living under the laws of the country as set out in the Constitution and the Amendments to that Constitution, and that can be done. The only difficulty with these things is the fact that they get a wrong attitude. I told the National Baptist Convention just the other evening that if I were black, I'd be as proud as I could be of my color. If I were red or yellow, I would feel the same way, and the idea was to get people to understand . . . that the man is what's in his head and what's in his heart. If he believes right and acts right, he doesn't have a bit of trouble.

The main difficulty is that they get these things off on a side issue, and the first question one of these Southerners will ask you is, "Do you want your daughter to marry a Negro?" Of course not, but you ask a Negro if he wants his daughter to marry a white man, and he'll say, "Of course not." The thing to do is to see that the mental, moral, and physical attitude of these people is that I'm proud of what I am. I'm going to try to make a good citizen, and if I do that, then I have a standing in the community, and it doesn't have anything to do with social affairs at all.

Now, you undertook to prod the thing along in '48 and took an enormous political risk in doing it. Obviously you didn't feel that leaving it to common sense and goodwill alone was going to accomplish the result.

No, it took the prod to get it started, but goodwill and common sense is the only way it can be finally settled. You can't settle it with bayonets or shotguns or things of that kind, except you've got to handle lawbreakers if they get into trouble, but the local law-enforcement officers—as they're doing now in Little Rock—ought to enforce that. It's not a case of forcing the people to do what they don't want to do; it's a case of persuading them to do what they ought to do and what's right.

Then you feel that this involves more leadership and that the country needs a spokesman on the point, and since you cannot have a spokesman for all the people except through the President, it's the President's job to do it?

It's the President's job to do it, of course. Now, the Governor of Arkansas could have avoided all this if he had wanted to take the attitude of being a leader for the welfare and benefit of the majority of his population. He didn't take that attitude, and he had to be forced into it. I think he's coming around to the viewpoint that he's made a mistake. I hope he is.

Well, you continue to make the point, Mr. President, that the Constitution and the Bill of Rights . . . combined make this the most flexible of all documents of government theory. Do you feel that the Presidency under . . . you brought up Jefferson. Of course, his concept was related to the agricultural nation, which we were, and now we're currently industrial. And we're going from industrial to automation, which is another level in the thing. Doesn't that change things around to where the Presidency becomes much more powerful as time goes on and that the Congress and the Supreme Court relatively drop in their level of importance?

No, I don't think that's true at all. I think the President's position as the Chief Executive, as Commander in Chief of the Armed Forces and the maker of the foreign policy, and as the leader of his political party is the greatest and most powerful office in the history of the world. I think the Chief Justice, as the head of the courts of the United States—he's not Chief Justice of the Supreme Court; he's Chief Justice of the United States—is one who wants to make the laws enforced in a manner that's intended. As I said once before, administration is two-thirds of the operation of the law. And the Congress is the legislative branch of the government which controls the purse strings. Now, the President, the Speaker of the House, and the Chief Justice of the United States, if they can be in harmony is one of the greatest things that causes this government to work as it does. None of them, not a single one of them, is superior to the other two. They are on an equal level, as the Constitution provides, and it takes an administrator in the Presidency to make that work, and he can do it. He, the President, with the Speaker and the Chief Justice, can make these things operate.

There's been a lot of feeling expressed recently that the Supreme Court is encroaching on the prerogative of the Legislative, and the Legislative is trying to overcome it by curbing the Supreme Court.

Well, the Legislative cannot curb the Supreme Court as it is set up in the Constitution. It would take an amendment for the Legislative to be able to curb the Supreme Court. But [in] a situation when the Executive or the Legislative, or the Court doesn't operate as it should, one or the other of those branches is going to take the leadership and prod them into doing what they ought to have done in the first place. That's all there is to it.

You worked very closely in coordinating with the Legislative Branch in that, before you made important policy pronouncements that concerned the Congress, you called in the leaders of both parties, and you kept them informed.

That's right.

Yet, in the steel case, you were up against another problem where the Supreme Court could easily undo what you were trying to do at that time. That was a major thing.* It raises the question as to whether or not either the President or the Congress could properly coordinate with the Supreme Court in acts before they are promulgated, or in acts while they are in the process of discussion.

In the beginning it was suggested—I think in Washington's administration—that the Chief Justice of the Court be called in before bills were passed to decide on their constitutionality. He refused, and he was right. Jackson, I think, took an attitude that he had just as much right to decide on the constitutionality of a measure as did the Chief Justice of the Court, and he had. And if he wanted to do it, he could, and he could enforce it. If you will remember, when one of the decisions was made by the Court in old Jackson's administration, he said, All right he's made his decision; I'll let him enforce it.† Only the [Chief] Executive can enforce it. He appoints the United States Marshals, who enforce the decisions of the courts, but that doesn't happen very often, and when it does happen, it usually works out to a point where there is a compromise on the subject. But each one of these branches of our government—that was the division of powers to keep a dictator from getting control—have certain objectives and certain things that they have to do, and when they refuse to do them, then they get prodded by the other branches of the government, which is a good thing. It doesn't hurt anything at all.

So this is what keeps them from running into the danger of having a dictator?

That's right. That's exactly what it's for.

Mr. President, you felt very strongly about the need for the American people constantly to know these things that you are talking about, and one of your aims and ambitions, since leaving the Presidency, is to get the young people to understand that. Can you tell us a little first of what has been your experience in talking to young people? How you found them?

---

*In April 1952, Truman seized the steel mills to prevent a lengthy strike over wages. His Secretary of Commerce, Charles Sawyer, assumed command of the mills. Truman emphasized that lessening steel production would endanger American fighting forces in Korea. Clearly, the President's sympathy for the steelworkers and his distrust of huge corporations also played a role. Almost two months later, the Supreme Court in a 6–3 decision declared the President's action unconstitutional. The majority held that the Commander in Chief did not have this power, which belonged to the Congress.

†Chief Justice John Marshall ruled in 1832 that the Cherokee Nation had land boundaries within which Georgia laws have no force: *Worchester v. Georgia,* 6 Peters 515. Georgia, supported by Jackson, rejected the court order and the President reportedly stated, "John Marshall has made his decision; now let him enforce it."

I found them vitally interested in their government and in its continuation and what it means. Now, I've been to a great number of universities around over the country, in the west and the north and south and east. I have had the opportunity to tell the youngsters my experience as President of the United States and what the Presidency stands for and what the Courts stand for and what the Legislative branch of the government stands for, and I find that they are vitally interested in the government. They ask some of the most intelligent questions that can be asked, and, of course, I try to answer them— sometimes not to their satisfaction, but it creates an argument and a thought in their minds which will make them better citizens. I don't know of anything better in the world that a man can do that's more helpful to the welfare of the nation than to get the youngsters to understand what they have and what they have to do to keep it, but I try to impress upon them that they didn't get this form of government for nothing. It was gotten through sweat, blood, and tears, the shedding of a lot of blood. In fact, we had to spend four years whipping ourselves before we made up our minds that we wanted this form of government. We've still got it. It's still the best government in the history of the world, and it always will be if the youngsters want to keep it up on the basis on which it was founded.

Mr. President, do you have any suggestions with regard to more American history or more history about our political institutions in the schools and universities?

I think the youngsters must and should be instructed on the problems of government, starting at the local level. You take the village and the city and the county and the state and the nation: They are all founded on the same basis—that's the Constitution of the United States. The more these youngsters can become interested in how the government works, from the ground up, the better it will be for the nation and for the future. I think they're all interested in doing a part in it, if they get a chance.

Were you ever interested in being the head of a university or a school?

Well, I've been invited a time or two, but my educational background was not such that I thought I was fitted for that purpose.

What do you mean by that, Mr. President?

I didn't have any college education, and I think when a fellow is the head of a university, he ought to have all the background in the world from an educational viewpoint. . . .

You've said that you didn't have a formal education. Now, what do you mean by a formal education?

Well, you see, . . . most men who are heads of universities and great colleges have a very long educational background; most of them are Doctors of

Philosophy and have earned Doctors of Law degrees, and most of them also had experience as teachers before they obtained all these degrees. They've usually obtained these degrees after they've qualified as instructors and teachers. Well, I didn't have that sort of experience. Although I've had one or two tentative offers to take over a university and operate it, [and] I've been told that it was an administrative job, I think that it takes experience in that line, the same as it does in politics. Unless a man has been through all the experimental stages that go to make up the operation of a great educational institution, he's not qualified to be president of one of them, any more than he's qualified to be President of the United States if he's been head of a bank in New York.

Mr. President, this bring me to the point I wanted to ask about: adult education. You're a shining example of a man who's been keenly interested in what's going around in the world, and not just what has happened in the past. You continue to be interested all the time. Don't you think that's one of the most important things that ought to be developed in the education of the country? That the adults go on studying?

Oh, yes. I think that's absolutely essential, because the education that a man receives in grade school and high school and in college, or a university, is a foundation on which he can build a real education. There isn't a leader in the history of the world who didn't keep on improving his knowledge of what things were necessary for him to use in the operation of what he was trying to do. That's true of every single man who's in history, and it seems to me that the best thing to do is to give these youngsters all the education you possibly can during their periods in the first eleven or twelve years of their school. Then, during that period, they've found out where this information is located, and if they're interested in any one special line, they keep on improving in that line. It doesn't make any difference what it is—whether it's banking or farming, or whether it's politics or any other thing. You never can quit improving your mind for use in what you're trying to do if you just keep working at it.

We're told that educationally we're also falling behind the Russians. Do you feel that we are?

No. I don't think the Russians have an educational institution yet that anywhere approaches ours. From what I can read and from what I hear from people who have been over there, they have a propaganda proposition which makes it appear that we're behind on everything. We're not. The only thing for us to do is keep on progressing for the welfare of our own country and to be sure that we're strong enough to meet those who don't believe in keeping their agreements. That's the only difference between us and the Russians.

Do you feel that we have managed to retain our self-discipline while educating our youngsters, instead of regimenting and coercing other people into certain ways of thought, as the communists have?

Well, yes, to a certain extent only I don't think we have used the hickory switch and the paddle as often as we ought to on the youngsters as they grow up.

Do you think we have gone too modern and too scientific in our bringing up of youngsters?

No. I think we've been too lazy in bringing them up. You know, it takes a mother and a father who are interested in raising a family to make a family. The greatest institution in the world is the raising of a family in the right way. In order to do that, they must be taught respect and discipline at home. It can't be done anywhere else, and when that fails—as I saw in the paper last night where youngsters have too many mothers; that is, too many baby-sitters—then trouble begins. It takes mother and father to raise a family, and they've both got to be interested in seeing that that family grows up to be good citizens. And they can make them that if they want to. But it takes hard work. I know, because I've tried it.

Mr. President, what is the most important single question that these youngsters ask you when you speak with them?

The most important question to them seems to be, What can I do to get along in the world from now on? And the answer that I give them is, "Decide what you want to do, and then try to find out more about it than anybody else knows, and you won't have any trouble."

Do they question you about the prospects for peace in their time?

Yes, they talk about peace . . . They like to talk about peace and hope it will come, but I always tell them that peace is a wonderful thing, and we all want it, but freedom and liberty are worth more than peace, and sometimes you have to fight for them.

Do you think that they get the difference between peace at any price and peace that you have to earn?

Yes.

You explain it to them?

A shining example to the world which I usually point out is that peace at any price usually brings trouble. You've got to be able to fight for what you think's right, and that's always been the case, from the beginning to the end. . . . Then, if you can't win it in the fight, you've just got to keep on working for what you believe is right. Now, you can take the history of the world from the beginning, and you find that the great things that have come out of it have been created by men who are willing to stand up and be counted in what they thought.

When you say "fight," you don't mean physical fight?

Well, moral or physical. Either one. Sometimes you have to shoot it out.

It has been done.

If it hadn't been for that, Nazi Germany would [be] in control of Europe right now. I don't know whether they'd have been any worse than the Russians or not, but they wouldn't have been any better.

So you still believe that peace in our time is a hope but not necessarily a realizable thing?

That's true. Unless you're willing to fight for it, you can't get it.

Session Nine

[A synthetic liberal is] one who poses as a liberal publicly, just like the old fellow my grandfather used to talk about who got up in the "amen corner" and did too much loud praying. My grandfather used to say when you see one of your neighbors doing that, you better go home and lock your smokehouse. And that's true with what I call synthetic liberals.

Let us get over to something that's on the personal side again. How did you keep yourself physically fit when you were President?

Well, every morning, before breakfast, usually about 6 or 6:30 or 7, I'd go out and walk a couple of miles. I still do it every morning. I was out this morning and walked for twenty minutes at 120 steps a minute. That's 2,400 steps, if I count right, and they're Roman-paced—*mille pacem,* you know, "made a mile." At two and a half feet apiece, I walked a mile and a thousand feet.

That's quite a walk. Do you get winded at the end of a walk?

No, no.

The people who walk with you do.

Some of them are not used to it. I've been doing it for forty or fifty years, and I'm used to it.

Did you do that as Senator?

Yes. I did it while I was a county judge and as a Senator, and, of course, on the farm I had all the walking I wanted to do with horses and ploughs and things of that kind.

Wouldn't you think that you had enough walking in that job not to continue to do a busman's holiday when you had a choice?

Transcript, Thursday afternoon, September 10, 1959, part one.

Well, you know, when you're on a job where you have to sit down all day, the best thing you can possibly do is to walk, especially after you're forty years old, because that exercises all the muscles of the body, a walk does. Legs were put on us to use. The present-day youngsters, and most people, will get in a car to go a block. They'd be much better off if they'd walk.

How about your diet, Mr. President? In the White House, and now, do you eat anything that you choose?

I eat anything that I choose, but not very much of it. It's much more important that you choose the main exercise from making a large belt by pushing back from the table rather than eating too much while you're sitting there. I noticed the other day that there was an article in one of the main magazines, I forget which one it was, in which the medical profession said that most of these weight removers were fakes, and that the best way in the world [to keep] from getting too heavy was by not eating so much.

Yes, I believe that the federal ... or rather, the Secretary for Health, [Arthur] Flemming, [does that] also.

I think he does what was said in the article.

That isn't going to help our food-surplus problem any.

Well, I'll tell you, we could solve our food-surplus problem in [a] way that ... those of us who know how to raise food surpluses can still keep on working and advising those who do raise surpluses how to do it.

Mr. President. Have you had any illnesses when you were in the White House or since?

No, I haven't had any serious illnesses in my life. I had an operation* for the removal of a gallbladder, and while the doctor [Wallace H. Graham] was at work at it, he took out the appendix. I don't know whether he took out anything else or not, but I've still got plenty left to work with.

That operation was quite an experience—the first time in your life when you really had a serious bout with the doctors.

Well, no, it wasn't the first time. It was the second time. When I was nine years old, I had an awful case of diphtheria, and they had me buried, just like they did on that operation, but I fooled them and came back.

You submitted to the operation after considerable discussion with the doctor on it, I gather.

*In June 1954, Truman agreed to make a surprise appearance, playing himself in the last act of Irving Berlin's *Call Me Madam,* then playing at Kansas City's outdoor theater. However, backstage on June 8, he suffered excruciating stomach pains, and Mrs. Truman took him home; two days later, gallbladder surgery was performed at the hospital: See Ferrell, *Truman: A Life,* 390, and McCullough, *Truman,* 943–44.

Oh, yes, yes. They made a thorough examination of the thing and finally decided that the gallbladder was infected. It was, and they took it out, and they got a handful of rocks out of it. The doctor wanted to give them to me for a souvenir, but I wouldn't take them. You know what he did with them? He sent them to Walter Reed Hospital to put in the museum up there, where they've got pieces of a great many Presidents.

I'll be hanged. They say they may have taken out your gallbladder but some of your gall is all over the Congressional Record.

Well, I could make a remark that's not properly used in polite society. The doctor made the statement that I had too many guts anyway, and he just took out a few, and it didn't have any effect.

You had quite a serious set-to.... Some of us remember that you were being given a rather doubtful chance of survival there for a while.

It was sort of like the election of 1948. Nobody thought I'd get well but me, and I did.

Any special introspective moments that you had during the time when you thought you were fading a little bit? You did look a little like you might have ...

I didn't think much about it at all because I never thought anything would happen but that the operation in the long run would be successful. They tried some antibiotics on me, which did not agree with me at all, and the surgeon's father—my White House doctor, the father of my White House doctor—was an old-fashioned family doctor. He came in one day when I was having a lot of trouble with these antibiotics, and he gave me a great big white pill like you'd give to a horse, and it had the desired effect, and I got all right.

Were you, to put it very bluntly, ready to go if you had to?

Well, of course. I'm always ready. I'm always ready to meet the situation, and, as I told the National Baptist Convention the other night, I hope I won't have to go in the back door when the Almighty gets ready to receive me.

Why have you kept a strict adherence to two doctors, one a general practitioner and the other a surgeon and general practitioner, father and son, all through these years?

That's been customary in our family. When we lived out on the farm, when I was a little boy, we had one old doctor who was always the doctor for the family, and they'd get on a horse and ride a couple of miles and bring him ... and he'd give us few pills, or whatever was necessary, and we'd get all right. Then we moved over to Independence, where my mother insisted that we ought to go so that we could go to a graded school, and we had another doctor that we had all the time that we were there. When we moved back to the farm, we didn't need a physician very much, although we used this same old man that we'd used when we lived there before. I became acquainted with Dr. [Wallace] Graham and his son when the son was a very small boy. I had the utmost confidence in him, never needed him very much for doctor purposes, only when I'd have a cold or something like that, he'd give me something for what the old English doctor said would keep the head cool, the feet warm, and the bowels open—he'd do that for me.

I was intrigued by your expression that you hoped the good Lord wouldn't have to receive you by the back door. Will you explain something of the meaning of that?

I was reading just the other day a late book on Stonewall Jackson, and one of the great Stone[wall] brigades said to the other one: "I wish the Yankees were all in hell." And the second one said, "I don't wish that at all, because old Jack would have us up to the gate and inside, and we'd all be hotter than we are now."

[Your] choice of doctors is rather interesting because at that time, we remember, there were a number of highly touted specialists who had their bags packed, and not out of any sense of notoriety, but out of a sense of deep interest and devotion to you. [They] were ready to drop their practices wherever they were, and they were East, West, and South. I knew of four who were all packed to come down and help out, and you discouraged them all.

They would have been very welcome, but I had the utmost confidence in the two doctors that I had ... the old practitioner that I'd known for fifty years and his son, who was my doctor in the White House.* I thought if they didn't know what to do, there were very few others that would. I was grateful to these people, though, for what they wanted to do. I figured it was a wonderful thing for them to feel that way.... You would find a great many in private life that would have been very happy to see me kick the bucket, but I fooled them just like I did in '48.

Without wanting to pursue it too far, there were some doctors who didn't quite share your confidence, ... and they were deeply concerned that your welfare should not be left to any unexplored possibility that might not be ...

I agree with that, and I thought it was very fine, but this physician who'd been my physician at the White House had been, I think, as fairly educated as a man could be. He'd been to every great school of surgery in the whole world—London and Edinburgh and Paris and Vienna, and Germany—and he

---

*The Army surgeon Wallace Graham had landed on Omaha Beach in 1944 with a hospital unit and was wounded in Holland. Truman, at Potsdam, asked Graham to come from Stuttgart's surgical unit and offered him the White House post. The conscientious doctor accepted after his hospital patients were discharged.

was well acquainted with all the approaches to these things. The only trouble with him, and we had the same trouble with him when he had to remove the tumor from Mrs. Truman, was that he was worried to death that something would happen where he'd be blamed for not having done the right thing. But he did do the right thing, and we came out all right.

And you also felt more comfortable with him?

Oh yes, because I knew him and had confidence in him. That's two-thirds of the doctor's ability . . . for the patient to believe that he knows what [the doctor is] doing and that he can go ahead and do the job. And I've always felt that two-thirds of a recovery is due to the fact that you have confidence that you're going to recover, and that you have confidence in the man who's trying to help you recover. That's all it amounts to.

Were you entirely preoccupied with the problem of getting out of your misery during the time? . . . Because at that time, you were cut off from all reading—one of the few times that you weren't reading anything.

That's true. I couldn't read anything much and, of course, I slept most of the time after the operation was over. I began to recover, [and] as soon as I could get on my feet a little bit, I read just as much as I ever did. I finally caught up with it, just like I do when I get three weeks behind with my mail here. I finally get caught up with it.

Was your interest pretty limited at that time? You . . . didn't want any radio in the room, and there wasn't any radio or television in your room.

No, that's right. I didn't see the necessity for it. I was in the hospital, I guess, about three weeks or four, and then I moved home and had everything available. We had radio and television and everything else when I got home.

You didn't even want an air conditioner [in the hospital], did you?

No, but they finally put one in, over my . . .

How did that happen? That's quite a story.

Well, my friends who were interested in my welfare insisted that I ought to have an air conditioner, and they put one in. I kept it turned on while people were around, and when they'd leave, I'd turn it off. So it worked all right.

Just for the record, could we amend that a little bit, because one of your very devoted friends couldn't get you to budge on the thing. . . . I remember distinctly that you said that so long as no one else had an air conditioner on that floor in that hospital, you didn't seem entitled to one, either.

No, that's right. And the only reason they got that done was to move me up two floors where there was one.

But they also had to do something else: You still resisted—just to bring this up to date—and they said, It's all right if you don't want one, but it's 110 to 114 [degrees] outside. Why should Mrs. Truman be subjected to it? And you said, Put one in!

That's right. It finally worked around just that way.

Now, getting back to the White House period. . . . Before that, would you mind if I get just to one point. . . . One of the most interesting things, I think, one of the things that will be very lasting is, you remember the prayer that you wrote* . . .

Yes, that's right.

Have you ever since that time, or since you've been out of the White House, written anything at all like that, or touched on that subject?

No, that covered the situation, and somebody found out about it . . . I think, got it out of your book, and it's been framed and hanging up here in the office for a long time.

But you haven't anything at all . . . any notes you've kept which touched upon this subject? I don't like to probe into faith, except . . . where it reveals your general philosophy of life. That's what I . . .

Well, if you're interested and want to read the speech I made just the night before last, or Tuesday night, I guess it was, to the National Baptist Convention—the Negro Convention of Baptists—you'll find that the faith's just the same as it always has been.

---

*   "Oh! Almighty and Everlasting God, Creator of Heaven, Earth and the Universe:

Help me to be, to think, to act what is right, because it is right; make me truthful, honest and honorable in all things; make me intellectually honest for the sake of right and honor and without thought of reward to me. Give me the ability to be charitable, forgiving and patient with my fellowmen—help me to understand their motives and their shortcommings [*sic*]—even as Thou understandest mine!

Amen, Amen, Amen"

Hillman, *Mr. President*, n.p.

Truman noted on the page below this prayer that it had been said by him "from high school days, as window washer, bottle duster, floor scrubber in an Independence, Mo. drugstore, as a timekeeper on a railroad contract gang, as an employee of a newspaper, as a bank clerk, as a farmer riding a gang plow behind four horses and mules, as a fraternity official learning to say nothing at all if good could not be said of a man, as a public official judging the weaknesses and shortcomings of constituents, and as President of the United States of America." Truman wrote out this prayer on August 15, 1950.

You have touched on your physical-fitness program in the White House, mainly walking and swimming.

Yes, I used to swim in the pool every afternoon, and then the sergeant who was working for the doctor, as his assistant, would—oh, about every other day—give me a rubdown, which is a very helpful thing. . . . I haven't been able to take those since I've been out of the White House, because I haven't had the time to do it.

That's a strange observation. You have less time now than you did when you were President?

That's correct. The time was arranged in such a manner that I followed a routine every day. Now I get up and do a tremendous amount of work between five-thirty and breakfast time, which is usually about a quarter after seven, and then in between there, sometime, I take a twenty-minute or thirty-minute walk. Then I come over here to the office and arrange things so as to keep everybody busy for the rest of the day, and spend my time studying what's happening around the world, in the papers and the *Congressional Record* and things of that sort. It takes all the time I have to spare. When I go back home, we have dinner at night, usually, and hardly ever go out anywhere. I spend up until bedtime catching up on my reading that I have neglected.

Now, you also had a problem of keeping yourself, for lack of a better expression, mentally fit. You had to be constantly on the alert. How did you do that in the face of all the pressures that you had?

I didn't let the pressure bother me very much, because I had certain principles I adhered to, and I didn't have any . . . I never felt any alarm about the pressures, because I'd been trained on that ever since I'd been in the political game, from 1922 until the time I went to the White House. The pressures in local government are much greater than they are in the Presidency, because in the Presidency you have secretaries and people to head off the crackpots and people like that who caused you more trouble than anybody else. People with common sense are not hard to deal with. They understand what the situation is and why that can't be done or why this can be done, but the crackpots are the ones that cause you all the trouble. The synthetic liberals are the ones that caused more trouble to the President than anything else.

What do you mean by "synthetic liberal"?

One who poses as a liberal publicly, just like the old fellow my grandfather used to talk about who got up in the "amen corner" and did too much loud praying. My grandfather used to say when you see one of your neighbors doing that, you better go home and lock your smokehouse. And that's true with what I call synthetic liberals. They're always pushing you for something they don't know anything about but what they think would make a popular proposition so far as they're concerned, if they could get it done.

You consider these people a problem to liberalism?

I do. They're not liberals; they're publicity hounds, and that's not what it takes. The word's been ruined, the word *liberal,* just the same as *democracy* has [been ruined] by the Russians. These people have made it appear that a man who's labeled as a liberal is usually a crackpot, but that's not the case. A person who should be a Democrat is always a liberal, if he's a real Democrat, because he's interested in the welfare of all the people and not just a few. That's what makes a liberal. The old man who was a Senator from Wisconsin was the best example of an honest-to-goodness liberal that I know of right at the present time. Roosevelt—Theodore—posed as a liberal, but the real liberal was Franklin Roosevelt.

Now why was he more of a liberal . . . now you talked about a man in Wisconsin. I assume you meant La Follette?

Yes, Robert La Follette, the elder La Follette, and then the younger Robert La Follette, too. Both the La Follettes. Bob La Follette was the same sort of man that his father was. . . . The reason I say that Franklin Roosevelt was the real liberal [is that] he succeeded in getting things done, and Theodore talked about them more than anything else. Theodore stuck with the old conservatives that had sent him down.

Then you have always considered yourself a liberal, in the pure sense of the word?

I consider myself a real Democrat, with a capital *D*. That's a political Democrat.

And being a liberal is just another phase of being a Democrat?

That's right. If he's the right kind of a Democrat, he's always a liberal. He can't be anything else. He looks out for the welfare of the people who have no other representation.

Why do we have so many shades of liberalism in the Democratic Party and still have it as a party with a capital D for Democrat?

The principal reason for that is that it's a matter of history. The party started with the difficulties and the differences between Alexander Hamilton and Thomas Jefferson. [Jefferson] always thought that the common people, if they had an opportunity, would make the best place in which to pose the power of government. That went along until the time of John Quincy Adams, and at the end of his term, Andrew Jackson came back and awakened the people again to the fact that they control the government. At that time the financiers had taken over the government, just like they had along in the 1920s, and he restored that control of the government to the people.

Then we had all sorts of troubles and a number of weak Presidents between Andrew Jackson and 1860. In 1860 [*sic*] they had the War Between the States, which was not necessary but which came about, and then Lincoln had the same idea that Jefferson and Jackson did: that the people were the source of power in a government, and that's what they ought to be. Then we had an interval after [Lincoln's] death that resulted in the same situation that had developed at the time of his election. . . .

Grover Cleveland came along in 1884 and did his part to restore the control of the finances of the government to the people. Then he was defeated by a minority vote in 1888 and was reelected again in 1892. By that time he had been associated with a lot of insurance companies, and his second term was not the liberal one that his first one was. In fact, he was for the election of William McKinley against William Jennings Bryan, who was the next liberal leader that the country had after that, and Bryan was in control of the leadership of the Democratic Party from 1896 until 1912, when he succeeded in bringing about the nomination of Woodrow Wilson. [Wilson] was another real honest-to-goodness Democrat, and he made a great many reforms which have been for the welfare and benefit of the people. Then, of course, the Irreconcilables . . . caused his defeat and caused his death. It was in 1932 that we reelected another man who understood what the liberal program meant, and that was Franklin D. Roosevelt, who, I think, is the greatest of all liberals in the whole history of the country.

Have you always felt that way about [FDR]?

Always felt that way about him.

I mean, you place him ahead of any of his predecessors in the realm of liberalism?

Well, I think we'll have to take them in this order: take Jefferson and Jackson and Abraham Lincoln, and Theodore Roosevelt was a talking liberal, and then Franklin Roosevelt came along and implemented the policies which never should have been allowed to get that way, the policies of Jefferson, Jackson, and Lincoln. So I don't . . . you can't classify them. I think there have been about six or eight great Presidents, six of them anyhow, and in my opinion—of course, I was alive when it happened—I always thought Franklin Roosevelt came nearer to being the ideal President than anyone we'd had during my lifetime, and I can remember back to the second term of Grover Cleveland, in 1892.

What special qualifications in FDR's armor and his disposition impressed you as his source of liberalism?

His bringing back the financial control, the monetary system of the country, to Washington. He took it away from the New York bankers, where it never should have been lodged. That's what old Jackson did, if you'll remember: He took it away from old [Nicholas] Biddle when Philadelphia was the financial center of the country, and then he worked out plans for the farmer and for the people who were unemployed.

Session Ten

[T]hey [bankers] didn't do anything but throw bricks at him [FDR] all the time, and of course I was on his side and trying to help him catch the bricks and throw them back.

Mr. President, you were giving some of FDR's qualifications and characteristics that made him a great liberal President.

He was very much interested in the welfare of all the people. . . . Not only did he do things for the farmers and the common everyday person; he rescued the banks when they were all in the worst sort of trouble. And he was very much interested in the training corps for the youngsters, which I think was one of the finest things—the CCC, if you remember, the Civilian Conservation Corps, that gave them some idea of making contributions to the welfare of the country. Then they had the Works Progress Administration which built a great many things around over the country which otherwise would not have been built, and he rescued these fellows that had brought on the panic with their high interest rates and things of that kind. Then, after they were all out of trouble, they didn't do anything but throw bricks at him all the time, and of course I was on his side and trying to help him catch the bricks and throw them back.

You keep referring to the restoration of control over fiscal policies to the government and control over the monetary resources of the country to the government, and you say that FDR had restored that to Washington after it had been taken away from there.

That's correct.

When was it taken away?

It happened in the panic of 1892–93, which was the result of what they called the "first billion-dollar Congress." One whole session of Congress in two years appropriated as much as $1 billion, and everybody thought that that

Transcript, Thursday afternoon, September 10, 1959, part two.

Panic of 1893 was brought on by that situation.* It was a combination of things. The labor policy and the crops' failure and one or two other things brought it about. The control of the finances of the country had been taken back to New York, I think as far back as the administration of [James] Garfield and Chester Arthur, and never had been brought back to Washington. But in 1907 there was another panic, if you'll remember, and Theodore Roosevelt called on J. P. Morgan to help straighten out the monetary situation of the country, and Franklin Roosevelt just moved the control of the finances of the government of the United States back to Washington, where it ought to be. Now this present administration has let it go back to New York. The Federal Reserve Bank of New York now controls the finances of the government, and that's the reason for these high interest rates. . . . I think Leon Keyserling [economist and vice-chairman of the President's Council of Economic Advisers, 1946–50] is still of the viewpoint that the control of the finances of the country ought to be in Washington and not in New York. Some of the rest of them didn't feel that way. I had a professor, Dr. [John D.] Clark from Wyoming, who was one of the ablest advisers along with Keyserling, but [Edwin] Nourse, who was there for a while, was on the other side of the fence. He wanted to see the bankers control the finances of the country, and I didn't. I didn't have anything against the bankers, but the control of the finances, just the same as the control of the rest of the government, ought to be in the hands of the Congress and the President of the United States, nowhere else.

You [retained] a number of FDR's advisers . . . after you took over the Presidency?

That's right. They all stayed as long as they wanted to, and they were all good men. I had trouble with one or two of the fellows that I inherited, including Henry Morgenthau and Henry Wallace, but the rest of them I didn't have any trouble with.

They seem to have gotten the impression somewhere—we just want to put that into the record without regard to its use—that you represented an important departure in the degree of liberalism as practiced by FDR. One heard that on many sides.

*Baring Brothers, a British banking house, failed in 1890 and forced British investors to sell off their American securities, thus draining gold from the United States. Also, decreases in tariff revenues due to the McKinley Tariff Act and the Benjamin Harrison administration's pension grants brought U.S. gold reserve below $100 million. In June 1893, the stock exchange crashed and the Panic grew, and the nation suffered for several more years. In 1894, Secretary of the Treasury John G. Carlisle tried to increase the gold reserve with a $50 million bond issue; however, only New York bankers subscribed. Finally, in 1895, President Grover Cleveland called on J. Pierpont Morgan and August Belmont for still another loan. Their banking syndicate provided a $62 million loan at a handsome profit. Again in 1907, Morgan's personal influence lessened the effects of a panic.

Oh, yes, you hear that all the time, but if you want to get the facts in the case, the best way to accomplish that is to read the message of September 6, 1945, which set out the principles which I intended to carry out. That's where the brickbats commenced to fly, after that message was sent to the Congress. And it's still good; it works just the same now as it did then.*

Now FDR, during his administration, when facing a little reaction to his program—I believe it was 1937 . . .

1937 and '38.

. . . ran into a minor reversal, a recession . . .

That's right.

. . . and then he proclaimed the need for taking a breather on the economy and that we were going to have a little time out from progress. You were in the Senate at that time. What was your reaction to it?

My reaction to it was very sad, because I didn't like it. I thought he was on the right track, and he finally got back on the track and went right straight ahead, and they reelected him again in 1940 for the third term to carry on these policies.

Then how do you account for Franklin Roosevelt's background, aristocratic as it was, privileged as it was, and coming out in front of his other associates by being the champion of all the common men . . . and the underprivileged?

Well, he had had a lot of experience as a member of the legislature of the State of New York and as governor of New York, and he understood the manipulations that can be made with the control of a government. He naturally felt that the man who had no pull in the makeup of our republic was the man who ought to be looked after. I always felt the same way, myself, because I started in the county here under the same circumstances, and I know that the people who don't have things and who don't have a chance to have any voice in the control of the operation of any government, from the bottom to the top, are the ones that ought to be looked after, because the rest of them [can] look after themselves, and usually do. They're the ones who harass the President and the heads of the local governments to get things that they're

---

*Truman's first postwar message, some 16,000 words and the longest since the Theodore Roosevelt administration, called for an all-out domestic program of twenty-one major advances that ranged from a minimum-wage increase, larger unemployment compensation, and tax reform to the establishment of a permanent Fair Employment Practices Committee, farmers' crop insurance, and federal aid for housing, especially redevelopment of urban slum areas. Conservative Republicans and Southern Democrats were stunned by this liberal document. Even Truman loyalists found the program distressing: Cf. McCullough, *Truman,* 468–69.

not entitled to, and the man in charge of the thing has to sit there and see that they don't get it, for the welfare and benefit of all the people.

In your first term, you felt that you had no choice but to carry out the mandate that FDR had as President.

That's right. I was elected with him in 1944 on the Democratic platform, and I tried to carry it out when I inherited the authority.

Could I bring you . . . forward to the period after you left the White House, or even before that? Somewhere in his book, Eisenhower said that you had talked to him about being a possible Presidential candidate.

Here's the way that conversation came about. He came in to see me one time when I was getting ready to send him to Europe, and I said, "I've heard that you want to run for President," and he said, "I wouldn't run for President under any circumstances." This was in '47,* I imagine, or whenever it was that he was sent over there to take charge of NATO. And he wrote a letter to a newspaperman in Wisc[onsin] . . . or in New Hampshire . . . which is the best essay I've ever seen on why a military man shouldn't be President. . . . I've got a copy of that letter somewhere in my files, and I never pulled it on him. He said under no circumstances did he want to run for President.†

Wasn't there a previous occasion when you were over in Potsdam?

No, no. This happened in the White House about the time [Eisenhower] was getting ready to go to Europe . . . for me.

*In 1950, Eisenhower left the presidency of Columbia University and became supreme commander of the North Atlantic Treaty Organization. President Truman is mistaken regarding the sequence of his discussion with Eisenhower about a presidential bid. The luncheon with Truman in the Blair House took place on November 5, 1951, and both men would deny they discussed a Democratic candidacy during that visit.

In 1948, Leonard Fender, publisher of the Manchester, N.H., *Union-Leader,* endorsed Eisenhower in an open letter. On January 22, Eisenhower, in an open letter to Fender, wrote: "It is my conviction that the necessary and wise subordination of the military to civil power will be the best sustained, and our people will have greater confidence that it is so sustained, when lifelong professional soldiers, in the absence of some obvious and overriding reasons, abstain from political offers . . . [M]y decision to remove myself completely from political service is definite and positive": as quoted in Stephen Ambrose, *Eisenhower, 1890–1952: Soldier of the Army and President Elect* (New York: Simon and Schuster, 1983), 463–64

†Eisenhower to Truman, January 1, 1952. Eisenhower wrote that he would not seek the Presidency and added, "[Y]ou know, far better than I, that the possibility that I will ever be drawn into political activity is so remote as to be negligible." On January 7 in Paris, after Senator Henry Cabot Lodge began an Eisenhower-for-President campaign, Eisenhower announced his willingness to accept the Republican nomination. At a White House ceremony in June, Truman awarded Eisenhower a fourth leaf cluster for his Distinguished Service Medal and praised him for "great and consummate skill, inspirational military leadership, indomitable spirit and the highest order of devotion to the causes of freedom" in guiding the Atlantic alliance: *New York Times,* June 3, 1952; McCullough, *Truman,* 888–89.

But you never offered him the . . .

Oh, no. I told him that if he wanted to run for President, I guessed everybody would have to be for him, and that's where that conversation came from.*

What did you mean by that, Mr. President?

I was thinking about General Grant.

In other words, the popularity of a . . .

Of a war hero. It's always that way at the top. There's only one in the whole history of the country who wasn't elected, and that was old Winfield Scott [in 1848].

Well, they keep insisting that you definitely encouraged him to seek the Presidency on the Democratic ticket.

Oh, no. I didn't do that. I didn't encourage him to seek the Presidency on the Democratic ticket, because I was going to run myself in 1948.

And you didn't think that he was qualified to run for the Presidency at that time?

I never thought a man with military training could make the best President.† I've always thought that, because his training is entirely different. It takes a politician to be President of the United States, and he's got to be the best politician in the country. When I define a politician, I mean a man who knows something about government. I am proud to be called a politician, and I think I know something about the government from the top to the bottom of it—from the bottom to the top, if you want to put it that way.

But during none of those years did anyone in your administration suggest to you that General Eisenhower might be a good successor to the Presidency?

No. No, they never talked to me about his being a successor at all. I wanted a Democrat, and I knew that Eisenhower didn't know what he was

*Eisenhower stated that Truman had called him to his office in 1948 and offered an arrangement whereby if Eisenhower accepted the Democratic nomination for President, Truman would run as Vice President. Eisenhower believed that Truman was using the celebrated general to provide victory for the Democratic Party: Ambrose, *Eisenhower, 1890–1952,* 458–60. In a Colorado Springs speech, Truman said he once believed Eisenhower was qualified to be President: *New York Times,* October 8, 1952.

†In his Colorado Springs address on October 7, 1952, Truman commented on Eisenhower: "I realized he was totally unfamiliar with politics. I knew he would have trouble in political life, as all military men do, separating the wheat from the chaff and the political phonies from the men who are really working for the good of the country. But he thought he would always stand up for things he believed in or the things his whole career has been dedicated to achieving": *New York Times,* October 8, 1952.

at that time. He didn't know whether he was a Republican or a Democrat. No military man does until he sees an opportunity to get somewhere by declaring his affiliation with one party or the other.

Some of these liberals that you designated as being synthetic liberals, including a son or two of President Roosevelt, had taken up the cudgels for General Eisenhower for the Presidency.

Yes, that was at Philadelphia. It didn't amount to . . .

It was before that, too, wasn't it, sir?

No, it was at the [1948] convention at Philadelphia. It started a little while before the convention met, and they, . . . like most of the other people who thought they were [what] you might call "in the know," . . . didn't think I had a chance to be elected, So they thought they'd pick somebody who could be, and a couple of the sons of Franklin Roosevelt got together and decided that they'd go with Eisenhower, but they never had a Chinaman's chance.* There was not any chance, you know. When the President in the White House decides he wants to be renominated, nobody can keep him from it.

What was the source of their disaffection, their dissatisfaction?

I never did know. I never did know.

What did they think Eisenhower would do that you didn't do?

I don't think they knew themselves. I think they just wanted to get on the bandwagon they thought would be helpful to them if he got in. I don't think they had any particular program or plan or any idea of right or wrong so far as the Presidency was concerned, because if they had, they'd have been for me.

Mr. President, what experience did you have with General [Eisenhower] previous to the time of any consideration of politics?

He was always extremely friendly. I was with him at Potsdam. He was at Potsdam, and I went down to Frankfurt. They put on a military review for me, and he gave me a globe, which I had in the White House all the time. I gave it back to him when he became President. He wrote his memoirs, and the inscription . . . to me is a fantastic one.† It's a beautiful thing, and there never

---

*Despite Truman's courageous—indeed, brilliant—decision to order the Berlin Airlift in June 1948, notable Democrats, including Elliott, Jimmy, and Franklin Roosevelt, Jr., together with Harold Ickes, Chester Bowles, Claude Pepper, Hubert Humphrey, and the newly formed Americans for Democratic Action, favored a draft of General Eisenhower at the forthcoming convention in Philadelphia. Party leaders believed that Truman's candidacy would take the Democrats to defeat in November.

†Eisenhower wrote: "To Harry S. Truman—with lasting respect, admiration, and friendship"; as quoted in Merle Miller, *Plain Speaking: An Oral Biography of Harry S. Truman* (New York: Berkley Publishing Group, 1984), 434. Eisenhower's book is not currently available in the Truman Library.

was a feeling between us, and I never thought there would be, even after he decided to be nominated for President. But the Republican inside boys—the fellows who wanted to get control of the government—got to him and made him believe that everything was wrong with me, and he believed it. That's one of the things that caused half his trouble. If he'd stayed with his friends, even if he wanted to be elected President on a Republican ticket, he'd have been much better off, I think, because there are a lot of things I could have told him. In fact, I did let him in there and showed him what the operation of the government is: what he had to do and the responsibility he would have. [I] trained all his men to succeed the ones in my Cabinet. But he got some sort of a notion that everything was wrong, and I never did understand it at all.

Mr. President, there are some reports that he felt rather hurt by the vigorous campaign that you made against him.

This was long before the campaign took place that he got this idea, for some reason or other, and I brought him in there and explained the situation to him. I let him sit in a Cabinet meeting and hear all the reports of the Cabinet members, and then, of course, when the campaign started and he stood on the platform [Milwaukee, October 3] and let General Marshall be called a traitor by that good-for-nothing [William] Jenner and [Joseph R.] McCarthy. Why, I took the hide off him out in Colorado Springs [October 7, 1952] the same day that happened,* and maybe that might have insulted him a little bit. I don't know.† But after the thing was over and he was elected and shown that he had never been in politics, he was still offended, I suppose. He did some little tricks that were not right in line with what a President ought to do to another. It didn't make any difference to me, because he's been trying to get right ever since.

*Angry and bitter about Eisenhower's silence in Milwaukee, Truman claimed in a prepared speech that, by canceling his praise for George Marshall, the candidate had surrendered to a "moral scoundrel" and "moral pygmies," without naming McCarthy and Indiana Republican William Jenner, and that Eisenhower's betrayal meant that, as President, he could not be trusted with controlling the atomic bomb: *New York Times,* October 8, 1952.

†In a Milwaukee, Wisconsin, speech in October 1952, Eisenhower asked his speechwriter, Emmet Hughes, to add a paragraph honoring General George Marshall, in Senator McCarthy's home state. Reporters were alerted to listen for the accolade. However, at the last minute, Eisenhower accepted advice from certain political advisers and left the tribute unspoken. On October 17, in a speech in Newark, N.J., Eisenhower made his first reply to Truman and other Democratic leaders about his silence regarding attacks on General Marshall. He made a brief reference to his wartime superior, calling him one in a group of "great American patriots": *New York Times,* October 18, 1952. When Eisenhower won the nomination in June 1952, Marshall sent a congratulatory note. As the fall campaign gathered momentum, Eisenhower's backers wrote to Marshall to back his protégé; and Marshall, similar to other American military officers in his generation, replied he never voted. To some backers he explained that his father was a Democrat; his mother, a Republican; and he was an Episcopalian: Forrest C. Pogue, *George C. Marshall: Statesman, 1945–1959* (New York: Viking, 1987), 496.

What were those, Mr. President?

Well, for instance, he came here to dedicate a bull on a post for the Hereford people—he's still on a post down there at the foot of 11th Street. He [Eisenhower] was at the Muehlebach Hotel, and I telephoned over there and told them that I would like to come over and pay my respects to the President, and I was very curtly told by the secretary, or whoever answered the telephone, that the President's time was all taken up. And the American Royal people gave him a dinner and didn't invite me to come at all. That didn't make any particular difference, but it's not a very nice way to treat a man in his home county, and I didn't like it. Nobody would like it under the circumstances. Then he did several other little tricks. The President-elect is always supposed to come to the White House and ride with the President to the inauguration.* He didn't show up. He came just barely in time to make the inauguration, and he rode up to the front of the White House and sent word in that he was ready to go to the inauguration. That's not very respectful to . . . and I made it very plain to him as we rode down that I was still the President of the United States and would be until twelve-thirty.

What was the occasion for your saying that to him?

Well, he made a statement on the way down there that he didn't come back for my inauguration in 1949 because he thought he'd get more applause than I did at the time it was carried out, and I said to him, "Well, I want to say to you, Ike, if I'd sent for you, you'd have come back, because you were under my orders." That stopped the conversation.†

One of the historians has made the observation that he couldn't understand why Eisenhower had gone out of his way to be discourteous and unfriendly to you. That it was all right, perhaps, during the early period, when he was not familiar with the Presidency, but as he got more familiar with the Presidency, his respect for you and his sympathy for you should have mounted with each day that he understood the enormity of the load and what you did in it. How do you account for that?

I can't account for it. I can't account for it, and neither can anybody else, and I'm not going to try to account for it.‡

Do you think that this is a weakness in his armor?

---

*During the later weeks of the 1952 campaign and furious about Truman's campaign attacks on him for his silence regarding General Marshall's patriotism and Joseph McCarthy's dishonest claims, Eisenhower vowed he would never ride down Pennsylvania Avenue with President Truman on inauguration day: McCullough, *Truman,* 912.

†Truman is mistaken. General Eisenhower rode in the inaugural parade past the reviewing stand, and the President waved his hat in returning the salute.

‡At President John F. Kennedy's funeral in November 1963, Truman and Eisenhower resumed their friendship.

I don't know. One of the so-called brain powers that was in the White House by the name of John Adams left the White House at midnight so he wouldn't have to ride with Thomas Jefferson to the inauguration, and long after that he got to thinking about what he'd done, and he was sorry for it. I don't think this fellow [Eisenhower] has ever recovered, although he had the Secretary of State, Mr. [John Foster] Dulles, invite me to come up there one time and discuss some things with him. At that time I was making these films with Ed Murrow* down in Florida, and I couldn't go, and I didn't go. I think once since then he asked me to come to the house, the White House, at one o'clock for a luncheon which would be confined strictly to people who were officially interested in the burial of the Unknown Soldier from Korea. Well, I didn't go to that, either, because I didn't see any reason why I should go there in the position in which he wanted me to come. I went to Fred Vinson's funeral [in 1953], and [Eisenhower] and Nixon were sitting in the front row, and they just barely spoke to me when I walked in.

They didn't shake hands at all?

I made them shake hands, but they didn't care about doing it.

Is it possible that—this is just speculation again, and I hear it referred to in places—that he had become the tool, the propaganda tool, of the Republican brain-trusters, and that this is consistent with the policy of first trying to destroy or vilify members of your staff and, at the same time, keep from giving you too much recognition in order to keep you down during this period?

Well, I have an idea that had something to do with it. And I think he believes all the foolishness and the crap BBD&O put out.

Is he lending himself to it knowingly, or is he being duped by it?

I think it's a combination of both. I don't think it was hard to dupe him. You wouldn't dupe me if I didn't want to be duped.

What puzzles me, of course, is how a man like George Allen [a friend of Truman's and a member of the Reconstruction Finance Corporation] could have so misled him and steered him.

I don't think George had anything to do with misleading him. I think it was the top Republicans like Brownell and those people and [Thomas] Dewey.

And [William P.] Rogers.

And Rogers . . . caused the situation, and there's no use arguing about it. It doesn't make any difference to me. The only difficulty is that it makes it rather embarrassing. I've been to Washington a dozen times, and never have

*Famous radio and TV reporter and host of the programs *See It Now* and *Person to Person* in the 1950s.

I heard anything from the President about stopping by the White House or anything of the kind. Now, when Franklin Roosevelt was President and Al Smith [New York's governor and Democratic candidate for the Presidency in 1928] came to town, he always asked him to the White House, and when I was President and Mr. Hoover was in town, I always asked him to come to the White House, and he always did. . . . I always felt . . . a man who had been President of the United States could always make a contribution if he was asked to help in certain lines, because he knows more about the government than any other man, naturally, because that's been his business.

Perhaps this isn't fair to throw at you now, but do you recall any other incidents in American history where a President might have called on a previous President . . .

Yes, I can give you a very specific instance of the case. In 1860, just before the Civil War, there were five Presidents alive, and Mr. [James] Buchanan called them to Washington to see if they couldn't prevent the outbreak of hostilities before the fourth of March. It was in conformity with Lincoln's idea, too. They didn't get anywhere, because the old man from New York, the smart boy [Martin Van Buren], refused to come. The man from Virginia, [John] Tyler, tried to get the four that did come together and accomplish something, but they never got anywhere. That's the only instance I know of where they had as many as five former Presidents alive, and the objective was to prevent the Civil War from coming on. It didn't do any good, but that's one time that they were called in.

Were they all two-term Presidents?

No, not a single one of them.

All one-term men.

Martin Van Buren . . . let's see if I can name them. There was Martin Van Buren and Tyler was next, and [Millard] Fillmore, and Franklin Pierce, and, of course, Buchanan was at the end of his term.

. . . You were speaking of continuity of government—in terms of giving some measure of tasks to do and things to perform in government to former Presidents, no matter what their political differences might be.

Well, I always thought it would be a fine thing if former Presidents on matters of policy—particularly foreign policy—could be consulted as to [their] associations with the people that keep the peace in the world. The heads of governments usually always, at one time or another, get together. I visited Brazil and Mexico, and nearly every head of state in the world came to the White House while I was President . . . the President of France [Vincent Auriol] . . . two Prime Ministers of Britain [Winston Churchill and

Clement Attlee] came, and the princess who was afterward the Queen of England was a formal guest of the President, and nearly every South American country was represented at one time or another at the White House personally, and came personally. Those associations are of vital interest to the peace of the world and to the carrying on of the international affairs of the government. That's the most important thing that the President could contribute his experience on for the use of the people who follow him.

Mr. President, in England they have the Privy Council, which is made up of members who have been either Prime Ministers or Cabinet Ministers or who have been distinguished statesmen in some field. They are supposed to form a special council of advice to the king or to the queen, and quite often the government will avail itself of the opportunity of getting in some members of the Privy Council for advice.

I think that's a good thing, and the reason that the British can do it [is that] they don't carry their personalities into their campaigns. One of the difficulties in this country is that they make personal matters out of campaigns. For instance, I was back in the Senate, after I had been out of the White House about a year—I went back there to address the Press Club—and, of course, the Senators on the Democratic side gave me a luncheon and asked me if I wouldn't come up and visit the Senate, and I did. . . . When I walked in at the west door of the Secretary's office, why, the Senator from South Carolina walked out of the other door. That's [J. Strom] Thurmond.* He's still there [in the Senate]. That was a most discourteous thing for a man to do, I think, because I had been a Senator for ten years, and there wasn't any excuse for his doing that.

Is there any remedy at all for this personal bitterness in American politics?

I don't know. I don't know. I never had any bitter feelings about any of my opponents. In fact, after I was elected, I was just as friendly with the opposition in the Senate—and the House, too—as I was with the people who were in control. There's no sense in a fellow carrying his political animosity into his personal affairs. I never did. I never did right here in Jackson County. I used to have the bitterest campaigns in the world, and the opposition was always just as friendly to me as they could be. They had a perfect right to come in and talk to the court any time they felt like it. They were courteously treated, and sometimes helped.

You were never personal in your campaigns. You were always . . .

*Thurmond left the Democratic Party and, as the Dixiecrat presidential nominee in 1948, won electoral votes of four Southern states. In the mid-1960s, he became a Republican and is now the longest-serving Senator in the nation's history.

No, I never did go into personalities in a campaign. In fact, in most of my campaigns I found it best not to mention your opponent because you just give him a chance to get a headline.

Isn't it rather peculiar, to say the least, that a general without any identification politically with any party would become one of the most partisan of Republicans in having achieved the Presidency?

It is, for sure, but you can't understand it.

And yet he's recognized by the press and some of these so-called wise men—[Walter] Lippmann, for instance—as being a nonpartisan in the true sense of the word.

There never was a nonpartisan in politics. I don't care who he is. The sooner that people find out that nonpartisanship doesn't mean a thing ... the only way a man can be nonpartisan is when he is President or the head of a government in a state or county or city and recognizes the fact that there are people on the other side that ought to be recognized and cared for. But when it comes right down to politics, a man's either one or the other. He can't be nonpartisan; he wouldn't be in the party if he were. When he's in any party, he's partisan; he's got to be.

You and FDR had gone out of your way to recognize the importance of the job ahead of the importance of the party in critical areas and critical jobs.

That's correct. That's always proper. I always tried to follow through on a situation of that kind, and did. I had bipartisan foreign advisers all the time, because when I was in the White House, and whenever anything of vital importance came up, not only did I ask the Big Four on my own side of the aisle of the Congress, I asked the opposition to come up, too, to listen to what had to be said. And in that way, we got all these tremendous things through without much opposition.

Yet we now have a case where there's not only studied discrimination but utter and complete disregard of ...

That's right. We haven't had a bipartisan foreign policy since 1952.

You don't think this is all the doings of the General personally? You think that he's been put up to most of ...

I think he's been put up to most of it by these partisan fellows who have been away from the food trough so long that they show how hungry they are by being mean to the opposition.

Other than returning control of our money matters to the bankers, has this administration done anything that you can point to that is new and in direct opposition to what you had been doing?

No. They've tried their best to discredit every policy that Roosevelt and I put into effect over the twenty years we were in power, and they have not been successful at it. They've always had to come back to the fundamental basis of the things that were set up on the right basis for the welfare and benefit of all the people. They've had to come back. They couldn't do anything else, foreign and domestic, although they've certainly padded the boards and bureaus in such a way that they have become partisan instead of looking after the welfare of the people.

Session Eleven

You take any man in a small position and put him in a job of responsibility, and sometimes he'll turn out to be excellent, and sometimes he'll turn out to be a damned fool.

Mr. President, I would like to touch on some personalities again to get your views of them. . . . In this period since you've been out of the White House, there have been certain personalities you have met who are still doing business. One of them is Jawaharlal Nehru. I'd like to get a little more [of your evaluation of him].

I have had always great admiration for Nehru, and I understand his background, I think, as well as anybody. But Nehru in this modern communist world is living in the time when he and Mahatma Gandhi were under the rule of the British Empire. The British Empire released them, and I don't think Nehru has ever learned, unless he has learned in the last week or so, that the communists are not to be trusted. They don't understand neutrality and peace at any price. The only thing that they understand is a strong force that can beat them in an opposition program, and I think that Nehru may now have discovered that situation. I like him very much. I think he's a very decent, able man with a headful of brains.

He impressed me, when I had him speak at the National Press Club, as being in secret an Indian imperialist, a man who talks so much of the past glories of India and wanted the world to remember that and talked in a way I doubt. . . . Can we turn to another phase that's expressed in the Nehru leadership? Here's a world in turmoil and at the crossroads and divided; the leaderships pretty well limited to a few passing elder statesmen. Where are the leaders to come from? You name the leaders of Russia, Germany, and England and our own situation. Where are the leaders for this world that desperately needs them?

Transcript, Friday morning, September 11, 1959.

They'll come to the top when the time requires it. That's always happened, and the main difficulty with the oldsters is that they never know when to give up. The best time for a man to step out of a position is when he has accomplished what he thinks is his program, and the main trouble with most of these people is they want to maintain control after they're past the time when they can maintain control.

But, Mr. President, the history of the world is replete with the important work that is done by oldsters, these elder men who have had the experience, after all. Physically they may not be at their prime, but mentally they seem to be reaching . . .

They always are mentally efficient, and the proper way to use those oldsters is for the leadership to listen to what they have to say, and then make up their own minds, which is what they always do anyway. The youngsters never learn anything except by experience.

Looking at our own situation, where do you see the leaders coming from? We have two parties, both of which have been having quite a struggle in finding men to lead them within our time.

Well, we have a number of very able governors in the United States. We have some very able Senators and some very excellent members of the House of Representatives. Out of all that number of leaders in the state and national setup we'll finally come up with a leader who'll take care of the thing, just like we did in 1932, when Roosevelt came to the top.

Why is it that we look to governors to succeed to the Presidency, and why have Senators had such a difficult time in achieving it?

I'll tell you, one of the reasons there is that Senators who have become Presidents have not been exceedingly strong men, and I can say that because I was a Senator myself, but the governors usually have had executive experience. Most of them make good executives, and that's the principal job of the President of the United States, although he has five others.

Mr. President, there has never been a Congressman who has been directly catapulted into candidacy or Presidential . . .

I can't think of one right now, but we'll have to look up the facts on that and be sure. Henry Clay came as near it as anybody else, although he finally went to the Senate, . . . but his reputation was made in the House of Representatives. He was never at a point where he'd accept a situation which might have made him President.

Nevertheless, . . . there's no reason why in the future, if some prominent Congressman, some prominent member of the House, should show up that he shouldn't be considered.

Well, Sam Rayburn was considered on three occasions, and he refused because he'd much rather be Speaker than President. And I didn't blame him for that.

Did he ever say so to you?

Yes. He said he'd much rather be Speaker than President of the United States, and I think maybe he was wise, because he's been a great Speaker— the greatest the country has produced. And there are a great number of great Speakers.

In terms of potential Presidential candidates that come to the top: Are they brought to the top, or do they normally, naturally gravitate to the top politically?

It's just a matter of gravitation. You can take any organization, whether it's a lodge or a political organization or anything of that sort. The man who does the work usually comes to the top. And that's absolutely true in politics, because when a man takes an interest in the government of his country and shows that he knows something about it, people are anxious to have him take charge and do things. That's customary in every line of business or anything else that goes on.

But the Presidency of the United States calls for a special kind of talent, a special kind of equipment, and a lot of facets all in one person. As you've said, all these jobs that fall upon him . . . how do you find a man with all those . . .

I don't think that's true, because you're looking at one who obtained the position without any special qualifications of any kind except a knowledge of history and a working experience with the legislative branch of the government and with local government. There are, I imagine, hundreds of men like that in the country, if we could just find them. But how are you going to find them? I don't know.

We would challenge that immediately on two grounds: One is that a knowledge of history doesn't come lightly to people and very few possess it in the sense you have it, and the other is that a feel for people, a feel for the world's people, is something that goes with the job now, and not many of them about us possess that special feel. Who among us possesses that feel now?

Well, we'll try to find him. I haven't seen him yet, but we'll find him.

Well, therefore, Mr. President, in talking about qualifications for the Presidency, you've got to narrow it pretty well to certain basic things without earmarking any man with having specific experience, because you had no experience in the executive side except when you were here in the local . . .

The county.

That's right. You had vast experience on the legislative side, and you did watch the budget and finances. Therefore, what qualifications, basically . . . what sort of man should you look for?

The first thing you've got to be sure of is that you have a man who's honorable, who understands the ethics as laid out in the definition of an honorable man by the Hebrews in the Old Testament and by the Greeks in the top of their glory, and by the Romans, as I mentioned yesterday. . . . You take any man in a small position and put him in a job of responsibility, and sometimes he'll turn out to be excellent, and sometimes he'll turn out to be a damned fool. You can't understand how the mental program is going to work in the head of any man. He's got to make it himself. And you have to take a chance. When you appoint men to positions of responsibility, a great many of them make good, and a great many of them do not. That's the difficulty. It's the human animal all over again. . . .

Isn't there some way to pre-test these men, to subject them to some kind of preliminary test, because we cannot afford to take chances if we can avoid them?

I don't know how you're going to find it out. Now, in the old days, they had succession by birth and position. Some of those men in that succession— I'd say about the same average as has happened with our Presidents—turned out to be wonderful men and great leaders, and a great many of them contributed to the welfare of the world. That's happened in the Presidency. It's a difficult situation. I don't know how in the world you're going to train a man to be President of the United States and be sure he's going to get there, because there's so many factors that cause a man to become President of the United States. I'll say that in the whole thirty-three men who have been Presidents of the United States, the percentage of greatness among them is greater than it was—or, I'll say, is as great as—in the monarchies that preceded republican government. I don't mean "Republican" with a capital letter; I mean the government of a republic.

That's interesting. In other words, you feel that the talent that the men had who were Presidents was equal to any talent of the monarchies?

There isn't any question about it, because we couldn't have become the greatest government in the history of the world without having had that talent in the men who were executives of that government. There are a great many of them that need complimenting. Some of those who are not considered the greatest were great contributors to the welfare of the country.

Could you name one or two, for instance, at this moment?

James K. Polk is one of the first that comes to mind, and I can say that old John Quincy Adams made a contribution to the welfare of the country, because after he became President and was defeated by Andrew Jackson, he went to the Congress and made a great contribution to the welfare of the country. I think that you'll find a great many of these men ... for instance, Rutherford B. Hayes, whose election was purported to have been stolen, turned out to be a very able President. You never can tell how these men are going to turn out.

Do the times bring out the greatness in a man, or does a man contribute of his own weight and importance?

The man meets the times, and if the times are kind to him, he becomes a great man, no matter what his position is at the time. But it's something that nobody can discover the proper approach to, for the simple reason you never know what a man will do until he gets in a place of authority.

Are you in effect saying, then, that greatness is latent in a great many people who will never achieve it?

I think that's correct. You remember what the statement ... that many a rose blooms unseen.

Wonderful. . . . In other words, you may test character and you may judge experience in the past, but you never are certain what happens to a man in the Presidency?

No. That's right. You're taking a chance. And I said a majority of them worked out all right. Some of them became great. Some of them were near-great. Some of them weren't any good, and we'll discuss them a little later on. . . .

And you have no suggestions on how we can possibly pre-establish his capacity?

One of the great things about our governmental setup in the Constitution of the United States is that we don't have to stand one we don't like more than four years.

Let me ask you an important question, then, Mr. President: Quite often a figure looms up as a compromise—or, in the recent parlance, as a dark horse—because he hasn't said anything to arouse any bitterness of all the factions. Is it possible that in such a man you might find a good President?

Yes. It has been done. James K. Polk is an example. He was the first dark horse, and he made good.

And he was a man who hadn't expressed himself very much on anything?

Yes, he had. He expressed himself on the things that really counted, and the thing that elected him was his viewpoint on the admission of Texas as a state. All the rest of them had fooled around and wouldn't do anything about it, but James K. Polk had been Speaker of the House of Representatives [1835–39], and he'd established a precedent behind that . . . or with that job that he had, as Speaker of the House, that really made him worthwhile as a bet to make a good President, and he made one.

What I'm getting at now is: Do you think that any man today who hasn't expressed himself clearly on some of the major issues, domestically or internationally, could possibly be considered for the Presidency?

Yes, it has been done. Warren G. Harding was one.

Yes. But, then, he was not a man . . .

And Calvin Coolidge was another.

*Well, Coolidge rose to fame, didn't he, through a police strike.**

Police strike, that's right.

And symbolized something. Harding was a compromise at the convention.

The greatest one who was a compromise candidate was Franklin Pierce. He was a brigadier general in the Army and took Mexico City, and he had no enemies on either side of the line. He was the man who . . . signed the bill for the repeal of the Missouri Compromise, which was one of the fundamental causes of the War Between the States.

The repeal was?

Yes.

This is a colorless man, a man non-committed and taken on chance, and he turned out to be dangerous.†

---

*As governor of Massachusetts in 1919, Coolidge criticized the Boston police strike with the assertion, "There is no right to strike against the public safety by anybody, anywhere, anytime." Acclaimed by President Woodrow Wilson, a Democrat, and the nation for his opposition to the strike, he won reelection to the governorship. He became a favorite-son candidate at the 1920 Republican Convention and Warren Harding's running mate.

†Pierce carried all but four states in defeating General Winfield Scott in the presidential election of 1852. Soon after the election, the Pierce family were in a train wreck, and their third and only surviving child, Benjamin, age eleven, died. Pierce named James Campbell of Pennsylvania, who was postmaster general, the first Catholic cabinet officer, and this brought on an intense anti-Catholic crusade and the establishment of the Know-Nothing Party. Pierce supported the Compromise of 1850.

That's right. Millard Fillmore was another one. I can give you a whole lot of stories about Millard Fillmore that are really worthwhile. They've just written a biography of Millard Fillmore* trying to make a great man out of him.

What I am trying to get at is that there are a number of personalities today who have not really committed themselves on any important viewpoint, or who are alleged not to have committed themselves, who may be considered for the Presidency. So I wanted to get some of your philosophy on the situation.

Well, the main difficulty with the Congress of the United States in the selection of a man to run for President is the fact that if he's been working as a member of the Senate or the House, he has committed himself on all the great issues that are before the country. You take the governors of great states: They don't have to do that. They're locally interested in carrying on the local government, and they're not called on to make public statements . . . or make votes on what the general public is interested in. That's one of the reasons it's difficult to nominate a Senator or a Representative for President.

In other words, if today you say some Senator or some Congressman is supposed to have no strong views, the best thing to do is to look at his record of voting.

That's correct.

The Cabinet has never been a stepping stone for the Presidency, although it has been a good training ground for the Presidency.

Except in the case of President Hoover. He was Secretary of Commerce and was nominated here at Kansas City for President of the United States. In times past, in the beginning, the Vice President was always considered the next man in line for President of the United States. You'll find that in the first five or six elections of Presidents that that was true [of cabinet members].†

And of course . . .

John Adams was a Vice President; Jefferson was a Vice President; James Madison was Jefferson's Secretary of State; James Monroe was in the Madison Cabinet; and John Quincy Adams was the son of a former President. Old Jackson upset that program. He went out and licked them all with the change of the nomination of the Presidency from the House of Representatives to a convention.

---

*Robert J. Rayback, *Millard Fillmore: Biography of a President* (Buffalo, N.Y.: Buffalo Historical Society, 1959).

†Twelve Vice Presidents have become President. Also, the office of Secretary of State served as an apprenticeship for the presidency for Thomas Jefferson, James Madison, James Monroe, John Quincy Adams, Martin Van Buren, and James Buchanan.

We didn't allow the Vice President too much opportunity to take part in the administration of the country up until the time of the present incumbent. You had the Vice President sit in on all Cabinet meetings.

Sure.

You initiated this exposure of the Vice President.

President Franklin Roosevelt initiated that, because I was invited to sit with the Cabinet every time it met for as long as I was Vice President, which wasn't very long. Then I continued that attitude, because I think the Vice President, as Thomas R. Marshall said, is only one heartbeat from the White House, and he ought to know what goes on.

President Roosevelt used Vice President Wallace on a great many other assignments besides his duties as . . .

That's correct.

But we now have a situation where there was from the very outset a studied campaign to train, expose, build, and project a Vice President for the successorship to the Presidency.

That's right.

What is your feeling about that?

They're trying to revive the attitude of 1796, and maybe they have revived it. I don't know. It's all right. If the Vice President is as carefully selected as the President is, always bearing in mind that he is the successor, then we'll get back on the track, and maybe we can train people then to be Presidents of the United States. . . .

You don't think, then, that exposing the Vice President to the duties of the President and to the functions of the President is a bad thing?

No. It's a good thing, and in my own instance . . . I had known a great deal about it, but after I was exposed to it, I still didn't want to be President. But it came to me in spite of all I could do.

Basically, to put it bluntly, a Vice President's major hope for the Presidency . . . is a matter of survival.

That's right—that the President may die, or somebody may shoot him. That's the reason the people who wrote the Constitution set up that office, and it's all right. It's the proper thing, and I sincerely hope that from now on the Vice Presidents will be as close to the world situation and the domestic situation as the President is. And [that the President will] keep his Vice President informed as to what goes on. That's the best thing that can happen.

But don't you give the Vice President a normal opportunity to foreclose on both parties, he having the inside track, where a President does not succeed himself, or his term expires?

Well, yes, he may have that situation, but it depends altogether on the man. The man's got to show that he has ability and his willingness to accept the responsibility of a candidate. They're ... just as hard to find for Vice President as they are for President.

But he may show ability. He may show a lot of capacity and enterprise, as the current Vice President [Richard Nixon] does, and not have the necessary other dimensions.

Yes, that's correct. That's absolutely correct. One of the main difficulties is that when a man has served long enough in government to find out what it's all about, he's too old to succeed to either the Presidency or the Vice Presidency. That was true of Alben Barkley.

Now, isn't another important characteristic and requirement of the President not only that he engage the imagination and the interest of our own people, but he must also engage the interest of the rest of the world? Certainly the free world.

That's absolutely true. I used to serve with a ... a very able and distinguished Senator from Washington. His name was Lew Schwellenbach, and he used to make some speeches in the Senate. I sat right close to him, and on one or two times when he made speeches, I said: "Lew, you sound to me just like a demagogue." "Well," he said, "let me tell you: If you want to get elected in my state, you have to do a little demagoguing."

After all, the consideration of whether you are a man who will have an appeal outside ... won't make too much difference so far as the American ...

No, the appeal has to be to the voters of the United States, and he has to have a fundamental honorable background in order to make that appeal, because people expect much more of the President of the United States than they do any other public-office holder. He's got to be clean in every direction. He's got to be physically fit. He's got to be morally clean, and he has to have a background that shows that he comes from ... that sort of a setup. It's a difficult thing for a man to be President of the United States. I don't care who he is.

But actually, the people, as people, don't select the potential President. This is the big problem—that certain sifting-down process and it's eliminative choice—is it not?

Well, yes that's true, but the men that are put up usually are put up by the two great parties, and they're put up with the idea that they'll be the best vote-getters. But you want to take into consideration that, in the long run, the people themselves select the President on the basis of . . . what he's stood for in the past and what his background is, particularly from a moral standpoint. The people of the United States want their Presidents to be ideal men. There are damned few of them. I wasn't one, but I got through some way or other . . .

What do you mean by that Mr. President? We challenge that.

Well, educationally, and two or three other . . .

Well, that doesn't have anything to do with morals, Mr. President.

Oh, well no. Of course, a moral background is absolutely essential, and all of our Presidents have been in that class. It's a wonderful thing when you take into consideration that people want their Chief Executive to be what they are not. They want him to be better than any of them.

Session Twelve

Because they [the people] don't want to pay the bill when it comes due. They all love the doctor when they're sick, but when they get well, to hell with him.

Mr. President, I want to get right back to where we . . . abruptly left off. That is on the question of the character of a man for the Presidency. You were saying "morally," but what you probably meant was character.

That's right. Well, a man can't have character unless he has a fundamental system of morals which creates character.

What are those?

In the first place, he's got to be honorable with his associates. He's got to be fair with the people with whom he's associated, particularly with his wife and family, and he must have a reputation that his statements are to be backed up to the end and that his word is good. You can't . . . no politician is worth anything unless his commitments, verbally and in writing, are as good as a bond would be for a bank.

Well, then, I would like to ask this one question: Throughout history, and certainly in recent European history, you have had statesmen and men who headed governments who were what might be called Machiavellian, or who couldn't be always believed, or who made sudden changes and turns. That's also been true in American history, hasn't it?

Not to any very great extent. The principal number of the people of the character you name are behind the Iron Curtain. You'll find that the . . . head of the British government, the Prime Minister, no matter who he has happened to be, his background and his word and his moral standing have been always excellent in, oh, I'd say, the last forty years—fifty years, maybe. And the main difficulty with the French government has been not with the head of the government but due to the fact that . . . France was divided into twenty or thirty

Transcript, Friday afternoon, September 11, 1959.

parties, none of which had any background which would cause them to stick with a program. I don't think you'll find there have been so many of the Machiavellian type in Europe since the old man wrote his book.*

The question of party division in this country has been puzzling a great many people and students as to precisely what the function of each one is to be in the future. How do you see the Democratic Party as it evolves in the future, and the other party?

One of the reasons for our good two-party system, which has worked very successfully for almost a hundred years, is the fact that each party is made up of certain lines of thought. There are crackpot liberals, there are honest liberals, there are people who think the welfare of the country comes first, and there are people who are bent over to the other side—and some of us thought they ought to join the Republican Party and be done with it. But that same thing's true with the Democratic Party. They have their lines of demarcation between various ideas of what the government ought to be. I've come to the conclusion that that's a good thing, because when the turnover is made from one party's control to the other's, the same pressures are on the new party [that] has come into control as were on the old one, because they have the same sort of a situation in their background. You see, a great majority of the members of the Democratic Party and the Republican Party inherited their ideas. They didn't learn them themselves. They just got them from father and grandfather as a result of the War Between the States. I am very strongly in favor of a two-party system, and to keep up that two-party system, we must have all classes of people in each party. Of course, I think the Democratic Party, when it's in power, is always for the underdog. The Republican Party, when it's in power, is for the top dog, which has been amply proved in the last eight years.

There are people within the Republican Party who don't admit to that.... Some of them have even tried to turn liberal. There have been liberals among the Republicans.

Oh, yes, a great many liberals among the Republicans, and I've always invited them to join the Democratic Party, where they belong.

Do you think they're liberal by delineation, or evolution? Because they certainly didn't get liberalism from their forebears.

No, but I think they've studied.... Most of them are able men, the ones you've mentioned, and they have studied what the welfare of the people means. As I say, and as I've said about several of them, they're Democrats and don't know it.

*Truman refers to Niccolo Machiavelli's sixteenth-century book *The Prince,* which explains that politics is amoral and the ruler can use any means, however unscrupulous, to achieve and maintain power.

Are the Democrats of the South—that's the principal problem—are they going to stay put, or join up, or press for a third party?

Well, the Democrats of the South are what's left over from the terrible Reconstruction period of old Thad Stevens, who was one of the worst old birds that ever lived in this country. You'll find the great men in the South in the present day, who do their own thinking, are just as interested in the welfare of the people as a whole as are the so-called liberals of the North. Eventually, when all this color proposition is out of the way in the South, you'll find you'll have the main leadership in the South that we had before the Civil War.

Do you think it could be helped along, or even cured, by the induction into the White House of either a President or a Vice President from the South?

Yes, I do. I think if a President from the South were to move into the White House, he would make just as great a President as one from New Hampshire or New Jersey.

Why?

Because his responsibilities, with the background that he'd have to have to be President, would cause him to do that.

Do you have any such persons in mind, that occur to you, that could have become ...

Yes, there are a half a dozen, but I don't want to name them, because it would make all the rest of them mad.

Do you feel that way about the possibility—this is possibly off the record—of a man of the Catholic church becoming President of the United States?*

Well, the main difficulty with that situation has been that the hierarchy of the Catholic church wants always to control the political operation of a government. That's the reason they've had trouble in France. That's the reason they've had trouble in Italy. That's the reason they've had trouble ... for the Reformation, which Martin Luther, the great man Martin Luther, gave them the best attitude that man could give them on that subject. I have no feeling at all about the morals and dogma of the Catholic church, but when the Catholic church gets to a point where it's in control, the government is always against the little people, and tolerance is not considered. That's true in Spain.

*This question probably arose because of Senator John F. Kennedy's attempt to become the Vice Presidential nominee at the 1956 Democratic Convention, and because of his private, later public, maneuvers to become the Democratic Party's Presidential nominee in 1960. In Session Nineteen, recorded two months later than this session, Truman states he is not opposed to a qualified Catholic's becoming President of the United States.

That's true in Colombia, in South America. In Spain, a Baptist can't be buried in daylight and can't be buried anywhere but in plowed ground. Well, now, I wonder what would happen if this great United States of ours would prevent Catholics from being buried in daylight and force them to be buried in plowed ground. We don't feel that way here, but whenever a religious organization gets control of a government of a country, you'd better look out.* You're in trouble—it doesn't make any difference whether it's Protestant, Catholic, or Jew.

Therefore, you feel that the problem of separation of church and state is the real issue?

The First Amendment is one of the best amendments to the Constitution, and that's it.

All right, sir. The Democratic Party seems to have had a tradition of having a national chairman [who is] a Catholic, and most of the principal governors and candidates for large office have been of that faith.

The idea of a chairman of the National Democratic Party as a Catholic originated, I think, probably, with Franklin Roosevelt, when he appointed Jim Farley to be chairman of the party. Jim was a good party chairman, but I don't think that has any effect on what we ought to stand for in this separation of church and state. I don't think the church ought ever to control the government. . . . I don't care whether it's Protestant, or Catholic, or Lutheran, or Jew.

And the tradition should be amended as soon as it can be brought about.

It doesn't make any particular difference about the chairman of the National Democratic Party or the chairman of the Republican Party. They're only the organizers of a convention that's going to nominate a President and the Vice President, and it's nice to have good men in charge, on either side. I don't think his religion ought to make any difference.

Hasn't there been a departure in the way chairmen of both parties have been conducting themselves in recent years, in terms of not confining themselves to the election of a President but making party policy?

No chairman of the Democratic Party or of the Republican Party is in a position to make policy. The policy of the party is made at the convention when they meet. That means that the majority of the people are represented, and when they make a policy, the chairman has to enforce that policy. It's not his business to try to make policy when the convention is not in session.

---

*However, an American Protestant cemetery burial was denied the deist Thomas Paine, and he was buried on his family farm in New Rochelle, N.Y., in 1809. Ten years later, his remains were removed to England, his birthplace.

Is it any of his business to interest himself in the candidacy of any one person?

He shouldn't. He's supposed to be neutral. He's supposed to arrange the Democratic Party so that it can win no matter who's nominated, and he oughtn't to have any candidate of his own to push.

Now, how do you see the Democratic Party evolving in the changing industrial age? Everything is going to automation; the emphasis is on more and more benefits for labor and more and more security for labor and more and more security for management. Where does the Democratic Party fit into that kind of society?

The Democratic Party will be what it's always been: the representation of those people who have no pull at the source of government—local, state, or national. The Democratic Party will always be what we might call "for the common people," and it's going to stay that way as long as I have any influence.

This is still the age of the common man, is it not?

It always has been the age of the common man, only sometimes he's been suppressed.

What do you mean by the common man?

I mean the ordinary fellow who has a small home, a small farm, a small interest in a business, and who is trying his best to raise a family on the basis of his income. And unless his income is protected, he'll be in a bad way.

You also would include, of course, the working man who doesn't neces- sarily have a small business?

That's the working man. That's the working man who depends on a small salary, who has a small home, who's trying to raise a family—they all go together. There isn't any difference between them.

Because you feel that basically these people of small income have a chance to earn their income—they're the basis of the whole economic structure?

That's right, and they ought to have a basis of income which will give them a chance to meet the payment for necessities, in what they have to have.

Would you name those as job security, home security, health security, and what other securities?

Well, they all go together. Things have come to the point where, in the national setup, which has become the greatest in the history of the world, all those things must be properly protected by the government of the United States, if the state governments don't do it. Some states do.

Do you think this is a primary government responsibility and function?

There isn't any question about it.

So that the difference between one party and another still gets down to the basic securities?

That's right. What I tried to do while I was President was, particularly, to have the health of the people properly taken care of, because they have invented all these various things to make people live longer and to make them easier to get well when they're sick. But they've made it so expensive, with hospitals' and doctors' charges. The American Medical Association was absolutely against a program to set up a situation where people could make a saving, and they have to be forced to make these savings, so they could pay their hospital bills and their doctors' bills. And they called that "socialized medicine."

But there are all kinds of . . . Blue Shield, Red Shield, No Shield . . . all kinds of plans to meet the problem.

No. They help though. They are voluntary. Unless you make people do what they ought to do, when the time comes, in the cases of health and service to the country—that's the reason we had to have a draft—why, they won't do it.

That's very interesting. Why do you think people who are so much concerned about the health of themselves and their own have to be compelled to do what is good for them?

Because they don't want to pay the bill when it comes due. They all love the doctor when they're sick, but when they get well, to hell with him.

So this is not a thing for individual choice or community option. You think this is a federal matter?

I thought so.

You still do?

I wrote a message on it, and I still feel that way.

Thus, primarily, because you think health now plays such an important role in what a country can do and what a people themselves can do . . . some reservation ought to be . . .

Keep people physically fit. When I got the reports on the registration for the draft in the Second World War, I found that between 34 and 36 percent of the youngsters were unfit for service, and two-thirds of that was brought about because they didn't have the proper medical attention when they were growing up. That's what I wanted to cure. When 34 percent of the youngsters are unfit, what do you expect from the next generation? The ones that were fit were taken in hand and shot at and killed, and those that were not fit were left back to make the next generation, and I was against it.

How do you go about taking a free people and compelling them to do those things?

You can't compel them. You have to convince them. That's what I tried to do, and haven't had any luck so far, but we'll keep working at it.

Well, the people were convinced. A lot of people obviously understood what you tried to get them to do, but ...

The American Medical Association didn't believe in it, because they didn't know what they were talking about, and they still don't.

Well, then, how do you overcome that?

Just keep working at it, keep working at it, and finally when the vast majority of the people understand exactly what they are entitled to and what they ought to have, then we won't have any trouble putting it over.

You think this is one of the primary things yet to be accomplished?

I'm sure of it, because health is the most important thing that an individual can have. If you go back to Jamestown and go through that old church and see the gravestones, you will find that the average age of those people was about 35 to 40. Think what that would mean today. We'd have a population of about half what we have if the anticipated life span was 35 or 40. I think it's way up toward 70 now. I'm one of them, because I'm 75.

[So] just as you cannot leave, for example, [cleaning up] pollution in drinking water to the voluntary will of the people, certain measures ought to be necessary and compulsory in connection with health?

That's absolutely true, because you take the situation of littering the streets and the highways in the country. Missouri finally had to pass a law which has a fine of $500 for dumping trash on the highway. I had the experience in my own place, out there we had this 600-acre farm. My sister and brother and myself planted trees and made the place look nice, and these city people would come out and dump their trash. Well, I had two staunch nephews who served in the Second World War. They took this trash back and dumped it on the people who'd put it there. You don't find people who are able to do that ordinarily, and now we've got the situation in line so that the trash movers ought to take care of their own trash. Now I'm figuring on putting up a sign on my front gate to litterbugs—please take your trash with you. Don't put it in front. I have to pick it up every morning, and while I like to take bendovers, I don't like to pick up your trash to do it.

That means that, to a certain degree, we'll always have a little bit of police in our state?

It must be necessary, because to some extent people have been brought up to get by with what you can instead of having a moral background that would say to them, I mustn't do this because it's wrong. The get-by business, I think, maybe originated in our military educational institutions. Whatever you can get by with is all right—I don't believe in that. I believe that you ought to have a background where what you do is right and not try to get by with something that's wrong just because you can get by with it.

Do you think that the Republicans are peculiarly and chronically conditioned not to be interested in all these problems that have to do with the plight of people?

Well, they have a viewpoint that's entirely different from the viewpoint of the welfare of the common people. They believe that there ought to be a ruling class. They believe that the welfare of the country can be handled from the top down, and the difference between them and us, as set out by Franklin Roosevelt, is that we believe that the welfare of the people starts from the bottom up. That's the only difference.

Isn't there a pretty large segment of the Democratic Party that believes the same way—let's say, about racial problems?

Oh, well, yes. As I said a while ago, both parties are cross-sectioned with people who believe one way and another, and there are, of course, some of the Democratic so-called aristocrats who believe in the Republican program. And they ought to join the Republican Party. I've always said that.

We've slowed down a little bit legislatively now, and some of the progressive fire that [was] built under the Congress by Franklin Roosevelt and yourself seems to be dying down.

I don't think so, because the very fact that they made the President accept the bill that he vetoed* shows that there are still enough good Democrats in the Congress to make that happen.

I don't think . . . one out of 105, Mr. President.

Well, I know. But you'll find that in every instance the vast majority of the Congress was for overriding the veto, and this situation of veto by the President—not on principle, but on policy of a Republican administration—doesn't mean that that's what the majority of the people believe. You study

---

*Two days before this interview, President Eisenhower vetoed a compromise bill for public-works projects to be done by the Army Corps of Engineers and the reclamation bureau. Although Eisenhower said the bill ignored fiscal responsibility, the Congress overrode his veto one day later.

the votes in the Congress, even on the vetoes, [and] you'll find the vast majority on the side of the people. The only reason they didn't have enough for two-thirds was because some of our Southern Democrats, and the Dixiecrats [states' rights Democrats] and the "Shivercrats," went along with the Republicans to uphold something that I thought, and that the majority of the Democrats in the Congress thought, was wrong.

In that case, wherever the President has vetoed and has been sustained in his veto, that doesn't mean he's been sustained by the majority of the people.

Not at all. It means that he's been sustained by those who believe in special privilege, that's all.

In other words, sustained by a minority, because actually . . .

A vast minority.

All you need is a third to support him.

You talk about a minority President. That's what he's been.

In that case, we are about to face another barrage of propaganda of peace and prosperity as the keynote and sole position and property of the Republican Party. How phoney is that?

Entirely phoney. All you have to do is ask the farmer and the little businessman, and then you'll get the answer.

That's not prosperity, and now they say, and they will continue to say it again, that wars are always coincidental with Democratic administrations and are absent in the Republican ranks.

How about Lincoln and McKinley?

Well, they . . . that was a little bit of both. But how about since then?

It isn't true. The only reason in the world that we had to get into World War I and World War II was due to the fact that we were attacked and had to defend ourselves. I'm not so much of the opinion that you ought to stand by and let yourself be slapped on both cheeks before you refuse to meet the situation with which you're faced, because eventually you're going to have to face it. The fact that the two last world wars happened in Democratic administrations was by accident and not the intention of the Democrats. I wonder what the Republicans would have done in the case of Pearl Harbor, when the Japanese murdered our youngsters without provocation and in peace time. I wonder what would have happened after the sinking of the *Lusitania* and the very fact that they began to sink and take our people off ships that were peacefully inclined. Would the Republicans have stood for that? I don't think they would. They all voted for the declaration of war in each instance. I don't think there were but a very small minority against meeting the situation as it came up, and when ... it's just like talking about Korea as my war. Korea wasn't my war. Korea was an attempt to make the United Nations stand up, and we did up until the time when the present administration surrendered to the communists after I had gone out of office.

The present administration is also making a big, big drive for peace, almost at any cost, is it not, sir?

I don't believe in peace at any price and never have. I believe that the best thing to do is to be sure that liberty and freedom are maintained. You'll find that some of the greatest philosophers in the country and in the world and in history believe that freedom of action and liberty of the individual are much more important than peace at any price. Nehru's found that out ... to his regret, I think.

Well, Nehru's found it out, and [Harold] Macmillan [who as British Prime Minister sought improved relations with Moscow] at this moment is taking his place, and he's out putting trade ahead of everything.

Well, trade, you know, has been the fundamental British economy. They want trade, and I don't blame them for wanting trade, because they are a country that can't produce enough to live on. They've got to have trade to make it work. But that doesn't necessarily mean that it's right. I think, in the long run, freedom and liberty are much more important than trade or anything else.

Is it fair to assume that the Democrats, because they are interested in the plight of the little man and businessmen, etc., that they are also equally interested in the survival of little nations and little peoples?

That's the reason for their interest in the survival of these small nations, and, of course, eventually the small nations, as was done after World War II in the organization of NATO [North Atlantic Treaty Organization], which put the free nations together—eventually those small nations will come to the point where they'll organize for their own protection, and then they'll be in a position to have a voice in the United Nations that will count.

Mr. President, what do you feel about de Gaulle's insistence that France be allowed to be a sovereign nuclear power? In other words....

Whenever France proves that it can overcome what it did in the Second World War and that it's a great nation again, as it was in the First World War, then I'll be for it, but not before that time.

Would you ask the Congress for authority, if you were President, to enable France to become that kind of a power?

Yes, I would. I'd like to see France back in the picture as one of the great nations, and they brought themselves to this position because—I shouldn't say that—but they had 1.4 million of their young men killed in the First World War [and] a great many thousands killed in the Second World War. The British had 900,000 killed, but that didn't cause the British to knuckle under when the time came for a fight.* And that's the trouble with France. I hope they'll come back, because the French are a great people and always have been.

Would you make it conditioned upon her not using this nuclear power with which we would equip her for colonial purposes?

I don't think she could use it at all unless their own change of front comes about to make France the great power it was before World War I. And when they do that, then they'll have common sense enough to know that this nuclear proposition is one that must be used with good sense and in a way so it won't murder all the people in the world, because they could start a world war, just like they have in times past.

Dave talked about asking Congress to help France. But what if France, with her scientists—and [France has] great scientists . . . supposing France is able to produce . . .

Well, France may find a scientific manner in which to produce these things, but it takes barrels of money to get it done, and they haven't got the money at this time. I hope they will have eventually.

Yes, well, I think they're about ready to explode one now, and I think maybe that's one of the problems with which we will be faced.

It'll be exploded in the Sahara Desert in the sand, so it won't hurt anybody.†

Yes, that's right. So in other words, [France] by that means will join the nuclear club, as it's called today. Would you be willing to use France as a wedge or weapon against Russian intransigence in trying to bring together the pooling of atomic energy?

When France recovers her position as one of the great powers, then I think that France, England, the United States, and the NATO powers will become the nations who are in control of the free world. When that happens, I'll be very happy.

---

*France suffered almost 2 million deaths; Germany, slightly more than 2 million; and the British Empire, 1 million. As John Keegan wrote: "The First World War inaugurated the manufacture of mass death." More than 10 million men were killed: Keegan, *The First World War* (New York: Alfred A. Knopf, 1999), 4–7. The United States lost about 51,000 as battle deaths, and 62,000 more died from diseases, mostly from a major flu virus.

†France joined the elite club of atomic powers with an atomic explosion in southern Algeria on February 13, 1960. President Charles de Gaulle cabled the scientists his gratitude for making France prouder and stronger.

Would you initiate such a move from the outside? Could the Democratic Party intervene in that operation?

I don't think so. I don't think it can be initiated from the outside, because the French are a very proud people—as Stalin said about the Poles, although he took them over—and eventually France will come back. It's been one of the great nations in the history of the world, and I'm hopeful that it will be still one of the four greats in the whole world.

Before you go, and we're going to have to release you for your appointment, do you see among the visible number of candidates for the Democratic nomination one who would measure up to your notion of what that man ought to be?

We have, oh, I think, five prominent men who are interested in getting themselves nominated for President—and I want to say to you, if they knew what they were getting into, they wouldn't be in such a hurry to get it. I am sure that when the Democratic convention decides on which one of those four or five men is the one to lead the party, that he'll begin to understand just exactly what he's up against. And you can't tell. He may turn out to be one of the great ones, but I have no special candidate now. . . .

Why doesn't the Democratic Party—this is a key question that Bill and I keep talking about—go to you for clear and definite guidance? Why is it avoiding you at a critical moment like this, when we have to find that one man who will get us out of all the trouble?

The Democratic Party is doing that. . . . I think that the situation is sort of like it was in 1912, when the special interests were at that time trying to obtain control of the Democratic Party. I think that we'll have the same trouble now, and if you'll remember, when the real climax came, there was an old man by the name of William Jennings Bryan that kept the country from getting into the hands of the people who would like to control both parties. That's all I'm hoping to do. I haven't any special interest in the matter except to see that we nominate a man who's not dominated by the ones who want to exploit the fellows who ought not to be exploited, and that's eventually what will work out.

What you're saying, then, is that the special interests are working both sides of the street.

They always have. They always have. They'll take any arrangement that can possibly be met. They took over Grover Cleveland in his second administration, if you'll remember, and then Cleveland was for McKinley. Then old Bill Bryan came along and expressed a liberal program, and it was the policy of the Democratic Party until finally, after twelve long years, we nominated a Democrat to be President of the United States who knew what is was all about. And his name was Woodrow Wilson.

Session Thirteen

But my sympathy was always with the fellow who didn't have the ability to do what the so-called top-notch social outfit in the country could do, and I never forget it.

Mr. President, if you don't mind, we're going to try to touch a little bit on what may appear to be trivia, but is personal.

No. No, you go ahead. It's all right. Whatever you do is all right with me. We can cut it out if you don't like it.

That's right. What we want is to get a little bit of the picture of the life you are living, since you will be really the first former president who will touch on what it means to be a citizen. In contrast with what we know about other former Presidents, we'd like to get a little bit of the picture of how you live, even if it seems for the moment irritating or trivial to you.

Well, it won't. You go ahead now. I understand what you want. We'll do it the best we can.

Mr. President, now you live in this big house on Delaware Avenue [North Delaware Avenue], and you and Mrs. Truman live there alone. You have no servants living in.

No. The principal reason is that it's almost impossible to obtain anybody to work on the basis that we've always had before, for the simple reason that all the old servants who were with us are incompetent physically and can't work for us. But we get along fairly well. We have two or three people to come in once or twice a week to clean up and to help Mrs. Truman get things arranged, so that the house runs almost exactly like it used to.

At any rate, your living is exceedingly simple. There's nothing elaborate or lavish about it.

Transcript, Wednesday morning, October 21, 1959.

No. No, I usually get up about five or five-thirty in the morning and go downstairs and do a round of work going through the mail and the newspapers that come to me. Along about seven or seven-fifteen, Mrs. Truman comes down and gets us a simple breakfast. We have breakfast and discuss things that take place during the day in the house and the yard and the people that are coming to work for us during the day. Then, about a quarter of eight, I get in the car and come over to the Library and sort out the mail that I haven't been able to sort the night before. I work on it all the time, and now I have help in the Library that takes the dictation and files the letters and things of that sort. Along about eleven-thirty, I go back over home, and Mrs. Truman and I have lunch together. A very light lunch. Then I come back over to the Library about one or one-thirty and finish up what I haven't been able to do in the morning and go back over home after I have signed all the mail and everything. [I] take a nap, and then, about five-thirty or six, we begin to get ready for dinner, which Mrs. Truman prepares. Then I go through a great many other documents that have accumulated during the day, and sometimes we look at television, particularly if Margaret [Truman] is on it. Then, about nine-thirty or ten, we go to bed and start over the next day and do the same thing.

Mr. President, let me ask you: Is Mrs. Truman a pretty good cook?

She has always been a good cook, but she pretends like she isn't. You'll find some of her recipes in all the national cookbooks. She has always been a good cook. Every woman in my family, from my grandmothers on both sides of the house all the way down, have been good cooks.

What are some of her favorite dishes that she gives you or those that you ask for?

Well, she is very careful to be sure that my waistline doesn't increase, because she thinks that might have a bad effect on my heart. I think that's what the doctors told her. We have, usually, for breakfast, toast . . . I have toast and bacon and maybe a soft-boiled egg or poached egg or some scrambled eggs, and she has about the same thing. She has coffee. Sometimes I drink a cup of coffee with her, [but] more often I don't have anything to drink at all for breakfast except water.

What are your favorite foods? Are there any special foods that you care for very highly?

When I was in the Army, a man kicked about the food. I was commanding officer of a battery, and I put him in the kitchen to make it himself. So it has not been customary for me to kick about the food, but I always have good food and what I like.

You're typical Midwestern in the fact that you like good food. If you have beef, you like your beef well done, don't you?

Well, yes. I like roast beef with the cut next to the end piece, and I don't like raw meat of any kind. I'm very fond of bacon, ham, sausage, and things of that sort. We usually have bacon and sausage for breakfast, [but] not together.

Mr. President, why . . . is there any special reason why the Midwest always prepares beef well done rather than rare, as they do in the East or other countries?

The principal reason for that, I think, is that the West—Midwest—furnishes the beef for the nation, and they are of the opinion that only coyotes and predatory animals eat raw beef. That's the reason we like it cooked.

May I go to the question of your walking? You still do the same number of steps per minute that you've always done?

Yes. My period of service in the National Guard and in the war, the First World War, it was customary for people on the march to do about 120 steps a minute. I still do that, not because it's necessary, but because if you're going to take a walk for your physical benefit, it's necessary that you walk as if you're going someplace. If you walk 120 [steps] per minute, that gives your whole body a good exercise. You swing your arms and take deep breaths and make 120 a minute. After you're fifty years old, that's the best exercise you can take. Of course, some of these old stiffs, you know, try to figure out that they can play tennis and that they can play handball or that they can do just what they did when they were eighteen, and very often it causes them to fall dead of a heart attack. I don't want to do that.

I would like to just touch on a very important phase of a matter of privacy. You would rather not have help live in with you in order to maintain a total sense of privacy and no intrusions.

That's true. We are of the old-fashioned cult that believes in home privacy, and we'd much rather do the things that are necessary to be done in the home ourselves than to have somebody that will go out and gossip about it. You know, a man who has been in the position that I've been in is subject for much gossip, and that's one of the reasons that it's very hard, indeed, to get help that will—well, as my mother used to say—keep their mouths shut when they ought to.

Have you had any betrayals of confidences either at home or in the White House from help?

Very, very few. I can't remember any of the real betrayals, but when a man is close to the Chief Executive of the greatest nation in the world, he is importuned by all sorts of people—particularly by these gossip magazines—to tell something about what went on behind the scenes. You can't blame them sometimes for breaking over, but we have had very few instances of that kind, in my experience.

Do you find the house you live in now is adequate for your needs? What I'm trying to get at is, how do you feel living as you do where you live?

It's a very happy arrangement. Everybody's pleased about it as can be. I had expected to rebuild the old farm home out at Grandview as it was when my grandfather and grandmother . . . both of my grandfathers lived there, and my mother and father lived there . . . but conditions developed, and the development of these places in the country where people shop, these shopping centers, so it couldn't be done.* It was taken over for a shopping center, and every time I go by there, I have a very nostalgic feeling on the past when I used to sow wheat and plant corn and harvest wheat and help my father and brothers to thresh it and plant corn and gather it in the same place where this shopping center is now. It's no longer the old home which was established by my grandfather in 1850. It's part of the city—what you might call the metropolitan situation—in a county that has grown outside the city limits of all the cities in it. But that happens, and we have to accept it as it is, but I can't help but wish that I could have kept that farm as it was in the beginning.

You often have the feeling, too, don't you, that you want to live where it is green and where you can look out on nature?

Yes. Yes, I do, and we're situated in our place in Independence where we have a very large backyard and front yard, and it's almost like it used to be at the Independence house. But at home on the farm . . . it is nowhere nearly as it was when I was a youngster and used to have the greatest time in the world on that old farm.

Now you say [that] you get up early in the morning, [and] you do your reading. Do you still continue to do a considerable amount of reading?

Well I do a great deal of reading between the time I arise, which is around five or five-thirty and until breakfast time. Then I'll do a great deal of reading in the evening when I go home after dinner. I still like to do it, because it's most interesting. I read a lot of newspapers; I read a lot of history books; and I get them by the dozens now since they found out I'm interested in history.

*When Truman's parents were married in 1881, they moved to Lamar, Missouri, where his father went into the mule and horse business. In 1885, a year after Truman's birth, they moved to a Cass County, Missouri, farm for two years before moving to Mrs. Truman's mother's farm in Grandview, Missouri. Because their children were reaching school age, Truman's parents bought several acres in Independence in 1890, and Truman's father carried on a general livestock business. He also farmed rented acreage outside Independence, where young Harry fed livestock, milked cows, and drove the herd daily to pasture two miles away: Truman to James Watkins IV, June 8, 1959, David Noyes Papers, Box 1, Truman Library.

Mr. President. I've noticed that you read a few more whodunnits now than you used to.

Sometimes I go to sleep reading a whodunnit when I want to get my mind off my troubles, but I don't care much for whodunnits. I'd rather make the whodunnits than read them.*

After all those years in Washington and getting used to the streets and the atmosphere of Washington, do you miss it now since you've been home?

No. I've never had any desire to go back to Washington and live. I was in Washington just a day or two ago, and it's just the same old place as it was when I was there for eighteen years. I never got the complex that I wanted to be a big shot in Washington or Virginia or Maryland. I think Missouri is a better state than [any] of them.

Now, just a jump in an entirely different direction for a second: You came from the heart of isolationist America.

That's right, and I never was an isolationist.

How is it that you have managed ... and people ask that all the time: Where did he get the feel for minority groups? Where did he get the sympathy that he communicates to them, recognizing their problems, their feelings? How did you develop that feeling for the plight of the minority group?

By experience. By experience. When I was college age, my father, due to circumstances, was not able to send me to college. I had to go to work. I went to work for $35 a month in a bank, and I found out what the bank clerks thought and how they were treated. Then, before that or after that, when I went back on the farm, I had a great many contacts with farmhands who came out of the little towns close to us when they worked on the farm.† Their usual wage was ten cents an hour. That would run up to $1 a day for ten hours or $1.20 a day for twelve hours. My father and I and my brother always increased that so that the men who worked for us received anywhere from $1.50 to $2 a day and their meals, which was, in those days, a very good wage and outside the usual pale. I have always been familiar with what happened to the

*In Session Seven, Truman noted the mystery writer Erle Stanley Gardner's gifts of books. During the Truman Presidency, Gardner wrote one new mystery novel, *The Case of the Fiery Fingers;* moreover, seven of his earlier books were reissued during the Truman years.

†In 1903, the Truman family moved to Kansas City, Missouri, where Harry Truman worked for the National Bank of Commerce. One year later, the restless family traded Kansas City property for an eighty-acre farm at Clinton, Missouri; they farmed for a year before returning to the Grandview farm. Leaving the bank in this year, 1906, Truman joined his father and brother in operating the family homestead. The father died in 1914, and a year later, his mother, Martha Truman, together with the two sons and a daughter, inherited the 600-acre farm: Truman to Watkins, June 8, 1959, David Noyes Papers, Box 1, Truman Library.

fellow who has no pull. These people were of the best stock that the country produces, yet they had to live almost in poverty. Yet most of them got along very well, raised good families, and some of those youngsters of those people who used to work for us have been graduates of universities and made good in every line of business in the country.

But my sympathy was always with the fellow who didn't have the ability to do what the so-called top-notch social outfits in the country could do, and I never forgot it. I never forgot the history I read on the same subject, which began when I was old enough to read, and I think that one of the best things that could happen to the education of a public official is to have to go through a lot of hardships. Then he'll understand what that other fellow suffers.

That's very interesting. May I just go back to a little detail about the farm? I remember, recall, very vividly your story about the difference between a horse and a mule. How a horse is eager to rush to water and food the minute that it's unharnessed. Would you mind repeating that . . .

Well, horses, most horses, even these big, heavy draft horses that are bred for pulling great weights, are full of vim and vigor and want to go faster than a mule does.

You were talking about these draft horses.

Well, when draft horses or horses that you work or drive usually are full of life, and when you come in from a drive or work, you must watch them very carefully to see that they don't drink too much water and be sure that they don't eat anything at all while they're hot. When you use mules, Missouri mules, sixteen hands high and 1,500 or 1,600 [pounds] in weight, you can drive them as hard as you please, turn them loose in the lots where the corn is in full sight and the water's plenty, and they won't drink too much and won't eat too much. They have really about [as much], or maybe more, sense than a man who's trying to take care of them.

What's become of the Missouri mule, sir?

He has disappeared. The tractor put him out of business. And, you know, there's a story [about] who had the first choice between the Swedes coming to the United States and the mules. Missouri had the first choice, and they took the mules. (Laughter). I've got forty-five minutes, now.

Fine.

Because this is an Independence thing.

All right. Would you describe your meeting with President Eisenhower at the Marshall services?

It was arranged after I arrived in Washington for a Colonel Kidd to be my aide and escort, as General [Harry H.] Vaughan was with me as my individual aide to escort me to the chapel at Fort Myers. We were supposed to be there before two o'clock, and we arrived promptly on time and were escorted into the pew, where I was supposed to sit with General Vaughan on my left and with the ambassador from Nicaragua on his left and a couple of generals whose names I didn't get. A short time after I arrived, General Eisenhower and his two aides came in—General [John] Pershing and a colonel whose name I've forgotten, but whose name we can find out—and moved in on my right. General Eisenhower said, "Good morning, Mr. President," and I said, "Good morning, Mr. President," and we shook hands.* We sat through the service, and then . . .

Excuse me, Mr. President. You said before that he extended his hand to you.

Yes, he did. He did. But the newspapers had it the other way around.

You felt that you should have greeted him first?

Certainly. He's the President of the United States, and I tried to give him every courtesy to which the President is entitled. As soon as the service was over, we all arose when they moved the casket out of the church and waited until the honorary pallbearers and the family had gone. Then one of the colonels who was in charge of the ceremonies came, and President Eisenhower moved out with his two aides and saluted me and said, "Goodbye, Mr. President," and I repeated the statement by saying, "Goodbye, Mr. President." Then I was escorted out by the aide that was assigned to me, Colonel Kidd, and followed the family and the casket out at another door. General Eisenhower—that is, President Eisenhower—went out at another door in front of the church, and I went out at a side door at the back of the church and got in the car and went on back to the hotel.

Did President Eisenhower give you a military salute as he was going out?

Just a country salute like I would give one of my friends out in the country. . . . I returned the salute.

How did the President look? Tired?

He looked rather tired, and I think he was tired, because the next day he left for Georgia for further rest. He had a terrible cough in the church.

*The New York Times front-page story on October 21, 1959, reported that the two Presidents had met for the first time in six years. Truman, seated at the Fort Myers chapel, stood up when Eisenhower entered and, according to this account, Eisenhower said, "How do you do, Mr. President?" and Truman replied, "How are you, Mr. President?" This news account also says that Truman told his friends that his differences with Eisenhower had resulted from the snub at the 1953 inauguration; Eisenhower's failure to defend General George Marshall vigorously from right-wing attacks; and the Muehlebach Hotel incident on October 16, 1953, when Truman's phone call and request to see the President for a few minutes' welcome was rejected.

I listened very carefully, and I think he was not over the cold that he had been suffering from.

Did he make any comment at all of any kind? No eulogies, no statements?

Not that I know of. He didn't make any in the church or anywhere else that I could see. None in the paper. He made a statement the day that General Marshall died, which was a very nice statement, but nothing since.

You did not go to the interment services?

No, I didn't go to the interment services because I was told very carefully by the colonel who was my escort that it was strictly a private family affair, and perhaps that's the reason even the President didn't go.

*Yes. All right. Now what accounts for the presence of the ambassador from Nicaragua there?**

There were several ambassadors there; he was just one among many. There were a great many ambassadors and nearly all the former officials who had served with General Marshall were there. This ambassador of Nicaragua was ambassador when I was President, and his wife went to school with Margaret. I suppose that's the reason he had a chance to sit with me.

These were by special invitations?

I don't know how this matter was arranged. I had no special invitation. I just simply went to the service because I thought I should, and I had been to see Mrs. [Elizabeth] Marshall in the morning, and she expressed the hope that I would be at the services. So of course I went, and evidently it had been arranged for me to go, because they had assigned . . . the Defense Department had assigned me an aide to see that I made all the rounds the way it should be done.

Mr. President, you said that when you read this statement about Marshall the second time, you almost had to stop because you were so moved by it.

That's correct. I couldn't help it.

And at the time that you saw Mrs. Marshall, both of you were somewhat moved very much the same.

Very, . . . and we didn't do much talking, although we discussed her grandchildren and mine before I left.

Let's move from this to another element that had to do with what we were talking about in connection with your domestic attitude toward help and your

---

*Dr. Don Guillermo Sevilla-Sacasa.

conditioning with the help that was being used on your father's farm. There's been a growth of snobbery in the United States in recent years. What is your opinion about this snob development all over the country that we see?

You mean toward the people that work with their hands?

No. Toward possessions—in other words, putting on the snob attitude for possessions.

Well, I don't like that. I think that's always been going on in the world, and to some extent it has increased after the Second World War. I don't think any man should be ashamed of what he does, no matter what it is. The man that's proud of his job has no trouble in this free country of ours, and I don't believe in anyone taking an attitude that he's better than somebody else because he apparently has a better job. It has been customary in this country for a man who makes good on one job that he can always expect promotion to a better one, and I hope that will continue. You don't have to be a snob to be in that condition.

Well, there's a snob development in industry. There have always been snobs. We now see it on the farm; we've seen it in labor; we've seen it in a great many places. Does it have any effect on the political complexion and the political climate of the United States?

It will if it continues long enough. We've got to continue to make it appear that any man—it makes no difference what his origin or where he came from—if he's an honorable man and has a decent background so far as his family is concerned, he's eligible to be President of the United States. That's always been my idea, and it's the idea of the teachings at the beginning of this republic.

The common man is losing some status now, is he not, in our present climate?

Well, if he doesn't look out for himself, he will.

How would you cure that?

We've got to inform the youngsters as they grow up that they mustn't under any circumstances feel that they're better than the other fellow because they have a better financial status in the community. It has always been the case that the people who live in the big houses always thought they were better than those who live in the small houses. I never thought so, and I guess that's one of the reasons that I had no trouble making the people understand what I believe.

Do you think that the leadership from the White House could have some effect on them?

It would, of course, and always has . . . had some effect on how people think. The expression of opinion by the President of the United States is always carefully listened to, and if he expresses opinions that are for the welfare of the people and the country and the people who do the work, you won't have any trouble with this country. I never did think you would have any trouble. I'm an optimist, and I'm going to continue to be that way.

You see no great danger signs so far as to any decline in our democratic attitudes toward each other?

No. No, I do not, for the simple reason that we've been through these periods before. They always come after a crisis, and eventually they straighten themselves out. Or we go through a difficulty like 1873, 1893, and 1929,* and then they straighten themselves out.

Could we jump from that to your first meeting with President Herbert Hoover in 1945? . . . [We] want to ask you just to clear up this thing: As I understand it, you were informed that Mr. Hoover was in town shortly after you became President, and that you asked the White House switchboard operator, Hackie, to put you through to the Shoreham Hotel where he was stopping. He answered the telephone. and you said to him, "Hello, Mr. President," and he said, "Who is this?" You said, "Harry Truman." Is that the way the thing went, as you recall it?

Yes. Then I asked him to come on over to the White House, and he came, and he had a way of coming into the White House. The first time he was there, Margaret was down in the lobby of the main part of the White House getting ready to go to school, and she said some big man walked in the front door and never stopped and walked right on through. She turned around to the usher and said, "Who is that?" And this John Mays, who was the head usher at the front door at that time—the doorman, really, is what he was—said, "Miss Margaret, that's President Hoover." But he always came in the front door of the White House and came down through the corridor that leads from the main building of the White House to the office for the simple reason that he didn't want to walk through the room where the newspapermen hang out. He was always welcome to do it, because that had been his residence.

Now, during that period, just to refresh your memory a little bit on it, you asked him to come to the White House, and he was reluctant to impose on you. He thought you were too busy. Didn't he say . . . that he didn't want to take your time?

Oh, yes. He said he didn't want to take up my time, and I told him that I had something that I wanted to talk with him about that I thought was for the welfare of the world. Then, at a later date, after that conversation, he

*Economic depression years.

came with Dr. [Julius] Klein, who had been one of his secretaries, and we discussed the starvation that was going on around the world, particularly in Moravia and in Tibet and in one or two other places in that part of the world. The difficulty that we were faced with was a drought through the Southern Hemisphere, which had ruined a great deal of the small grains that are used for food. I asked President Hoover if he wouldn't try to get the situation lined out so we could feed all these people and allow no one to starve to death. He made a trip to South Africa and South America and to Indonesia and to the rice-raising countries over there, and we accumulated enough food grains per people so that none of them starved. We had to use the American Red Cross by sort of an ultimatum to the Soviets in feeding these Moldavians, who are in Romania and Czechoslovakia. We got that done, and no one starved for lack of food.

I have here in this institution of mine [the Truman Library] presents from the various people who were fed. There's a wonderful mahogany table and a dining-room suite from the President of the Philippines [Elpidio Quirino], because we helped to feed them after they had been devastated by the Japanese. I have a picture of the Grand Dalai Lama of Tibet in his Shawl of State, which I doubt very much if anyone else has, because we fed them.* I have presents . . . I had an Order of the Holy Sepulchre, Knight of the Holy Sepulchre, which was organized by the Empress of Constantinople who was Constantine's mother, sent to me by Queen Helen of Romania on account of the fact that we had fed these people in Romania known as the Moldavians. There are various things here in this institution from the people who showed their gratitude to the President, although I was not particularly entitled to any gratitude. We were doing just what was right, and in order to get that job done, the help of the former President of the United States, President Hoover, was indispensable. He did a wonderful job in that line. He knew how, because he had fed the Belgians in the First World War. He was acquainted with the approach to these things, and I don't think anyone could have done the job as well as he did.

Just a matter of detail. In your first meeting that you arranged with President Hoover, you found him rather reluctant to impose on you and take your time because he was pretty much out of the public eye and out of circulation—a very obscure figure at that time. Then you said to him, "Well, if you're too busy to come here, I'll come to see you." Is that what you said?

That's true.

Following which, he said, "Well, of course, I'll be glad to come to see you at your convenience." Thereupon you said, "Well, I hope so, because there's a car on the way now to get you." Did you do that, sir?

*In March 1959, the Dalai Lama fled from Tibet, and in September, he asked the United Nations for immediate intervention against the Chinese occupying forces.

That's right. That's right. Every time he came to Washington, I always saw to it that there was a car at his disposal, and I always told him that if he wanted to stay at the White House, he could, but he never did. He'd rather stay at the hotel, same as I would.

*Mr. President, have you ever talked to him spontaneously in conversation about the attitude that President Roosevelt had toward him?**

No, no. I never brought the subject up at all. I was very anxious to have things on a very friendly basis with him, because I was sure that he could do the job that I had in mind for him to do. We never talked about unpleasant things at all.

You never even discussed with him the thought that you have had in your mind, and have developed so strongly since, that ex-Presidents, former presidents, should be used ...

Well, I've always thought that former Presidents should be used. While I was in the Senate, I talked to a great many of the members of the Senate and suggested to them that former Presidents and former Vice Presidents should be given the privilege of the floor in the House and in the Senate and the privilege to sit on committees and discuss things that were before those committees in our upper legislation in either house, without the privilege of a vote, which would not have unbalanced the state setup on the two senators for each state. But I never got anywhere with it.

But the first reason that motivated you to reach for the telephone and call Herbert Hoover was that you wanted to extend to him the courtesy that was due to a former President?

Well, I felt that was the thing to do, because I have always thought that when a man holds the office—and I thought that long before I held it or ever thought of holding it—ought to have every courtesy that can be extended to a former Chief Executive of the greatest nation in the history of the world. Now, you take most of the foreign countries—their Prime Ministers and their former monarchs. If they retire, they are treated with the utmost courtesy. I thought the same thing ought to happen here, because the men who have held those positions as Speaker of the House, Vice President of the United States, and President of the United States have an experience and a chance to become more familiar with the government of the United States than any other people in it, and their information ought to be used.

Can I go briefly into one thing? Immediately upon leaving the Presidency, didn't you have a sort of automatic reaction to what you were doing? As a matter of fact, when you set yourself up in Kansas City, you went on

---

*At President Franklin Roosevelt's White House, Hoover was persona non grata.

seeing people, you went on answering letters. Wasn't that a little bit automatic, because you had been so busy doing that? What I'm trying to do is to probe into your feelings on ...

I understand, but it was not any effort on my part, because I'd been doing that since 1922, and it was just a habit to see people and to answer the correspondence that people would send to me. I didn't feel any burden of it, although I had some difficulty in having the ability to obtain enough help to carry it on. But we finally got through without any serious trouble. During the period when I had to go to the hospital for the first time in my life on a real hospital case, I accumulated about 10,000, 15,000, or 20,000—maybe 100,000—letters and never got them answered. I always felt very badly about that. We answered as many as we could, but we couldn't get 'em all answered. And it accumulates now. Every time I leave, the mail piles up. I'm behind right now because I've been out of town for two or three days, but we finally catch up.

Mr. President, wasn't there a little sense of loneliness or a little sense of sadness at suddenly going from President to private citizen?

No, not the slightest. You see, I'd kept up my contacts with the people here at home. I'd been coming home at regular intervals, and I had a state and county full of friends, and I associated with them just like I did with the people back in Washington. The thing that was most satisfactory to me was the relief from the tremendous responsibility as President of the United States. To tell you the honest truth, on the first go-round, I certainly enjoyed that relief and I still do.

But you, nevertheless, did feel a sense of an involvement with those affairs which had been associated with ...

Oh, yes, of course. The people kept questioning me about them, and the newspapermen everywhere I'd go asked me questions on my viewpoint on various approaches to things. I always tried to tell them just exactly what I thought, but I never tried to make a statement of what I would do if I were somebody or other. I have always made it a point never to answer hypothetical questions of that sort.

But emotionally you couldn't quite get yourself away from the fact that some of the major events that were going on, and still are going on, were part of the events in which you played such a role.

No, no. You never can get away from that. It's part of the setup. You just can't get away from it.

The sense of relief from the enormous, crushing burden of the duties of President didn't last very long, did it?

(Chuckling) Well, I don't know. I've been very much relieved that I don't have to make decisions on some of the things that have been happening lately.

But weren't you troubled and irritated at some of the bad decisions that were made on those problems?

I was terribly worried on the lack of decision. It was not the decisions that were made—it was the lack of making any decision that always worried me. . . .

Now to go back to Herbert Hoover for just a little more color. When he came to see you the first time when you established a relationship with him, did you ask him to come to the front door of the White House or to the side door?

No, no. I asked him to come to the White House, and he could use his own judgment on that, because he'd been in there often enough to know how to come in. . . .

What was his attitude and his feeling, his general attitude toward you for having established this relationship?

Very cordial. He was always very cordial. I can remember sometime after that—that's when he was the opposition speaker at the Gridiron Club in Washington, where they have a lot of fun and rib each other to beat the band—Mr. Hoover made one of the nicest speeches that was ever made from that side of the table. He had been asked before or after that, I forget which, if he would make the keynote speech for the 1948 Republican Convention. He made the statement that he would make the speech if they wanted him to, but if the Republicans thought he was going to spend his time attacking the man in the White House, they were mistaken. He wouldn't do it.

[How about] your judgment of President Hoover after your meeting with him and after the assignment you gave him in the government? Do you think he performed better [in the years after] he was in the White House than he [did] as President?

I don't like to go into the analysis of the Presidency at this time, because there are people working on that phase of his career. As a citizen of the United States and as a man who had in his heart the welfare of the country, I think President Hoover was just like all the rest of us. He wanted to do exactly what he thought was right. I might say that I think that one of the difficulties was that he, in a political way, started at the top instead of at the bottom, and it would be just like my starting into his engineering career without knowing anything about engineering. A man has to know politics the same as he does any other business, and I think the principal cause of Mr. Hoover's trouble and the cause of the troubles of a great many men that started at the top, including Henry Wallace, was that they didn't know the political setup from the ground up.

But you consider him to be a man of capacity and considerable ability.

I think he's not only a man of capacity; he's a man of integrity and an honorable man. I think very highly of President Hoover and always shall think very highly of him on account of what he did for me when I was in trouble with this starvation period.

I think we wanted to get into the question of Adlai Stevenson. . . . Why do you now think in that respect that Adlai Stevenson lost out the first time he ran for President?

Because he didn't know anything about national politics and didn't want to learn.

Did he have the qualifications for the Presidency?

Oh, yes. I think he had the qualifications, except for one thing that I've discovered since then: He rather lacks the power of decision, and that's what a President has to have more than anything else.*

Did he show those qualities as governor of Illinois?

He apparently made a very good governor of Illinois from all I could learn—at least, I thought he was a great administrator and was so informed by his constituents. But I've come to the conclusion that his difficulty in making decisions and his prolonging the fact that great decisions have to be made promptly is one of his failures to be able to connect with what it takes to be the Chief Executive of the United States. . . . He's got to have the power to make decisions on the basis of the facts as he knows them, and the prompter that they're made, the more promptly that they're made, the better off the country is and will be. Sometimes you make wrong decisions, but you always have the power to change them and make another one.

Is there anything else that is lacking in Governor Stevenson to qualify him for the Presidency other than his inability to make decisions?

---

*In April 1956, David Noyes wrote to Truman regarding Stevenson's speech to the American Newspaper Editors' Association on hydrogen-bomb testing and warned the President that Stevenson "is encumbered with psychological difficulties which may add up to a personality defect." Noyes also said that, despite his high intelligence, Stevenson was chronically unable to deal with the obvious, and that there seemed to be a "serious question of his capacity for sound judgment and the aptitude for making timely decisions and then resolutely to carry them out": Noyes to Truman, April 17, 1956, PPF, Name File, Box 109, Folder 1, Truman Library. Before Noyes went into West Coast businesses and advertising, he published a small-town daily and weekly in Illinois. A clever writer, he warned Truman to avoid Eleanor Roosevelt, who was dividing the Democratic Party in 1959: "She chose an outside perch—from which she keeps chirping away and sniping at you": Noyes to Truman, December 12, 1959, PPF, Secretary Office File, Box 31, Folder 3, Truman Library.

He has a hard time understanding what Lincoln thoroughly and completely understood—that the Lord wouldn't have made so many common people if He didn't love 'em . . .

Mr. President, just one more question as far as Stevenson is concerned. You saw him a number of years later in Chicago and, as I recall it, as you told me, you had told him quite bluntly and frankly that he had an idea that you were corrupt.*

That's right.

Can you recall that?

Yes, yes. I recall it, and he denied the fact that he felt that way about me, but he felt that other people in the administration might not be as honest as they should have been. Well, it's amply demonstrated over the history of the country that there are always people in every administration, in every organization—banks or anything else you go into—there's always somebody who thinks he can get by with something that he oughtn't to do. I don't think there were a greater number in the administration in which I was head than there had been in previous administrations and that there have been in this administration which followed me.

What was the exact word that you used, Mr. President, in trying to characterize what he thought of you or what you thought he thought of you?

Well, I asked him if he thought I was an albatross around his neck. He didn't say he didn't feel that way, but he denied that he had any idea there was anything wrong with me personally. But he's the man that made the statement out in Oregon that there was a mess in Washington that ought to be cleaned up. Of course, the Republicans grabbed that like a fish grabs the bait and used it for all it was worth.†

---

*A handwritten letter by Truman to Stevenson called Stevenson's reply to the editor of the *Oregon Journal* a "surprising document" that makes it seem that Stevenson is trying to beat the Democratic President with his mention of the "mess" in Washington. Truman wrote: "There is no mess in Washington except the sabotage press in the nature of Bertie McCormick's *Times-Herald* and the anemic Roy Howard, snotty little *News*." He also added that the only national mess was being made by Dixiecrats, Taft Republicans, Nixon, Noland [Knowland], Harry Byrd, and seniority chairmen of key Congressional committees. Frustrated, the President warned Stevenson: "There are more votes on 'Skid row' than there are on the 'North Shore' [of Chicago] for the party of the people." With bitterness, Truman wrote: "I'm telling you to take your crackpots, your high socialites with their noses in the air, run your campaign and win if you can. Cowfever [Estes Kefauver] could not have treated me more shabbily than have you": Truman to Stevenson (not sent), President's Secretary File, Box 334, Truman Library.

†In August 1952, the *Oregon Journal*'s editor sent Stevenson a question as to whether he could "clean up the mess in Washington." Stevenson signed the reply prepared by an assistant, which stated: "As to whether I can clean up the mess in Washington I would bespeak the careful scrutiny of what I inherited in Illinois and what was

In every one of his acts, starting with the setting up of separate head-quarters in Springfield [Illinois] he has shown pretty clearly that he wanted not to be associated with you.

Oh, yes. That was, I think, the advice he had received from his friends—that the further away he could get from an association with me, the better off he'd be politically. Well, I don't know whether that was correct or not, but, anyway, he set up a separate headquarters in Springfield and had one in Washington. Neither one of them was able to run and do any good with the political campaign which was then going on, although I got out and went everywhere and did the best I could, just the same as if I'd been running for President.

Isn't that a pretty clear indication that he hadn't quite understood and appreciated the big things that were achieved during your administration and was more or less content to make his judgment on the little things, as so many of the opposition papers did?

That's right. He was inclined to take what the opposition press, and most of it was opposition, had to say about what was going on. . . .

Was it in light of that experience in '52 and some of the things you saw come out in the campaign that you felt that the Democrats had to look elsewhere in '56 for a candidate?

That's right. That's the reason for it, but I didn't find out in time, because I kept trying to get Stevenson to say that he was going to be the candidate. He had a perfect right to be the candidate if he wanted to be, but he never would give me an answer affirmative or negative.

That was in '52?

In '55. That was in '55. And then, if you remember, he came out on the atomic bomb when the thing was at its worst point, and it was just as bad as calling my administration a mess in Washington.* I didn't think that a fellow

---

accomplished in three years." Republicans did indeed publicize Stevenson's implied agreements that the mess existed. Stevenson's reply outraged Truman: see Ferrell, *Truman: A Life,* 376–77; and McCullough, *Truman,* 906–7. In 1956, Stevenson, after reading proof pages of Truman's *Memoirs,* explained to Truman that the "mess" reference was an inadvertence, that the quotation marks were left out of Stevenson's reply either in dictation or in transcription: Stevenson to Truman, January 10, 1956, PPF, Box 109, Truman Library.

*On April 21, 1956, in a brilliant speech that Stevenson himself had prepared for the American Newspaper Editors' Association, he urged the United States to take the lead in ending hydrogen-bomb testing, saying that this was a matter of principle, not politics: cf. Harrison E. Salisbury, *New York Times,* October 16, 1956. Just weeks before the election, Stevenson stated that ending H-bomb testing would be the first order of business if he won the election. On October 15, in a speech in Chicago, he promised to seek world agreement with the Soviet Union, Great Britain, and other atomic powers

who could not see the public welfare first, and the welfare of the nation in the hands of the Democratic Party, ought to be nominated for President. I went to Chicago to try to get somebody else nominated, but I got licked, and then I went out and tried to elect [Stevenson].

But before that, in July, after you had returned from Europe, you had a meeting with him at the Blackstone Hotel, at which time you briefed him on what you observed as the problems confronting the world in the danger zone.

That's right.

And you also pointed out to him at that time that in order to qualify for the Presidency and have a chance at winning it against the incumbent, you would have to get platform space on the peace issue with him.

That's correct. That's right.

What was his reaction after you gave him the fill-in on the world situation as you saw it?

I was trying to get him then to say that he would be the candidate in 1956, and he wouldn't say it.* He said he didn't know whether he wanted to run or not, and he probably felt that he had to be drafted again, which he was.

He was already engaged in some primaries at that time?

That's right. But he hadn't made up his mind whether he was going to accept the nomination or not, even in '56.

Even though he entered some of the primaries?

That's right.

The only other point I have to ask about is the incident where Roger Tubby reports that, after you got through with this long session with Stevenson, he asked you, "What is wrong with me, Mr. President? What am I doing wrong?"† Then you asked him to come to the window with you, and you were up on either the fifteenth or sixteenth floor, and you saw a lone figure in front

---

to end testing, especially because these explosions send Strontium-90, a powerful poison, into the atmosphere. Stevenson's nationwide speech on October 15 was reprinted in full in the *Times*. Stevenson's advisers believed his H-bomb declaration to be the most important promise in his election campaign: cf. Johnson, ed., *Papers of Adlai Stevenson,* 6:110–21, 281–87.

*Soon after his July meeting with Truman, Stevenson wrote a note of gratitude to him in which he explained that he was more interested in the Democrats' winning than in who would win. Thus, Stevenson found if difficult to do what Truman suggested— "Make up my mind that I want the job and say so": Stevenson to Truman, July 18, 1955, in Johnson, ed., *Papers of Adlai Stevenson,* 4:529–30.

†By September 1952, Roger Tubby had succeeded Press Secretary Joseph Short, who died in late summer. Truman worried that he had given Short too much responsibility, affecting his health.

of a revolving door. You pointed at that figure and said, "Governor, you'll have to learn how to reach that man."

That's right.

And when you parted, he, on the way back to his office with Tubby, is purported to have said to Tubby, "What do you suppose he meant by that?" Now, is that how you have the report on that situation?

I'd heard about it. The two things I had in view was the fellow couldn't make up his mind to get into the revolving door, and after he got there, he was afraid he didn't know how to get out, and he was a common, everyday citizen. I wanted [Stevenson] to get used to that sort of people.

You don't think then that Stevenson should be another Bryan—get a third chance to run?

Well, if you remember the history of Bryan, he didn't ask for a third chance, the third time. He was nominated in 1896 in Chicago and made a great campaign. He was renominated in Kansas City in 1900, and I was there as a page and I saw that procedure. In 1904, after listening to all these people who thought he wasn't any good, the Democratic Party met and nominated a conservative that was more conservative than William McKinley. His name was [Alton] B. Parker, and he got licked by a much greater majority by Teddy Roosevelt than Bryan had ever been whipped in '96 and 1900.* And so, in 1908, there were no Democrats on the horizon who appeared to be able to make the grade, and due to the fact that the Democrats were all very friendly to Bryan, he was nominated again in 1908. But he was defeated by Theodore Roosevelt again. No! By William Howard Taft.

William Howard Taft.

With Roosevelt's backing. Then Roosevelt fell out with Taft, if you remember, and split the party, and Woodrow Wilson was elected in 1912, which, to some extent, overcame the last sixteen years before that.

But there are ample candidates today whom the Democrats could talk to rather than turning, as they did in 1908, back to Bryan.

Oh, yes. I think so. Well, you see, this is the time for another candidate, anyway, if we follow Bryan's example.

Oh, I see. That's interesting, very interesting. . . . But haven't the Democrats always had a tough time finding candidates—more so than the Republicans?

---

*In 1904, Roosevelt received 7.626 million votes; Parker, 5.084 million. In 1896, Bryan received 6.647 million votes; McKinley, 7.035 million. In 1900, Bryan again was defeated by McKinley, by 6.358 million to 7.219 million votes. In 1908, Taft won with 7.679 million, against 6.409 million, votes.

Always have. I can remember, I was old enough to remember, in 1896—let's see, I was twelve years old at that time. When the Chicago convention met, Missouri had a candidate. His name was "Silver" Dick Bland. He was a congressman from Missouri. He had the inside track, and the convention, for some reason, allowed a delegate from Nebraska to get up and make a speech on the gold and silver issue. Bryan's famous "Crown of Thorns and Cross of Gold" speech was made, and he was nominated unanimously, and poor old Dick Bland never got anywhere.

So those days are not to be repeated now that we have radio and television and public participation?

Well, I think you're as mistaken as you can be. I think those days can be repeated, and I think the proper thing would be for us to remember the history of these conventions and to try, if we can, to build up a candidate in the Democratic Party—he's got to be built up—who knows what the score is and in whom we can have confidence to do the things that are necessary when he becomes the President. The job grows bigger and bigger all the time, just the same as the country grows bigger and bigger, and we've got to meet the situation with the time. But history will repeat itself as we go along, just like it always has.

This is a very tough question: How would you insure the country against an unfortunate choice of a President in critical times like these?

You can't. You can't insure it. The only thing that can be done is to do the best possible to try to get a man who can do the job. In most instances where that has been done, the country's found a man, and I'm sincerely hoping that we'll find him this time.

Would it be possible to have a council of ... to use that expression ... to use an elder statesman, a surviving former President always subject to be summoned ...

I can give you a historical example on that. There was a time when we had five presidents alive in the most terrible period in the history of the country, just one hundred years ago now. Those five presidents didn't do a dime's worth of good toward stopping the Civil War, although they tried with all they had.

Why did that happen, do you think? Because there was division, or because they were ignored?

Principally because they were ignored. And then there's another thing: When a fellow is out, he's not as well thought of as when he's coming up. The next generation has to always be producing people to carry on what's been left to them. I don't think that these so-called elder statesmen know very much, anyhow. Those I've come in contact with don't.

With one notable exception . . .
(Laughter)

President Hoover. . . .

Mr. President. It is said that Eisenhower resented some of the things that you said in the '52 campaign. Have you any idea or notion what those things might have been?

Yes—I think probably the speech I made at Colorado Springs after he stood on the platform and let General Marshall be called a traitor.* I'd skinned him from the crown of his head to the heel of his foot, and he might have felt that that was a personal matter, which it was and ought to have been. But I've been skinned many a time on things on the other side of politics, and I never carried any grudges on.

---

*In Milwaukee during the 1952 Presidential campaign.

The President with David M. Noyes, his longtime friend, counselor, speechwriter, and editor, proudly holding a special award from the American Cinema Editors. The organization voted Truman the Outstanding Television Personality of 1964 for his contribution to contemporary American history with his television series *Decision: The Conflicts of Harry S. Truman*. (Courtesy of David Noyes)

Three days after the successful 1944 Presidential election, President
Roosevelt; Vice President-elect Senator Truman; and a disheartened
Vice President Henry A. Wallace return to the Capitol during a rain-
storm. *Photo credit:* Abbie Rowe, Department of the Interior (Courtesy of the Harry S. Truman Library)

President Truman presents
General Dwight David
Eisenhower with the third
oak leaf cluster for his
Distinguished Service
Medal at the Pentagon in
early 1948. General Omar
Bradley became the new
Chief of Staff of the U.S.
Army. A few months later,
Eisenhower was sworn in
as the thirteenth president
of Columbia University.
Photo credit: Abbie
Rowe, National Park Ser-
vice (Courtesy of the
Harry S. Truman Library)

President Truman waves from his armor-plated Pullman Presidential car (first outfit-
ted for President Franklin D. Roosevelt in 1942), named the Ferdinand Magellan,
on June 3, 1948. Departing from Union Station in Washington, D.C., Truman was
beginning the 9,000-mile round-trip to the University of California at Berkeley,
where he delivered the Commencement Address and received an honorary degree.
Photo credit: Abbie Rowe, National Park Service (Courtesy of the Harry S. Truman
Library)

In November 1948, shortly after the Presidential election, President Truman discusses the European Recovery Program with Secretary of State George C. Marshall; Paul G. Hoffman, president of Studebaker and the program's administrator; and former U.S. Ambassador to the Soviet Union and Great Britain W. Averell Harriman in the Oval Office at the White House. (Courtesy of the Harry S. Truman Library)

Shortly after dawn on October 15, 1950, and just one month after General Douglas MacArthur's brilliant landing in Inchon, Korea, President Truman meets the general on Wake Island in the Pacific to discuss the Korean war, possible Chinese intervention, and additional threats from communists in the Far East. *Photo credit:* U.S. Army Signal Corps (Courtesy of the Harry S. Truman Library)

Four days before Christmas 1950, Secretary of State Dean Acheson provides President Truman with an analysis of his sessions in Brussels with the Foreign and Defense Ministers of the North Atlantic Treaty Organization nations. *Photo credit:* Abbie Rowe, National Park Service (Courtesy of the Harry S. Truman Library)

One month after the 1952 Presidential election, won by the World War II hero General Dwight David Eisenhower, President Truman confers with the brilliant though reluctant Presidential candidate of the Democratic Party, Governor Adlai Stevenson, at the White House. Stevenson failed to carry his own state of Illinois. *Photo credit:* Abbie Rowe, Department of the Interior (Courtesy of the Harry S. Truman Library)

Portrait of a relaxed President Truman as a plain American citizen back home in Independence, Missouri, some three months after leaving the Presidency to Dwight David Eisenhower. *Photo credit:* Leo Stern (Courtesy of the Harry S. Truman Library)

Maneuvering for the Democratic nomination for President in 1960, Senator John F. Kennedy visits President Truman in mid-November 1959 at the Truman Library. Truman's earlier apprehension about a Catholic being elected President had moderated; however, he continued to worry about the influence of JFK's father, Joseph Kennedy. (Courtesy of the Harry S. Truman Library)

Two months after becoming President in 1969, Richard Nixon sent the White House piano as a gift to the Truman Library. During his brief visit with President Truman, Nixon played the "Missouri Waltz," a melody the frail eighty-five-year-old Truman did not recognize. Bess Truman and Patricia Nixon, however, enjoyed the music. (Courtesy of the Harry S. Truman Library)

Session Fourteen

[MacArthur] thought he was a bigger man than the President of the United States, and if his brigadier generals or his colonels had treated him the same way, under the same circumstances, . . . they'd have been court-martialed, and that's what ought to have happened to him.

If you had to deal with General MacArthur all over again, what would you do about his repeated defiance of the authority of the President and of the civilians' control?

Well, the general in the field—he's a sort of a proconsul for the government of the United States—is necessarily responsible to the President, and when he doesn't . . . carry out the program of the President, then he has to be relieved. I was very patient with General MacArthur because I should, I think, have relieved him sooner, and I know that Franklin D. Roosevelt should have relieved him much earlier than the time came for me to have to do it. But I always hate to ruin the reputation of a man who has been in the service of the country for forty-nine years, and I think that's what his period was. There wasn't anything wrong with the program, and it would have to be done. I'd probably do it a little more promptly if I had to do it over.

Would you have recalled him to the White House, in view of his rank and his position, and dismissed him or relieved him from the offices of the White House?

I invited him to come to the White House long before this took place—in fact, long before the trip to Wake Island. He said conditions were such in the Far East that it was absolutely necessary for him to stay there, so I met him at Wake Island, which was only a short distance from Japan. When I first invited him to come to the White House, he should have come, and then there wouldn't have been much trouble. I think, in all probability, I would have relieved him then.

Transcript, Wednesday afternoon, October 21, 1959.

What is there about a military personality in times of national stress that gives him such a powerful hold on public opinion and public following?

It's necessary to have able military men to carry out the program when you're in an emergency. We certainly were in an emergency so far as Germany and Japan were concerned at that time, and so I have the same feeling that everybody else has that a great military man is a necessity. You take any controversy or any war you want to read about, you'll find a person who's most talked about and who's most necessary is a man who understands how to move military forces so they'll meet the emergency. That's customary and it's necessary, and you can't help it.

Don't they get built up to where they begin to infiltrate the political mechanism of a democracy such as ours and complicate it?

That depends altogether on the man and how he works. You will find that to be the case with most of the great generals who were war leaders in their time, but sometimes they get a superiority complex. I think Winfield Scott was a shining example of what can happen to a man. So was McClellan, and MacArthur is the one in our time. You'll find in between that and before that that our generals usually were men of integrity and men who understood their positions, and they had no trouble with them.

Do you consider him one of the great strategists in the military sense?

I considered him a great strategist until he made the march into North Korea without the knowledge that he should have had of the Chinese coming in. That's what caused most of his trouble.

Then you did not encourage his political ambitions at any time nor did you discourage them?

No, no. I didn't discourage him. I didn't encourage him, because all these generals often know history as well as I do, and so I didn't try to educate him on that subject.

And you still feel that a general's capacity for administering a civilian economy such as ours is not necessarily the best?

No, for the simple reason that a general in command of a military force is a dictator, and a President of the United States or the head of any other republic can't afford to take the attitude of a dictator. He has to get the people to agree with what he wants to do and then go ahead and do it. Generals—most generals—can't understand that.

But [MacArthur] did seem to express some of that in his administration of Japan.

He was a good administrator in Japan, and he did a very good job in restoring Japan. But his business was to be a military leader under the command of the President, [and] he didn't keep in touch with the President as often as he should have. It took a long time to find out exactly what the trouble was.

Mr. President, there's a very interesting study made by John W. Spanier on the Truman–MacArthur controversy in which he backs you up completely on the position you took and says that it was historically inevitable and correct.* He goes on to say, "This need for a field commander more in sympathy with official strategy becomes even more urgent in view of the latitude the United States has traditionally granted its military officers."† And he says that "one of the essential things is that no government can allow a military officer to challenge its whole foreign policy publicly. Such toleration would undermine its authority to determine the nation's policy, divide the domestic support it needs, and alienate the allies it desires." And just one more quote here. He says, "Necessity may, therefore, compel a re-examination of the American tradition of military freedom lest it excuse us into disaster in limited warfare not only military strategy; but, on occasions, even military tactics have important political repercussions."

That's a very excellent analysis and it's as true as it can be. If you'll read the history of the country or if you'll read the history of any other country, you'll find that that statement is correct.

And he says that "the military as well as their civilian superiors will have to recognize that clause of which is a definition of war as a political tool means that military operations are not only subordinate to political aims, but that there is no such thing as an autonomous sphere in which military operations are conducted in a strictly military manner unencumbered by outside interference." He goes on to say that "General [Matthew] Ridgway is the only one who took part in the Korean War that understood war in this broader sense—even better than James Van Fleet, Mark Clark, [Charles] Turner Joy and MacArthur."‡

Yes. That's as correct as he can be. Ridgway was one of the ablest men that was mixed up in this thing and if he'd been there in the first place, in all probability, there would have been no trouble.

Why don't you get that passage where MacArthur refers to the position of a military leader as distinguished from a temporary, civilian President or anyone else who is there for just a short time? ... Here, here is the place: "MacArthur drew a sharp distinction between his loyalty to the state and

---

*John W. Spanier, *The Truman–MacArthur Controversy and the Korean War* (Cambridge, Mass.: Belknap Press, 1959), 203–205.

†Ibid., 274–75. This quote in the transcript and the ones that follow in the next two paragraphs include the substance of Spanier's analyses, but not the exact wording.

‡Van Fleet, Clark, and Joy echoed MacArthur's proclamations for a military victory: ibid., 275.

those who temporarily held its power. He did this in testimony before the Senate Committee. He said, 'I find in existence a new and heretofore unknown and dangerous concept that the members of our armed forces owe primary allegiance or loyalty to those who temporarily exercise the authority of the Executive Branch of the Government rather than to the country and its Constitution which they are sworn to defend. No proposition could be more dangerous.'"*

And no proposition could be more dangerous than that viewpoint of the government of the United States. That's what the trouble was. That's exactly what the trouble was. He thought he was a bigger man than the President of the United States, and if his brigadier generals or his colonels had treated him the same way, under the same circumstances, what would have happened to them? They'd have been court-martialed, and that's what ought to have happened to him.

And, incidentally, this came out clearly . . . this defiant position came out clearly only as the hearings before the Senate came out, and the Senators suddenly realized that MacArthur had taken a very defiant position on a constitutional question. . . .

He didn't know what he was talking about when he made that statement. That was a terrible thing for him to do, because that gave away exactly what he was trying to do—to be a dictator and to tell the President what to do, and the President was there to tell him what to do. That's what the Constitution provides, and he was sworn to support and defend the Constitution.

At any rate, this writer sums up that both [Georges] Clemenceau [Prime Minister of France during World War I] and Truman proved and showed that war was too important a business to leave to the generals.

That's absolutely true, because, as the old German [Karl von Clausewitz] said, it's a political approach to settle things that can't be settled without a fight. That's all there was to it.

In other words, you are even more convinced than ever that you should have relieved MacArthur when you did, and sooner if you had thought about it?

Well, here is the situation that you must take into consideration: I could not become familiar with all the things that had happened previous to the time that I was sworn in as President of the United States. I had to take things on faith and try to carry out the program to win the war both in the Pacific and in the Atlantic, and that's exactly what we did. Had I been familiar with all the things that had taken place between Commander-in-Chief

---

*However, MacArthur's startling statement came from his speech to the Massachusetts Legislature and was reported in the *New York Times* on July 26, 1951: as quoted in Spanier, *Controversy,* 235.

Franklin Roosevelt and Proconsul MacArthur, the thing would have been settled much sooner. But I had to take things as they came, and when the time came that it had to be settled, I settled it. That's all there was to it.

And once you made that decision, you had no special qualms about doing it, even though you knew there would be a considerable public reaction?

Not the slightest, because I was familiar with James Madison's trouble with his commanding generals or colonels or officers in the War of 1812. I knew exactly what had happened to James K. Polk, "Old Fuss and Feathers," and Winfield Scott. I knew exactly what had happened between Lincoln and five of his field generals—McClellan, in particular. This was just another case of McClellan trying to run the country from the field.

While you're in that mood, could you tell us exactly why you entertained such deep disregard and misgivings for Richard Nixon?

Well, the thing that causes my disgust with Richard Nixon is the program that he had carried on in California against a certain lady Senator, who was a good one.

Congresswoman.

Yes, a Congresswoman, Helen Gahagan Douglas.* She was running for Senator, I think.

That's right; she was.

And then the thing that he did to the Congressman whose district he took over—he almost ruined that Congressman for no good reason. He was almost as bad as McCarthy in those days in the way he campaigned, and I don't like that kind of business. I never made any personalities out of my campaigns.

Incidentally, this book by Spanier [mentioned] Senator Nixon at the time that you removed General MacArthur. First of all, Senator McCarthy called the President a "son of a bitch who must have made his decisions while he was drunk on bourbon and Benedictine"†...

(Interrupting) I have no taste for Benedictine. No, go ahead.

McCarthy called upon the American people "to fight the President's decision lest Red Waters may lap at all [of] our shores." He warned, "Unless the public demanded a halt to 'Operation Acheson,' Asia, the Pacific, and Europe may be lost to Communism." Senator Nixon proposed that the Senate

---

*Nixon defeated Democrat Douglas in the 1950 Senate race after a bitter campaign during which Nixon, the victor, charged Douglas with communist tendencies.

†McCarthy's term was "sonofabitch": as quoted in Spanier, *Controversy,* 212. The quotes in the transcript agree with the substance of Spanier's text but not the precise wording.

censure the President and call upon him to restore General MacArthur to command. "MacArthur's dismissal," Nixon stated, "was tantamount to rank appeasement of World Communism."

Oh, of course, that's the biggest lie that ever was told, and everybody knows that, because McCarthy was finally censured by the Senate itself for just such conversations, and if Nixon had kept it up, he'd have had the same dose of medicine.

Incidentally, isn't Nixon now ... isn't he one of those leaders now in trying to appease or play along with world communism?

It would appear so, but, then, we can't tell about that until we see what the result is. You see, these political men who take advantage of whatever comes along to help their own political welfare are not thinking so much about the country as they are their own interests, and he's thinking about running for President.

*The congressman you had in mind who was eliminated by Nixon, ... who ran against him in his district was Jerry [Horace Jeremiah] Voorhis.**

Jerry Voorhis. He's one of the finest men I ever met. . . . It's a terrible thing, you know, when character assassination gets in the campaign or election in a free country. I'll say this for the British: They never, as far as I have been able to find out, attack the character of their opponents. They run on principles and on the reasons for being elected for the welfare and benefit of the country. Now, it's become a fashion since McCarthy was such a rabid rabble-rouser, and since Huey Long was in the same class, to attack the character of people who oppose them and do everything they possibly can to destroy them through the fact that people have a certain system of morals. You never find these birds exposing their own moral background for the welfare of the public. The trouble with most of the people whom these fellows have hurt

---

*In 1946, Nixon launched red-baiting attacks on Congressman Voorhis in the California race for the House of Representatives and won the contest. Voorhis had been a member of the Socialist Party in 1920. Nixon knew Voorhis was not a communist sympathizer with communist support; in fact, communists opposed Voorhis because he had denounced Soviet aggression in Eastern Europe, and in 1940 he had sponsored the Voorhis Act, which required communists to register their affiliation. Twenty-five years later, Voorhis wrote an angry, bitter appraisal of Nixon and the 1946 election, blaming Nixon and his campaign manager, Murray Chotiner, for lies and half-truths: Jerry Voorhis, *The Strange Case of Richard Milhous Nixon* (New York: Paul Eriksson, 1972), 4. But in 1947, Voorhis wrote: "The most important single factor in the campaign of 1946 was the difference in general attitudes between the 'outs' and 'ins.'" In addition, Voorhis, too confident about being reelected, did not campaign heavily in California early on; he stayed on in Washington, D.C. Voorhis also noted his last visit with Nixon, just before Voorhis left office, and wrote, "We talked for more than an hour and parted, I hope and believe, as personal friends": Jerry Voorhis, *Confessions of a Congressman* (Garden City, N.Y.: Doubleday, 1947), 334, 349.

has been because they were decent and wouldn't do what their opponents did. That's the only trouble.

You don't feel that Mr. Nixon has learned and mellowed from time and experience?

Not unless he thought it would help him politically, he wouldn't learn anything.

That means that you don't consider him fit for the Presidency?

I never have and never will. I don't consider him fit for the Vice Presidency. The only reason he's there is because the powers that be in the Republican Party were afraid of McCarthy.

*Of course, Nixon has tried in many months to disavow that he had ever called you a traitor. He keeps on repeating and saying that what he meant was a "traitor to the Democratic Party principles rather than a traitor to the nation."**

That's a word that shouldn't be used except in its connection with disloyalty to the government of the United States or any other country that ever a man belonged [to]. He can't get out of it in any other way. The statement that he made in Texarkana, Arkansas, or Texas, or whichever side of the city he was in, was a plain statement that I was a traitor, just as the statement of Jenner up in Wisconsin was that General Marshall was a traitor.† I want to say that the man who could have stopped all that never opened his mouth. He knew better than to take things like that for granted.

Let's get over to a pleasanter thing: You had a very nice visit with the President of Mexico.

Yes, I did. I had a very pleasant visit with the present President of Mexico.

What is his name?

I can't pronounce it. I can't pronounce it. He's a wonderful man.

Morales! [Mateos]‡

No . . . no . . . no. No, that's not his name. We'll have to get it for the simple reason that it's pronounced in a little different way from the way it's spelled, and we don't want to mispronounce the name of the President of our

---

*In Texarkana, Texas, on October 27, 1952, Nixon accused Truman, Acheson, and Stevenson of being "traitors to the high principles in which many of the nation's Democrats believe": see Ferrell, *Truman: A Life,* 391, and McCullough, *Truman,* 909.

†In Senate debate in 1950 over Marshall's confirmation as Secretary of Defense, Republican Senator Jenner of Indiana called Marshall "a front man for traitors."

‡Adolfo López Mateos, President of Mexico, 1958–64.

sister republic. When he was down at the ranch of my good friend, Senator Lyndon Johnson, he expressed the desire to the Senator that he would like very much to see me—that he wanted to see me more than any other man in the United States. Of course, I was highly complimented at that, and I went down there to see him and had a very pleasant visit with him. His purpose in coming to the United States and to Canada was to show his friendliness to his two sister republics in North America—and between the two sister republics and to Canada. I was very much impressed with him. I think he's a fine man, and he has a fine family.

How was his English? Could he . . .

He couldn't speak English at all or he didn't attempt to. He had an interpreter with him. He had the same interpreter with him that was with President Alemán when I was in Mexico.

And he did express his interest in you? For what reason?

Well, I don't know for what reason except that he made the statement to the interpreter that I was the most popular American in Mexico, and I guess that was the reason, maybe.

Why would you be so popular in Mexico?

I had a very pleasant visit in Mexico [March 1947] while President Miguel Alemán Valdes* was in the President's chair down there and in being shown some of the wonderful things in Mexico City—the pyramids of the Mayas and things of that sort. The Secretary of State† in the Mexican government at that time asked me if I would object to putting a wreath on the monument to the Niños Héroes—that's the child heroes who jumped off at Chapultepec and committed suicide rather than let the American general, Winfield Scott, capture them. Of course, I said I'd do it. I thought it was one of the finest things in the history of the world when those youngsters, for the love of their country, were willing to jump overboard, as the ancients used to do, rather than to surrender. That's the reason for it. I didn't have anything in view except to recognize that heroism isn't confined to one country or one race. In every race and every country, you'll find things just like this, even this hero thing. That's how it came about. But I wasn't trying to match character with the Mexicans; I was only doing something that I believed in.

Do you think we are now fully discharging our obligations to Mexico?

I don't know. I don't know. The President seems to be very well satisfied with the relations between us.

---

*President, 1946–52.
†Jaime Torres Bodet, Secretary of State, 1946–48.

What is your feeling about South America, Mr. President, because the Mexican President has a feeling, as he expressed in Washington, that the South American organization—or that Organization of South American States—ought to do more to help South America economically, to do more to bring about mutual assistance and aid.

I'm in complete agreement with that and acted on it when I was President.

Do you think we're doing enough to further the development of our South American neighbors?

Well, I don't know about that. I don't know what's been carried out since I left the White House, but I had made a suggestion to the ... What is the name of that organization to which you referred? The Association of the American States?

Organization . . .

[To the] Organization of American States on two immense projects. One was to change the overflow of Lake Titicaca and those high 13,000-foot lakes. I think there are three of them in which the overflow runs to the sea through the Madeira River.* To change the course of that river and send it to the Pacific from that 13,000-foot height, which is perfectly feasible, it would go down that 13,000 feet, and it would make power enough for Bolivia and Peru and Chile, and then give Bolivia a seaport on the Pacific for the use of that water and that power. It seemed to make a hit with some of the leaders in all those countries. And then the development of the two great rivers on the east side of the continent, the Paraguay and the Paraná rivers.† There are a couple of falls on those two rivers that have more water over the fall than does Niagara, and they're higher. If they could be developed as they are now developing the Zambezi in Africa, it would be one of the finest things that could happen to South America. Brazil itself has the greatest undeveloped resources of any country in the world. It could as easily support 340 million as it supports the 40 [million] or 50 million who live there now.

Then those resources that are not yet developed should be developed? How can they be developed since they, themselves, don't possess the means to do it with?

They are working on that situation, and have been right straight along. There have been several people in this country who have investments in Brazil, which is creating a development of that sort. In south Brazil is an area ... as large as the State of Texas which has a soil that is thirty-six feet deep, and it will grow anything outdoors that will grow in the temperate zone.

---

*This 2,013-mile-long river in western Brazil forms at the Bolivian border and flows northeastward to the Amazon River.
†The Paraguay flows south from Brazil into the Paraná in Paraguay.

When those things are developed. . . . You must remember that Brazil has the greatest forest resource of any country in the world except Siberia.

Yet we see the ironic thing of Brazil sending a mission to Moscow to try to arrange some facilities and some trading and some help from the Russians.

Well, people who have great things to do will grasp at anything that they think will help. I want you to remember when the British and the French and the Germans poured hundreds of millions of dollars into this country for its development. Had that not been done, [the United States] never could have been developed. But as soon as it was developed, it finally turned around so that when they got into trouble—that is, the French and the British—those resources which they had invested in this country gave them the wherewithal from this country so they could win. And Brazil may eventually be developed by themselves and by us and by Britain and France and Germany, as well as anybody else. I sincerely hope they don't get tangled up with the Russians, though, until we get Russia a free government.

In a look to the future, do you see the possibility of a development, or at least an idea, like they have had in Europe—a United States of Europe? Is there a possibility of a United States of North and South America?

No. I don't think that's possible because of the difference in languages. You see, in Brazil, it's Portuguese—that's the language of the country. And in the other South American countries, it's Spanish, as it is in Cuba and Puerto Rico and in Mexico. It's a very difficult thing for people who have a language barrier to understand exactly what the other fellow means when he talks, and it takes a very careful and skillful interpreter to give the same meaning and emphasis to the words in one language to the words in another language. That's one of the drawbacks. But there's no reason in the world why we can't be friendly with them, why we can't help with their development, and why we can't let them have the benefit of the development that's made in their country. You take that wonderful city down there, São Paulo—it's called the "Chicago of South America." And its growth has been phenomenal due to the development of resources back behind that city.

Now, one final question: You don't expect communism to get an important toehold anywhere in the Americas?

No, I don't. I think as long as the Americas have a moral code based on the Sermon on the Mount and on the twentieth chapter of Exodus, there's no chance for communists to get in to do anything about it.

Do the [Americas] have that code?

They have. Yes, they have.

Mr. President, if I can get into another field: You have frequently said that even the private letters, the notes, all the private things that a President does are equally important as official papers and what he stands for.

I think that's true. You know, one of the great things about the publication of the papers of George Washington was the fact that he was a very meticulous bookkeeper. He kept track of every transaction that he ever had, no matter how small or how large. And while the actual correspondence and papers of George Washington would cover ten, maybe twelve, volumes, the publication of the complete set of Washington's papers took 150 volumes, and that's because he kept track of everything. There are some very interesting things in those volumes and papers that most people would have thrown away. The same thing was true of Jefferson: Jefferson's papers, you know, were scattered because the Congress took it on itself to decide which of Jefferson's papers were official. Now Princeton University is spending about $200,000 or $300,000 trying to get all those papers that Congress decided were not official together again.*

Mr. President, do you then also feel that the letters and the private papers of a former President, as he goes on, have some importance to shed light on him as a man, as a President, and on the period in which he lived?

And on the development of the character which he has to assume as Chief Executive of this great republic. You see, things happen which sometimes add greatly to the development of the man who is responsible. There are things that happen sometimes to kind of make him deteriorate a little bit. We should know all the ups and downs through which he has to go in order to be a good Chief Executive.

I'm talking now also of the period after he has ...

Oh, yes. I think that's important as well as the other period because it's a most difficult thing for a man to settle down to what's called "private life" after he's been in a position of that sort, and the former Presidents of the United States have been sorely neglected. You take James Madison, James Monroe, and two or three of the Presidents in between them, and Abraham Lincoln, and several of the Presidents since then have been sadly neglected. Most of them, all of them, had the idea that they should not exploit the fact that they had been in that office. James Monroe and James Madison almost starved to death for that very same reason. That shouldn't happen. That doesn't happen in most countries, where they take care of the men who have spent their lives working in public office. No politician, unless he's rich before he goes into the

*Julian Boyd, Lyman Butterfield et al., ed., *Papers of Thomas Jefferson* (Princeton, N.J.: Princeton University Press, 1950–[1997]). Thus far, twenty-seven volumes have been published, bringing the series to 1809.

game, can ever have a retirement fund of his own that will keep him in the style at which he ought to live had he been the Chief Executive. . . .

Do you think that there's some significance in why this nation turns its back so suddenly upon a man who is elevated to high position and then proceeds to forget about him?

It's customary in republics. They've always done it. If you remember, some of the men who made the greatest contributions to the Revolutionary War were sadly neglected, and some of [those] whose efforts made great contributions to the setting up of the republic were allowed to die in poverty. That's been true all through . . .

Is that ingratitude or just plain carelessness?

Carelessness. It's carelessness. Well, it's ingratitude, too, but you never want to count on gratitude when you do favors for the simple reason that a man who does favors for gratitude is always sadly disappointed. Barkley [Truman's Vice President, 1949–53] had a favorite story in which some old fellow for whom he had done a number of favors went back on him when he needed him most, and he asked him what was the matter. "Well," he said, "you ain't done nothing for me lately." And that's the attitude of most of them.

I suppose, too, that the average man is so preoccupied with his own problems that he doesn't stop to think about the people who have enabled him to get benefits.

That's true. And there's another thing we must bear in mind: Up until our republic was formed, the rulers were always amply taken care of in their places while they were in office, and after they left the office, they were all pensioned and properly taken care of. I can give you shining examples of it if you want them, but a republic never thinks about what happens to the people who helped the most, and I suppose that's just a natural human trait.

Well, then, Mr. President, do you think that in our education we ought to stress more to the young people the significance of this so that they won't be discouraged from going into public service . . . they won't be discouraged from doing anything but pursuing money-seeking careers?

I think that's a good thing, but you want to be very careful not to get the idea into the minds of the coming generation that that's the proper way for them to get ahead and stay that way. Hoping to get a—we'd say a pension— after he gets through with his public service is not the proper way. They ought to be properly taken care of, of course, just as we've started out now with this old-age pension business and the care of the children and things of that kind with those who are not able to take care of them. They ought to do the public officials the same way, and, in most cases, they are coming to do that. But we must instill into them that the honor of serving all the people is much greater than any monetary remuneration that they can possibly get.

It's very important to get that over to the young people.

I think it's vital, and that's what I'm trying to do.

In that spirit, could we turn to another young man who has a slight touch of Nixon in him: Jimmy Roosevelt? He's just written a book, which he calls "A Testament of Love" — which should have said parenthetically "And Money, Too." ...

Well, you know, I'd rather not ...

Not take up any tape time with that?

Just cut that subject, because the mother of this young man is one of the finest women that ever walked, and we don't want to do anything that would reflect on her or her family.

Fine. But he is ... it's in his record ... and is going to go unchallenged if we omit it. He will have the final say about what gets said. But it's for the record now, which will be privately unpublished for a long time. He said these slighting remarks purported to have been said by his father about those who were in line for the Vice Presidency in 1944 and all were very sharply dismissed as inconsequential or nuisances. You don't believe that ever took place, do you?

No. I don't. I don't think it ever took place.

Because Jimmy's record for reporting is not exactly the best — accurate reporting, I mean. ... Also, in his book Mr. President, *he says that he considered in 1948 the possibility of Eisenhower as a Democratic candidate. He says, "for which Mr. Truman has never forgiven me."*

That's not true. I didn't hold it against him. I just thought he didn't have any sense when he made that statement. That's all I thought about it.

Yes. One of the notes here is to ask you what it was you said to him at the Ambassador Hotel in Los Angeles when he called on you in 1947, when you were making your first Whistle Stop.

On that first trip to Los Angeles, he had made some of these snide remarks that he's publishing in a book now, and he came up to see me with a whole bunch of his California friends with whom he wanted to make a show. I took him in the back room and told him that he ought to have his head punched,

---

*James Roosevelt and Sidney Shalett, *Affectionately, FDR: A Son's Story of a Lonely Man* (New York: Harcourt Brace, 1959).

because if his father hadn't had the support of the people whom he was try-ing to malign right then and there, he'd never have been President in the first place, and that if he felt like taking it to the conclusion, that's just what he'd get. And he went out with the others so he wouldn't get punched.

Well, Bill [Hillman] tells me [David Noyes] that there is a letter from Mrs. Roosevelt commenting on the book, suggesting certain minor corrections, but there's nothing in that letter to her son which suggests corrections involv-ing you in it. How do you account for that?

I don't think that she wanted to tell. . . . she has always taken the attitude that her children and the children of everybody else ought to be allowed to do as they pleased. I don't believe in that, but, then, that's her theory, and it makes no difference to me. But the thing, in the end, that worked out is the fact that if some of the crackpots who were then trying to get control of the Democratic Party got control, they wouldn't have made a hero out of Franklin Roosevelt like I did.

You have gone on in your feeling that Franklin Roosevelt is a very great man, and you've never lost the opportunity of stressing that, despite the fact that when you took office many of the Roosevelt holdovers—and I talk about the lower echelon as well as the upper echelon—did nothing at all but make snide remarks about . . .

Oh well, that's customary. I didn't pay any attention to that because that's true locally, and it's true statewide, and it's true nationally. I never paid any attention to that because I knew exactly the feeling that they had. They'd lost their leader, and they were down in the dumps, and they were afraid the coun-try would go to the dogs with a new man who didn't know much about it, they thought. But after they found out—the vast majority of them—that the policies and the ideas of Franklin Roosevelt were to be carried to their logi-cal conclusion, then they quit that, and I never held it against any of them. Not even Jimmy.

Could we touch on a subject here that we've left unresolved? Why did you think at the time that Stevenson was wrong in injecting the hydrogen bomb into the 1956 campaign?*

There wasn't any place for a thing of that kind. That was part of the for-eign policy of the United States. The decision that I had to make while I was President of the United States was whether we should go on with the devel-opment of the use of atomic energy, of which the hydrogen bomb was the top-notch thing for power and for destruction, and it had to be carried to a conclusion if we wanted to keep ourselves as the leaders in the free world. The objective, of course, of all this development in the long run was to make

*Cf. Session Thirteen for Stevenson's views.

its use for peaceful purposes, and, as you remember, I tried and tried and tried to get the Russian government to agree to a pooling of all those things under the control of the United Nations for the use of all the world when we had a monopoly on it. If we'd stopped without the development of the hydrogen bomb, we'd have been only half through, and I think we're only half through now. There'll be more of it to come if we keep on with the proper development of that atomic energy.

... Well, Mr. President, may we reserve any further questions on the hydrogen bomb and the atom bomb until you have had a chance to look at a book which has just been published by William L. Laurence, the science editor of the New York Times,* *who has done a very remarkable job of synthesizing all the facts from the very beginning of the experimentation on fission and fusion down to the latest events? He pays you the proper tribute in all the actions that you took, but I think it's a good thing to get a bird's-eye view. . . . [Now we] just want to get into this text the political implications of Stevenson, not the discussion of the hydrogen bomb.*

Well that's all right.

You've just said that he had no business injecting [the hydrogen bomb] into a partisan issue. This was not a partisan issue?

Not a partisan issue and should never have been, and it wasn't as long as I was President.

That's important. That's a very important point. . . . [About the] business of our [lagging in the] race with Russia and the space technology: The president's advisers and spokesmen and news publications . . . criticize him [President Eisenhower] for having allowed us to drift into a second position, [but] they switch the blame to you for having failed during your administration to give due recognition to its importance.

That's just as untrue as it can possibly be, because the very first thing I did as soon as the United Nations was set up—as I stated a while ago—was pool the development of this tremendous power in such a way that all the world would profit by it. I kept at it, and I think the Russians vetoed it 265 times.

---

*Laurence, *Men and Atoms.* Laurence, a science reporter (later science editor), for the *New York Times* beginning in 1930 won the Pulitzer Prize in 1937 for his report on the Harvard Tercentenary Conference of Arts and Sciences and again in 1946 for articles on eyewitness accounts of the bombing of Nagasaki. Laurence also reported in this book Professor P.M.S. Blackett's theory that America used the bomb for political, not military, reasons—that U.S. officials wanted to bring about Japan's surrender before the Soviet Union could enter the war: ibid., 142–43. Gar Alperovitz would elaborate on this theory in his book *Atomic Diplomacy: Hiroshima and Potsdam* (New York: Simon and Schuster, 1965).

What about missiles and rockets and space technology?

They started to get up a guided-missile proposition. The Air Force had one, and the Navy had one, and the Marines had one, and the Army had one, and I finally sent for K. T. Keller, whom we should interview, and put him in charge.* He took seven people and coordinated the whole thing or we'd never had a guided missile of any kind. And you can see now that some of these people who have been turned loose again have more failures than they do have of the things that have worked. But that matter has to be handled from the top. Whenever you divide these things up with rivalry among the people who are supposed to be working for the same end, then you have all sorts of trouble, and you have to have a strong man to coordinate those things. As soon as I left the White House, in two or three months, they fired K. T. Keller, and if he hadn't gotten them together, we wouldn't have had any missiles of any kind.

Mr. President, you had a major problem trying to fuse the military forces into a working unit. Congress didn't go along on the plans as you ...

Not at all. No, they didn't.

Do you feel that there should be a tighter amalgamation of all the armed forces, instead of all the separate businesses?

There isn't a doubt in the world but what the whole thing ought to be tightened up so that the President, as Commander-in-Chief, can deal through the Secretary for Defense, and the Secretary for Defense should be a man strong enough to make all of them behave. That's what it takes in the long run. I had correspondence with every single commanding general in the field, a stack of correspondence that high—I don't know whether it's been destroyed or not—all of the opinion that we ought to have a Secretary of Defense who had control of the defenses of the nation, just the same as the Secretary of War did when Washington set up the first defense program. The Secretary of War had control of the Army and Navy and Marines, and, of course, the Navy is a bunch of eager beavers, and they got separated from the Secretary of War. That was the first split. Then they finally got the Air Force in the same fix after it came along and became powerful. We [need to] get the idea over that the Defense Department of the government of the United States is a thing that's just as important as any other department, and that it ought to be in the control of a man who knows where he's going and why.

*Kaufman T. Keller, skillful chairman of the Chrysler Corporation board of directors, became the guided-missile director under Secretary of Defense General George Marshall in October 1950. An expert on production, military and civilian, the sixty-four-year-old Detroit industrialist continued as chairman of Chrysler while bringing guided missiles out of the experimental stage. From 1950 to September 1953, he advanced guided missiles from "drawing board to military reality": cf. *New York Times,* October 26, 1950, and ibid., January 13, 1954.

Do you think that the race between us and the Russians in that category is lost to the Russians now?

No. No, I don't think so at all, and never have thought so, and don't think so now.

Well, it's admitted now that they possess a much greater thrust than we have and that they have solved the fuel problem, and we have not.

The great idea of that, of course, is to get all the money they can appropriated for their use, and I think if you look into it, we probably have the same fuel. [If we] had an emergency so that the thing could be done as an emergency, they wouldn't get away from us, and they won't when the time comes where we have to do it. I don't have any worries about that at all.

In other words, this country operates mainly when it's under pressure, and that's in an emergency?

You don't suppose that the President of the United States could have spent $2.6 billion in making a thirteen-pound bomb if there hadn't been anything going on in the world to force him to do it. It'll come around when the time comes. But the thing that we've got to do is to get this thing in shape so that the demand for its use in peaceful terms will force these things that we're talking about—not for destruction, but for construction.

Now the question is being raised by many scientists about the handling of [J. Robert] Oppenheimer and other men like him by this administration, and the wanton disregard of their usefulness by kicking him out. [The Atomic Energy Commission suspended the brilliant atomic-energy physicist from government work in 1953 as an alleged security risk.] It had some effect, did it not?

It's wrong. It's wrong. It's absolutely wrong. This discouraged the men who are devoted exclusively to things of that kind in trying to do anything, and it's absolutely wrong. I don't think they did the right thing in trying to smear character—assassinate these men who had done this thing for us and who were willing to go ahead and do more if they had let 'em alone. Because there was some communication between scientists in other countries, we didn't gain anything by letting them out. They found out anyway, and they always do in a thing of that kind. There's only one thing. I remember, I've got some vases back here behind me that were made by the Phoenicians 3,800 years ago. They're the first ones who found out how to make glass, and they kept that secret for 1,500 years. We kept ours for about ten years, that was all.* There's more communication now than there was in the time of the Phoenicians, and this thing here could have been worked up just as easily as

*The Soviet military exploded a first atomic bomb in 1949.

possible had the Russians not been so obstreperous in trying to conquer the whole world for an unmoral government, one that has no morals—communism, as they call it. It isn't communism at all.

All right. Do you think that we have lost some ground in our leadership or our opportunity for leading the free world?

I don't think there's any doubt about that, and there isn't any sense in it. When the emergency becomes strong enough, we'll come forth with a leader who will do the job, just like Roosevelt did.

What would have to be done in order to get our industry and all of our institutions focused upon this one problem, short of an emergency? In these times, what would you do?

Well, the first thing that you'd have to do is to elect a President who knows where he's going and who can make people perform. That's the first thing you've got to do, because this thing centers in the head of the government of the United States. Then he's got to coordinate all these things so as to give us the same position in science that we had when World War II ended.

In other words, we have to give the same charge to industry and our whole economy about this as we did in connection with the atomic bomb and everything else, as we did in the war?

That's right. There are plenty of men who have their hearts set on accumulating all the money they can, unless they're guided in the right direction to do all the work they could toward scientific development along the same line.

What are the chances at this juncture of our nation's electing a Catholic as President of the United States?

I don't think the time has come, as yet, when that can be done. One of the difficulties with that situation is that if you want to get into the subject, the Catholic church is ruled from the top down. They have an idea that the Almighty turned the running of religious affairs in the world over to St. Peter. I don't think they were turned over to St. Peter any more than they were to anybody else, and that's the reason I'm a Baptist. You don't want to have anyone in control of the government of the United States who has another loyalty, religious or otherwise. That's what the difficulty is. That's what it's always been. That's what brought about the Reformation. Had it not been for the Reformation, there wouldn't be any church at all in the world, because the Reformation brought morality back to religious control. I haven't got anything against a Catholic as a Catholic. They believe just the same way we do, but they have a loyalty to a church hierarchy that I don't believe in. That's what the trouble is.*

*Almost a month later, in an interview on November 16, Truman was less anxious about a Catholic becoming President.

Mr. President, just by way of reinjecting a thought, because you suggested it by way of your comment: Supposing you have a chief of staff or a chairman of the combined chiefs of staff who is also a Catholic?

That's a different matter. He's not in control of the government. He takes orders from the Commander-in-Chief.

Well, MacArthur didn't.

He did in the long run. He wasn't a Catholic, anyhow.
(Laughter).

All right. Where is the opposition in the country coming from? Is it coming from the Protestant states or is it coming from other . . .

It's coming from the general run of the people. I've talked to a large number of men who are honest-to-goodness Catholics who are of the same opinion that I am that it's a bad thing to have a man in control of the government, locally or nationally, who has two loyalties. He's got to be in control of the government in such a way that he's not a favorite of any organization, Catholic or otherwise. France has had that trouble ever since King Henry IV, and they've always been in trouble over it. They're having that same trouble in Italy right now, and the reason for the Reformation in Germany was because they couldn't stand [Albrecht] von Wallenstein and the enforcement of the laws of the Catholic church. That's the reason Gustavus Adolphus was able to bring on the Reformation.

One of the candidates prominently mentioned answered that by declaring forthrightly that he felt his first obligation would be to the United States; that he would be bound by the Constitution; that he would recognize no other overriding power.*

That's all right, and that's what they ought to do. There's no reason why that shouldn't be done, and he oughtn't to have to announce it if that were absolutely true of the hierarchy.

Did he denounce something in doing it?

I don't think so. . . . I don't think that he had to renounce anything at all, because the Constitution provides for complete separation of church and state. We don't have a state religion. And the British don't adhere to [their state religion] very much.

It's more or less a perfunctory.

That's right.

*John F. Kennedy.

Now in '56, when a Catholic [John F. Kennedy] was being suggested or nominated for the Vice Presidency, the first support came from the totally unexpected State of Georgia, and then Texas.

The headquarters of the Ku Klux. . . . the Dixiecrats trying to beat the Democratic Party, in my opinion. That's what I analyzed it for.

Well, the polls in the South at this particular moment show a surprising percentage of people favoring a Catholic for President.

Well, I don't think they'd favor it at the ballot box.

May I get to a question here, now? It's one of your favorite topics. Your position has been once again vindicated, and that is the question of polls. They had a poll just before the British election which showed that the Conservative government was not only tottering, but that the Laborites would likely come in with a majority of thirty-five to fifty, and they were proved absolutely accurate [sic].

Just a repeat of 1948 for the poll business, that's all.

What is your analysis of that? Why is it that people take samples, and these samples can be so way off base?

I'll bring it home to you very concretely. Suppose you're walking along the street and some nice-looking young lady or young man stops you and asks you who you're for. You'll stop and think a minute and try to figure out who she wants you to be for, and you'll say, Well, I'm for this fellow or that fellow. But when it comes time to vote, you've had a chance to analyze the thing, and nobody's got any business investigating the way you vote or how you vote. So when you go into the polls—the voting polls, not the pollsters' [polls]—you get to thinking about the situation, and you change your mind and vote for what you think is right. That's what most people do when they have an absolutely secret ballot.

Isn't the [pollster's] poll, in a way, rather an imposition on the public? Isn't it an attempt to sway the public and to mislead them?

I don't think they've ever been able to do that. The first great poll, if you remember, was [taken by] the old *Literary Digest*. Don't you remember that, when they polled all the people in the telephone book, and the people who didn't have telephones knocked the socks off them? That's what happened in 1948.

(Laughter)

Hoover was elected by a big margin.

That's right.

George Gallup himself is now seriously qualifying the validity of his poll and the use to which the poll should be put—[that is,] not for purposes of trying to find a candidate.

In a business way, the poll is very good, because people will tell you what kind of a gadget they like, and what kind of a car they like, and what kind of a house they like to have. But when it comes to government, they're rather secretive. Most people are very jealous of their privilege of privacy when it comes to deciding what they want to do about the government, and that makes all the difference. I don't think these pollsters have ever come to that conclusion.

That's a major point and needs to be said, because in England ... up to the last election [as was mentioned earlier], the most accurate poll and almost infallible poll came from there because they had such a concentration of opinion, such a concentration of people, and they were never off more than 1 percent or a fraction. The polls there, up to this last election, were regarded as completely valid, and this one crossed them up so completely that they didn't know where to look. . . . There was a major election involved . . . and that really threw them off.

That's right. That made a difference.

Before we run out, I have a few personal questions to ask you, if I may. Since you have devoted most of your life to public service, and since you've been giving so much of yourself to getting things done for your fellow man, do you miss now being in a position to do it?

No, I do not, for I am in a position to do it. I help people just I always did.

(Laughter)

But you have to do it by indirection now?

Yes, of course. It can be done by indirection, but not really by indirection, because when the facts are put up to the people who are in control, most of them are reasonable and honest and want to do the right thing.

You continue to get requests for all sorts of things, from supplying texts for other people's writing projects to jobs, Social Security, and personal appearances. You have to turn down most of them. How do you do it?

Most of them are out of the question. They don't expect an affirmative answer. Principally, they want a reply, and that's what they get is no.

Well, Mr. President, by character you are never at any time what I would call a dawdler or a loafer. You don't want to just sit back and take it easy.

No, I don't. I never had that ambition.

So it has been no problem since you left the Presidency to keep on going at a high pitch, because you continue to go at a high pitch.

Yes, and I like it. I don't know what I'd do if I had to sit down and twiddle my thumbs. I just couldn't do it, that's all. I've got to do something.

What has given you the outlet for all the immense energy you have and the desire to express yourself? What has been your best outlet so far?

Well, the best outlet, so far, has been public appearances and the correspondence that is carried on from this office. [That's] the outlet which [has] allowed me to express my opinion publicly so that lots of people could see it and hear it. I got that idea, if you can bear with me for a minute, from the fact that after the White House was opened to the people to see, I got the boys of the radio and television and took them on a trip through the White House, and everybody in the country saw the White House from the inside. Now, there's only about 1 percent of the population that ever has a chance to see it. We did the same thing the other day in going through this institution [the Truman Library] that we're trying to set up here for educational purposes. It wasn't as successful as the one through the White House, because that was devoted exclusively to that purpose. I didn't have the means or the ability to get the same sort of a trip through the Library as I did through the White House, but people are interested in what public men have been doing even after he quits doing it. That's one of the reasons it has worked out all right.

People are curious, but you're also curious about people, aren't you?

Yes. Whenever I have a press conference, I get more information than the fellows who are questioning me, because I've found out just exactly what their bosses are up to when they ask me those questions.

Do you have any preference as to the kind of people you would like to rub elbows with when you're out?

I pick my own associates, like anybody else does. That's customary. You don't have to associate with people that are not of the kind that are not interested in what you are, but I never turn anybody down who wants an interview if I have time to give it to him. But I don't give any private interviews. Whenever I have a press conference, I have everybody come. They don't have to come, but if they don't, they sometimes lose out.

I was just going to ask you whether a President in office should be as detached or shielded from the people for reasons of security as he so often is.

Yes, I think it's necessary. I didn't think so at first. I used to tell those boys that if anybody tried to shoot me, I'd take the gun away from him, put it down his throat, and pull the trigger. They said, "Mr. President, you can't get at him," and I found that was true when they tried to do it.

You tried during the early days to walk across Pennsylvania Avenue and even have the traffic going normally until that didn't work out so well.

Well, in the first place, when we were living at the Blair House, they tried to make all the lights red when I went to cross the street. I made them stop it. I made them turn the lights on normally, just like they always did, and I waited for the green light, and I make them wait for the green light now when I'm out walking.

And you kept in touch with people regardless of the fact that you were being protected and shielded?

Oh, yes. The only reason for the shielding was the fact that there a great many people who have obsessions. Now, we had a special man at one of the gates at the White House where all these so-called crackpots were sent. He was a genius in handling them, and most of them just need a talking to. Some of them we had to send to St. Elizabeth's.* But a crazy man when he has an obsession is just as likely to shoot his mother as he is anybody else, so those are the ones that you've got to watch out for, and it's a very small percentage. But they come to the White House just like bees go for sugar.

In terms of your personal staff—this is a toughie, because we have to ask something about if you had to do it all over again—what would be your personal preference and your measuring yardstick for the kind of staff you would again pick for the Presidency?

The hardest thing in the world to do is to be sure that you get people of integrity and people who are willing to work, no matter how much work there is to do. You can't tell whether a man will do that until you try him out. It's a case of elimination, just like everything else, and I tried my best to get men to fill the positions that I thought they were best fitted for. And if they weren't, why, then I had to try again. That's the same with everything. That's just as true of business and industry as it is in politics. The hardest thing in the world is to find a man to fill a place when you need a man.

You had your share of brickbats at some of the members of your staff by the press, as well as [by] some of your friends who were very much concerned about some of the behavior of some of the people.

That's customary. That's customary. I used to run the county here, and I had the same trouble with my county employees.

But you were very quick and highly resolved in the judgment you rendered when you were chairman of the famous Senate committee that had to do with the conduct of affairs—not the war, but the . . .

*A psychiatric hospital in Washington, D.C.

Of the staff.

And there you acted when some wrongs or corruptive things were uncovered. You never hesitated, and you always had a unanimous decision.

That's right.

Everyone considered that that portion of your committee's performance— that phase of it—was one of the great things, because nobody had to wait too long and nobody had to guess as to what you were going to do when you caught them red-handed.

It was the same way in the White House whenever I caught anybody doing anything.

Session Fifteen

But the cost and expense for the ordinary person to get the proper treatments for his physical well-being is beyond the reach of the people in the middle income bracket. The very rich can get them. The very poor are taken care of by the welfare organizations.

The big question is, if you had to do it over again, would you have retained precisely the same caliber of staff and the same personnel as you had with you during your terms in the White House?

I would have tried, of course, to improve the staff all I could. Whenever I found out that there was anything wrong with any of them, why, usually I got rid of them, transferred them, and those who did anything wrong were prosecuted. The mink-coat girl's husband* was sent to jail. The fellow who was interested in all these crazy ideas with regard to the Greeks was finally convicted, and every single one of the Internal Revenue men who went wrong—there were 117 of them—were prosecuted and convicted for what they had done where they were wrong. At the same time that was being done, there were 600 bankers in the United States who were convicted for the same offense that the 117 Internal Revenue men were convicted for, but you never heard anything about that in the papers.†

The job of the President has become complex. He has so many agencies and so many in the government. Have the facilities of the White House and

Transcript, Thursday morning, October 22, 1959.

*E. Merl Young, an examiner with the Reconstruction Finance Corporation, gave his wife a $9,540 mink coat paid for by an attorney for a company that had received an RFC loan. He was later convicted and jailed for perjury. An assistant attorney general with the Justice Department's tax division, T. Lamar Caudle, also received funds from a lawyer who dealt with this division. Truman fired Caudle in November 1951, and Caudle was convicted for income-tax evasion.

†By December 1951, 113 Internal Revenue Service staff members, including 6 regional directors, were fired.

the facilities available to the President kept up with the growth of the immensity of the Presidency?

I don't know whether that's happened during the last six or seven years or not, but I know this: When I went to the White House, it was almost impossible for the President to obtain the information that he needed to carry on the job. So I had Admiral Leahy and two or three of my staff work on a program accumulating and coordinating information which the President should have. The situation, at that time, was that the President had to hunt around for information. You see, the State Department and the Defense Department, the Department of Agriculture, and the Department of Commerce all had foreign relations. They all received immense numbers of messages. I finally got those things all coordinated. That's when they set up the Central Intelligence Agency, and after it became a successful working organization, then the Congress tried to legislate the matter so that it was not convenient to the President. I don't know if that's been changed or not. But unless the President has complete information on world affairs, he can't make sensible decisions.

With all the decisions that a President has to make, are these facilities adequate so that he can personally make these decisions without having to depend on advice and direction from the branches of the government or the secretaries or its staff?

It's absolutely essential that he have advice, but he doesn't have to have directions, because he makes the directions.

The President, then, can, even with the growth of government and with the growth of the responsibilities of the Presidency, still make personal decisions without having to take directions from anyone?

He can make the decisions. It doesn't make any difference what comes up. The final decision is made by the President of the United States, and they're not personal. They're decisions of the head of the state, the executive officer of the United States, the man who makes the foreign policy of the United States and who tries to inform the Congress what the domestic policy ought to be. Nobody can make those decisions but the President.

What I'd like to get back to, Mr. President, is the period since you left the White House and up to now. . . . What are your feelings and reflections about the political campaigns you have done during the period you have been out of office. How have they been different?

Well, they haven't been seriously different from the campaign of 1948. I've tried to follow the same pattern in the hope that it would be helpful to the man who was running for President, but no man can carry on a political campaign for somebody else with success. The man himself who is the head of the ticket must carry on the campaign. That's true from the county to the Presidency.

The last election that you went on a tour was the Congressional election. What was the reaction of the public at this time?

Very cordial. It was very cordial. I never had any more cordial receptions than on that campaign than I did in 1948.

Mr. President, with the growing use of television, does this Whistle Stop Campaign or this personal appeal to the public at various points become less necessary? Or is it still necessary, in your opinion?

It's still absolutely necessary, because a man never is himself on a television program. He can only be himself when he personally meets the people. The people want to be met, and unless they are met, they don't understand what the man stands for.

In other words, you get a stimulus from the crowd and the crowd gets a stimulus from the speaker?

That's absolutely true, and the facts in the case are that the people in front of a man who is running for President can analyze his character when he's there personally. That can't be done on television or radio.

Do you think the people instinctively are able better to judge a man by looking at him and hearing him in person than through any other medium?

That was amply proven in 1948. I'm not bragging; I'm just stating a fact.

Do you think, therefore, that in the future men will have to make as strenuous campaigns as you did in '48, which was very strenuous?

Yes. I think that's true, and that's the reason I'm against a Presidential primary, because he can't make two campaigns.

You think, then, that the Presidential primary uses up a lot of energy and a lot of appeal which ought to be directed to the public only at the time of an election?

I know that from experience, because I had to make four campaigns for two Senatorial elections in Missouri, and I know that if it was made on a national basis, there's no man in the world that could stand two campaigns like the one I put on in '48.

Do you think, then, that the working of a democracy will not be at all set back if you do not have primaries for a Presidential candidate?

I'm sure of that, and I want to say to you that in that period television and radio are all right, because that gives a man a chance to get international acquaintance with people during the period before the nomination. After that, he's got to make the campaign for President personally and on the road. If he doesn't, I don't think he has any luck getting elected.

In this last Congressional campaign in which I saw you talk to people through the Midwest and the North, you found the public just as interested in seeing the individual as ever.

Just the same, exactly, because that campaign, if I remember correctly, started at Fort Wayne, Indiana . . . in which we put on a program of most interest. They had a dinner in the center of a great big auditorium that seated 14,000 or 15,000 people. There were about 700 people who paid their way in for the dinner, and I was very much afraid that the galleries wouldn't be full. But when it came time to discuss the issues, those galleries were jammed. We elected a Democratic Senator from Indiana [Rupert Vance Hartke]. Then we went straight to Nebraska for the next appearance, and they had the biggest dinner in Nebraska that they'd ever had, and we elected a governor in Nebraska [Ralph G. Brooks], we elected a governor in Iowa [Herschel C. Loveless], and we elected a Senator in Indiana, because the people understood what was wanted.

Mr. President, you're a natural fighter. You're a natural champion of causes, and you don't mince words. But what do you think of the reputation you've gotten, looking back at it now, of . . . contained in that slogan, "Give 'em hell, Harry!"

That started out in the Northwest, in Seattle, Washington, when we had a tremendous meeting there in 1948 and some man with a great big voice made this statement from the galleries, "Give 'em hell, Harry!" and I told him at that time, and I repeated it, that I never gave anybody hell. I just told the truth on the Republicans, and they thought it was hell.

Nixon and some of the others say that they're going to adopt your style of a slashing attack. Is that a correct description—a "slashing attack"?

Well, it's an attack based on principles. It's not an attack based on individuals. I don't think Nixon can carry on a campaign without slander and without character assassination of the individual on the other side. I never in my life have done that. I never said anything against my opponent personally at all. I attacked their principles and their actions as public servants, not as individuals at home.

I just want to get to one more question in that connection. Friends of Eisenhower's say that he has been upset by some of the things you've said. You answered that in part yesterday, but one of the things I think that he was upset about was your accusing him of taking the tactics of these racial Nazi attitudes. Do you recall that at all?

No. The thing that I was put out with him about was when he stood on the platform with Jenner and McCarthy and allowed General Marshall to be called a traitor. In Colorado Springs—the day after . . . the same day that he did that—I went after him for not protecting the man who had made him.* And that's the only thing he's got against me.

. . . What about the problem of conventions? You've witnessed two conventions since you left the White House. How do you think they get along in terms of focusing on the man who ought to be nominated?

Well, that's American democracy at its highest. You take these conventions apart, and they are the most interesting things in the history of the country. They started way back in Jackson's administration, where he insisted on a Democratic convention instead of allowing the Congressional caucus to nominate a man for President. That's where the difficulty came about—that's 1824—between him and John Quincy Adams and Henry Clay. That thing has continued since, and it's one of the greatest ways in the world for the people to find out exactly what the party stands for.

[Is] the party really in control of all the presentations of candidates? How do you overcome the problem of the favorite son where so many come and it gets confusing?

Any favorite son has a right to be presented to the convention, and when he's presented, he has to get up and show what he has. If he doesn't show it, he's out.

Then you think that's a better way than having state primaries, where the favorite son is always in a position to crowd out somebody who is more of a national figure than the favorite son?

No. I'll tell you what the trouble is [with] those primaries. . . . They nominate their favorite son, and the delegates who are elected for the convention are tied by that nomination and can't go for the men they like. That's the reason I don't think a fellow who's nominated in the primary in his state—and the state conventions ought to nominate the man—is a man who is in the way of allowing the delegates to find out the facts and then be for the men they want to be for. Now, every state convention nominates somebody for President or agrees to support somebody for President, and, at the same time, some of the states make a unit rule, which forces the minority delegates to be for the person who is nominated by the convention. That has the same effect as the primary. I don't believe in the unit rule, and I don't believe in the primary, for the simple reason that these conventions take the place of the old legislative caucus which nominated a man for President, and he had to be the man

*In Colorado Springs on October 7, 1952, Truman told the crowd that he was disappointed by Eisenhower in this Presidential campaign.

who was put on the ticket and elected. The objective of a convention is to give all the delegates a chance to express their opinions. When they can't do that, then it's just too bad, if that splits the convention.

Just one more thing here about state primaries: As I remember it, you advised Adlai Stevenson in 1956 not to engage in a contest for state primaries.

That's correct. I did.

And he got into a very involved campaign with Estes Kefauver, and it developed into quite a hassle.

That's right.

Now, how do you feel about that situation in light of what transpired in '56?

I think I have the same opinion. If I were a candidate for President, I wouldn't get in a Presidential primary in any state.

Why did Stevenson choose to disregard your advice to him not to engage in the primary? Did he ever tell you?

I suppose he thought it wasn't good. I don't know. I didn't ask him.

But you did tell him specifically . . .

I told him to stay out of the primaries.

Do you remember when you told that to him?

Oh, before they started.

Did you give him a reason for staying out of the primaries?

The same reason that I've just given. The man gets into a Presidential primary, and he gets defeated. The same thing happened to him that happened out in Oregon when Dewey beat [Harold E.] Stassen.

Mr. President, in connection with your statement that the state conventions and national convention are, in effect, a substitute for the legislative caucuses, either in the state or in the nation, which had previously nominated candidates, the question that occurs to me is: Do you feel that these state conventions are really made up of representatives of the party?

Oh, I think they are. You see, that starts in the precinct in the county and the state, in most states. You'll find that the people in these state conventions— and I've been to many a one—are just as good people as there are on Earth, and they are people who listen to reason even when they are controlled by bosses. I know from experience.

Do you think that they are really representative, then, of the Democratic . . .

There isn't any question about that. If the Democratic Party isn't properly represented in these conventions, it's because the people are too lazy to go to the county meetings and the precinct meetings and the state meetings to set themselves up as representatives of the people. I don't have any sympathy with anybody who quarrels with what's done when they don't take any interest in it.

But there have been several occasions, haven't there, where some men have taken control in certain areas who were not nearly representative of the sentiment of that particular area?

Well, I think that might have been true in some instances. I don't know of anyone from experience.

To get pointed about the present situation, there's a certain situation in California. There have been in Illinois; there have been in New York. There's a quarrel among different factions of the Democratic Party whether those now running things are really representative.

Well, if they're not representative, it's because the people don't take enough interest in it. I went all over the City of New York when they were getting ready to nominate their leaders. I went to meetings in every district and borough in New York, and I found the people there just the same as they are out in Jackson County. The men that they thought would do them the most good were the ones behind which they worked. It all depends on what a fellow does in his own district. Now, one of the best stories I ever read was about a political meeting in Colorado where a young man heard that a committee meeting was going to take place that had always been handled from the house of the fellow who had always run things. This young fellow got about two dozen of his friends to go to that house, and he upset the whole applecart. It can be done anywhere when a fellow wants to take charge of it. And that's what makes free government.

You're speaking of free government. One of the big problems in connection with election to the Presidency—nomination first—and the election of governors and senators is money. How do you get these enormous funds together that it takes to elect a man to office? Isn't that a very serious challenge to free choice?

I don't know how you get those funds together, because I never had any. I never had enough money to run a campaign in Missouri, in the county. I never had enough money to run a campaign for the Senate in the state. And I never had enough money to run a campaign for the Presidency. But we won.

So you don't think that it's always money that wins out?

It isn't.

What does it take, sir?

Well, it takes an individual who understands what the people want. That's worth more than all the money you can get together.

How does he get his story over to the people without needing a lot of money?

He just goes out and tells them. Sometimes he has to go into debt. It took me about ten years in the Senate to pay off the political debts I made.

In money?

Not money. I mean expenses and things of that kind that took place. Nobody ever gave me any money in any campaign that I could use for myself. I had contributions, of course, just like every man who runs for office does. But those contributions are very small and inadequate, and they paid telephone bills and things of that kind. But it took me ten years in the Senate to pay off all the debts I made while I was running for the Senate twice.

Now the National Committee is in debt as a result of not being able to pay the television expenses of the candidate of four years ago, and they weren't able to pay for the one before that. How do you get out of it without going to people of privilege and means and saying, Please bail us out?

The only way to get out of it is to win. When you win, you won't have any trouble.

May I ask you this? When you use the expression "what the people want," just what do you mean by that? Of course, you're not suggesting that you cater to everything they want. After all, a leader must suggest some course.

A leader has a program, and he should make it perfectly plain what his program is. If the majority of the people agree with him, then he's got to go ahead and try to get the program over that he agreed to do when he was a candidate. And, of course, you can't please everybody. If you start to please everybody, you please nobody.

What the people actually want, then, is leadership?

Just fair treatment by a leader that they can depend upon.

. . . In terms of the two parties, as you see them functioning a generation from now, how do you see the alignment? Are the liberals still going to be on the Democratic side, and are the conservatives going to be with the Republicans?

If the liberals decide to leave the Democratic Party, they'll get in the same fix that they were in 1948, and that's what they ought to have, because the only party that ever did anything liberal for the public was the Democratic

Party. And if they want to be conservatives and vote the Republican ticket, why, then, they get what they deserve—just what they have in the past.

The present leader of the Republican Party undertook to moderate them and even follow in the footsteps of the Roosevelt–Truman policies, but that didn't seem to last very long. How do you account for that?

I can't.

Try.

I can't account for it. He didn't get anywhere with it, I hope.

. . . Well, is it that the Republican Party cannot go accepting where it is now, or that the Democrats are the party that can accommodate the most people with the most benefits?

Well, you see, the Republican Party—the present Republican Party, and that's not a proper name for it—was originated in the differences of Thomas Jefferson and the Secretary of the Treasury.

Hamilton.

Hamilton. And Jefferson then organized a party which was known as the Democratic Republican Party, and the Republicans stood for those people who believed in a republic instead of a monarchy. Then, when Jefferson was elected in 1800, it was the custom to have the second man on the ticket be the Vice President. He and Aaron Burr were tied on that situation, and it had to go to the House of Representatives, and Jefferson was finally made the President. He had organized a party by handwritten letters called a party of the republic, and he called it the Democratic Republican Party. From Jefferson, Madison, Monroe, John Quincy Adams, until 1824, when the controversy came about between that theory and Old Andrew Jackson, we had a Democratic Republican Party in control of the government. The Federalists had folded up. After the election in 1824, Jackson had more electoral votes than any other person, but there were four other candidates, including Henry Clay and, of course, John Quincy Adams, and the situation went into the House of Representatives, and Adams was elected President of the United States. Then he made Clay his Secretary of State, and old Jackson always accused Clay of selling out to John Quincy Adams. I don't know whether he did or not, but that controversy is still going on. At any rate, in the next go-round after 1824, Jackson was nominated by a convention outside of the legislative outfit, and he called it the Democratic Party election. That's where it originated, but Republican and Democratic, at that time, went together. Jackson was nominated and elected in 1828, and he was reelected in 1832, and then Van Buren succeeded him. Van Buren was an able administrator and a fixer, and a fixer can't get along very well in the White House. He had trouble because Jackson paid off the debt of the United States, and that caused a panic, believe it or not. The Panic of 1837 put Van Buren in a bad light, but he really was a good President, in spite of his ability to fix things. If you go through all these things, you find there's no difference in the human setup or arrangement that creates the heads of state in a republic. That's what we're working at.

What do you mean by a President cannot be a "fixer," that he can't succeed at that?

He can't be a "fixer" when he becomes President. He's got to represent the whole country and do what he thinks is best for the nation. When he becomes a party partisan as President of the United States, it doesn't work. . . . Although he ought to stay loyal to his party that put him there. . . .

Do think that the South is a drag on the Democratic Party?

No, I don't. I think the South is getting religion. You see, they've urged industry to come to their states, and when they get organized so that industry is there, we'll have them converted to the fact that the Democrats do 'em more good than anybody else. You see, this Southern bloc was brought about by the situation after the War Between the States known as the Civil War. It was called the Reconstruction program, and they have had a terrible time getting over it. My mother and father never did get over it, but I saw that the best thing for the world and for the United States was what Lincoln did to make a nation out of this country. And we're gradually teaching the Southerners that that was the best thing for them, although they're like my mother—they don't like Lincoln. But he did the best thing that ever happened in this United States of America.

And you think that there is a great future with the South?

There isn't a doubt in the world about it. The Southerners are just as fine people as you'll find anywhere else in the nation, and when they come to the conclusion that race and creed and color don't make any difference in what's in a man's heart, then we won't have any trouble.

What future do you see for the Republican Party if it is to survive as a party?

Well, they've got to find a program that will do what they tried to do in 1856 and what they tried to do in 1860. They have got to find a program that will be for the best interests of all the people of the country. And if they can find it . . . they won't find it on Wall Street or Madison Avenue.

How can management ever give its support to the Republican Party if the Republican Party takes the cause of labor and the cause of the little man that the Democrats now seem to have embraced?

Well, that would probably be a good thing. That'd be a good thing because management would then find out that the people that work for 'em in a free republic where a man can vote for what he pleases is their best asset.

Does the United States need a two-party system in order to have its democracy revitalized?

Yes! Yes, it does. You've got to have a two-party system. You've got to have an opposition to keep the people in control on their toes. Because if you don't, the first thing you know, they'll become . . . as I've always said, when the underdog gets on top, he's worse than the top dog was before.

Mr. President, there's talk lately about whether management should take a part in politics. I always had the impression they were in politics all the time.

They always have been. They always have been.

I want to know what they mean particularly by that. That they actually should identify themselves with a . . .

No. What they're trying to do is to work behind the scenes and control both parties. When they try to do that, why, they get what's coming to them. They ought to be on one side or the other.

May I just drop in an extraneous thing here? They've just formed a thing they call the Institute on the Strategy of the Cold War, and into that institute have come all the heads of all the biggest corporations in the United States, the generals, the admirals, and the military convocation of experts in the field, and they're going to go up and down the country to take a lead in educating the people on the problem we face with Russia. At the same time, this is the strongest congregation and aggregation and concentration of the America-Firsters, the tough-minded businessmen, the du Ponts, General Motors. What do you see in that kind of a . . .

Well, the thing that I see is that they're commercially minded. They hope that by doing something of the kind, they can sell their goods and chattels to China and Russia. I don't think they can, but if they can, I'm for 'em. But you'll find that those people have always been for the welfare of the people that control all the institutions that have to do with money and education and things of that kind. If you don't watch 'em, they'll try to put the whole country on the side of the people that we've always been against. Those people are not for the people who need help. It's a wonderful thing, you know, that this Russian* came over here. It made the difference between the people who worked and the people who sell goods and who employ the workers because they want to get a market for what they had and they didn't care what happened to the country.

---

*In mid-September 1959, Nikita Khrushchev came to the United States on a state visit. He addressed the United Nations on September 18, where he urged nations to disarm down to police units within four years. At meetings at Camp David, he and Eisenhower discussed the future of Berlin. The Soviet spacecraft *Lunik II* made mankind's first trip to the moon on the eve of Khrushchev's visit. Apparently, the launch was timed for this visit.

You think there is the chance of a labor party evolving in the future in the United States?

No. No, I don't. I hope it won't. The very fact that we've been great, politically, is due to the fact that we have a two-party system made up on each side of the aisle, as I call it—in the Senate, with the majority and minority on either side—made up of people who have ideas along both sides of the question. That's the reason we've never had any trouble in the turnover from one party to another in the control of the government in the United States. That's what makes us great. And if we get all the opposition on one side and all the conservatives on the other side, then we're going to have more trouble than you can shake a stick at. Now, I want this thing to stay in a divided way so that whenever the Democrats lose or the Republicans lose, people that take over are not going to upset the whole idea of the progress of the government of the United States.

And you think they won't do that because they will have them in their ranks—feelings all the way from the left to the right?

That's correct. In both parties. That's what makes our country great, a two-party system who quarrel with each other but who are not far apart on the welfare of the country.

Do you think that some of the outstanding personalities that used to pop through in the past and rise to the top and become enormously effective figures in the House and the Senate and governors' offices are no longer with us? You don't hear about them, anyway. There aren't too many of them around.

No, that's true, but they'll come up again. That's always happened.

How do you account for the lack of a very important national voice in the Senate of the United States today?

I can't account for it.

But there isn't any?

There ought to be. There ought to be one, but I'm afraid there isn't.

You don't know why they've suddenly been silent?

No, I don't, but that's happened in various periods, just like it's happening now.

In other words, it's just a question of a lack of talent or a lack of men rather than principle?

Well, it's a lack of men who are willing to take a chance. They want to be in with the top dogs. Whenever a Senator decides that he's for whatever happens, no matter who's in charge, then you have trouble.

Well, you've had the recent example of [William A.] Proxmire leading a revolt against the majority leader, and Proxmire found himself completely silenced and crushed without achieving anything.*

That's right.

Was that a good thing to do?

Well, it was all right for him to make a try, but personally he hasn't got what it takes to put it over, and that's what the trouble is.

In other words, it finally gets back to the old stories since mankind began: You've got to have a man, or you've got to have men.

That's right.

These are not the men who necessarily had the ability to conduct a filibuster on one of those monumental issues from time to time?

No. There have been ... when you go into history, there've been some very great men who stayed in the minority, but who finally came up with what was necessary for the welfare of the country when they kept up because they were right. You take George Norris. The TVA is due to George Norris. And you take the old man La Follette. He was one of the most able of the "bolsheviks" and men who were against the government, and he had a son who was equal to him. But they were succeeded by McCarthy. So how are you going to account for that? People got tired of them, that's all.

Do you think that the country can take just so much agitation and so much irritation to get itself forward, and then it has to take a little breather?

That's right. And if it doesn't take the breather at the right time, you have a 1929.†

Then you think that the period of Franklin Roosevelt was a period when the country was getting tired of normalcy and getting tired of all the other antidotes they took after the First World War?

They weren't getting tired of normalcy. They were getting tired of a forward-looking President. Normalcy was Harding.

Yes.

They were getting tired of a forward-looking President. Having studied history all the time, that's what I thought in 1952. I thought they wanted a change. And they got it. And they're sorry.

You deeply felt that people were ready for another change? ... What did you base your decision or your appraisal of the people's attitude on other than your very acute ear to the ground?

---

*Democrat William Proxmire served as Senator from Wisconsin, 1957–89.
†Stock-market crash and beginning of a severe economic depression.

Their attitude toward Korea. In the Congress, when the Democrats were as hard to get along with as the Republicans were when I was President, I based it on the same situation that happened in General Grant's administration for the campaign of 1872 and on the campaign of the "Plumed Knight" from Maine.

Blaine.

James G. Blaine against Grover Cleveland. The same thing was going on, and it seemed to me that the people ought to have a chance to decide that they didn't like the people who'd done the most for 'em, and that's the reason for it.

Well, there are facts beginning to come to the surface that you miscalculated a little on that, sir.

No, I don't think so. I don't think so. They got what was coming to them, and I knew they would. . . . I think they needed a little somebody to take them backward, and that's what's happened.

Well, Mr. President, in addition to your feeling that you've never believed in the philosophy of an indispensable man . . .

That's right.

Therefore, it was true you also felt, as you saw the signs of the times, that the people who were not really understanding the benefits that they were getting were bound to turn on the people who had been leading them to certain things, and that there was bound to be a change.

Well, of course. Whenever a fellow gets prosperous with the help of somebody else, he has a yen on to show that fellow that he can do it by himself. That's the same thing that happens in the country.

Mr. President, you also had an accumulation of twelve years of campaigning against FDR, eight years of campaigning against you . . .

That's right.

And you had a newspaper brainwashing campaign that more or less left the people in a state of being mentally drugged. Now, do you think if you had had a more fair representation of what you were trying to do in the press that your decision would have been the same, or would you have made the same decision?

I think I would have had to make the same decision because the press is just a reflection of what people are thinking. They have to sell papers. They have to sell advertising. When I have a press conference and these young men who are just as fine as they can be ask me questions, I know exactly what their bosses are thinking about. You know, I had a press conference every week, and sometimes two, and I could find out what people were thinking. Not because they wanted me to find out, but because I could analyze what the questions of these boys meant. It meant that the whole press of the United States wanted to change so that they could do as they pleased, and they got it, and now what do they . . .

You don't mean to say that McCormick, [Harry] Chandler, Roy Howard, and [George Randolph] Hearst are always saying what the people are thinking?

Oh, no! No, no! I don't think they ever say what the people are thinking. But they influence people in such a manner that they don't follow out their own thoughts. It's a publicity brainwashing proposition.

In other words, you think that the representation which is made to the public of what is going on has, after a number of years, a certain influence on the people just [like] a drop of water on a stone?

There isn't any question about it. I can give you a concrete example right here at home. In this big suburb of ours, they've been working and working and working to upset a party control of the city government. Well, they got it, and now that people have got tired of it, they've thrown it out. That happens. That's part of the game.

But on the whole, you think that the Democratic Party is keeping pace with the development of the times and the emergence of a new era in our economy?

Oh, I'm sure of that. The Democratic Party is the only one that's lasted for one hundred years, and sometime or other, when we have a little time, I'll analyze this situation and tell you why I think that's true.

What would you recommend to the Democratic Party now what it ought to do that it is not doing in order to keep itself up?

Well, the Democratic Party has got to stay on the side of the little fellow who has no representation in Congress or in the White House or anywhere else and try to arrange things so that little fellow who has no representation will be as well treated in the Congress and in the Executive branch of the government as the fellows who have lobbyists there. I've said that a hundred times over the United States.

Well, you've omitted civil rights from your little injunction here to the Democratic Party. What about civil rights?

Civil rights is fundamental. Civil rights only means that every citizen of the country has the same right to express his views in public and in private as anybody else, as long as he doesn't injure anybody. You'll find the booklet that was gotten out at the end of my administration, which says to . . .

That's your Civil Rights Committee?

Yes.

"To Preserve These Rights" ...

"To Preserve These Rights." That's not the word, but then that's it. It's a booklet about that thick, and they took all the funds away that I had to make further investigations on the subject. This Republican Eightieth Congress did, but we got that book out and it's still a gospel of civil rights. It ought to be read by everybody.*

You've omitted communism as a right. Can a communist go up and express his views under your interpretation of civil rights?

Why, certainly. Certainly. He ought to be allowed to express his views, and if he does, he's through, because the people understand him. They won't express their real views, but a communist ought to have the same right to say what they have to say as anybody else. Then if the people are fools enough to want to go under a dictatorship, why, that's their fault.

But you ought to leave that decision to the people?

That's right. That's the way we've always done. . . . That's correct. The argument over civil rights is always put into a situation where there's no reason for it to be. The first thing you hear when you talk to people who are violently opposed to a civil-rights setup is, "Do you want your daughter to marry a Negro?" Then if you ask the Negro if he wants his daughter to marry a white man, you get exactly the same answer. When my Assistant Secretary of State who was at the United Nations† was in Copenhagen and he was sitting by one of these wives of some of the State Department people over there, that's the question she asked him—if he wanted his daughter to marry a Negro. And he said, "I certainly do, because I am one." And the conversation ceased.

Let us take a jump to the future. What do you see for the United States as a force for the future? First, at home: What do you see transpiring on the home front?

Well, the resources of the United States have only been touched, and if they're properly conserved and used for what they ought to be—for the welfare of the whole country—this country can support 300 million people just

*The landmark 1948 report "To Secure These Rights" shocked Southerners, especially their representatives in the Senate. Truman continued to emphasize equal opportunity for all persons.

†Ralph Johnson Bunche (1904–71), who became the first black person to direct a division of the State Department, in 1946. At the United Nations, he researched race relations and colonial administrations, beginning in 1946. For his leadership on the UN Palestine Commission, he was awarded the Nobel Peace Prize in 1950.

as well as the 170 million that it has now. Our resources, properly conserved, are almost inexhaustible.

What do you think is essential for the moment to keep the economy going and growing? Would housing be one of the things that . . .

Well, the thing to keep the economy growing is to have people in charge of the policymaking section of the government that understands that an expanding economy and a growing population go together. There is plenty of room for the population if the economy is not held back by the people who call themselves conservatives. That's what they've been trying to do by holding up the forms that are necessary for the development of the country in housing and in the development of the resources of the country in such a way that it can't expand. You have to expand the economy of the country as the population expands, because the youngsters coming on have to have some place to go and some sort of a job when they get to the point where they need it. The only way to do that is to expand the economy, and that can be done.

So you see the need for expanded housing, both private and public?

That's correct.

What about public health?

Public health is a peculiar situation. You see, the scientists have discovered ways to control nearly all the plagues which the human race suffered up until this time, and they've discovered ways to meet that situation. But the cost and expense for the ordinary person to get the proper treatments for his physical well-being is beyond the reach of the people in the middle income bracket. The very rich can get them. The very poor are taken care of by the welfare organizations. But the man in the middle, who is the greatest taxpayer of the whole outfit, can't meet the situation when his family gets in a position where it has to go to the hospital and stay there. My idea was to set up a program where people would have a backlog with which to pay hospital bills and with which to pay the doctors. And you know the people who beat it? It was the people who would profit by it—the hospitals and the doctors.

Do you think that that kind of a public-health program is ruled out for the future in view of the opposition?

No, I do not. I think that it's going to become absolutely necessary because the people who have the most votes are going to vote for it when the time comes.

Well, do you think that this is something we ought to do just for ourselves, or ought we do that with the facilities we have and with the advancement we have for other nations that don't have it?

We have been doing it. We have been doing it. That's part of the Point IV Program that's improved the health in these Point IV countries 100 percent.

Do you expect that in the future we will have some kind of a public-health program that will protect the people who are not now receiving protection?

I am as sure of it as I sit here. That doesn't mean that the government will control it when these people pay in their money for a backlog so that they can afford to go to a hospital and have a doctor. They'll have a perfect right to decide on the hospital they want to go to and the doctor they want to have. I don't see anything socialistic about that.

But at any rate, you feel that that is not only coming, but it's necessary? And it's necessary also that you push for a fight on it?

It's absolutely necessary, and I'm going to fight for it until I die. I hope that won't be soon.

We're going to prevent that with modern medicine.

That's right. That's right.

Mr. President, what about higher education in this country that is now within the reach of those who deserve it but can't afford it?

I think those youngsters who show the facility for higher education ought to be helped to get it, because education and the development of the brain power of the country is absolutely essential for the future. In order to get that done, there are plenty of youngsters whose economic conditions prevent them from taking the courses in the higher educational institutions. That situation ought to be provided for, and it can be without any trouble.

In order to achieve a better opportunity for civil rights, you get immediately involved in the courts and the administration of justice. How do you feel about the administration of justice in this country? Do you think the courts should be streamlined and modernized? And do you feel that there's too much snarled-up, technical procedure and it's much too costly for the average citizen?

Well, there's certainly too much snarled-up procedure, and the cost, of course, of litigation is just in the same line with the cost of medical treatment, but there's a difficulty in connection with that. There is hardly enough money in the tax setup of the country to meet all the lawsuits that might be filed by people who don't understand that a great many of their troubles can be settled by negotiations. That's one of the things you've got to instill into the people—that sometimes their difficulties can be settled if the people on each side have a little common sense and they have an arbitrator who can settle it. You've had a great many cases—for instance, a fellow lost his farm in Iowa suing over a calf. When he won the suit, he didn't have anything left, and the calf was grown and he couldn't use it.

Would you then suggest, Mr. President, some sort of new machinery or setup of arbitration which might be voluntary that would take the pressure off courts?

Yes, and I think the courts can do that. I think they could educate people so that the confidence that we're supposed to have in our judges—they're all honorable men—could set up an arbitration program where the suit didn't amount to too much money, then have it settled in that manner. I think both parties would be highly pleased to have that done.

Well, don't you think there's a feeling among lawyers and judges that the courts belong to them rather than to the people?

Yes, and that's the thing that we've got to overcome. It's natural that the courts and it's natural that the lawyers feel like they've got a corner on justice. They haven't. Sometime or other, we'll wake up to the fact that justice belongs to all the people, just the same as the control of the government of the United States.

You used to do something about it during your Presidency, when you called in the district attorneys of the Department of Justice.

That's right. I had a meeting almost every year with all the district attorneys, and I made it perfectly plain to them that it was their business to enforce the first ten Amendments of the Constitution as well as enforce the law against criminals, and it was as much their duty to see that a man got justice as it was to prosecute him.

Do you think the answer is in the government, in the state—in the federal government or the state—or can the lawyers themselves bring about a solution to it? How would you go about getting it solved?

The lawyers could bring a solution to it, but they've got to be pushed into it by people who are fundamentally injured by the manner in which the justice courts are carried on. We had a situation right here in Jackson County where we had justices of the peace, and the nickname for that organization was "justice for the plaintiff." A man who owed a bill didn't have a Chinaman's chance in one of these courts. They were eventually abolished, and we put in municipal courts where a man has the same right, whether he has an attorney or not, as he would have in the higher courts.

To go back to the doctors for just a second. We have ... the medical business ... we have the problem of a shortage of hospitals, a shortage of doctors, and a shortage of medical schools. Now, should we leave that to the medical profession, or how do you go about correcting that?

No, we shouldn't, because when the Baptists wanted to build a hospital here in Kansas City, a suburb of this town from which we're talking, every single doctor and every single hospital in town opposed it, although there was a tremendous shortage of hospital beds. Well, there were too many Baptists in town to be overcome by that, so they built the hospital anyway.

In other words, the answer in some degree comes from the community itself.

That's right. The community's got to do it. Nobody else can do it but the community.

And not the federal government?

The federal government, if they wanted to take a look at the thing, could arrange things so that the hospital facilities in every community would be increased to the point where they'd be of use to the whole population and not to just a few that can afford to pay for it. And that's my theory on this tax for medical purposes that I was working on when I was President.

Well, I'd like to get to a vexatious question. In view of all this expanding thing, what about the expanding taxes that we have in this country. Do you think it will reach a saturation point? Are there any sources that could be tapped?

Well, I always had the opinion, and I wrote an article on it when I was the presiding judge of the County Court of Jackson County, that the tax burden ought to be borne in a manner so that every section of the government—local, state, and national—would have a certain tax base. It was my opinion that the local taxes for city, county, and schools ought to be on the basis of the fundamental basis of the whole welfare of the nation—that is, the land tax. The states probably could get along with a sales tax, and the federal government ought to stick to the income tax, so that there would be no cross-purposes in the levying of these taxes. But I didn't get anywhere with it.

So you have today a vast duplication of taxes, tax upon tax piling up on our hands?

Yes, you have. You have the state making a sales tax on the road situation. You have the federal government levying a tax on the same basis. You have the state levying an income tax, and the federal government levying an income tax, and it's getting very difficult for the local governments to find some place where they can get the money to run the government.

Well, then, probably what you might need is a sort of a new constitutional convention to get together to work out some plan or some suggestion to the Congress to act.

Well, I don't know. I don't know how in the world you'd ever get it done, for the simple reason that we had a terrible time with the income tax. You know, in the Civil War we had an income tax. Then they got a very conservative court and decided it was unconstitutional. You had to pass an amendment to the Constitution to get into effect again. But some way must be found to equalize all these taxes. If one section of the government is going to collect them all and distribute them to the rest of the sources of government, like the state and local, then that's one way. The other way would be to divide the things that are to be taxed between the local, state, and national governments. I don't know how you're going to do it. It may take a Constitutional amendment.

The role of small business and the role of government and public power such as REA and TVA,* et cetera—is that going to expand, or do you think it should be kept where it is?

Oh, it's got to expand for the simple reason that there's no way in the world for people like . . . who are served by rural electrification to be served by the utilities on a basis that people can afford to pay. That's the reason for it.

---

*Rural Electrification Administration and Tennessee Valley Authority.

Session Sixteen

Formosa [Taiwan] is a part of the defense line which is used to draw the line against the communist world, and I think they'd [U.S. leaders] have to defend it.

Mr. President, [we were] just asking about this incident in which you talked with President-elect Eisenhower about his not attending your 1948 inaugural . . .

It was '53. January 20, 1953.

Yes, that's the inauguration.

That's right. He was invited to come to the White House and go down to the inauguration with me in the car. He didn't come into the White House. He came down by the White House and sent word in that he was ready to go, so I went out and got in the car with him. On the way down there, we had discussions of various things, and there was one incident that has never been told in which he made the statement that he didn't come to my inauguration in 1949 because he was sure that more than half the people would be applauding him instead of me. I turned around to him and said, "Ike, you'd have come if I'd ordered you; don't worry about that," and that ended the conversation until we got to the Capitol Building. Then we were in the room waiting to go out onto the platform in the Capitol when he said that somebody had caused his son to come to the inauguration. He thought it was just a way to embarrass him. I said, If it is, I embarrassed you, because I ordered your son to come, and he ought to be here.

Why didn't the President come in? Is it customary for a President-elect to come and call on the outgoing President?

It's customary for the President-elect to come to the White House and usually have coffee or tea and a sandwich or two and then go down to the

Transcript, Thursday afternoon, October 22, 1959.

inauguration, which takes place at noon. But he didn't show up. We had things all ready for him, but he didn't come.

And this was the time he wore the Homburg. . . .

He made the statement in New York he was going to wear a Homburg hat. I didn't care what he wore. So as not to embarrass him, I didn't wear any hat, I don't think.

You didn't wear a cylinder hat?

No. The President should wear the most formal of formal clothes when he's going to the inauguration, but I think this was done for popularity purposes. I didn't pay any attention to it. It was all right with me if he didn't want to wear the customary dress. I was willing to go along with him because he was very soon to be President of the United States.

What was his mood in the car?

It was cold, as it was the other day at Marshall's funeral.

I want to ask about whether when Franklin Roosevelt was inaugurated in '33 . . . did Herbert Hoover stay in the House and Roosevelt call on him, or did the same thing happen then?

No, no. Roosevelt went by the White House and paid him every courtesy, and they rode down together in long tails and high hats, just like they should.

It wasn't too courteous, though. It was rather cold.

I don't know. I wasn't there. I wasn't at the inauguration at that particular time.

All right. Now, we have some things to get at, and they're pretty basic things. You were discussing before what you would do or what you would propose for the health, housing, and education of the nation—the higher education of the nation in the future—and you've also discussed the complex and confounding tax problems which are beginning to pile up on the country. Now, let us switch to the Orient, because there is, . . . apparently, developing future trouble. How do you view the big switch in the Orient, with Imperialist Japan now adopting the ways of peace and democracy, and hitherto peaceful China going military, warlike, totalitarian, and imperial?

I think China is going through the same stage that Japan did when they assumed the same attitude, and I'm as sure as I can be that the Chinese are a very, very able people and that they will come out of the situation, just as Japan did, on the side of free government.

How do you see the aftermath of Chiang Kai-shek's passing? What will happen to Nationalist China and Formosa?

The only reason that Chiang Kai-shek had to move over to Formosa was because his generals surrendered to the communists. They surrendered all the equipment that we'd sent him, and they used that equipment to run Chiang out of China.

Do you think that Red China should be admitted to the United Nations, and if not now, when?

I've never been in favor of admitting them. You can't very well admit them until they have shown more interest in the welfare of their neighbors and people by whom they are expected to set an example, as they did in times past.

If Nationalist China should be without a leader, it would obviously cease to be of any significance in the affairs of the United Nations or in any of the affairs of the Orient.

The only reason for the Nationalist China situation is due to the fact that they were one of the five great powers who set up the United Nations, and it's very difficult to eliminate people who helped make an organization. That was long before Chiang Kai-shek's generals surrendered to the communists.

Do you think that the United States would be in a position of having to defend the integrity and the independence of Formosa, even if there were no Chiang Kai-shek about?

Formosa is a part of the defense line which is used to draw the line against the communist world, and I think they'd have to defend it.

So you still see a divided China for quite some time—until Red China mends its ways and becomes a civilized member of the United Nations.

That's true.

Do you think there's any hope for that?

I doubt it.

So you don't think that that is here.

It's not an immediate proposition that we have to worry about, because I don't think the Chinese under its present government will mend its ways any more than Russia did under Stalin.

They're on the march now, and they're going to keep going until they exhaust themselves or something stops them.

I feel that's the truth, the outline of the thing. That happened with Genghis Khan. He had to march all the way to Vienna before he learned his lesson.

Let us switch for a moment, again, to the domestic scene. What do you see in store for the American farmer, particularly the family farmer?

It looks as if every effort has been made in the last six or seven years to eliminate the family farm and make it an industrial proposition, just as they have in Russia. I don't believe in that. I think the family farm was the foundation of the country. I think we're going to have to have the family farm, and I don't think there's any way in the world to completely eliminate it. Of course, now, the difficulty with the farm situation has been that the increased productivity in the soil brought about by the proper rotation of crops and fertilizers and the improvement in the grain production—for instance, hybrid corn and wheat and oats—is much greater than it was in times past, and one acre will raise as much as ten acres used to raise. So I don't know what the answer is. I hope it's good for the farmers.

You don't feel that the government of the United States could ever turn its back upon the farmer either in terms of support or, if necessity brings it about, subsidies—additional subsidies to keep them going?

I think the United States government is going to have to keep the food producers in business. How it's to be done is a matter that ought to be worked as scientifically as possible. Now I had a Brannan Plan when I was President of the United States, which, in my opinion, would have eventually worked the thing out. But it was ridiculed out of existence.

Do you feel that they ought to cooperate a little bit more among themselves in the way that the National Farmers Union has brought about cooperation?

I think the National Farmers Union has done more to create a situation among the farmers to get them to help themselves than any other organization we have. The other organizations of the farmers are just organizations of capitalists who want to put the farmer out of business.

How does the Department of Agriculture function? Since your administration, the budget for the operation of the department has gone up enormously.

Five billion dollars. It has gone up from $1.1 billion to about $6.4 billion.

What is that money going for, sir? What are they doing that they haven't been doing?

I haven't the slightest notion what they've done with the money, because they seem to be against the crop program which we had in force. They had a soil-bank proposition, which they thought would keep the farmer from raising crops, and they paid great money to big farmers. But the little farmer didn't do any good with that sort of an arrangement. I think that's what's gone with the $5.5 billion.

*A good many of the farm organizations have been in sympathy recently with Secretary [Ezra Taft] Benson and ... with the [Charles F.] Brannan Plan.**

I don't know of any farm organizations—those that know what they're talking about—that are in sympathy with Benson.

Farm organizations, in a sense, are not exactly representing the best interests of the farmer, in your judgment?

One or two of 'em are not, but some of 'em are.

All right. Now, how do you view the evolution of the American labor movement? What is in store for the bullying, arrogant type of labor leaders like Hoffa and [Harry] Bridges?

I think they eventually will get their comeuppance. Their situation is just like every other situation where a man gets power and gets too big for his breeches. He soon has a come-down. The difficulty with the labor movement is the fact that they've been able to collect too much money in one place, and when any man—I don't care who he is, whether he's a banker or a laboring man or somebody else—gets control of too much money, why, it makes a fool out of him. That's what's happened to the Teamsters' Union.

The labor movement has come through some pretty difficult battles they had on their hands in order to achieve some measure of economic security, but there are so many laws on the books now having to do with the social security and the underpinning of the people's economy. Is there as much need for a big labor union and the things they do as there used to be?

Yes, there is. The National Labor Relations Act, the Wagner Act, is what put labor on its feet, and the law as it began to work, of course, needed amendment.† But it didn't need the Taft–Hartley Act for that amendment, as they are very conclusively finding out. But the labor boys thought they had something, and they voted for it, and they got what was coming to them.

---

*As Secretary of Agriculture, Brannan proposed canceling commodity-price supports and, instead, provide income-maintenance payments to family farmers in order to protect operators of small farms. Opposition by the National Farm Bureau Federation and other Republican groups resulted in the plan's demise in 1949.

†This July 1935 act created a national board that gave labor new protections against unfair employer practices. It also upheld employees' rights to join a labor union and to bargain collectively.

How do you differentiate between Hoffa, Bridges, and John L. Lewis in terms of labor leadership?

John L. Lewis was a fellow who thought he was kind of a king, but he found out that he wasn't, and he adjusted himself to conditions. And another thing in the difference between John L. Lewis and Hoffa and Bridges: Lewis was honest and the other two weren't.

You think that Lewis fought, even though harshly and sometimes arrogantly, but he had in mind the interests . . .

He was always fighting for his people, and these other people have been fighting for themselves and exploiting their people. That's the difference.

What would you do with those people? How would you deal with them?

I made a recommendation in the veto messages, both of them, of the Taft–Hartley Act on how to handle that situation was to see that their funds are properly investigated and that they have to make their reports at certain times on what they do with the money, and why they do it, and that the dues of the members should be on a basis where it would accomplish the purposes for which the union was set up without creating a great fund for exploitation by the heads of the union. That's the difference.

In that case, what do you think of unions' spending or contributing money to a political campaign?

I think it's all right if it is done in the right way.

. . . They could collect funds, but not treasury funds?

Not treasury funds. It's not treasury funds they should appropriate. I remember the railroad unions in 1940: They collected $1 apiece for $8,800, and that's all the money I had to run the campaign with, but they didn't take it out of the treasury. And they shouldn't take it out of the treasury. That's the point.

Mr. President, I have with me here a match-holder showing you and Richard M. Nixon linked arm in arm. It's called, "Harry S. Truman and Richard M. Nixon Bury Their Hatchet in a Steinway, Official State Piano, at the National Press Club All-Star Musicale in Washington—'Missouri Waltz' by Mr. Nixon, and 'California, Here I Come' by Mr. Truman—Duo-Duet Medley."

It didn't happen.

It did not happen?

It never did happen.

How was this . . .

That picture was made when Nixon met me on my first visit back to Washington to escort me into the Senate for the purpose of occupying my seat in making a speech in the Senate. That was in 1953, shortly after the Republicans went in, but no such thing as they tell about on that match thing took place.

Mr. President, what I want to get to is your return to the Senate during the time that you've been out of office ...

This was the first time that I was there to make a speech to the Press Club, and I had lunch with the Senators, the Democratic Senators. They asked me to come over to the Senate, and that was the first time I had been there since the 1952 election. The next time I went there was after 1954, when Nixon had called me a traitor, and I wouldn't go into the Senate after that unless he got out of the chair. They finally put Barkley in the chair, and I went in. That was the second visit.

That was the second visit? You have made one or two other visits since then, haven't you?

Oh, yes. I've made several visits since then.

But Nixon was never in the chair?

Was never in the chair when I went in.

Did he realize that? Was that by prearrangement, or ...

If he didn't ... If he didn't realize it, I wouldn't have gone in.

In other words, the only way that you could have possibly buried the hatchet with Mr. Nixon was to have it buried in his back?
(Laughter)

Well, no. If he'd gone on after that meeting as he should have and hadn't gone down and around over the country and called me a traitor, I wouldn't have had any feeling against him. I didn't care what he said in the campaign of 1952. It was in '54, in the Congressional election, when he got so bitter and so mean, just as he did against Helen Gahagan Douglas and his opposition when he was running for Congress against Jerry Voorhis.*

---

*As noted earlier, in 1946 Nixon defeated the five-term liberal Democratic Congressman Jerry Voorhis. In 1950, using Hollywood-style media-campaign tactics with innuendos about presumed communist sympathizers, Nixon defeated the liberal Helen Gahagan Douglas for the California Senate seat. Douglas, a former Broadway and opera star and a New Deal Democrat, was first elected to the House of Representatives in 1944; she voted against Truman on aid to Greece and Turkey in 1947 because she believed the assistance should be routed through the United Nations. Joseph Kennedy gave his son Jack $1,000 to forward to Nixon for her defeat.

... Do you recall any memorable discussions with any Senators during the time you returned to the Senate since you've been out of the White House, Mr. President?

No. I've had several meetings with Senate committees, and that was all a matter of record on the various subjects—the United Nations and things of that sort—and I appeared before the House committee on the appropriations for NATO and the Point IV Program. I spent an hour or two with that committee, and the whole committee was present, and they all had a chance to ask questions. The Republicans had prepared what they thought was a very embarrassing program for me, and I think I converted all of them. It became as polite as it possibly could be.

You were also asked to testify on the question of this two-term limitation of the President?

That's right. That's right.

As I recall on one occasion, Mr. President, just before Senator Taft died, when he was still hobbling about, you had quite a warm meeting with him on the Senate floor.

On the floor of the Senate. He was on crutches and standing there, and I went over and spoke to him. One of the Republican Senators from Kansas [Andrew F. Schoeppel] was there. Taft said, Harry and I have always had the viewpoint that he'd make the best Democratic candidate and I'd make the best Republican candidate for the reason that we each think that the other would be easiest to defeat.

Do you recall any other incident with any other Senator at all in that nature or anecdotal?

No. No, I don't. When I went into the Senate after the meeting when Barkley was in the chair, why, the Senator from South Carolina walked out the other door as I came into one, but I thought that was all right.

Oh, yes. Have you had any difficulty with any of the Dixiecrats since that time?

No, no. I haven't had any trouble with any Senators. I've never had any trouble with any Senator.

Along that line, if Senator Taft had been nominated and elected President in '52, would he, in your opinion, have carried on a program of conservatism and withdrawal, or would he have gone along with the established policies?

Oh, no. I think he would have carried on a program of conservatism, but he would have been as decent and nice to his predecessor as a man could be, because he and I were personal friends on the floor of the Senate. You don't have to fall out with a man because you don't agree with him on politics.

But you do feel that he would have changed the policy materially?

Oh, yes. He would have gone as far "right" as the Congress would let him.

In that respect, we had a narrow escape, probably. Now, Mr. President, getting back to the ... not the right to strike, but the sanity or the wisdom of it, of striking under our present setup. We're now going through the one hundredth day of a steel stoppage. You've had some experience with that kind of thing.

Yes, I have.

What is your opinion with respect to these strikes on a vast scale in view of our importance in the world today—in a free world—in a growing and expanding economy?

It's not a good thing when a nationwide strike takes place, and there ought to be some way to stop it and force negotiations. I followed through on a program of that kind, and the steel fellows who are now in trouble took the matter to the courts. There was a decision by the courts, six to three, and the minority report . . . the minority opinion should be the law today. Of those six opinions (there were seven altogether), Justice [Felix] Frankfurter had to write two, and none of them had any sense. But they called it a majority against what I was trying to do, which was to prevent just what's happened in the last hundred days. I think even the steel people are rather sorry now that they went to the court with that sort of an approach. If you'll read the minority opinion on that case, written by Mr. Justice Fred Vinson, who was the Chief Justice, you'll find out exactly what the law ought to be, and someday it will be just that.

In other words, Mr. President, you feel that some sort of compulsory arbitration should be necessary in a strike which affects . . .

Which is nationwide, of course, for the simple reason that industry is controlled to some extent by the laws of the land. . . . It's the antitrust law and the other manipulation of the market that's controlled by the Securities Exchange Commission. That is, when you have a Securities and Exchange Commission that tries to enforce the law, which we haven't had for some time, that's the difference. I wanted the powerful labor unions to be under the same sort of control as those two ideas which confront industry. If that could be done, then they'd all be treated just alike, and the little unions would have the same rights before the union court as do the little people who want to sell stock.

Forced arbitration is exactly what the unions don't want. They've been fighting that thing very bitterly.

I don't care anything about forced arbitration. All I want to do is to have the government in a position to make the country run when somebody tries to stop it, and that's what I did all the time while I was President.

Today, the government in . . . arguing its case in Philadelphia on appeal from the union, argues that a government has no right to confiscate a steel company that it deems necessary to the operations of our security program, our defense program.

That's correct.

Isn't that what you tried to do?

Yes, that was the program. I hope that everybody will read Mr. Justice Vinson's minority opinion on the suit that was brought against me by the steel companies. I think they wish that they had never brought that suit.

Then you think that the strike as a weapon by the unions is outdated as far as achieving the results?

No. No, no. I don't think so. I think the strike is a necessary thing, but when it becomes national in scope—for instance, when they can tie up all the railroads, when they can tie up all the shipping things, and they can tie up all the steel that's necessary to keep the country running—then it's gone too far.

You've been pretty consistent on that, because, as I recall, during the time of the railroad strike you were ready to move in, too.

I did move in, and then they quit.

Now, this is on the right-to-strike business. You made your point very clear on that. . . . Can we go back over into the foreign field? Do you view the future of Germany as a force for peace, or is she likely to revert to her former way?

If Germany continues to have a government [like] the one we have under Chancellor Adenauer, I think Germany will be a force for peace. I think Germany's had two lessons on the subject, and I think Germany is very anxious to have peace. I think if Germany and France and NATO countries keep up their attitude toward trade between themselves on a basis of one country, there will never be any cause for any disturbance.

And you don't see any danger emanating from East Germany or a possibility of its merging permanently with Russia?

Yes. Yes, there is a very great danger in connection with that. If some demagogue should come along and succeed Adenauer and decide that Germany ought to be reunited and do what Hitler did, we'd have the same thing over again. I hope that won't happen. I think . . . I hope that the Russians will wake up to the fact that the next time Germany decides to invade Russia, nobody's going to stop them.

Historically, all three—[Otto von] Bismarck, Kaiser Wilhelm [II], and Hitler—got into power and did all their mischief with war in the process of reuniting German countries.

That's correct. That's absolutely correct.

Processes, historical processes, could be repeated.

Could be repeated if we're not careful.

You don't see any chance that Western Germany might ever unite with Russia in any kind of an association?

Not unless they had a demagogue in control who wanted to do what Hitler and Stalin did. They united but didn't stay united.

Germany, historically again, is easily led and easily misled.

I think that two lessons, maybe, will be enough. I hope they won't have to have a third one.

What does the United States do, having had two involvements in this thing, to prevent it before it gets out of hand, like the last two things did? Certainly, the second one got out of hand.

Stay strong and keep the United Nations going in a manner that the police force of the United Nations can prevent any such thing from taking place.

You have frequently talked, especially in the last few months, about the possibility of the Russian people eventually awakening and getting . . .

I think when they get educated enough and understand what goes on west of their western lines, nothing can hold them down.

Mr. President, I want to get back to this question of the Russian people. You feel that in time they can't escape the inevitable progress which comes to people, and that is to seek democracy or to seek . . .

I'm only thinking about the French, the British, and the American people. They've all been through that stage, and they all came out all right. I think eventually when the Russians find out what liberty means—individual liberty—they'll do just what the rest of us have done. They've never had any freedom; since the time of Ivan the Terrible, they don't know what it's like. So as long as these Communist Party people can ride them into dictatorship and make them believe that they're getting something, why, that long will they stay in favor.

You think then that in that sense, colonialism is passing out as a form of imperialism? But is there not another form—a more subtle form—of colonialism shaping up at the present time?

It's a dictatorship that you're talking about. You see, colonialism was brought about by the opening of the wild countries of the world in Africa and South America and North America. When those countries were properly opened up and the exploitation began, the people just wouldn't stand for it. But it will take the Russians some time to come to the conclusion that they want something other than what they have. That's the difference.

Mr. President, we are often asked how we square with our freedom of government and the respect for freedom of others and encouragement when we make deals with a government like Franco's in Spain.

I never was for it. I never liked Franco. I don't like him now, and I never will like him. He's the same kind of a dictator as Hitler and Mussolini were.

Still, you had to deal with him.

I didn't deal with him. I didn't deal with him at all. He was recognized, but we never made any deals with him at all, because I didn't like him a bit. The deals have all been made since I left the White House.

But they've got a great big lot of fortifications there. Were these initiated during your period?

They were initiated immediately after I went out of office.

You would not have approved of them?

I would not have approved of them. I never did approve of them. I don't like him, and I still don't like him.

What do you foresee for Spain in the future?

I was for the republic that Franco overthrew. If you'll read the book of the ambassador who was over there on my appointment, you'll find exactly the situation as I believe it was and as it developed.*

You mean Claude Bowers.

Bowers.... Claude Bowers's book on Spain.

And you think that the government in control of Spain is of a temporary nature? Is that it?

I can't tell. I don't know. The Spaniards are emotional, and you can't tell exactly what they're going to do. I think they had a good government before

---

*Claude Bowers, *My Mission to Spain: Watching the Rehearsal for World War II* (New York: Simon and Schuster, 1954).

Franco went in there, but they charged it with being a communist government. And, of course, the Russians got in and made it look like it was communist. If the Russians had stayed out, Franco would never have been able to get in.

Nevertheless, Mr. President, we are today using Spain as a very important NATO base.

I agree with that. They're doing that. There's no question about it.

We've spent hundreds of millions of dollars in support of our activity there, and this, obviously, was an important economic transfusion to Spain. Could she go along without aid from the outside?

No. No. Spain's one of the poorest countries in the world and the most downtrodden people when you get in and look at it right carefully.

What would you suggest, then, as the outlook for Spain in the future?

I don't know. I don't know whether Spain has any outlook or not. But you remember the same was said about our Central American countries, about Mexico, and about Puerto Rico, and they came out of it all right.

What about what's going on in the Middle East now since your administration? Many changes have occurred there.

The most difficult situation developed in the Middle East when the present administration of our government allowed the British and the French to lose control of the Suez Canal. After the thing was all over, they moved the Sixth Fleet in the Mediterranean to the eastern Mediterranean. If the Sixth Fleet had been moved over there in the first place, we'd have had no more trouble with [Gamal Abdel] Nasser and his Middle East policy, for the simple reason that he's another exploiter and he thinks he can do what Hitler and Mussolini did. But he hasn't the resources; nor has he the people that can do it.

Acting as the devil's advocate, how can you justify the British and French going in to take military action and our fleet moving into the Mediterranean when that is what we're trying to avoid?

It could have been avoided in the beginning if the proper negotiations had been carried out. When Nasser found out that he could split the Allies, he went to work. I would never have allowed that to happen, because the thing could have been negotiated in a way that would have been all right, because the British and the French owned the canal. They built it.

Could you illustrate it in terms of your own dealings with [Mohammed] Mossadegh and Ibn Saud [al-Rahman al-Faisal Al Saud] in the days when they were acting up?

Yes. We didn't have any serious trouble with them when they found out that we were in dead earnest to get justice. That's all we were ever after. We didn't want any overwhelming control of anything. All we were trying to do was to protect the investments that had been made in those countries. They wouldn't have been developed if it hadn't been for those investments. The same thing is true of Egypt. The canal never would have been built if it had been left to the Egyptians to do it.

The Arab world didn't move, although they had cause to move, on Israel during your administration, since Asia recognized Israel, which was important to them, and we were depending upon their oil, which was very important to us at that time.

Well, here [is] the situation in that. Way back in 1924, that's when Lord [Arthur] Balfour made a statement after the First World War that Palestine should be home for the Jews who had been persecuted all over the world, and the British kept fooling along and never did anything about it. When it came time to do something and set the thing in shape, then I agreed to go ahead with it, and we got it done. There's no reason for any displaced persons in the Near East if the proper development of the countries over there is made.* The Tigris and the Euphrates rivers would support 40 million people, and the Nile would support 20 million more than are there now if it were properly developed. You know the difficulty with the Arabs? They don't want to work. They let the women do the work. When I get in a crowd of women with my wife along, I always say that they have one bright idea—they let the women do the work! But when you want to get something done, you've got to have people who are willing to work. That's the reason Germany is so progressive. They work, and they're willing to work. The Belgians and the Dutch are the same way. We've had difficulty with the French on that same line, but the French are coming out of it. De Gaulle has taken some of the wine away from them, and he's making them work. That's all they need.

I'd like to get back to the question of investments in the country so that I can get straight the flavor of what you mean by "to protect investments." You, of course, are so far away from that conception that you have to send gunboats to protect investments. You certainly are of the idea that dollar diplomacy is abhorrent.

Absolutely.

What . . .

Here is the situation. Whenever investments such as the ones that were made in the East and Near East for the development of their oil production,

*On October 11, 1946, Rabbi Philip S. Bernstein, at President Truman's request, met with him at the White House to discuss the conditions of Jewish displaced persons. Bernstein congratulated Truman and generals Joseph T. McNarney and Mark Clark for assisting the victims of persecution residing in displaced persons' camps in Europe. Truman noted his recommendation to resettle 100,000 Jewish persons in Palestine, despite Clement Attlee's anger about this: Bernstein to Truman, January 21, 1958, Bernstein Conference Notes, PPF, Secretary Office Files, Box 20, Truman Library.

and investments such as are made in South America for increasing their production, those investments are usually protected by treaties with the two governments. In the case of the Central and South American countries, we don't have to enforce those treaties anymore, because they keep their agreements, and that was all that was the matter in the Near East with regard to the Suez Canal and with regard to the oil investments in Arabia and in the . . . what's the name of the country? . . . in Jordan.

Are we going to be seriously hurt in the event that the Arab world decides to cut us off from the world and shift over its interest to communism?

I don't know what they'd do for a market. The Russians couldn't take it. We're using a large part of their oil, as are our friends and allies. I don't know what they'd do with the oil. What would they do with it if they took it over? Plug the wells and let them stand?

They would, in turn, . . .

That's all they'd have left.

No. They could, in turn, market the oil to Europe, which needs it, only on their terms.

No. Europe is getting all the oil it needs and not taking more than half of what comes out of the Near East. We take nearly half of it, and in the long run they would certainly have to have a market that would keep their wells operating. I don't think that there's any danger of their throwing us over as operators of their oil after we've developed it. We've developed all the oil in the Near East, you know, and . . .

Looking at it the other way now, we have Venezuela with a growing supply of oil. Some of the other South American countries are getting oil. Canada has got it coming out of its ears. Are we . . . would we cut off the Middle East oil in order to take up the economic slack of Canada and Venezuela, for instance?

It could be done, but I don't think it's necessary. I don't think it's necessary because . . . Oh, I'll say at the beginning of the First World War, the production in the United States of 2 million barrels of oil was considered overproduction. We're producing 6 million barrels of oil a day and are still short, for the simple reason that we've done away with coal as fuel for operating machinery of all kinds.* To tell you the honest truth, if we ever get this

---

*U.S. crude-petroleum production in 1917 was 3.35 million barrels; however, in 1959, this production reached 2.75 billion barrels. In 1916, Truman, as treasurer of the Morgan Oil and Refining Company, was buying and selling oil leases out of Kansas City. The company went out of business after the declaration of war by the United States. Truman joined the Army, and the other partners abandoned the company: Hillman, *Mr. President,* 193.

atomic-energy thing going, we won't need oil, either. Then what are they going to do?

Is it going to be possible to take atomic energy and control it? They've had some trouble in containing it so that it doesn't break through.

It can be controlled, because it has been done on these submarines that we've put out, and they're working on an aeroplane right now. Eventually, we'll have engines on the railroads, just like they have these diesels that will run almost forever with one charge. That's the thing I think these oil fellows are contemplating, and that's the reason they're trying to get control of the operations of atomic energy, and I don't want them to have it. I want it to stay in the hands of the people.

Do you see that far away, or is that in the immediate future? This development of atomic energy for . . .

It will come about . . . along about the same way in which oil took the place of coal, and that took a period of fifty or sixty years. That's probably what will happen here. That's the reason I'd like to be alive in [the year] 2000 and see what they're doing.

Could you take a look at the year 2000 and see what we'd be like having atomic energy running our plants, our motor cars, our railroads, our airplanes? What'd it be like?

We wouldn't have nearly as much dirt on our skins as we have now with oil and coal. That's the only difference I can see.

But the human heart would still be the same, and the human brain.

There wouldn't be any difference at all. The human animal would be behaving just exactly as he has for 10,000 years.

Therefore, Mr. President, from your general philosophic view of the world, the problem always remains the human beings.

Absolutely. The human animal has to be guided in the right direction under the moral codes, and then there has to be some machinery to make him behave and live with that moral code.

And you think that there always should be balances and adjustments so that when the underdog becomes the top dog, he will be reminded.

He ought to be treated just like the top dog was before when he doesn't behave himself.

You've lived a long and very active life, and you have looked at all sorts of people in all sorts of places, and you have a sense of history. Morally and spiritually, are we pretty much the same as we were during the days of the birth of Christ, or are we changing?

No. If you go back that far in a period, I don't think there's been a radical change. I think the generations in this country ... each one is in better shape than the one before. But when you study the history of what they call the Pax Romana, until they broke up, they went through the same periods that we're going through. They had depressions, and they had the various things that the poor people didn't have, and they had rebellions, and some of them didn't get enough to pay for what they were doing. But in the long run, they had a very able and good setup, and so have we if we don't let it go to pot.

Do you see us, then, getting to a point where we can have a universally prosperous and a universally peaceful world?

Yes, I do, if we keep working at it. It'll have to come, because if they use these horrible weapons that we now have on hand in this great country—and all of them are going to have them—it would be just a complete destruction of the whole human race if we had an all-out war like we had in the First World War and the Second World War. Because in an all-out war, you'd wipe out every city in the world, and think what that would mean. That's what MacArthur wanted me to do to China, and I wouldn't do it.

In other words, the problem is still the problem of how to avoid war, because as weapons have become destructive, the problem of war becomes even more terrible.

That's right.

Now, how should we lead the world? Who's going to lead the world? It isn't the United Nations that can do it.

Oh, yes, the United Nations can do it when they develop the leadership to do it. But until that time comes, the free world must produce the leadership to keep the United Nations in shape so that when the time comes that it can control things, it will have the leadership to do it. I think it will appear.

Should that leadership in a national sense be spearheaded by the United States?

Yes, it ought to be. It ought to be. When it isn't, why, then we're in trouble.

Then the future role of a President of the United States is not only the leadership of our own people, but to provide some of the direction and the help for the emancipation of other people?

He should be the leader of the free world. The President of the United States should be the leader.

That's a new role for the President of the United States. Would you explain that a little bit, sir?

It was inaugurated by Franklin D. Roosevelt, and I tried my best to carry it through. I don't want to comment on what's been going on since.

How did Franklin Roosevelt initiate this new role as the leader of the free world?

He was following the lessons he'd learned with Woodrow Wilson. He was in the Navy, and he finally became the nominee for Vice President in 1920. He'd been through all that period, just as I had, and he knew what happened when it fell through. We finally wound up with isolationism again and a Second World War, and if you wind up with isolationism again, as the right-wing Republicans would like to do, we'll end up with that destruction that we've been talking about.

Mr. President, could I get a little bit clinical here and ask you . . . you are very optimistic. Is that due to your disposition, or is it also buttressed and fortified by your knowledge of mankind and men and in your belief in men?

It's caused by my knowledge of history principally. . . . Pessimists never made anything work. They're against everything. They never want to do anything, because they're afraid something will happen that they don't know anything about. An optimist is a man who wants to take advantage of conditions as they are and make them better. And that's all there is to it.

That is your philosophy?

That has always been my philosophy.

Are you buttressed by your knowledge of history in the belief that that's possible?

I know it's possible, because you take the great leaders in the historical past, where the men who were willing to try to do things that would improve conditions in the world and improve the situation in which they lived, and it came out all right. When they got men like Hitler and Mussolini and Franco, the conditions in their countries never did improve unless they had good luck and a rich uncle who took care of them.

Mr. President, can I just drop for a moment into a personal side again? Since you have left the White House, your mail has continued very heavily. Can you characterize [it]?

Yes, I suppose I get the biggest individual mail in the State of Missouri, and it keeps coming. I think the principal reason is because I've always made it a point to answer my mail, and people are interested in what I'm doing and what I expect to do, and most of them want to find out what I think about things around the world. Sometimes I can tell them. Most of the time, I can't.

Why do you feel it necessary to answer all the mail, or most of the mail, you get?

Just plain courtesy. That's just plain courtesy. When a man doesn't answer his mail, he's a boor, and my mail has to be answered in one way or another. It's just as easy to say no in a letter as it is personally.

Why do you like to read letters that are vilifying you?

I like to find out what the crackpots are thinking. It's a lesson, you see, to find out how their minds work. Most of them won't sign them, but when you find one that does, he usually gets a reply and a "thank-you" letter for having sent me his viewpoints.

At any rate, you don't always want to hear letters of praise or . . .

No. No, no. When a fellow gets to the point where he has to be told what he wants to hear, he's a gone-gosling and he can't be a good public servant.

Do you find that most of the letters that you get that are upbraiding you for one thing or another have to do with any particular act of yours as President?

No. No, no. They're, for instance, letters on what I may be doing, or what I've said, or a speech I've made, by people who, of course, never would agree with me. Some of them are courteous and tell me why they don't agree. Some of them get obnoxious and nasty. They don't get an answer. It's those that are honestly in disagreement with me that get the answers. Those are the kinds I like to receive gone-gosling because it tells you what all the people are thinking as your friends.

And it is the lot of a President to adjust himself to having to expect that no act of his will ever be completely popular?

That's right. No President ever was completely popular. There never was but one President who was considered completely popular, and his name was James Monroe. There wasn't anything to do in his administration and he didn't do it.* So there you are.

---

*Truman omits the major territorial additions to the United States in the Florida Treaty with Spain, in 1819, which was designed and secured through careful negotiations by the Secretary of State, John Quincy Adams. Adams was also responsible for Monroe's message in 1823 regarding North and South America. In 1816, Monroe won an overwhelming Presidential election, with 183 electoral votes to his opponent's 34. His 1820 candidacy went unopposed, and he received 231 out of 232 electoral votes. Historians have termed his administration the "Era of Good Feelings."

You have found, haven't you, Mr. President—and I think you can say this without immodesty—that more people have begun to understand what you tried to do and what you achieved?

I think that's true. And that goes on for any President. Fifty years after he's out of office—I haven't been out quite that long—but you'll see now people are beginning to understand exactly what the aim of Woodrow Wilson was. They're beginning to find out what the aim of Theodore Roosevelt was. We know now in the first administration what the aim of Grover Cleveland was. And you also find out what the Presidents who didn't do anything . . . what their aims were. It takes a long time for those things to become settled. But a man of action always causes trouble.

But a man of action can't wait or shouldn't wait for what the verdict of history will be. He hasn't got time for that.

No, no. He's got to make a decision and go ahead with it and do what he thinks is right after he gets the best advice he can. And if he doesn't do that, the country would go to pot.

Could you name the aimless Presidents?

Yes. I've written an article for the magazines on the Presidents that I think are great. There are about a half a dozen of them, and I've been urged to write an article on the Presidents that I think were not so great. I think that could be done without hurting anybody's feelings, because those Presidents didn't do anything. We can start with John Adams. And Madison, as an administrator, was not a very great success, although he followed one of the greatest of the great Presidents, Thomas Jefferson. And you take the man who followed Andrew Jackson [Martin Van Buren], who was one of the best politicians that ever walked, and he was not considered a success. He was followed, of course, by William Henry Harrison, who only lived a month, and John Tyler was his successor. John Tyler was a Virginian who'd been nominated on the Whig ticket, and as soon as old William Henry Harrison died, the head of the Whig Party, why, Tyler fired all the Whigs and hired Democrats and got into more trouble than you could shake a stick at. The same thing happened with Zachary Taylor, who didn't know anything about administration. He was a general in the field and won one of the greatest battles in the Mexican War—the Battle of Buena Vista, where he said to Captain [Braxton] Bragg, "Give them a little more to drink, Captain Bragg!"* and that won the battle. He was succeeded by Millard Fillmore, who was an Anti-Mason and a Know-Nothing and was elected on the same ticket with old Zachary Taylor. He was succeeded by

---

*Taylor supposedly called out, "A little more grape, please, Captain Bragg." This quote may have been devised during the 1848 Presidential campaign rather than on the 1847 battlefield: cf. David Lavender, *Climax at Buena Vista* (Philadelphia: J. B. Lippincott, 1966), 51.

Franklin Pierce from New Hampshire, who signed the bill repealing the Missouri Compromise, which was one of the greatest of the contributions to the cause of the War Between the States. He was absolutely a do-nothing President. He'd been a brigadier general in the Mexican War, and whenever there was a big fight, he was sick. He was followed by James Buchanan, who, I think, was the best do-nothing President that the United States ever had. He could have stopped the Civil War in South Carolina just as easy as old Jackson did it about twenty years earlier. Jackson told them if they didn't enforce the laws in South Carolina, he'd come down there and hang every one of them, and they knew he'd do it. And that's all James Buchanan had to do. And then to get . . . after the War Between the States, we had General Grant who was not a good administrator and who surrounded himself with people who didn't know how to do an administrative job. He was followed by Rutherford Hayes, who was a good man and tried his best to pull things out. But he got in on a stolen election, and his moral background on that account caused him all sorts of trouble. Then the fellow who succeeded him was assassinated—Garfield. And Garfield was followed by the best-dressed man that ever was in the White House [Chester A. Arthur] and was the best-looking man, with sideburns and all that kind of business.* He didn't care much about doing anything. Then we had along a good deal later—I don't like to get too close to modern times— we had Harding and Coolidge. Coolidge was a [double] for Franklin Pierce. He didn't have to do anything, and it wasn't necessary for him to do anything. He carried on the government, and that's all that was necessary, and he liked it the way the thing came out. They tell a good story on him. When this fellow wrote the book debunking George Washington, he was told about it, and he turned around and looked out the window in the White House office and he said: "Well, his monument is still there. I guess it will stand."

(Laughter)

That's one of the greatest things he ever said.

That's wonderful. Now that's an amazingly concentrated bit of history, and it's very, very exciting.

If you can get people to study these people without any prejudice, then you'll find that the Presidents who did things and who pushed the country forward were always followed by Presidents who didn't do so much, because people didn't want anything more done. They didn't like him, and I can say that because I followed one of them.

We don't accept that and we'll delete that part of it because . . . That part of it will be privately unpublished forever and anonymous, but I would like

---

*Chester A. Arthur (1829–86), a graduate of Union College and a lawyer, served as quartermaster-general of New York during the Civil War. Appointed port collector in 1871 by President Grant, he was removed by President Hayes seven years later for violating an executive order.

to get to a personal thing here, which is very germane to this business of doing things. Disregarding the last sentence of your statement, the fact is that you were probably as driven to doing things and getting things done, both administratively and executively, as any occupant, including your predecessor. That's personal privilege, here. How do you . . . this was never quite brought out. You were one of the best listeners in modern times in the White House chair, and yet you were the least influenceable man that was in that chair. You had everybody come around and give you all kinds of advice, but then you invariably used your own judgment. Now, how did you do it?

Well, here was the situation. Whenever it was necessary for me to know about things—any legislative matter or foreign relations or things of that kind—I'd try to get all the information I possibly could from every source that was possible. Then, I would be happy to listen to everybody else who had something to say on the subject. That's one of the reasons we set up the Central Intelligence Agency—so I could get all the information I could, and then, if the other people who had studied that same information wanted to give me their viewpoint, I was glad to have it. Knowing the background of the situation myself, if I didn't think they were right, I didn't pay any attention to them. If I did think that they were right, they were usually in agreement with the decisions I made.

So in a sense, you approached them with an almost closed mind, didn't you?

Yes.

Your mind was pretty much made up while you were listening to their advice?

But not made up for good.

I see.

It was not made up for good. I would listen to them, and sometimes they would furnish me with an idea that would make it much more easy to do what I had to do. I knew what I had to do all the time.

Excuse me, sir. You don't recall any particular incident in which you wanted to take one course and were influenced by any advice that you got to do the opposite?

No, not in a policy matter, but sometimes in appointments—that would happen every once in a while. Like a person that was interested in a fellow who was going to work for him and I had to make the appointment, he might know something about him that I didn't. Then that would go by the board. But when it came to national and international policy matters, usually there was never any very serious disagreement unless somebody wanted to turn the clock back. Of course, the leaders on the Republican side of the House and the Senate would always, naturally, want to turn the clock back, but they were easily convinced that they couldn't do it, and then they didn't want to do it. That was even when we had a Republican Congress in foreign affairs.

Mr. President, you had, and Roosevelt had, more Republicans in government than certainly the subsequent government had Democrats. Why did Roosevelt, or why did you, feel that you should have Republicans in the government?

Here was the situation. When we got into the Second World War, it was necessary to have the country completely united. In order to get that done, why, Mr. Roosevelt appointed a Secretary of War and the Secretary of the Navy who were of the opposite political party.* He did that because he wanted unanimous support in carrying out the program that had to be carried out in an all-out war. After he passed on, I continued the same policy in the hope of getting a United Nations program set up and a foreign policy set up that would work. I knew if they started a situation as it was in 1918, '19, '20, and '21, we'd never get it done. That was the reason for it. I always had an opinion, and I still have it, that when the President needs key men for his administration, he must get those who agree with him as to policy and as to politics.

You found, didn't you, that Stimson was one of the great Americans?

Stimson was one of them, one of those men, and Robert Patterson was another one. And [Arthur] Vandenberg was another. I could name you a great many others.

Vinson was . . .

Vinson was . . . You mean the . . .

Fred Vinson.

He was talking about Republicans now.

Oh, I'm sorry.

He's a Democrat. He's Democrat, but you'll find out that the vast majority of those people, when the emergency came, no matter how bitterly partisan they were—with one or two exceptions—and I'll except the demagogues.

[Robert A.] Lovett was one of them.

Lovett was another one of the men who was one of the best public servants I ever had around me, and he succeeded to the Department of Defense.

*Henry Stimson and Frank Knox.

I never looked at a man's politics when I wanted to fill in a key job. I tried to find the man that could do it. I didn't care what his politics was.

In every department?

Every department. Every department.

How did you fight off the patronage dispensers when you were doing that?

In the key jobs, . . . they weren't after the key jobs; they were after jobs for precinct workers, and you don't have any trouble finding them.

All right. One more personal thing. . . . When the chips were down and you were in deep difficulties in terms of events that would crowd you and tend to depress—like the day you fired MacArthur and the whole world descended on you, or like the day you had to make the move to march on Korea and with the bad news—how did you keep from blowing up a little bit?

Well, here was the situation. When those things came along like MacArthur, and Korea, and one or two others—the Berlin Airlift—I'd studied the situation and made up my mind, and I didn't worry about it. I said we'd go ahead and do things this way, and we did. That's the way it happened. If you're going to fail to make up your mind in an instance of that kind, you're going to walk the floor and worry yourself to death. Then you're no good to do the job. Then if I did wrong, to hell with it. We'd start over and do something else.

Mr. President, as President you used to keep frequent memoranda. . . . Have you continued that?

Not so much. I keep some some memoranda, but not very many. The correspondence I've dictated is the best memoranda I have now.

And you certainly get, as you said before, a great abundance of correspondence. You also get many invitations. I notice a very good expression you had here at a speech you made yesterday. You said that every organization within a hundred miles has sought to obtain you as a speaker before their group because "I was chief President on Pennsylvania Avenue."

That's right.

But you could lengthen that one hundred miles to longer, couldn't you?

Oh, yes. It's all over the United States the same way. There are certain organizations that it's necessary to appear with, and when a political campaign is coming up, it's necessary for a man who's been in the position as the leader of his party to go out and help the people who are trying to restore that party to power. But you'll find that these luncheon clubs and things of that kind, they're always trying to take you to a place where they'll have three or four customers, and a fellow who's been President ought to at least talk to a hundred.

Now, did you ever write a memorandum or memoranda to yourself when you were about to make an important decision in order to gain perspective on the act which was to follow?

No. No, I never did. When I made up my mind on a thing of that kind, I went ahead and did it, and I never did any writing on the subject. I've made several memoranda on things after they happened, but not before.

In other words, they were summations of your actions in order to be able to remember what you did.

That's right. And not only that, but maybe I might want to make another decision and straighten it out, and I wanted to see what it looked like.

Session Seventeen

Had the Russians gotten into Japan, we'd have had exactly the same situation that we have in Poland and East Europe. When I found out their attitude and their actions, they did not get into Japan. And they couldn't get there, because we controlled the seas.

...In 1956 in the campaign between the two Presidential candidates, the issue of [further testing of the] hydrogen bomb became a campaign issue.

Yes, by Stevenson, and it shouldn't have been put in the campaign at all.

Were you consulted about the theme of the hydrogen bomb as one of the issues in the campaign?

No.

It was not suggested in the platform of the Democratic Party?

No. No. No one was consulted on the matter that I know of. But the objective of that whole setup was to keep us ahead in these powerful weapons, and that had started way back as far as 1946 or '47.

Mr. President, I recall when I was along with you in your campaign in 1956 that, as you saw Stevenson making his statement that we ought to do something about damming any further testing, you categorically stated that you didn't intend to be stultified by what Stevenson said on that matter.

Well, no. I told him that progress was not made by stopping when you had an approach [to] something that ought to be developed and that we ought to go ahead with it just because that was good sense, just like we did the first one.

But then at no time during that campaign did you go along with him, because you never discussed the matter?

Transcript, Friday morning, October 23, 1959, part one.

Oh, no. I immediately made a statement that he was wrong.

But didn't you amplify on that statement from time to time in your private meetings—that although you supported him in your campaign for his election, you did point out that the testing of the hydrogen bomb for further development was not a political issue but a security matter?

That was emphasized all the time. Not only was it a security matter, but it was a matter which would result in the further use of the atomic explosions for peaceful purposes. I thought we ought to control as much of it as we possibly could.

But you further went on to suggest, as I recall it, that the testing of the hydrogen bomb and its development and its further extension for military purposes could be best determined by whoever was President at that time, because he had available to him information that no one on the outside could possibly have.

That's true.

And therefore, this matter should not have been taken to the . . .

It ought not to have put into the campaign at all. There wasn't any reason for it. It didn't make anybody any votes and I think it lost some.

So that as a political issue it boomeranged, too.

That's right.

Mr. President, on the general basic philosophy, Laurence suggests that as a result of the control and harnessing of this hydroelectric [sic] bomb, this nuclear bomb, it is a positive force that makes peace inevitable, as it totally eliminates the basic elemental reason that has led to all the major wars in history—the have-nots coveting the possessions of the haves. For in the nuclear reactor, as the atomic power plant is known, man has at last all the energy he needs to create the wealth and leisure and spiritual satisfaction in such abundance as to eliminate forever any reason for one nation to covet the wealth of another. What do you think of such basic philosophy?

I want to tell you this. I hope that the ideals expressed in that paragraph are true, but the human animal hasn't changed a bit, and covetousness is one of them. You know that one of the commandments says, "Thou shalt not covet thy neighbor's wife, or his ox, or his ass," and it hasn't changed any. If these idealists can get these things over . . . It takes idealists to make the world work, because eventually some of the thoughts that they put out will come about. But when it comes to physical, common, everyday things, most men are jealous of a fellow who's successful.

Yes. Mr. President, I would like to go to one of our unfavored authors, Mr. Walter Lippmann. This morning, in his column, he says, "In this country *there exists the same difference of opinion about negotiating about the Berlin situation as exists in France and Germany." "It is led", he said, "by members of the Truman administration, by Mr. Truman himself, Mr. [Dean] Acheson and Paul Nitze.* Their thesis is . . ."*

I don't know Paul, but go ahead.

"Their thesis is . . ." Can I get that remark, Mr. President?

I say, I don't know Paul, but go ahead.

"Their thesis is that the status of West Berlin is not a negotiable question, that the right policy for this country is to refuse to discuss the status of West Berlin and to defy the Soviets to do anything about West Berlin. They think, it would appear, that the Soviet government will be overawed by our firmness. And if it is not overawed, they are prepared to fight some kind of 'limited' war." And then he goes on to say, "These retired Truman officials, like old soldiers, are in my view trying to relive the battles in which they won their fame and their glory. But while they are right in insisting that the Cold War will go on, their preoccupation with their own past history is preventing them from grasping and dealing with the new phase of the Cold War. A rigid and unchanging diplomacy, which is what they advise, will not work in the present phase of the Cold War. It will not work because it compels the country to oppose all moves toward accommodation." What is your opinion about that?

I think it's just a column that had to be sold, and it makes good reading, and that's all there is to it for the simple reason that the only objective of myself and my friends has been to have the Russians agree to the commitments which they made at Yalta and Potsdam for the reuniting of Germany and to give free governments to Romania, Bulgaria, Hungary, and Poland. That's all there is to it. And if these people want to leave these countries who were our friends all through the program under the heel of the dictator in the Kremlin, then that is what Mr. Lippmann is talking for.

In other words, all this suggestion of accommodation, isn't that a pretty dangerous philosophy, because every time you get pressed, you have to accommodate . . .

You can't make an accommodation with Russia that they'll keep unless you have the strength to make them keep it. That's all there is involved in it.

You think that Mr. Lippmann is letting himself be carried away by his own concept of a situation with which he is not as familiar as those who had to deal with it.

---

*A young economic adviser in the State Department early in Truman's Presidency, and later director of the Policy Planning Staff at the State Department.

That's true. And he's a lot older than I am, and you know what happens to old men when they get to the end of the line.

Chronologically, he's been older than you are since the day he was born. The other point about Mr. Lippmann and his following, and he's got a following, is that what he seems to lose sight of is that you cannot divorce the past from the present if you're going to deal with the future, and that your main point is that unless they keep those agreements into which they entered in the past, there can be no future in any negotiations with them.

That's correct. Because they wouldn't keep those agreements, either. The agreements they make, they won't keep.

In other words, if you start accommodating them from time to time, then what assurance have you that they will keep those agreements?

You accommodate yourself out of business if you do that.

During your administration, there were no special provisions made for rigidity in thinking or . . .

Not at all.

Or concerted thinking. Each one was encouraged to act and think independently?

That's right.

And you did not impose your views on anyone else?

That's right.

And neither did anyone else impose his views on you?

That's right, and that's the way it ought to be.

Of course, there was no cabal of soldiers or thinkers who are now working overtime to keep your former policies from being brought up to date?

Not at all.

In other words, you do not favor a rigid course in order to be rigid. You are prepared to follow a course which can bring about an agreement by the Russians which the Russians will keep.

Yes. If we can get them to keep their agreements, we wouldn't have had any trouble in the first place. The only way that you can get them to keep their agreements is to be stronger than they are.

And there's a vast difference in your thinking, Mr. President, between being firm and being rigid?

That's right. You've got to be firm when an agreement is made; you want to carry it out. If it isn't carried out, you ought to have the means to see that it is carried out, and there's no rigidity about that. There might be renegotiations if they found out that they couldn't get what they wanted.

Mr. President, since it is apparent that at the present moment, and for some time to come, there is no possibility of East Germany and West Germany being reunited, would you in any way favor the recognition of communist East Germany?

No. No, I would not. Because if you recognize communist East Germany, you're going to bring on another Hitler and take it away from the Russians. That's what the Russians are afraid of. They can't stand before the Germans. Whenever a force even half their size meets them head on, they just can't stand. That's what the trouble was, and if they had kept their agreements, they wouldn't be in any danger of that situation.

In other words, you have said before, and I think the government has since said, that this country is always willing to guarantee both Russia and Germany against the aggression of each other?

Yes, that's correct. That's absolutely correct.

And there was no reason, actually, in having the United States and Russia enter into a hydrogen-bomb race if they had responded to your original call to come to terms with the United Nations?

That's right. I made the proposition, when we had a monopoly on it, as you know, for the world to benefit by the discovery of the use of atomic [energy], and the Russians vetoed it every time, because they have no idea of a concert of powers for the welfare and benefit of the world. They want to conquer the whole world, and we just can't let them do it. That's all.

Isn't it also a fact that the only reason why there is any chance . . . this is something which Mr. Lippmann seems to overlook . . . why there is any chance at all to negotiate with the Russians now, or why they're making signs that they could be negotiated with, is that during the period when they were intransigent and completely unresponsive and vetoing, as you've just said, you had to build our strength and you had to work with our Allies to contain them?

That's right. We did.

Because if they had acted upon their program at that time and hadn't been stopped, there would have been nobody to negotiate with in the first place. They would have . . .

There would have been no free Europe or anyplace else. There would have been no free world.

There's just one more thing from Lippmann, and then we'll leave that old rag alone. We're wasting tape on him. "It is true," says Lippmann, "that the great international measures of the war and of the Truman administration—lend-lease, the Marshall Plan, NATO—were pushed through Congress by popular terror and fear. But that cannot go on forever. The time has come, now that the postwar era is ending, when our leaders will have to learn how to persuade and convince the people, not merely to frighten and stampede them, into doing what is necessary for them to do."

He has a completely wrong approach. The idea was to help the people who had been responsible for the creation of the free world to a recovery. There was no idea of a military program involved in that at all. For the first time in the history of the world, the great victor made it possible for the enemy to recover. And that's never been done. Mr. Lippmann misses the whole reason for these very things that he names. He tries to make them military. They're not at all.

In other words, Mr. President, one of the things that many of those who have analyzed your administration point to is the great reversal in all history of the willingness of the victor to help.

Help the vanquished. Suppose Russia had obtained control of Japan. Suppose that Russia had obtained the whole of Western Europe. What would have happened? Would there have been any recovery? Ask Mr. Lippmann how he would have handled that situation if it came about! I don't think we ought to pay any attention to him, because I don't think he knows what he's talking about.

That's right, Mr. President. The only reason I bring it up is because some of these arguments come up. . . . I just want to conclude this Lippman thing by saying that it appears to us that Lippmann, himself, is the old soldier fighting the old battles by taking a position of . . .

There isn't any doubt about that. That's what he's always done. You see, as editor of Pulitzer's paper, when he lost his job, he was frustrated, and he's been that way ever since.*

I just wanted to get back to a statement you made in 1948 when you were fighting that man for the office and you talked about atomic energy. You said, "This is a force." You were worrying about its getting into the hands of the privileged again and going back to business.

---

*Walter Lippmann (1889–1974) joined the editorial staff of the *New York World* in 1921 and three years later became editor. In 1931 he moved to the *New York Herald Tribune,* and his internationally syndicated column, "Today and Tomorrow," was carried in more than two hundred newspapers, with an estimated 38 million readers. He won Pulitzer Prizes in 1958 and 1962 for his columns. He also wrote twenty-six books, many of them on political philosophy.

That's right.

And you said, "This atomic energy is a force which holds great danger for catastrophe in the wrong hands. At the same time, it holds great promise of a better life in the right hands. Everyone must understand clearly what is involved." And this is exactly the statement that you have been trying to evolve here this morning—that what you were worried about was not only its not falling into the wrong hands and be there as a threat, but you were also concerned with making the most of its potential for the benefit of humanity.

For the welfare and benefit of the most people, that's the idea.

While we're on this subject, could we get back to Berlin in terms of what might have been a situation more to our liking and less threatening, as it is now, if you had had a hand in originally shaping our decision of what to do with Berlin?

I'll tell you what the situation developed. Of course, you must have confidence in your Allies. We had confidence in France. We had confidence in Germany, and we had confidence in Russia, and the confidence in Russia was misplaced. We found that only by the action on Berlin and East Germany and Poland. For that reason, the Russians were kept out of Japan. Had the Russians gotten into Japan, we'd have had exactly the same situation that we have in Poland and East Europe. When I found out their attitude and their actions, they did not get into Japan. And they couldn't get there, because we controlled the sea.

In other words, you didn't want to make any changes at all from the commitments that President Roosevelt and Churchill had made?

Those commitments were made beginning in Quebec, when the first conference took place. Then the Atlantic Charter came along, and then they had a meeting at Casablanca and in Cairo and in Tehran and then in Yalta.* Potsdam was the windup meeting, and the only thing that we could do at Potsdam was to implement the agreements that had been made beforehand, after the Germans had surrendered. Of course, no one had anticipated that the Russians would take the attitude which they did, not to do what they'd agreed to do, in all these conferences which had taken place previous to our meeting in Potsdam. Now, it's too bad that Germany was divided the way it was, but, you know, at that time, Hitler had caused Germany to be the worst, low-down government in the history of the world. And these people—all of them, including Russia—were trying to do something to prevent Germany's revival on the basis of the Hitler program. That's all there was to it.

---

*Quebec, August 1943; Atlantic Charter, August 1941; Casablanca, January 1943; Cairo, November 1943; Tehran, November–December 1943; and Yalta, February 1945.

And even when Churchill talked about moving into the areas where the Russians were scheduled to go, do you think that he felt that Russia was going to be tricky? What do you think was the purpose?

I think he was still thinking about the landing in the Black Sea Straits in the First World War. I think he always had an idea that the European situation could be settled by starting from the Baltic Sea or from the Black Sea and coming up through Central Europe. I think that's what he still had on his mind. But he'd agreed with Stalin and Roosevelt on a certain program, and I didn't feel that I was in any position to break an agreement that the United States was a party to. I tried to keep every single one of them while I was in the White House.

In other words, Churchill was following the traditional British strategy of always trying to maintain a balance on the continent by balancing off one power against the other? And the British also had a history of always wanting to keep the Russians back?

Oh, yes. They kept the Russians out of India for a century. And they kept them out of Iran or Persia for a century. They kept them away from the Black Sea Straits after the winning of the First World War, and that was the policy that was in view so far as Churchill was concerned, and he was entitled to it. But that policy should have been expressed and worked on when the meetings in Tehran and Yalta were taking place.

In other words, it was then that he should have taken a position rather than at a moment having committed himself?

After the commitment was made, of course, it couldn't very well be changed when the war was over. But I think Churchill had a notion, and I like him very much, that he could influence the former Vice President in going through with a program which Britain had been following for three or four centuries. And I myself told him that this agreement had been made, that he was a party to it, and as far as I was concerned, I was going to keep it.

Mr. President, how is it . . . and the question is often asked that, with the signs that were beginning to develop of Russian misbehavior and the lesson we already had in China as a result of your great experience with your mission to China through General Marshall . . . that we still misjudged the Russian potential in terms of troublemaking to the world and did not take all the necessary steps to prevent it?

It took a year to find out that the Russians were not going to keep their agreement, and when we went into Berlin, that was when we found out that they had no intentions of keeping any agreement. That was what kept them out of Japan and the Japanese war—their attitude toward Berlin and the Black Sea Straits.

In other words, you had a very clearcut feeling and a very definite feeling that the Russians were playing fast and loose, and therefore you were not going to risk anything further so far as Japan was concerned?

That's correct.

There's also a point being made that you felt that Russia . . . and you and President Roosevelt felt that Russia . . . having had a narrow escape from total disaster, would not so quickly forget her brush with a disaster and embark upon a campaign of world domination?

But she did. She immediately forgot it, and the reason for that was the situation which developed in the military setup in the world—the very fact that we had to squeeze our military organization to nothing—brought about by the Eightieth Congress.* That was one of the things that the Eightieth Congress did, which caused this whole thing to develop. It was the refusal of the appropriations necessary to maintain a military front that would let the Russians know that we'd fight if it was really necessary.

In other words, as you look back now, you feel even more strongly that one of the fatal steps which induced Russia to be difficult and to take on a bold air of spreading out was our missteps in demobilizing so swiftly?

That's correct, and you couldn't help it. You couldn't help it. The people at home caused that very demobilization that brought about this very thing that caused the Cold War. They were told at the time that that's what would happen, but it didn't do any good. They went right ahead.

To turn for a second to the United Nations: During this entire period since the forming of the United Nations, all of these patterns of Russian policy were becoming pretty clear on the floor of the United Nations, and yet during that period through the exercise of the veto, the United Nations had not, of itself, been a force for peace enforcement or world conciliation.

They couldn't go any further than they did until the great powers—that is, Russia, the United States, Britain, and France—finally decided they were going to have to meet the situation head-on. Then they were stopped.

Had the United Nations been the force that it was planned to be and drafted to be, could the Korean breach have occurred?

No. No, it could not. That's the result of the upset of the League of Nations. When the League of Nations was upset, that was a precedent on which the Russians were working.

*1947–49. In his 1948 campaign, Truman harped on the phrase, "This Do-Nothing Congress."

In other words, the Haile Selassie experience with the League of Nations was almost* ...

Exactly what the Korean situation was with the United Nations.

And you feel now that this was the reaffirmation of the United Nations as a peace enforcement agency of the world?

It had to be sustained, because the United Nations set up the Republic of Korea, and if it had been allowed to go by the board, there wouldn't have been any United Nations any more than there was the League of Nations after Haile Selassie's experience with them.

Let's jump from that to a domestic situation that has to do with a thing called inflation, which is now with us and which we've been fighting ever since the war. The point has been made that in 1948, you petitioned Congress for measures to give you price and wage controls in order to [keep] the runaway economy from overtaking us and to put some kind of a check on inflation that was then in its development. Then, in 1950, when you had to go to the Congress to get enabling legislation with which to carry on the action in Korea, you omitted at a time of emergency asking the Congress for price- and wage-control legislation which would have enabled you to check inflation during that period.

They had the information. It was given to them. It was still standing, and they refused to act on it, and then they called it a totalitarian proposition. They didn't do anything about it. That's what the trouble was. You talk about inflation being a price–wage proposition. It's not so much a wage proposition as it is a price proposition. When a $2.37 wage increase is made on a ton of steel and the price of steel is raised $14 a ton, who's then contributing to inflation? It's not the fellows who have to work for their living; it's the people who profit by what they do, and that's not socialism, in spite of what Mr. Eisenhower says.

In other words, you think there's been profiteering in wages rather than wages profiteering in ...

There's been profiteering in prices rather than wages. That's the point.

Yes. A question. I was going to ask maybe the same one you wanted to ask. It's this: Do descendants and children of the President continue to have and face the same difficulties that they faced when their parents were in office? ... In other words, do children have a hard time because ...

---

*Benito Mussolini's tensions with Haile Selassie's Ethiopia escalated in February 1935, and by December of that year, Italian bombers had destroyed Dessye Palace. The League of Nations' March 1936 ultimatum to Italy was ignored, and in May, Mussolini proclaimed victory and the rebirth of the Italian empire. In July 1936, the League of Nations abandoned Ethiopia.

Yes, they undoubtedly do. Even the collateral descendants of . . . the brothers and sisters of Presidents . . . have difficulty. They're harassed. They have no protection, and most of them, not having been in the place itself, have difficulty in finding out just how to meet these things. When the children of a President make mistakes, and they make no more mistakes than the children of ordinary parents, they have to face a difficult situation in publicity and harassment and things of that sort, and my sympathy is with them. I never say anything seriously detrimental about the children of Presidents, except the son of Fillmore and the son of Abraham Lincoln, who tried to destroy their papers. That's the only time I've ever made any remark about any of them. They have something to face that no other people have to face, because the limelight's on them no matter what they do.

Even after their parents leave the White House?

Long after their parents leave the White House.

There is a social problem involving a kind of democratic dynasty that's beginning to develop around each President, is there not?

Yes, that's true. They have difficulty. People try to promote them and use them for their own welfare and benefit. And politicians do the same thing, because when a man makes a great name in the Presidency of the United States, of course, that name, politically, is an asset if it's properly used. And they're always trying to promote these youngsters into doing things that they ought not to do as sons and daughters of the President.

You feel that all of these descendants have but one problem—how to meet their obligation? And that they have no special privileges in a democracy?

That's right, and some of them can't understand that. You can't blame them for that. That's human.

All right. Now you've been blessed with two grandchildren, and you're seeing them in their most delightful formative periods.* In your moments of contemplation, sentimentally, what do you wish for them?

I want them to be good citizens. I want them to forget that they had a granddad who was President of the United States and go ahead and make a name and record for themselves. That has been done in other instances.

Do you intend to take any part in helping to guide them a little bit?

---

*Clifton Truman Daniel was born on June 5, 1957. On May 19, 1959, Margaret had a second child, William Wallace Daniel. Two more sons were born: Harrison Gates Daniel on March 3, 1963, and Thomas Washington Daniel on May 28, 1966.

Well, of course, that all depends on what their mother sees in the thing. I don't think the grandparents should interfere in the raising of the grandchildren where their mother and father are involved. These youngsters have a good father and a good mother, and I think they'll understand how to raise their children. It can't be done with undue interference from the ancestors, and I'm not going to do that.

They are going to be raised in an environment on both sides of the family of public information and public service, right tradition. Would you want them encouraged to be sampling this thing as they go along to see if they would want to follow in grandfather's footsteps?

The thing that they have got to do is to adjust themselves to conditions as they go along. I hope they'll have first-, second-, third-, and fourth-grade teachers who will put them in their place when they try to be smartalecks on account of the fact that they're descendants of a man who has been in the White House. If that happens, I know that's what their mother and father will do. They'll come out all right as good citizens, and due to the fact that their name is somewhat different from their ancestor's name, they won't have as much trouble as they would have if they had the same name. Take the Roosevelt family as an example. They're always watching what they do because their name is Roosevelt. That's true of Theodore Roosevelt's family; it's true of Franklin Roosevelt's family; and it makes it a very difficult situation. I don't know whether a President ought to have any descendants or not.

Why do you say that, Mr. President?

For the very reason that we've been discussing. It's difficult for them, because while we're not a monarchy, they look at them in the same way they do the descendants of the hereditary monarchs of Europe. They oughtn't to do that. They ought to be treated just like any other citizen. They ought to have the same chance to make their own way that everybody else has. I hope that is what will happen to my grandsons.

I have a question here: What kind of a society . . . what kind of a world do you see them coming up in? How does the America that they're going to live in look to you?

Just as much greater as this period is than the one that our grandfathers lived in, in my opinion. I wish I could live fifty more years and see how it comes out.

What changes do you see in working hours, working conditions, transportation, and all those things?

I'm sincerely hoping that the time will come when the whole world can have enough to eat and enough to wear and a place to live and the ability to raise a happy family if he wants to. That's all we live for.

But you don't necessarily think in terms of shorter hours or decrease of labor, because you think that labor is important?

When a man doesn't work, he doesn't get anywhere, and a man who counts the hours and watches the clock never gets anywhere, anyhow. But there are a lot of people who like to do that, and they ought to be allowed to make a living if they want to make a living by the clock. But a man who works all the time usually accomplishes what he wants. I was talking to a young man down in Texas who handled the meeting while I was there, and he said, "You know, Mr. President, I found out when a fellow's willing to work, they'll let him do it and give him the responsibility."

Do you see the possibility of these two grandchildren of yours being involved in a war of any kind? Of any extent?

Of course, we all hope that that won't happen, but that's what the descendants of the men who fought the Civil War thought. But the two greatest wars in history were fought a short time after that, comparatively, when you take into consideration that the time of forty, fifty, or sixty years doesn't amount to much in the history of the world. We can't tell what will happen. But I hope, if an emergency comes where the welfare of country is involved, that they'll do their duty and try to furnish everything that they possibly can to save the United States.

In other words, you want them to be trained for whatever is necessary to take their positions alongside the other . . .

That's right. Mentally, physically, and every other way.

May I ask, Mr. President, what your feeling is about the type of education that the coming generation should get in view of the fact that science has transformed the world, actually, in uncovering the ways of harnessing the forces of nature.

The fundamental education is practically the same as it has been since men began to read and write and learn. The fundamental education of the youngsters hasn't changed much from the time of Hammurabi, 2,500 years before Christ, to the present time. If they get the proper fundamental education, of course, the scientific part of the thing will come along, because if they want to go into that, all right. If they want to go into something else—if they want to go into finance or business; if they want to run a farm or anything of the kind—the background of knowledge on what's happened before in whatever they're going to pursue is absolutely essential. Then they can begin to look forward and see if they can't improve on what the old people did. That's what's been taking place in this country right along.

In other words, you want them to be educated in the basic things such as reading, writing, and knowing what the world is? What is your opinion about the necessity of a moral code?

A moral code must be fundamental with the whole business. It's necessary that for the world to continue, the majority of the people have a moral code. We have one of the best moral codes in the history of the world. Of course, these youngsters in whom I am vitally interested will be brought up on a moral code as well as a practical educational code.

In terms of their main characteristics, would you want them to be more socially minded in the sense of being interested in the lot of other people, or would you want them to be also very successful in a material sense?

They can be both. They can be both. A man doesn't have to be unsuccessful in a material sense because he's interested in the welfare of the people around him who are not so well fixed as he is. I'm just as sure of that as I sit here. I had an old grandfather who made his way—two grandfathers, in fact, who made their way in the world—from the start to the finish. They both were very successful, but they never forgot their neighbors. When one of my grandfathers died, we found a whole handful of notes of people to whom he'd lent money, and he'd never received a cent of interest or return on it. He was helping his neighbors.

Which one was that, Mr. President?

The old man who carried the train across the field—across the country to Salt Lake City and San Francisco once.* The other grandfather was the same way. He was always willing to help his neighbors, and it never hurt him any. It didn't hurt him any at all.

In other words, [in terms of] material success, you'd rather they were not self-indulgent in their own comforts?

I don't want them to be misers and consider that the accumulation of property and money is the main thing in life. Of course, they must have enough to live on, and I'm sure that they'll have the ability to arrange that. But while they're doing that, if they are more successful than other people sometimes are, they ought not to forget how they got where they are by neglecting the people who are not so successful. They ought to help everybody where they can.

In other words, you put a strong emphasis on being useful to others as one of the measures of success?

That's the basic thing in a republic. People must be willing to see to it that every phase of the population is as well treated as he hopes to be.

---

*Truman's maternal grandfather, Solomon Young, became a wealthy freighter and led wagon trains west probably in the 1840s, when he was in his thirties. His other grandfather, Anderson Truman, came from Kentucky and took up farming.

You said at one time that one of the most important conditioners for a democrat—with a small d*—is that he be at some time or other exposed to adversity.*

That's true. If he doesn't suffer adversity, he never appreciates what happens to people who do suffer it. When a fellow's been through adverse things, as all these ancestors of mine that I've been talking to you have been, they always have a kindlier feeling and softer hearts than those who never have any trouble.

Do you have any plans for subjecting your grandchildren to a little bit of adversity?

No. No, I haven't. Personally, like every fellow of the previous generation, [I hope] that they won't have any adversity. They'll have to bring that about themselves and come out of it as best they can if they cause it.

But nature and circumstance will take care of that.

That's true.

Speaking of adversity, what we were leading up to is the session you had with Averell Harriman in 1952 on that very subject. It was when, so the report seems to indicate, he approached you for your advice, and perhaps your encouragement, to his ambitions for the Presidency in 1952 that you brought up the subject of adversity with him. Do you recall exactly what the conversation was between you and him?

No, I don't. I know it was discussed, and Averell seemed to have the right attitude toward it. He did. I think he's really, honestly, what you might call a real liberal person in regard to the welfare of others. I don't think Averell's fortunate inheritance has in any way spoiled his attitude toward people who are not so successful as he has been.

The story is that when he approached you, you demurred a little bit by suggesting that, of course, you would not discourage anyone, but that his particular background involved so much privilege that he was hardly conditioned for the Presidency on the Democratic side. And you said that he . . . one had to have adversity in order to really develop the feel for that high office on the Democratic side. When he demurred, in this way, you then capitulated on the point, because he said to you, "Mr. President, I've had the greatest of all adversity: the adversity of overprivilege."

That's true. But you must take into consideration this situation. [The] settlement of the Middle West and the Southwest and the Far West in the country was brought about by the fact that the pioneers had difficult, very difficult, times. The country now has become rich and prosperous, and there are hardly any segments of the population that don't have a much better situation than was had by the people who landed on the Virginia and New England and North Carolina and South Carolina coast. During that time, it was the fellow who had made good with all the adversity who was considered politically expedient. Now that condition is changing to a very great extent. But the men who have attained political precedence through the fact that they are successful usually have the heart to understand that there are people in the world who are not as successful as they are, and I don't know that the old tradition ought to be applied to this modern age. Just because a man's successful ought not to prevent him from being a political leader if he has the heart to understand that his business as a political leader is the welfare of all the people.

You did, however, make a suggestion to Mr. Harriman, did you not, that before anyone should try for the office of the Presidency, he ought at least to have some political experience in an elective office?

That's right. He ought to. Any man who aspires to public office ought to have a background of political effort to get that office. In order to have that political background, he must have worked in the precincts in the county and the state in which he lives in order to become familiar with the program, which is necessary to be followed for a man who's successful in political office. And that's just as important as it is to train a man to be president of an insurance company. You don't go out on the street and pick up a man to be president of an insurance company unless he's had some experience in how that company runs and what it means to have a program of how mortality tables work. And in politics, you must take people who've had experience if you expect to have an administrator who knows what to do and how to do it.

To change the point to another period: When Woodrow Wilson's period was up, and this was the end of an era of world war, there followed three Republican Presidents: Harding, Coolidge, and Hoover. Some historians take the position that normally in '48 you were not entitled to succeed yourself, because the country was not only moving away from you and FDR, but it was moving away from this excitement or something to level off. You fooled them, but then in '52, we got one who was a Republican—or, at least, so designated. Do you see now the next two or three cycles—this may be off the record here—that history will then repeat itself, and that we will get a succession of Republican Presidents?

Oh, it will undoubtedly repeat itself, but if the party in power doesn't understand, that's a possibility. You see, people get tired of being held in harness. That was what was the matter after Woodrow Wilson's administration. They were very tired of the draft. They were very tired of having to do what they didn't want to do to save the country. And they went through another period where they had freedom of action, and they ran the country into the doldrums. We've got practically that same situation now if we're not careful to see that it doesn't happen again. That's the reason it's necessary to understand the background of history. I sincerely hope that the men who are Presidents in the next fifteen or twenty years or twenty-five years will understand the background necessary to keep the republic of its own free will and accord from going to pot. That's what happened to the Roman republic. It became too prosperous. It became too fat, and then they had to go into a dictatorship, and they never got out of it.

It's beginning to seem that we're going to have a house divided again. We're obviously going to have another Democratic Senate, that's statistically so, and maybe another Democratic House. Is that unprecedented in history?

No. No, it isn't. No, it isn't. There has never been a time after a President is elected . . . he usually takes in a House and a Senate with him, because a third of the Senate always has to be elected at the time, and if the majority in the Senate is not overwhelming, it can be changed along with the House at the same time the President goes in. There's one instance back when Zachary Taylor was elected when a Legislative branch was elected against the President. That same thing happened in 1956, but it doesn't usually happen.* You see, that's only twice in 106 years. But it doesn't make much difference whether the President has the Congress with him or not. If he's a leader, he'll make it work. Roosevelt had opposition Congresses. Even some of his people who ought to have been with him were against him. I had an opposition Congress in 1946, and we got some of the best foreign-affairs programs put over that were put over during that administration. . . .

*In the House, there were 112 Democrats, 109 Whigs, and 13 Free-Soilers. Democrats in the Senate had a majority of 10. In 1956, Democrats carried the House and the Senate for the next four years.

Session Eighteen

One of the best things I ever heard was Will Rogers' statement to the DARs [Daughters of the American Revolution] that were telling him how many of them were descended from colonial people who were way up there in the economic scale and that they landed at a certain time, particularly the landing at Jamestown, Virginia . . . Will Rogers said he was very happy that that was the case, because his ancestors were there to meet them. He was about one-fourth Indian.

We were dealing with the role of the Truman grandchildren and what their position in society was going to be if you had any say about.

Well, my statement—I think part of it is on the other record—was that all I wanted them to do is be good citizens and do their part in the community, and if the country came to an emergency, to furnish the services necessary to show that they are citizens of the country. I don't care about trying to tell them what they ought to be or what they have to be or anything of the kind. That's going to be up to them. It doesn't do any good for the old folks to interfere in the raising of a family of the next generation. That's the job of the mother and the father of that generation. Of course, grandparents have a special interest in the grandchildren, but they ought to keep their noses out of the raising of the children.

You were referring to that situation in connection with the new estimation you make of men of wealth in terms of their ability to appreciate the lot of those who don't possess wealth and be able to serve them sympathetically and with devotion.

I was trying to make it plain that conditions have changed radically from the time the country was settled, because the people who came to the colonies in Massachusetts and Virginia, North and South Carolina, and Georgia were people who were trying to find a better position for themselves. They were

Transcript, Friday morning, October 23, 1959, part two.

all poor; they were all down in the dumps as far as their welfare was concerned; and they moved westward under the same conditions. People from all those eastern colonies moved west because they thought they could better their conditions, and it became a tradition in America that a man to be in high political office must have come from a log cabin or something of that kind. Well, there are no more log cabins. We've got to take men for what they're worth, no matter what their financial condition or their economic condition may be. If they've got it in 'em, they can be just as good as the fellow who was born in a log cabin if they're willing to work at it and try to do it right.

In this same vein, a good many of our tourists are going all over the world giving the impression that we are rather economically overprivileged—that we are on a spending spree and we put materialism ahead of everything else; that we show off and spend and are reckless about the use of money.

You know where that came from? It was originated by Richard Harding Davis, who tried to make out that one American was worth a dozen of any other race or creed or color, and we've got to get over that.* They'll find that the people of all countries are of the same stripe if they get down and study the thing very carefully. There's no reason in the world for the showoffs to represent the people of the United States, because most of the people of the United States are just good, honest, everyday hardworking people. When these people who accumulate enough money, sometimes too suddenly, take trips abroad and try to show off, they don't represent the American government or they don't represent the American people. I hope the foreigners or the people whom they visit will find out if they'll come over here and take a look that the general run of the people are just as easy to get along with; they're just as kindly. They have no sense of being better than anybody else, although they want, in their communities, to be honorable and upright and have positions of standing. If we can get the people in other countries to understand that we're not trying to make a, well, what you might call a whole bunch of showoffs who want to make out like they're better than anybody else in the world, the sooner then we'll have a better feeling with all our allies and our friends.

Mr. President, we have had several successions of generations of different peoples and races who have come to this country, and each have had their own problems. At the present moment, there seems to be the problem of integrating Puerto Ricans. You have had a special contact with the Puerto Rican

---

*Davis (1864–1916), who was born in Philadelphia, became a famous American journalist, editor, novelist, and war correspondent who covered the Spanish-American War, the Boer War, and the Russo-Japanese War. He died of a heart attack shortly after returning from the trenches on the Western Front in World War I, where he reported on the suffering of noncombatants and destroyed cities.

situation because some wild-eyed Puerto Ricans attempted to assassinate you during your Presidency. What do you feel? Do you think that their problems are insurmountable?

No, I do not. Puerto Rico is overpopulated, and some of that overpopulation has been moving out into the United States, because they're citizens of this country. The fact that we set up a self-government in Puerto Rico and gave them an opportunity to do their own developing down there has made them among the happiest people in the Western Hemisphere. Some of those who have migrated to New York and other cities in the North have found some difficulty in getting along. But you'll find a vast majority of them are just as good people as any of the other people in the community.

What do you think of cultural exchanges between ourselves and not just the people behind the Iron Curtain, but all nations. Have we done enough of that?

No, but we've been at it for quite a long time. It's a very good thing. There's hardly a week goes by that I don't address some students from some other country who have come over here to study in the schools that are particularly interested in that program, and I find them to be just the nicest kind of youngsters, and they're as anxious as they can be to find out all they can about the country. That's one of the best things that we can do. . . .

How do you feel about the cultural development of the United States?

I think it's progressing. I think that the cultural development of the United States is one of the greatest things in the history of the world. It's called the melting pot. We've taken the Irish, the Italians, the English, the French, the Germans, the Swedes, the Norwegians, the Danes, the Greeks, and the other parts of Western Europe and put them together and have made a population which is made up of all of them, If you go back at least two or three generations, you'll find that the grandparents or great-grandparents came from one or the other countries, and you can't tell these youngsters of the present day from the native-born Americans. And I mean by "native-born Americans" those who came three hundred or four hundred years ago, when the first settlements were made on the eastern coast. One of the best things I ever heard was Will Rogers' statement to the DARs* that were telling him how many of them were descended from colonial people who were way up there in the economic scale and that they landed at a certain time, particularly the landing at Jamestown, Virginia, which was the first one, if I remember correctly. Will Rogers said he was very happy that that was the case, because his ancestors were there to meet them. He was about one-fourth Indian.
(Laughter)

*Daughters of the American Revolution.

Mr. President, do you think that in terms of our . . . one development, . . . we have had medical development in this country that's been extraordinary. Do you think that we ought to do something on an organized basis to share that with the rest of the world?

Oh, yes, I do. I've always thought that. And the rest of the world has things in the same line to share with us, and that's one of the finest things that can happen. But when it's shared, it ought to be shared on a basis where the people that need it most can make the most use of it, and that's not the case at this time in this country. I've been working on that ever since I became a United States Senator from Missouri.

What did you do as Senator from Missouri in connection with this?

I tried to get an arrangement made so that the public-health organization could be expanded in such a way that the people could have the benefit of all these wonderful things that have been discovered for the prolongation of human life. What I was after was to get the people to set aside a savings fund so they could go to the hospitals on the basis that the hospitals have to have the money to keep running and that they could pay their doctor bill. That was the only objective, and they had a right to select the hospital; they had a right to select the doctor that they wanted. Yet the American Medical Association got a complex which caused the defeat of that program, and I thought to myself that they were cutting off their noses to spite their faces, and they were.

In other words, you didn't interpret patriotism in the sense of acute nationalism, where whatever we achieved and whatever we did was a proud possession to be limited exclusively to the people of this nation?

No, no. In public health, everything that can help the human being to have a better life and be more healthy ought to be a worldwide program.

Well, you [went] along with Point IV and all the other programs of your administration. Wasn't that part of the new, broad view of the responsibility the United States felt at the same time that it made these enormous strides for improving the lot of other people?

That was the intention. If you read the message, . . . and the reason it's called Point IV is because it's the fourth point in the message of 1949 after I was elected [inaugurated] on January 20, . . . you'll find that the objective was to help people help themselves. There was no intention to try to make them believe that what we had was the best thing in the world, but if we had something that would help their situation, we wanted to make them perfectly welcome to use it. That was the objective, and that's the way it worked.

It was rather an extraordinary thing even for a generous country like the United States, after having gone through two terrible wars, to undertake a program in face of another ideology setting itself up where it was going to siphon off from other nations for its own development. We were going to siphon off from ourselves and make a transfusion to other nations.

No, not necessarily siphon off from ourselves, because the expense of the Point IV Program is very, very small. It only needs instructors to show the people of the other countries who can make use of it our engineering ability, our ability to organize, our medical background and what we have to offer that will make people more healthy, and our inducements to them to increase their food production and things of that sort along the same lines that we'd been able to do with our agricultural colleges here in this country. It was a matter of information and teaching and help. It didn't have anything much to do with the expenditure of money.

Mr. President, there was a thing in connection with that. The charity, the care that starts with the charitable disposition to save people from want and to rescue people, is what charity normally does. This was an undertaking to improve the lot of people. That's a new philosophy.

That's right, and it wasn't charity at all. It was to help people to help themselves improve their conditions, and they can do it if we show them how.

Where in the history of the United States was the birth of this idea originated? Where did this start, this interest in the lot and the improvement of other people?

It started, in my opinion, when the settlement of the United States west of the Allegheny Mountains took place. People always helped each other. They were willing to help each other, and the people from the colonies and the states from which they came were willing to help them . . . improve their situation. We also had help from Britain and France and Germany and the investment of funds over here to help the development of the Great West. That was the idea behind this Point IV Program.

In other words, in a sense, it was the philosophy of the Middle West, which developed . . .

That's exactly right. It developed in the Middle West entirely.

And that has become now a permanent feature of the American character and the American outlook?

Developed principally in the "Show Me" state, Missouri. Missouri helped to settle all the other Western states and made a contribution to them in one way or another, and that's where I got the idea. . . .

How did we help in the settlement of all the other Western states?

Their treks to make a settlement, most of them started from here. All but the Mormon trek—it started from Council Bluffs, Iowa, and we sent them up there to Iowa from Missouri. The idea was always to see if there was not something better just over the horizon, and they kept going and finding that place over the horizon and making settlements. The first thing you know, we had the whole West the most prosperous place, I think, in the whole country. And it's growing so fast that I think they're going to forget what they had from the East. Maybe they won't. I hope not.

So in a sense, the growth and the interworkings of the states, particularly the State of Missouri, had a lot to do with flowering this whole idea of . . .

That's true. All those great trails which took the first settlers to the West originated right here in Independence, Missouri. When those people carried their trade goods to the Far West and as far southwest as Chihuahua and Mexico, it made a very friendly feeling with all the peoples concerned. One of the things that we have to be ashamed of is the treatment of the Plains Indians while that was going on.

In that connection, Mr. President, can you recall now some of things that have guided you and things that you heard your father and your grandfather and all those that you knew of your living ancestors in their philosophy?

Their philosophy was to be kindly to their neighbors, to help them wherever it was possible, and then, in return, the neighbors always returned the favor when it was necessary. It was a custom in this part of the world, especially with the farm owners, to exchange work, and there was no financial consideration in connection with it. If a man had a hundred acres of wheat and another fellow only had forty, they'd exchange work just the same as if they were on an equal basis.

And basically that philosophy, you feel, has been carried over into American thinking and American conscience?

I think it has. I'm sure it has. If you study the Marshall Plan and the Point IV Program, that's exactly what they are.

We've had missions of all kinds. These missions you speak of as the country moved westward, there were all kinds of religious missions right in their wake. There were economic elements who were working to follow trade, but for a long time we've been sending missions from the United States all over the world—not only those who originated in their own work, but we've started some of our own, like the Moody Bible Institute and those. As against the religious missions or the medical and economic missions, which would you encourage?

I'd encourage them all. They're equally necessary. You have to have them all if you're going to get successful results.

Isn't there some question, just to develop this point a little, as to whether a right to encroach upon the religious rights or preferences of other people is a good thing or a bad thing from the standpoint of our relations with those people?

A very good thing, because we have a lot of Baptist missions in Russia, and we're teaching them morals again, which is what they need worse than anything I know of.

After all, too, Mr. President, we remember that it was Paul on his mission that started the spread of Christianity.

There isn't any question about it. Paul and Barnabas's trip to Asia Minor started the thing.

That raises a very important point, because we're dealing now with an anti-Christ, anti-religious-of-any kind society that seems not only to be growing, but also to be attracting other nations. And a lot of their work has been done as the result of exploiting the failure of the church, and particularly the Catholic church. Would you say that this failure of Christianity is in part responsible for the growing success of communism?

I can't consider that there has been a failure. I can't start out with a premise that there has been a failure. There have been difficulties, just like difficulties come with everything else, but it's my opinion that the moral code of the Christian church is about as good a moral code as there is in the world. There are moral codes in existence in other parts of the world. The Mohammedans are very, very nearly based on the same code as Christianity. The Buddhists have a moral code that is excellent, and so have the Confucians in China. But we think we have a better one, and if we can argue with them and convince them that that's the case, they usually adopt it.

These moral codes have never quite succeeded in preventing a war by a people that practice those. You have it in the Middle East. These Mohammedans, or Muslims, are very involved . . .

It has always been the part of the hierarchy of every religious organization to be careful to instill into the common membership that the other one is absolutely wrong. There has been more blood shed over Christianity than any other one thing that ever came into the world. And the Mohammedans contributed to that because they like to fight the Christians, and the Christians like to fight them, which is all wrong. There isn't any sense in it at all, because when you get right down to brass tacks, they all believe in the honor and the welfare of the individual, and sometime or other, we'll come to the conclusion where we can sit down side by side and let the other fellow do as he pleases. We do that right here in this country. We've got all brands of Protestants and Catholics and Greek Catholics and the Church of England in this country, and we don't cut each other's throats because we don't exactly interpret every verse in the Bible just alike.

One of your great aims while you were President, an aim that you couldn't carry out, was to try to get all the great leaders of the world's different religions to adopt a certain common front.

That's right. That's right. I wanted the moral forces of the world to make a common front against the unmoral forces, and we got pretty well along with it. It made quite an impression on a great many of the countries and the leaders of the religious sects in various countries. The people who were most violently opposed to it were the Protestants right here in the United States.

And they, of course, apparently were afraid of the Roman hierarchy, weren't they?

That's right. That's what the difficulty was.

Would you mind repeating one of the things I've often heard you tell? It's the story, I believe, about the Prime Minister of Pakistan who said that if you'd come to his country, you'd see the tomb of Christ. [Liaquat Ali Khan visited America in May 1950 and addressed Congress. Columbia University awarded him an honorary degree.]

That's right. He was the Prime Minister of Pakistan. He came to see me, and he said if I would come to Pakistan, he'd take me up into Afghanistan and show me really where Christ was buried. He said His tomb was up there.

When you visited the Pope [Pius XII], did the question of universal religion or the bringing together of the religious sects come up?

Yes, it came up. We discussed it. It had already been discussed by Myron Taylor,* who was the representative of the President at the Vatican. Myron Taylor had discussed the matter with the Archbishop of Canterbury and the Archbishop of Cheshire in England and with the head of the Huguenot sect in France and with the head of the Lutherans in Holland. And in Germany, the Bishop of Berlin, [Otto] Dibelius, I believe was his name, had had the matter put up to him. They were all very careful listeners. Some of them were not impressed; some of them were. Then, when this discussion came to a head in the United States, the Protestants in this country were the ones who caused the most trouble and caused the upset. The efforts were not carried through,

---

*Cf. Myron Taylor, ed., *Wartime Correspondence Between President Roosevelt and Pope Pius XII* (New York: Macmillan, 1947). In 1949, Taylor retired from this post, and two-and-one-half years later, Truman, likely with an eye to the 1952 election, nominated General Mark Clark, a notable Mason and Protestant, as ambassador to the Holy See. Because of Protestant clerical rage, Clark withdrew his name, and a furious Truman recognized that he did not have sufficient Senate votes. No replacement was named until 1984: Hamby, *Man of the People,* 572–73.

but I think it would have been a wonderful thing if that could have been carried through. The Metropolitan of Istanbul ... was very much interested in it, as was the Pope.

Do you think some time in the future that thing ought to be taken up again?

I think it's going to have to be done unless we want the moral code of the whole world upset by the communists.

Are the communists going to sit still for this, or are the communists going to continue to gain in their regressive measures, as they have in Hungary and Poland and elsewhere, of religion?

I think enough missionaries in Russia, as the Baptists are doing now, will keep them from doing anything upsetting, because the general run of the people in Russia are just as anxious to have a moral code to lean on as we are.

Why do the people need missionaries to awaken in them the natural instinct that they all have anyway?

Why did the Hebrews need prophets to keep reminding them that they better stay in the groove or they'd come to a bad end? That's just the human animal over and over. I don't know why. In the long run, they come to neglect the very fundamental thing which made them great. I don't know why that's true, but it is.

You believe that religion is still a very necessary force to sustain the moral and to check the possible tendency toward immorality?

I don't think there's any doubt about it. The great leaders of the world have all been leaders of a moral approach to a way to live, and that's what it amounts to. I had a chance down in Dallas just the other day to talk in a Methodist church on the background of our government and where it originated. I began with the twentieth chapter of Exodus and went through the Sermon on the Mount and showed them where the prophets were all preaching the same thing that we're trying to live by.

But did all of our Presidents practice and profess any serious involvement in any particular religion?

Every single one of them belonged to some religious sect in the United States or other.* There's never been a Catholic in the Presidency, but there's been a man in the Presidency of nearly every ... Protestant sect.

Who was the most devout President?

---

*Presidents Jefferson, Lincoln, and Andrew Johnson did not have religious affiliations: cf. Joseph Nathan Kane, *Facts about the Presidents: A Compilation of Biographical and Historical Information,* 6th ed. (New York: H. W. Wilson, 1993), 336.

I can't remember. Most of them had to swear a little bit once in a while to make things go.

Was George Washington a devout churchgoer?

He was a good Episcopalian, but he knew more words—as many words as any other general that ever commanded an army.

Was anyone ever in the Presidency who adopted . . . or who had undergone a change of religious affiliation while in the Presidency?

I don't think that happened until quite recently.*

I see. Enough said!
(Laughter)
Could we then get to the Presidency itself? What is happening to it during this twentieth century? How is the Presidency of the United States evolving both from the standpoint of authority and centralization and [from the standpoint of] its importance in our government?

I don't think there has been any serious evolvement of the Presidency. I think the Presidency has always been just what it is now. The operation of the Presidency has depended entirely on the man who's in there to do the operating. George Washington was the first President. He had the most trouble, of course, because he was trying to set up a nation, and he was the most abused man in the Presidency. After his administration and after John Adams's administration, it became perfectly apparent that there was an attempt being made to make a ruling class in this country, and Jefferson overturned that. Then things went along until the financial interests of the country began to feel that they could control it. Jackson took care of that when he came in. Then people began to feel that they ought to have all the authority at home that was centered in Washington, the city of Washington. That brought about the War Between the States. Lincoln happened to be a man who understood the Constitution and who knew what ought to be done—which the principal thing was to save the Union. You remember, he said he would be for slavery if it would save the Union, and he'd abolish slavery if it would save the Union. After his time, the financiers came back into power again, along in the [1890s], and the great industrial organizations like the railroads thought they could control the country. Then along came the Interstate Commerce Act and the Anti-Trust Act, and the financial head of the government eventually . . . the same thing happened that happened in Jackson's time, when he moved the control of the finances of the government into the hands of the big bankers. Woodrow Wilson came along and remedied that with the Federal Reserve Board. Then, during the 1920s, it went back, and Franklin Roosevelt came along and brought the headquarters of the finances of the country to Washington, the capital of the government.

*Eisenhower joined the Presbyterian church after he became President.

These people are from the same line of those who think they're better than somebody else and know better how to run the government than anybody else. I don't believe in that. I think every one of these powerful organizations ought to be in complete control by the government of the United States and by the government of the various states. Every once in a while, somebody has to come along and wake the country up, just as I was telling you about religion a while ago, to be sure that the government is what they think it is.

Mr. President, there's so much talk from time to time, and it certainly has been sharply emphasized from the Roosevelt administrations through yours down to the present, of the cost of government. The people are making so much ado about the huge deficit and about the ...

Do you know the reason for that? There are a great many people who want to go back to the time of Alexander Hamilton, with a population of about 3.1 million people in the country. They have the idea that the federal government of the United States can be run at the same price as it was in Washington's administration. I can tell you an example of how things happen. The Secretary of the Treasury in Jefferson's administration [Albert Gallatin] went home with a headache and couldn't sleep all night because the country had a debt of $80 million. Well, at that time, when they had that debt, there were about 5 million people in the country. There are probably 170 or 180 million people in this country, and the government itself and the operation of the government naturally grows in conjunction with the population, the way that business and the banks and everything else increase. You've got to meet the situation. You couldn't run the Chase National Bank in New York on the same basis that you ran the Manhattan Bank back in 1800.

In other words, the increase in the national debt doesn't necessarily mean that you're increasing the liabilities of the nation?

The increase in the national debt was brought about, of course, by two world wars, by the fact that the people were not willing to assess themselves— that is, to tax themselves to meet the cost of the thing as it went along. Of course, when a debt of that kind accumulates, if it's not properly handled, the cost of the operation of that debt becomes almost unbearable. Then you're bound to have trouble. I think eventually we can easily work out of the situation when the assets of the United States government are ten to fifteen times what the public debt is. That's a greater backlog for the soundness of that debt than most bankers are willing to accept for the ordinary fellow. If he has assets of twice what he's trying to make a loan for, why, they're perfectly willing to make it to him.

In other words, the collateral is there, and it's solid, and there's no problem?

Why, of course. I don't think it's any problem at all. And I know it can be handled, so it won't be any problem if he gets somebody who knows how to do it.

Mr. President, on the point of the Presidency, you expressed yourself as considering it subject mostly to the personality and the whims, almost, of whoever happens to be the occupant of the White House.

That's just as true as it can be.

... We were suddenly thinking, Mr. President. Where does that expression, "I'm from Missouri! [Show Me!]" come from?

It came from the West. When the Missourians went West, they were always the butt of ridicule. They would ask a man where he was from, and if he said he was from Missouri, they'd say "Oh, yes, you're one of those birds that has to be shown!" And then they had an ugly word that they called the Missourians, which we won't put in the record.

About what period was that? Do you recall?

Oh, before the Civil War, when the trains ... when the communications began to be carried between the West Coast. You might say anywhere from '35 to '49.

Was there any reason why the Missourians were not being well received?

They were always considered skeptical. That's one of the reasons.

Oh, I see. How about the contrariness? That's another dimension.

That's part of it. That's part of the whole thing. You see, when a Missourian had to be shown, he was not to be taken in by every Tom, Dick, and Harry that came along.

... Let's get on to this very important meeting, historically, that you had with Princess Elizabeth at the time of her visit to the United States. ... There was one thing that we need to refresh your mind on a little bit, and that is the immediate moment when she got off the plane, and you were there to receive her.

That's right.

The report we had was that she ... was frightened to the point where she froze, and she apparently indicated to you that she was going to have a little trouble making her little talk, and that you sidled over to her and very quickly said to her in these words, "Daughter ..." Did you use the word daughter?

No.

You didn't?

No, I didn't. I always addressed her by the title to which she was accustomed ... [I told her] not to be uneasy about the situation—that everybody was friendly to her, and all she needed to do was just to tell them what she had on her mind, and she wouldn't have a bit of trouble. After we got up on the stand, when I introduced her, I said (under my breath), Now, go ahead. Nobody's going to hurt you at all. And everybody will be happy with what you have to say, and then she didn't have any more trouble.

I see. You did refer to her as the fairy princess, and you did add a little about the fact that as a youngster, you were always dreaming of meeting a fairy princess.

Yes.

And now you'd met one.

But that statement was made at the White House when she presented me with the overmantel as the present from the King [George VI]. Then's when I introduced her as the fairy princess, which as a youngster I had always dreamed about.

I see. What did she say to you directly? You escorted her to the Blair House when you came back, or whatever it was.

... I think that's the morning that we had a family breakfast—nobody but our family and she and the Duke. She told me that that was the nicest affair that she had attended since she'd left home.

You have had warm relations with British royalty ever since?

I always had. I always had. The King, her father, came to see me when I came back from Potsdam, and we spent an hour together on the *Renown* and also on the *Augusta*. The King gave a luncheon for me on the *Renown*, and we had all the distinguished men who were along.* But he and I had a private conference all to ourselves. He was a very able, sensible man. He knew what was going on, and he wanted to find out what had happened at Potsdam, and I told him very frankly what had happened. He understood. He didn't have to have anything explained. You state the case to him, and he understood exactly what you were talking about, because he kept up with things.

Mr. President, you were going on to say you put her up at the Blair House, and then you talked to the chief of protocol regarding a party.

A party for the youngsters. That is, the children of the people who were associated with the White House, like the members of the cabinet and those

---

*Truman flew to Plymouth, England, in August 1945, immediately after the Potsdam Conference. There he boarded the heavy cruiser *Augusta,* which had carried him to Europe. He met King George VI aboard the battleship *H.M.S. Renown.*

members of the staff. Any of them that had youngsters under seventeen or eighteen were invited to bring them to the Blair House, and they had a reception for them. [Princess Elizabeth] telephoned over to our side of the house and asked [my daughter] Margaret if she wouldn't come over, and Margaret went over to see what was wanted. She asked Margaret if she should wear her tiara, and Margaret said if she didn't, there'd be a terribly disappointed bunch of youngsters. So she wore it.

All right. Let us jump very quickly to another very important conference you had, which needs to be filled out a little bit more, and that's the meeting you had with the chairman of the Federal Reserve Board at the time that you were laying down the policy again that the interest rate on the federal debt had to be kept down and the guarantee of parity—that is, the face value of the bonds—had to be continued by the Federal Reserve as a policy . . .

. . . That's right.

. . . with instructions which were supposed to have been as follows. That you said to him [William McChesney Martin], "Before I appoint you, after which I would have no recourse except to ask you to resign, but I couldn't fire you, I'm going to have to have a commitment from you on how you're going to conduct and carry out the policies of this administration as far as money policies are concerned."

That's true, and he agreed to go along with the policies I wanted, and I never had any more trouble after that. And the bonds never went below par as long as I was President. We never had any trouble financing the federal debt at all, and we always financed it below the going rate for commercial paper.

Just for a change of pace here, do you have any one single regret in all the years that you have been in public service? Major regrets?

There are a great many things that could have been done better, but I don't know with the information and the circumstances at the time how the situation could have been done any differently. Of course, a man can contemplate a thing after it has happened and he sees the results and wonder why he didn't do something else. But I never thought about those things. I went on from where the incident took place to the next one, and if I found out that I'd made an error, an appointment that I could not call back, I went on and tried to get the thing remedied by doing something else. It doesn't do any good to cry over what's already been done. You've got to go straight ahead all the time. Of course, when you make a mistake, and everybody's bound to make 'em, the best way to do is to correct them and admit that they've been made. That's all there is to it.

In some areas, you had not a choice of right or wrong, good or bad, but a choice of evils, didn't you?

That's right. And we had to take the one that we thought was the least harmful. I think that's the best way to express it.

That's very good. Could I change over here to the business of origination of legislation? Should it originate with the Congress under the present executive setup, with the Bureau of the Budget and all the facilities it has for research, or should it originate with the Congress and be brought to the President?

The President's duty as set out in the Constitution is to inform the Congress on the state of the Union and recommend such measures as he thinks are necessary to meet conditions as they are. That's the policy that's been followed ever since the government was organized. When the President makes his recommendations to the Congress, those recommendations are the first order of business on the agenda of the Congress. Appropriation bills, of course, he tells them how much money he ought to have to run the government. Then he talks about the policies that are necessary to be followed in foreign affairs. He talks about the policies that he thinks ought to be put into effect in domestic affairs, and he recommends legislation in each case. For some reason or other, the Congress has had the habit of asking the President if he won't send them outlines for bills, which has been done, oh, ever since I can remember. As nearly as I can find out historically, I think that policy originated in very early times, and it's always been followed.

The President is a part of the Legislative branch of the government. That's the reason he has a conference every week with the floor leaders of the House and the Senate. When he does that, he explains to them what he has in view by certain things which he has put in the messages. He sends down many messages in addition to the message on the State of the Union, and nearly every one of them will require some sort of legislative action. The Congress, of course, is at perfect liberty to introduce any legislation, themselves, that they want to, and they do introduce anywhere from 8,000 to 12,000 bills at every session. But there is only a very, very small percentage of those that are even considered. A vast number of them just die in the committee, because that's all the Congressmen expect. They want to show what they had done. They've got a perfect right to do that, and I've done it myself when I was in the Senate.

You have vetoed a great many bills. This administration has vetoed more than 145 so far, and there's a unique situation there where only one of all the bills that has been vetoed by the President has been overridden by the Congress. The situations are different in the two instances, are they not? Between your vetoes and the present?

Oh, yes. My vetoes were principally when I had an opposition Congress. Of course, these vetoes are for an opposition Congress, and they're vetoed against policy. You see, I set out the policy, and when I had a Congress of the same political stripe as myself, I got most of the things done that I wanted. But sometimes they passed legislation, particularly in the Eightieth Congress, that was terrible for the country, I thought, although some of it was passed in the next Republican Congress when the present occupant of the White House came in. But the President's theory of government is to carry out a policy on which he's been elected. When he tries to carry out that policy, of course, he has to veto certain bills, which are sometimes passed for the purpose of putting him in a bad light with the country. Most of the bills which have been vetoed lately have not been for that purpose, because there has been no recommendations along the lines of even the Republican platform of 1952, and that's what the difficulty is. I think I've made it perfectly plain in my statements around the country that this government, by veto of bills that are in the public interest, is not for the best interests of the country.

Isn't there a peculiar switch there, that when a bill is introduced by the Congress in opposition to a President's wishes, all he has to do to have his veto sustained is have one more than a third?

That's all.

If, on the other hand, a President suggests legislation and it passes by a majority, it's in.

That's correct.

So any legislation that is introduced by the President has a better chance of survival than legislation that's introduced by a legislature where it's not quite in harmony with the President's views.

You'll always find that . . . , when bills are introduced and referred to committees, the first thing that the [committee] chairman does is to find out what the attitude of the White House is toward that proposed legislation.

Mr. President, I've seen you campaigning on many occasions, and it seems, as you've gone along, that you've gotten stronger and more assured in your appearances. How do you like talking to the public?

Oh, I like it, all right. I like it, all right. But if I had my way, I wouldn't do as much of it as I have done in the past, because it's a very strenuous program to continually address large crowds of people. The difficulty, particularly since I've left the White House, is that there is not the protection that a President has. People are kept at a distance when the President is talking, unless he wants to see somebody that he sees in the crowd and has them brought up. Take last night at a small meeting that I had at the Muehlebach Hotel. After it was over, I was practically mobbed by everybody there, and it was mostly Republicans, and they all wanted autographs. They wanted to know what I was going to do and how hard it was to get to the Library and things of that sort. I just had to fight to get through the people to take me out of the place, because they were pulling both of my arms off shaking hands.

Yes. That has happened very frequently, and I recall the most arduous one was recently in Boston, when you were so pounded on your back and your hands.

That's right. I had a terrible time getting out, and that's always the case in Boston. They mob me every time I go there—in a friendly manner, you understand. It's not hostile.

Yes. One of the problems, then, since you've left the White House is that whenever you speak, it's much harder work?

Yes, it is. It's very difficult. Usually, they have arrangements made so that we can get out by a back door or a side door. We don't want to hurt anybody's feelings. All these people are as friendly as they can be. They merely want to say that they've had a chance to talk to and shake hands with the fellow who's been President of the United States.

Do you recall today your first speech, or when you made your first speech?

Yes. I recall it very vividly. It wasn't a speech. It was a thoroughly rattled fellow on the platform who couldn't say a word. It was when I started to run for the nomination for eastern judge in Jackson County. They had a meeting down at Lee's Summit. They had all the candidates there, and when it came my turn to talk, I couldn't talk. I was scared to death!

But you gradually got so that you could . . .

I got used to it. I got used to it.

You still are a little bit nervous every time you approach the platform to make a speech?

There isn't any question about that, because unless you are worried about what the effect is going to be, you don't get ready well enough.

All right. Could I jump to a very important subject here: the President's press conferences and your opinion about the new method of allowing full quotation of the President's statements for a press conference? Do you feel that that method is more conducive to keeping the public informed than a careful sifting and a rephrasing of the President's statements for clarity?

I never thought it was well for a direct quotation . . . for the press to be able to make direct quotations from the President at a press conference. The objective of a press conference is to inform the country what is going on and what the President thinks about certain things. When it comes to the point where they're going to transcribe it and make a show out of it, why, it's not a press conference. I got used to press conferences when I was on the committee to investigate the national defense program. I had a press conference every week, and sometimes every day whenever any important things were coming up, but I learned very early that the press men want information. But sometimes, if you're not careful, they'll want to make a kind of a headline by embarrassing a fellow whom they're questioning. I soon got used to that, and it didn't happen very often. But I think the early handling of a press conference, which was established in toto by President Roosevelt, is the best way to handle them. That's my experience I'm talking from.

Why the indirect quotation, though? Why not a straight quotation, a direct quotation?

The objective of the indirect quotation is to make the person who's quoting the President amenable to amendment if he makes a misstatement on the facts. That's the principal reason for it. Of course, if they're going to make a direct quote of the President ... they're going to have television and radio and things of that kind, they'll have to make direct quotes. But I never was for making a show out of the Presidential press conference.

What do you think has been the result of President Eisenhower's going over to the other extreme of allowing ...

I don't think it has helped him a bit. I really don't. I really don't think it's helped him a bit, because the handling of a press conference is a job that requires extreme skill. It was always my experience that I could find out more about what the editors and publishers were thinking and what the public was thinking by the questions they asked than they found out from me by the answers.

You were also concerned, weren't you, that some answers given to spontaneous questions [were] therefore spontaneous answers [and] might be harmful to the country?

Yes, and they garbled many a one, as you remember. The "red herring" incident was nothing in the world but a garbled statement by a fellow who wanted to cause me embarrassment. That was the case.

Yes. You didn't use the expression "red herring." Somebody questioned you.

Somebody asked me if what the Congress was doing was not on the order of a red herring to drag something across the tracks so they wouldn't have to go ahead and do what was necessary. I said yes, and that's all there was to it.

And then they hung the red herring on you?

Well, of course. And that's exactly what it was. I afterward said that that's exactly what it was. It was nothing but a red herring to keep from working on legislation that should have been worked on.

On the same subject, with the advent of radio and television, do you think it is possible for the President to avoid being directly quoted?

If he's going to set up a show with radio and television, he's going to have to be directly quoted, because he is directly quoted when people look at him on television. They can see what he's doing, what he says, and how he looks, and everything of the kind. I never felt very keenly toward that sort of a situation. Of course, now the news broadcasts and the television news broadcasts have become great rivals of the ordinary press reports of incidents as they take place. I may be behind the times. It might be that if I were there to do it over again, I'd do it the same way.

Both you and President Roosevelt used radio and television not as press-conference vehicles but as opportunities for making direct reports to the people and presenting to them certain very important problems which you were considering, or [for] explaining to them decisions that you were about to make or had made?

That is absolutely the case. At least once a week, every once in a while within ten-day periods, President Roosevelt would make what he called "fireside chats." He had those prepared, and they were handed to all the press people so that they had it at the same time that the broadcast was made. I did the same thing, and they worked very successfully.

You kept the public very carefully informed on everything that was going on, as you informed the Congress and everybody else?

That's correct. When I sent a message to Congress, sometimes it required legislation in other than legal language, and that is what was done.

In other words, your objection or dislike at being quoted directly [on] spontaneous answers to spontaneous questions was not because you desired to suppress information or to suppress anything, but you were anxious to see that it was not only accurately gotten down but also that nothing was done to harm the conduct of the government.

That's right. So that it was not garbled. You see, those were strenuous times, and a great deal of the period was . . . of that twenty-year period after 1938 . . . in wartime. It was very difficult to keep from causing trouble with our Allies and everybody else. It was very difficult to keep from letting the enemy know exactly how we were situated. That was one of the reasons for that. It might be, when there's no emergency in the world, the proper thing to [do is] directly quote the President, but I'd have to get used to it. I don't like it now.

All right. . . . What do you see in store for the United Nations as an instrument? How do you view that in the future as a force? . . . Is there anything further that we as a nation could do to insure the continuity of the United Nations?

I think it has been very well supported by this country, and I hope it will continue to be supported by this country and all other countries. Then it will be a going concern and will be for the best interests for peace in the world. That's my idea and always has been.

And it's here to stay, in your opinion?

I know it is. If it doesn't stay, we just might as well get ready for another debacle and have all the world torn up by a turmoil that will wipe out most of the human animals on it.

I have a question here that I would like to follow through with: How do you explain the election of a Republican President and a Democratic Congress over so long a period and so important a time?

I can explain it very easily. When a man is a leader in wartime that is a field general and he's successful, he becomes a hero to the people, and they think he can do no wrong. That same thing held true with General Grant, even after his first two administrations were considered no good. He was almost nominated again in 1880. People have hero worship in their bodies and in their minds, and you can't get rid of it. That's the principal reason for it. They didn't like what he was doing, but they didn't want to hurt his feelings by firing him.

Would you say then that the election and reelection of President Eisenhower was not a party victory but a personal victory?

Personal victory. Of course it was. Of course it was, because there had only been one other fellow who had the same experience he did with the Congress, and that was Zachary Taylor under exactly the same circumstances.

Then the election of Eisenhower was not as a Republican, but as a glamorous figure?

Yes, as a hero of World War II.

Do you think that the Democrats could under even circumstances, equal chances, come up with a victory this time, even if there was no law to prevent Eisenhower from running again?

I'm morally certain of it. I'm morally certain that it can be done, because they found out just exactly what they got themselves into by too much hero worship.

You've gone up and down the country, and that is the sentiment that you've been running into?

I find it all over the country just the same way.

I have seen a very interesting article calling you a much more mellowed and kindlier individual. Would that be a suggestion that you're not as fighting an individual?

Not the slightest.

Session Nineteen

The Japanese citizens who've been here for two generations were terribly mistreated in the Second World War, and I think the proper thing is the development of Asia itself in a way that will take care of their population.

Mr. President, will you take these five [persons], one by one . . . some of the things that you would like to say about them, and then we'll put them together?

The presiding officer at this meeting is the Honorable Adlai Stevenson who is the former governor of Illinois and twice the nominee of the Democratic Party for President. He is a very fine man and was a great governor of Illinois. He has had a great deal of experience politically, and I sincerely hope that that experience has done him a lot of good.

All right, Mr. President, let's start with Senator [John F.] Kennedy.

Senator Kennedy is the young Senator from Massachusetts—a very able Senator and one that seems to be very well liked in the Senate. He has had some very important political experience, particularly with regard to the labor situation. His residence is Massachusetts, which is rather far east for the Middle West, but, if he keeps on displaying his abilities, I am very sure that he will receive the consideration that he deserves at the convention.

What about Senator [Hubert H.] Humphrey?

Senator Humphrey is one of the ablest liberal Senators in the Senate. He has been to Russia. He's been around over the country in a great many places. He has a very wonderful intelligence, a keen intelligence. He seems to understand the conditions with which the country is faced. He lives in Minnesota, which is rather far north for those of us in the Middle West and the Far South for complete consideration as a President of the United States. But you never can tell what may develop. I think I proved that in '48.

Transcript, Monday morning, November 16, 1959.

What about Stu Symington?

(Lowered voice) There's another one. The governor of California.

That's right. Pat Brown.

Pat Brown is the able governor of California. I like him very much. He seems to understand the whole political situation and what it's all about. He was attorney general for the State of California for quite some time and was overwhelmingly elected to be governor of that great state. He's doing a wonderful job as governor of California. I've had several interviews with him, and I think he understands the political situation better than anybody that I've met for a long time. But California is in the same situation as Minnesota and Massachusetts are. They're on the borders of the United States, and the great voting center is in the middle of that great country.

We're getting to Mr. Symington.

The Senator from Missouri, the Honorable Stuart Symington, is a personal friend of mine. He liquidated the surplus property that was left over after World War II, some $40 billion of it, and did a very able job of it, with no breath of scandal. He then liquidated the Reconstruction and Finance Corporation [*sic*] at my suggestion, and I finally made him Secretary for Air, in which he served very efficiently. He's a Senator from my state, and it's rather embarrassing for me to tell you just exactly all his qualifications and what he might do under circumstances with which we are now faced. I like him very much, as I do all the other members of the organization of the Presidential candidates which I have named. At the convention, I think that the Democrats will have a chance to select the man who's best qualified to be President. And that's what we're going to be forced to do if we expect to win this next election.

Isn't it going to be rather difficult for you as the former President not to incline just a little bit toward one or the other, because you are in the unique position of being able to mark the paper to that very high office on the basis of experience?

Well, here is the situation that will have a greater effect on these things. The delegation from Massachusetts, naturally, will be for Mr. Kennedy. The delegation from Minnesota, with its able and distinguished governor, will naturally be for Senator Humphrey. The delegation from Michigan, with its two very good United States Democratic Senators, undoubtedly will be for the governor of Michigan [Gerhard Mennen Williams], who has been elected four, five, or six times as governor of that great state and who has turned it from a Republican, backward-looking state to a Democratic, forward-looking state. That same thing will happen with regard to the other candidates who are up for consideration. Stuart Symington comes from Missouri and is a

United States Senator from Missouri. He occupies the seat which I occupied in the Congress of the United States. You'll have to draw your own conclusions as to what my inclinations might be when the time comes for an announcement.

But at any rate, you are going to make an announcement before the convention meets, are you?

I hope to be able to make an announcement before the convention meets, unless some difficult situation should arise, such as asking me to make a keynote speech at the convention—in which case, I couldn't announce for anybody.

Do you still feel that the three principal barriers or considerations in connection with a candidate for the Presidency—religion, geography, and national origin—should continue to have any weight in the choice of a candidate for office?

No, I do not. But I don't have anything to do with setting that out. It has weight in selecting a candidate for office, and there's no way to overcome it. That's been the case ever since the first Democratic Convention was held in Baltimore, Maryland. . . .

Mr. President. If I may, I'd like to get quickly . . . to go back to some personal matters and then to go on to other things. You've had a very important event in your life when Margaret married.* Would you mind talking a little bit at length, if you wish, about how your feelings were for her and the marriage?

Well, of course. I was, naturally, and so was her mother, very much interested in that event because our whole hope was for Margaret's welfare and happiness, and when she decided on the man she had agreed to marry, both Mrs. Truman and myself were very happy and very hopeful that he'd be the sort of a man that we thought Margaret ought to have. And I may say to you that it's turned out just that way, and we are very happy with our son-in-law and always have been, ever since Margaret was married.

Did her choice come as a surprise to you? Because down through the years, even when she was tiny, there had been so much talk about [whether] she was going to marry this man or that.

That's true—especially while we were in the White House. There was hardly a week went by that somebody wasn't set up by the newspapers as the

---

*The Trumans' only daughter, Margaret, married Elbert Clifton Daniel, then an assistant editor of the *New York Times* and earlier a foreign correspondent in England. They were married on April 21, 1956, at the Trinity Episcopal church in Independence, Missouri.

man whom Margaret had picked for her husband, but that didn't happen. This all came about after we left the White House, and I am just as sure as I can be that the marriage of Margaret and Clifton Daniel was one that was a love affair between both of them. It has shown that conclusively since.

Did it come as a surprise at all to you?

Of course it did! The old man's always surprised when his daughter picks a husband.

Mr. President, now you have two grandsons. That was a very exciting experience, too, wasn't it?

It certainly was. One of the most wonderful things that can happen to grandparents are grandchildren. These two young men seem to be perfectly happy and healthy and seem to be full of vim and vigor, and I am very sure that when they come out to visit us this coming Christmastime, we'll have one of the best times we've ever had in our lives.

Mr. President, may I ask this? You have frequently spoken about the problems of children and the grandchildren of the President. Can you give us a little bit of a lengthy story about what you recall of the children of past Presidents and the problems they face?

The children of Presidents . . . the children of rulers of any country are always in a severe limelight, and it's very, very difficult for them, and it's difficult for any President's family. It doesn't make any difference whether it's to the third and fourth degree related. My brother had four boys and a daughter, and my sister was a very strong part of the family. She never married because she stayed with her mother until her mother died at [age] ninety-four. But all those members of my family were continually in the limelight, and the limelight was aimed at them for the purpose of finding something wrong, not something right. They never found anything wrong. Never in the world did a single member of my family, nor did a single member of Mrs. Truman's family, in any way ever embarrass me as President of the United States.

It's a very difficult role for the relatives of the first degree or the second or fourth degree to live after a member of the family becomes the head of the government of the United States, on which the strongest limelight in the world is cast. I am as lucky as a man can be. Not a single one of my family ever caused me the slightest embarrassment, but it must have been a terrific strain on all of them, because it didn't make any difference what they did, no matter if they just turned around on the street, why, some reporter had something to say about it. But they never did in any way cause me the slightest embarrassment. They never did anything that I thought was wrong, and I am as happy as I can be about that. I think that that's a record compared with some of the administrations which have been in the White House of the United States.

Can you cite some examples of difficulties which others have had?

A great many of the Presidents had no really close relatives or had no children. But those who did have children always had some serious difficulty. The one that comes to mind, particularly, is John Tyler, who had two sets of children. He had seven children by his first wife and seven by his second wife—all wonderful people. But those two sets of children didn't get along. Some of his second set were still living in Washington [D.C.] when I was there. I was acquainted with a couple of them, and they told me very frankly that they didn't care much for the first set of their father's children and that things were not exactly as they should have been in that part of the family. It wasn't true, but that's the way families operate as they go along. The son of Millard Fillmore burned all his papers. Why, I don't know. The son of Abraham Lincoln, Robert Lincoln, who was the president of the Pullman Company, was discovered in New Hampshire by Nicholas Murray Butler burning his father's papers. I've come to the conclusion that Fillmore's son and the son of Abraham Lincoln were rather ashamed of the origins of their fathers, and they wanted to be sure that the things that didn't show that they were aristocrats to begin with were destroyed. That's my own opinion. It doesn't amount to anything at all, but that's what really happened.

General Grant had some children who behaved remarkably well. You never heard of any sort of a maneuver of any of Grant's children doing anything that was wrong. Grover Cleveland had three children, I think, but the son of Grover Cleveland decided that his father didn't know the right road in politics, and he became a strong, old-line Republican and a lawyer in Baltimore. I think maybe he's still alive, but he was, I think, very much ashamed of his father's career as a Democratic President of the United States, and that's too bad. Theodore Roosevelt had a number of children. All of them were fine people. They never caused him any embarrassment at all. He had a daughter by his first wife. Then he had several sons and other children. I think he had six children all together, and one of those sons was killed in the war, the First World War, over in France. They always acted honorably by the reputation of their father, and they are still doing that. I am acquainted with Theodore Roosevelt, Jr., and some of his children, and they are just the finest people you want to meet.

Woodrow Wilson had three daughters. One of his daughters is the mother of the dean of the Washington Cathedral. They were the finest kind of people. I don't think any of Wilson's daughters ever caused him any embarrassment whatever. The [Franklin] Roosevelt family is still alive, and they have to speak for themselves. In fact, I think Jimmy Roosevelt, the oldest son, has written a book on the subject, and they tell me it's a very interesting document.* I don't know anything about the inside workings of the Roosevelt

*Roosevelt and Shalett, *Affectionately, FDR.*

family. I liked 'em all and knew every one of 'em personally. One of them went off the reservation. John turned out to be a Republican and came to Independence one time and made a Republican speech to thirty-five people. He didn't attain anything. I think that was on account of his marital connections, and I never held it against him. At the present time, there is one son of the White House now, and he's a very fine man—John Eisenhower. He has behaved remarkably well, just as my family did, and I feel very happy that that's the case. . . .

Now the reverse of the medal, Mr. President. What handicaps do you think that the children or descendants of Presidents have?

They have this handicap: They can't do anything without being in the public eye. They can't do as they please. They can't have their marital relations without front lines, headlined pages about it. They can't go into any kind of a business unless they're accused of having promoted positions which their relative had in the White House. It's a very, very difficult situation. My sympathies are with them always.

And, of course, many of them are compared frequently to the President.

Why, naturally. Naturally. That's customary, but, then, you must always remember that in the selection of a President or the ruler of any country, there is difficulty to find the man able and capable of doing the job. We've had great Presidents. We've had Presidents who were not so great. We've had Presidents who didn't care whether they were Presidents or not, and we also are expected to have that situation continue, because we are a free government. That's true of governors; that's true of Senators. If you go through the list of the Senators of the United States—there have been a great many of them— you'll find very few of them who were outstanding. Most of them were just the ordinary run of people, as it should be in a republic.

It shouldn't be the custom of the publicity agents of the country to try to compare the children of the President [to] the President, because they don't have the opportunity, and there's very little chance of their ever having it. There have been only two families in which two members of that family were President of the United States: That's the Adams family and the Harrison family.* The people were not as happy as they should have been with the successors. But that's part of the setup in this republic of ours. The worst thing about the Presidency is in some instances where mud has been thrown at the President's wife. I don't think there was anyone in the whole history of the country as unmercifully persecuted as Mrs. Abraham Lincoln, and she didn't deserve it. Other Presidents' wives have had mud thrown at them, but you take the general run of the Presidents' wives, they've been much more carefully treated and much more respectfully treated than have the Presidents themselves.

*Presidents John Quincy Adams (1825–29) and Benjamin Harrison (1889–93).

You have said, sometimes, a President really shouldn't have any children. Is it because of that?

I've often thought that those Presidents who didn't have any children had less embarrassment than those that did have.

Why is it that a President has so much difficulty in deciding on a successor, or in even being able to find a successor suitable to carry on the work?

The principal reason is that we live in a republic, and it's not really the prerogative of the President to decide on his successor unless he wants to support a man that he thinks will carry on his program. In a monarchy, of course, the oldest son, the oldest daughter, or whoever happens to be in succession are the ones under consideration. But a President, actually and theoretically, has no more right to select his successor than any other man in the government of the United States, and the convention usually takes care of that.

But you had a little difficulty in '52 finding someone suitable, and FDR had it on two different occasions. There is some feeling that the reason he continued to succeed himself is because he couldn't find anyone to carry on this work that he had begun.

That may have been true. I don't know for sure whether that was true or not; but, then, of course, the President of the United States is the head of the party which elected him, and he naturally has some say in the convention when it meets at the end of his term as to who shall be the nominee. But very few of 'em have ever had any luck in obtaining the people that they really wanted for successors. Old Jackson succeeded in nominating Martin Van Buren the first time, but after that, the convention took care of the thing on its own hook. The same thing's been true of Republican Presidents. They've had very little luck in naming their successors, except in the case of Theodore Roosevelt when he named William Howard Taft. Then, when Taft didn't go along with him and he fell out with Taft, he split the Republican Party and caused the nomination and election of Woodrow Wilson, which was one of the finest things that ever happened to the country. So maybe a thing of that kind may be for the welfare of the people. You can't tell. No President can really select his successor, although most of them when they're in control of the party machinery try to do it. Sometimes, as was Theodore Roosevelt, they're woefully disappointed with what they've done.

. . . We have a different situation in our country now. We have gone from being a self-contained nation to where we are now a world power or we're a world leader, a leader of the free peoples, etcetera, and it takes a special kind of experience and a special kind of a man to carry on the Presidency in that sense these days.

Well, that's what a lot of people think. But I think I'm a shining example of the fact that that's not absolutely necessary. Sometimes it can be carried on by somebody that knows nothing.

We're having, off the record, a rather shining example of someone who is not carrying on and doing a last-minute job at salvaging it.

No, that's not a shining example. That's a continuation of examples that have been set . . .

However, when you have talked about continuity of government, you don't mean the continuity of the man or the continuity, necessarily, of any policy of an administration. What you mean, isn't it, Mr. President, is that certain parts of government just transmit easily, and that men succeeding each other should keep in touch with each other?

Yes. It's a continuity of the Constitution as was put into effect by George Washington, and it was finally continued by Abraham Lincoln and Old Man Jackson and Grover Cleveland. That continuity has been remarkably well done in spite of difficulties through which the country has gone, and I think it will continue that way. That's the reason I'm spending a lot of time trying to explain to the younger generation in the schools and colleges what they have and what they have to do to keep it. The reason for the organization of the government under which we live—it's a remarkable thing that this government is the result of all the experience from the . . . oh, from way back in the beginning up to now. When the men who sat in that Constitutional Convention—they were not old men—they called them the fathers of the government, and most of them were in their forties. I don't think there were but two of them who were beyond fifty years old. They had studied the history of the government. They knew it from the beginning, and it's very seldom that you find even a Congress with a dozen men in it who know how government originated or what its use is. But we've been exceedingly happy and lucky in this fact that we've had a continuing government since 1789 which has been for the welfare and benefit of most people. When it gets off the beam, why, they're in a position to turn it over, because they can elect whom they please to be President and head of the government.

Do you think we have reached the peak of our development and that we are now getting into a state of decline? Have we lost some of that original pioneering spirit that made us a free people and a . . .

I can tell you . . . I can cite you a shining example of that trend of thought. It was in the paper this morning about how we were going to the dogs. In the 1840s and '50s, the Duke of Wellington and Lord John Russell were Prime Ministers of Great Britain. Each of them made the statement, if I am not mistaken, that they were glad to pass on because the British Empire was going to the dogs. For the next forty or fifty years, the British Empire attained its greatest period. I think that's what we're faced with. I think we've got the greatest period in history facing us. I'm not at all pessimistic about what will happen, because I'm just as sure as I can be after talking to all these youngsters . . . I've talked to thousands of them, looked in their faces, and I'm perfectly willing to turn over the welfare of the country to this coming generation. I think they know a damn sight more than we did when we started.

What is your view of America? What do you think of when you think of Americans, Mr. President?

I think of the government of the United States as the greatest government in the history of the world, and its continuation is absolutely essential for the welfare and benefit of the most people in the world. There has never been a government in the history of the world on the winning of a war who's been willing to rehabilitate its enemies instead of robbing them and killing off their population and putting them out of business. That's the first time in the history of the world that that's been done, and that's the result of the Marshall Plan and the Point IV Program. If and when these people understand exactly what the victors in the Second World War really did, I don't think there's any chance in the world of our going backward. I think we're going forward along that basis which is based on only one thing, "Treat others as you'd like to be treated." We never wanted to go into either one of those wars. We were forced into both of them, and when we came out, we did our best not only to help our friends, but we helped our enemies.

In other words, Mr. President, when you think of America, you think in terms of the government that it has, which helps distribute the greatest amount of goods to the greatest amount of people, but that it is also a generous America that . . .

That's right. They're the most generous people in the world. All you have to do is to read any morning paper and find out where some person has had all sorts of trouble, and the first thing you know, everybody in the whole neighborhood and sometimes over the whole country is trying to help them out. Everybody takes an interest in a pup when he gets caught in a pipe, and they'll go and try to help him out. And if that's the case, I don't there's anything to worry about the heart and the welfare of the American people, because it's right.

How do you find an American, then? We talk about a Frenchman; we talk about an Englishman; we talk about a Russian, a German. What's an American?

I don't like to call a citizen of the United States or any citizen of any other republic in the Western Hemisphere "Americans." The citizens of the United States are a mixture called a "melting pot." They're made up of all the races in Europe and other parts of the world and they've come out with a generation,

I think, that's better than any generation that ever came about. If you want to talk about 100 percent American, you must go back to the inhabitants of the United States at the time that the people landed in Massachusetts, in Virginia, in South Carolina, North Carolina, and the people who landed in Peru and Mexico. In those two countries [Peru and Mexico], they found one of the greatest civilizations that the world has ever seen, particularly the Incas in Peru. In the United States, the Indians, they call 'em—they weren't Indians, they were North Americans and South Americans. Columbus thought he'd discovered India, and that's the way these people came to be called "Indians." But you'll find some of the greatest patriots in the history of the world in those Indian leaders who were fighting for the welfare of their people. They were the 100 percent Americans.

Then you would feel that these so-called DARs and super-patriotic organizations are a little bit out of line?

No. I think it's all right to have them around, because they instill into the youngsters a feeling that they have the greatest country in the world, and it helps....

May I just try to get one further note? Stanley Baldwin, who is Prime Minister of England, said that when he thought about England, he thought in terms . . . he thought in certain picturesque terms about the fog over England or the colorful and beautiful scenery of his land. Do you think in terms at all of America . . . of this country, especially, in any particular phase?

I think of this country always in terms of people—people who are making the country what it is. It's wonderful to have beautiful scenery. It's wonderful to have recreation places and things of that sort, and I'm glad we have them. We have some of the most beautiful ones in the history of the world, particularly here in Missouri. But the people make the country, not the scenery or the fogs or anything else.

May I then switch you over to another projection here? How do you feel about the future of Germany?

I'm very optimistic about that for the simple reason that Germany has had two terrible lessons in what it means to try to be the aggressors in regard to their neighbors. The Germans—the ones that we have in this country—are kindly people. They're some of the best stock that we ever had in this country, and I'm just as sure as I can be that if Germany has the will to get along with its neighbors that it appears to have now in [its] agreements with the six-nation program—with [its] free interchange of goods—eventually, Western Europe will come out of this situation in a manner which will continue the civilization which caused this country to be great, because we've got parts of the civilizations of every country in Western Europe which made us great. We also have immigrants from every part of the world nearly. We had the importation of people from Africa, and some of those descendants of the African slaves which were brought over here are some of our best citizens. I had one of them in the State Department.* I made one a federal judge in Philadelphia, and I made several of them ambassadors to various countries. They've turned out to be just the same sort people that the rest of the world is when they have the proper opportunity, the proper education, and the proper association.

In other words, the traveling back and forth, the opening of a frontier, the opening up of trade, the making of trade treaties—those are all producing a condition in Europe that is like that of the United States where the people are becoming interrelated, intermarried, and . . .

That's right. I think that's what eventually will work out. At least, I hope it will.

In that relationship, what do you feel about the future of Russia— the Russian people?

The Russian people are good people. . . . [W]hile I was President, I had reports from people—Russians themselves—who had emigrated to this country and had gone back to see their people and their relatives, and the fundamental basis on which the Russian people live is all right. They're good people. I've talked to several men who've been in the Navy in the Black Sea and other places, and they said whenever they made presents to the youngsters of Russian people, they always wanted to make a return for it. When they have had a chance to understand what free government means . . . you know, the Russians have been in totalitarian government ever since Ivan the Terrible, and it's been a terrible government all the way down. But the general run of the Russian people, from their troops to Moscow, they're good people. Whenever they find out what free government means, I don't think we'll have any trouble with them. They'll do just what the French did after Louis XIV and the time of Louis XVI.

You feel pretty much about people of all races in all categories as being essentially good?

I do. I'm sure that's true, because why would we have all these great philosophies by which men are supposed to live if that hadn't been the case? You take the Chinese: They had a philosophy of government and of living together under Confucius. You take the Hindus: They have a philosophy that's almost parallel with the one under which we live. The Buddhists have the same thing. You take the Mohammedans: They got their whole fundamental basis of law and order from the Hebrews, just like we did, and it goes to show that in the long run they fathered two opposing trends of thought. One of them believes in material things; one of them believes in spiritual things. Eventually,

*Ralph Johnson Bunche.

the people who work under a spiritual approach to this thing and have a moral code—we have one of the greatest moral codes in the history of the world—they usually come out all right. I think every people in the long run want such a code, and I'm an optimist. I don't try to make out like I know all about it, but I know that's true from my viewpoint. Maybe I'm wrong.

Mr. President, this tribute you got this morning is overwhelming, you say, because there's nothing you can do for them in making ...

That's true. You see, they come in here and present me with a plaque and a gold card. This evening, I'm going over to a dinner, where they're going to do the same thing and make a $5,000 contribution to the Library, and it's all as a result of what's happened in the past. That's what makes it so good. There's nothing I can do for 'em now.

You've had quite a week. You've had kind of an interdenominational week. How did it go?

Well, on Tuesday, I went over to Liberty to talk to the students of the school over there. There are about 1,200 of them. They're Baptists. It's a Baptist school.

What school's that?

William Jewell College. I talked with them on what the President does and what he has to do and then let them ask questions. They asked me some most intelligent questions. Then, on Friday afternoon, a panel made up of representatives of every one of the organizations of the Catholic young people that were here came over to the Library, and the Bishop from Kansas City and St. Joseph [Missouri]—he's the same man—and the Bishop of Rochester, and two or three monsignors were in charge of them, and they spent their ... I told them that this Library was set up for a historical program for the study of the Presidency, and they asked me questions.* The first one, of course, was, "Would there be anything against a Catholic being President of the United States?" I said if he was qualified, religion ought not to interfere, because the First Amendment of the Constitution of the United States made the church and state absolutely separate.† Then we went on from there. Then, on the next morning at eight o'clock, I talked to about 6,500 of them at breakfast on the Presidency. Then, yesterday morning, I went to Columbia [Missouri] to dedicate a plaque at the Jewish chapel down there in honor of Eddie Jacobson, who was my friend and partner during the war and afterward. This morning, we have had various people in here who are interested in talking to me on

---

*Bishop John P. Cody of Kansas City, Missouri, and Bishop Lawrence B. Casey of Rochester, New York.

†See Session Twelve and Session Fourteen for Truman's anxieties regarding a Catholic becoming President.

various subjects. It's a great thing, I'll tell you, but it looks as if now that I am strictly nonsectarian. The Baptists on Tuesday, the Catholics on Friday and Saturday, the Jews on Sunday, and Monday, I'll probably have every religion represented at this presentation of this plaque tonight. . . .

. . . We are now at a point of asking you where you think Israel is going to go, since you had a lot to do with establishing this state.

I am of the opinion that the Israeli Republic will continue, and it should, and the reason I feel that way is because if the proper development of the Mesopotamian valley is made and the development of the Nile River is made, there'll be plenty of room for Israelis and Arabs in that section, and they ought to get along together. I've got a plan, which I think would be a very satisfactory one, to take the elevation of the Mediterranean Sea and transfer enough water over to the Dead Sea valley for the creation of a power program which would make the whole eastern Mediterranean coast an industrial situation. Then, if the Mesopotamian valley is developed as it was in the time of Babylon and Ninevah, it'll support 40 million people. The Nile valley will support 20 million more than are there now. Then you'd have the whole integrated, industrial setup. If that were done, you see, . . . a siphon could be engineered that would take care of [the 1,260-foot fall between the Mediterranean and the Dead Sea] so that power could be created that would make an industrial center of the coast of Palestine—that is, the eastern Mediterranean coast—all the way from Aleppo down to the mouth of the Nile. I have always been of the opinion that there wasn't any use of the Arabs and the Jews fighting with each other, because they're first cousins anyway.

Do you think that the fighting is likely to subside, or do you see any kind of an armed conflict in the Middle East?

It's going to take leadership to keep the armed conflict from taking place, and we've got to have the leadership.

From where, sir?

It has come from the United States.

What role do you see for Japan in the Orient?

Japan is one of the most progressive nations in the whole world. You remember when they were awakened by the trip of our admiral over there . . . Admiral [Matthew] Perry. The Japanese then began to realize that there was something besides the Oriental view of things. They became one of the great powers and were one of the four great powers in the First World War. Then they did just like every organization that comes up very quickly. They began to think that they were greater than anyone else in the world, so then, of course, they had to be brought down, which was done in the Second World War. They are still one of the most progressive peoples in the world, and if their progressive instincts are guided in the right direction, they will be one of the greatest of the countries for peace in the world that we have. The Philippines and the development of Japan will make that part of the world part of the bastion which will, in the long run, convince the Chinese that they're on the wrong track.

You think there's room enough in Japan to accommodate Japan's needs for its people?

No, I do not. No, I do not. They're going to become a completely industrial nation, and these other nations, like India and Indochina and China itself, will have to depend on Japan for industrial progress. It can be done if we can get them to understand each other and go ahead and do the work like they ought to do.

We have two new states [Alaska and Hawaii] now, with lots of room at least in one of them. Would you invite some of them to come over?

No. I tell you, there's a kind of an objection. The Japanese citizens who've been here for two generations were terribly mistreated in the Second World War, and I think the proper thing is the development of Asia itself in a way that will take care of their population. I think it can be done.*

What is your feeling about China, Mr. President?

China now has gone Russian, and the Russians, I think, are afraid of them because they have 650 million people to Russia's 200 million, and Siberia is not populated. The only place for China to expand is in Siberia, and that's where one of the world's trouble spots is. That's the reason that Khrushchev is trying to be so friendly.

Mr. President, I'd like to get back again to something personal. We've asked you these questions before, but perhaps you have another feeling about it today. What advice would you want to give to your grandchildren?

(Quite amused) Well, Bill, the advice to grandchildren is usually wasted. You know, if the second and third generations could profit by the experiences of the first generation—we'll take this time as first generation—we wouldn't have a lot of trouble. But those youngsters all know they're smarter than their ancestors and that they can improve on them. They do just like this present administration did. They throw out everything the former generation had and try to start out on their own, and they have to have that whole experience that the other generation had. And that's what this last administration did in politics.

---

*In his 1948 State of the Union message, Truman called upon Congress to provide legislation regarding the claims of Japanese Americans who had been confined in relocation camps during World War II because of their racial origins.

Could I ask you specifically what you think your grandsons' education should be?

I think he ought to be educated in every line, particularly in humanities. He ought to know all about the things that constitute reading, writing, arithmetic, geometry, trigonometry, Latin, Greek, and things of that sort, and then he ought to be informed on the history of the modern world from the time of Genghis Khan to Ivan the Terrible and the last of the Roman Empire to now. Then he's got to make up his own mind what he wants to do. I got most of my ideas on how the world runs from the King James version of the Old Testament. It's one of the greatest historical documents in the history of the world. Every trouble that the human animal has is set out, and its remedy is in there if you know where to find it.

In other words, you believe a Bible should be read?

Why, of course. It ought to be read. I read it fifteen times—maybe more—before I was fifteen years old.

What's your feeling about your grandsons in public service, in public life?

I think they ought to go into public life, whether they do it from a private position or whether they do it as a profession.

And one more question about military service, because you have always felt . . .

They ought to have it. They ought to have it. I told the youngsters yesterday that I always thought that everyone ought to have military service. I tried to get into it before I was twenty-one but couldn't because my mother and father were unreconstructed Southerners, and they were afraid I'd have to wear a blue uniform. And I did when I got into the service at twenty-one.*

I don't know whether we have time for this one: I would like for you to tell us why you prefer to live in a small town.

Because in a small town, you know everybody and his connections, and you know their sisters and their cousins and their aunts. When you live in a big town, you don't know anybody. It's just the same as living in the desert.

What is the benefit of knowing everybody in a town?

They're always friendly, and they can always give you support and advice when you need it, and they're always ready to help you if you're in trouble.

---

*In June 1905, Truman became a charter member of Battery B, 1st Battalion, Missouri Field Artillery of the National Guard, and continued training until 1912. In April 1917, as a first lieutenant, he helped organize the 2nd Missouri Artillery: Truman to Jaime Watkins, June 8, 1959, Papers of David M. Noyes, Box 1, Truman Library.

And, of course, your grandchildren are being brought up in a big city.

I'm going to take care of that! I'm going to take care of that. (Much laughter)

Over and above the communion, the social factor, in a small town where you do know your people, doesn't it pose some problem where you want to have in your post-Presidential position a measure of privacy?

Oh, yes. Of course it does. But, then, when a fellow's fool enough to become a notorious character, he has to take what comes.

You don't like to be exhibited in a church, but you don't mind being exhibited in your own town?

No, no. I don't want to make an exhibition of a religious program for the simple reason that I don't think that's fundamental. Religion starts in what you believe and what you act, and when you try to make a program out of it for public use, why, it's wrong.

Then the symbol of the President no matter where he goes or what he does is a permanent thing that is not necessarily related to his continuing in office?

That's true. You can't get out of it.

Mr. President. You have in the past talked about one or two superstitions you have, as everyone has, even if lightly taken. You haven't gained any new superstitions, have you, since your return?

(Amused) No. No, I haven't. . . . Those superstitions are superficial. Let's put it that way.

Very good! That's interesting. How did you come by some of those super-stitions?

Oh, just hearing the old wives talk. We had old Negro cooks who had been slaves, and they instructed us in things not to do and what to do and what was what and so forth. They knew all the changes of the moon and why it went on, and we listened. Then, after I had a chance to read the background of what made the moon changes, why, it didn't have any effect. But it's nice to talk about.

One more thing about a more basic subject: When you were in the course of making important decisions—really big ones—did you at any time sit down with members of your family and talk?

No, no. I talked to Mrs. Truman about everything that came up, but the major decisions were accomplished after a long study of all information available, no matter where it came from. In the long run, the jump decision that I made in the beginning was usually the right one.

What do you mean by "jump decision"?

Immediately make a decision when things are put up to you, and you don't want to tell anybody that you've made that decision, but you want to get all the facts and not try to get those facts to support what you think you're going to do. [You] get all those facts and put them together and, in the long run, if your heart's right and you know the history and the background of these things, it'll be right. . . . You'll find nine times in ten [that] the decision off the cuff, in the long run, is the correct one.

That's an intuitive decision?

That's right. It comes out of your mind.

In other words, your experience has been that nine out of ten decisions which you have made swiftly and immediately, although you may not even have told it to your associates or assistant, have been right?

Well, when Dean Acheson called me in Independence and told me that North Koreans had invaded South Korea and asked me what to do, I said, Get the United Nations agreement that we're going to prevent that from happening. I was thinking of Ethiopia when that happened. If I hadn't known about Ethiopia, I'd have had to study everything in the world to find out about it. And we did the right thing!

And everything was confirmed? Every bit of information?

Every angle that we did: . . . I called them all together, had them sit around the table and find the conclusion was just . . . because the history shows that that was the right thing to do.

Then your judgment came into play immediately as to what was the right thing to do and what would have been the wrong thing to do?

That's exactly what I thought.

Session Twenty

In the War Between the States, Lincoln had to fire five generals. The only man who stayed through the whole difficulty was Robert E. Lee. Every effort has been made to debunk him, and they've had no luck in doing it.

Mr. President, one thing that I'd like to talk to you about is the so-called battle of the generals that we have seen since the end of the war, in which the generals accuse each other of either ineptitude or difficulties in carrying out a campaign. What is your overall impression of this?

It's customary. You never want to let it worry you. It started back, way back, in the beginning of history. You'll find the difficulties between Caesar and Pompey and all the rest of those great men of that time were exactly what they were between the generals of the Revolutionary War. There was only one man in the Revolutionary War that they couldn't attack, and they charged him with doing things that could have been done better by somebody else and almost fired him at one time. And that thing was true ... that same situation was true in the war with Mexico.

Excuse me, Mr. President. What general were you referring to in the Revolutionary War?

Washington. General Washington. He's the only one that they couldn't upset. Then they abused him like a pickpocket after that. And the same situation developed in the Mexican War between Winfield Scott and Zachary Taylor. In the War Between the States, Lincoln had to fire five generals. The only man who stayed through the whole difficulty was Robert E. Lee. Every effort has been made to debunk him, and they've had no luck in doing it. The same thing was true of Stonewall Jackson. They found fault with what he did. They found fault with [William T.] Sherman, and they found fault with all the other generals who were mixed up in that war. If you remember in the Spanish-American War, the admirals got into a fuss—Admiral [William T.]

Transcript, Tuesday morning, November 17, 1959.

Sampson and [Commodore Winfield Schley]—as to who had won the battle of Santiago. It didn't make a bit of difference. They won the battle, but they talked about it, I think, for ten years. The same thing, of course, . . . happened in the First World War, but not to such an extent, because we weren't there long enough to cause trouble. We were over there at the final windup of that war, and General Pershing was in complete command. He did a whale of a good job, and nobody has thrown any bricks at him, although some people tried. . . . You'll find these controversies will go on indefinitely. Then, when history is written, the facts in all probability will come out, and we'll find out who really did the job.

Mr. President, have you any opinion about any of the leading generals or admirals of this Second World War?

I certainly have! My opinion of General Marshall is that he was the brains and the man who really made the military organization work, both in the Pacific and in the Atlantic.

What about some of the Allied officers?

The Allied officers were all good men. But, of course, you must understand that when the newest of the Allies, the United States, was put in complete command of the situation, it was a hard pill to swallow for those men, who knew that there was no military talent in the United States. But they were fooled, they were mistaken. And they're going to keep talking about it for a long, long time to come. But I don't think it will do any harm to the reputations of those men who really made great contributions to the winning of the war. That's particularly true of General Marshall, General Bradley, and General Eisenhower.

What is your feeling about General Eisenhower as a man and as a soldier?

He was a good soldier. He did a good job. He coordinated the Allies, kept them together, made the crossing of the channel and the landing in South Africa, and came out of the situation, I think, in very, very good shape.

What about any of the admirals of the war?

Admiral [Chester W.] Nimitz was the greatest of the admirals in the war. Eddie [Ernest J.] King was the Chief of Naval Operations, and he was a cranky old man. I used to have difficulty with him all the time, but he did the best he could and, I think, handled the Navy in good shape. But the greatest of the admirals was Admiral Nimitz.

How much do you think that generals or admirals are able to plan out in advance the conduct of a war? Don't they also have to be subject to the whims of events and unexpected events, especially?

There isn't any question about that. But they're the only ones who are capable of working out a military program with the idea of winning the objective which they had in view. In this last war, [the objective] was to wind up Japan and Germany in such a way that they could not do what they did again.

Mr. President, do you recall at this moment anything about what General Marshall may have said to you which you haven't so far talked about?

General Marshall was always in conference with me right straight along before the Germans surrendered, which they did a short time after I took over. Then General Marshall went to China and did a wonderful job over there. If he had had the right support from the bureaus back home, I think he would have been successful in that program. He became Secretary of State and did a remarkable job for me. Then he became Secretary of Defense, and he was one of the ablest administrators that I ever came in contact with who had a military background.

What was his character? Could you describe it at all?

He was absolutely reliable. He was an honorable man, and his word was just as good as his bond. He never forgot what he said.

Didn't you try to persuade him to leave a record or memoirs?

I sure did. That's right. I tried to get him to go ahead and arrange things so that the facts could be known—the conditions through which he had to go when he was Chief of Staff of the United States and, really, Chief of Staff of all the Allies, as far as that goes. But he never would do it. He was of the opinion that the facts would come out. But along toward the last after they began attacking him politically, he had made up his mind that he'd go ahead with it, but he didn't live long enough to finish it.

Was he pretty frail when he left the service?

Oh, he was, yes. He had been in bad health for quite some time, long before he retired. Then, when I called him back into service, he had a great many difficulties physically, but it never affected his mind in any way.

You went to see him at his home several times since his retirement?

That's right.

Anything occur there while you were with him?

Oh, we always had the warmest associations, and we spent a great deal of time talking about things that had happened and the misinformation that had been put out in regard to some of them. That was the reason I was very anxious for General Marshall to set down his viewpoints from his position, and I am as sorry as I can be that he didn't have a chance to finish.

Did he have anything to say to you about his protégés and your successor?

No. He never talked about individuals. If I'd ask him a point-blank question, he'd answer me with two or three words as to whether I could rely or I couldn't rely on them, and that's all he ever said.

Didn't he get somebody to take down some notes from him, or did he dictate some notes?

Yes, he did. He did. The papers and all the things that were accumulated in General Marshall's office from the time that he started with General Pershing back in the First World War are accumulated at the Virginia Military Institute. There has been a gentleman in charge down there who has been working to coordinate those things, and he was the one that was working with General Marshall in a manner which we hoped would be General Marshall's memoirs, but they never got it finished.

May I ask you now about Secretary Stimson? What was your opinion of him?

He was a great man. Secretary Stimson was one of the men who understood the world situation as well [as] or better than anybody I came in contact with. He was absolutely honorable, and you could rely entirely on what he told you. I can give you an instance of this. I was making investigations in the Senate as chairman of the committee investigating the national defense program and I found out that the United States government was spending immense amounts of money at Pasco, Washington, and down in Tennessee on the Manhattan Project. I sent some investigators to take a look and see what they were doing. Secretary Stimson called me up and said that he would like to talk to me about the situation, and I told him that I would be glad to come down and see him. He said, "No, I don't want you to do that. I'll come down to your office." He came down and told me of the importance of this project and that it could cause an immense amount of difficulty if anything should occur that would put it into the limelight. I said, "All right, Mr. Secretary. If you tell me that the thing ought not to be looked into at this time, I'll follow your suggestion." And that's just exactly what I did, and I made no mistake, because, after all, it was the atomic bomb.

He was the first one to see you after you became President—no, the second one. [James F.] Byrnes was the first.

It's hard to tell who the first person I saw was after I became President. If I'm not mistaken, I think it was the Secretary of State, Mr. Stimson . . . uh, [Edward] Stettinius. Stettinius. And then, of course, I called all the cabinet members in before the swearing-in ceremony took place, and then we had a cabinet meeting right afterward, which was made up of all the members of the cabinet that had served with Mr. Roosevelt.

Why did the Secretary of War [Henry L. Stimson] leave your service?

Because of his health. He didn't live very long after he left. He left under my protest. I didn't want him to go, but he had a man as Undersecretary of War who was a very able person, and that was Bob Patterson. He served with me for a long time after that, and I had just as much confidence in him as I did in any other cabinet member.

You continued your relations with Secretary Stimson after he left the service?

Oh, yes, we were in correspondence on various things all the time concerning things that had happened—both pro and con—and I have quite a file of correspondence with Secretary Stimson.

Mr. President, Dave had a suggestion. You have named those Presidents which you thought were strong and those that were not so strong. Would you mind looking back over history now, quickly, as Dave suggested? Who were the great justices of the United States?

There were a great many of those justices, but they are in the same fix as a great many of the Presidents. Their policy and program has never been followed through. Now, the only reason that we know so much about Chief Justice [John] Marshall was because Senator [Albert] Beveridge of Indiana took a personal interest in him and wrote a biography of him, which has made him one of the famous justices. We've had a great many other great justices, and we know very little about them, but the present Chief Justice now is trying to get that worked out so we will know who were the great justices of the court during its period of operation from 1789 to today. And we'll find out a great many things about the justices of the court that we are not now familiar with, because that is a dry subject. When the court makes a decision on a majority vote and they all turn in an opinion, you never know which one is correct. Only the technical lawyers ever look at those decisions. I'm sincerely hoping that when Chief Justice Earl Warren gets through with the project that he has in view, we'll know a lot more about the courts than we do now.*

How do you account for an ostensibly impartial body taking two opposing attitudes, one being conservative and the other liberal, and was accentuated by the famous team of [Oliver Wendell] Holmes and [Louis D.] Brandeis?

That's part of our system of government. We were just talking about the fact that both parties in our two-party system were made up of all branches of thoughts, from liberal to conservative, and it's good for the country. The

---

*Justice Warren wrote *Current Constitutional Issues* (New York: Da Capo Press, 1971); *The Republic, If You Can Keep It* (New York: Quadrangle Books, 1972); and *Memoirs* (Garden City, N.Y.: Doubleday, 1977).

arguments that those justices have over the decisions that they have to make is one of the best things that happens in this country.

Now, is the Constitution a conservative document or is it a liberal document, according to your . . .

It is both. It's both. It depends on the interpretation. It took the court a long time to find certain words in the Constitution which made it a liberal document. It didn't take some of the courts very long to decide that it was a document for the benefit of special privileges, and those things are good for the country because we try by trial and experience to find out what is best for the country. And that's the way it should be. You can't do it if you had somebody whose final word is law.

Was it made deliberately flexible, subject to the adjustment of the Constitution to the times, or does it work out that way?

I think it worked out that way. I think the intention of the men who wrote the Constitution was to have a document that would be a lasting instrument of government, and it has been. But I don't think they had any more idea than we have today of what the future would bring forth, of how the Constitution would work out. It worked out to be one of the greatest documents of government that ever was written, and it was founded on the knowledge of these men who wrote it of governments which had previously existed. Their objective was to make a free government with an instrument that had a certain number of checks and balances in it so that no one man could get control and turn himself into a dictator, and that hasn't happened in this period of time from 1789 until now. It's the oldest existing government in the world, founded on the greatest document on government, in my opinion, that ever was written.

How do you feel about the Congress deliberately initiating legislation to override the opinions of the court?

They do that all the time. You see, the courts decide on the wording which the Congressmen put into law, and when the Congressmen change the wording of the law in such a way that it may meet conditions that they think were not met in the first law, then the court goes along with it. But the Congress should never have the right, categorically, to override the decisions of the court. I made that statement the other day when I was talking to these youngsters over here at Liberty—that if you wanted to give the Congress the authority to override the court in the decisions that they made, we wouldn't have any court. It was set up that way, purposely, so that that could not be done. They'd have to have a Constitutional amendment to do it, and I think the people in the United States have too much sense to pass a Constitutional amendment like that.

Mr. President, do you think adequate justice has been done to the lives of all the Presidents in the recordings of their lives?

No, I don't. No, I do not. I think one of the shining examples is the life of Andrew Johnson. Had it had not been for [Lloyd Paul] Stryker's willingness to go ahead and make a tremendous amount of research and put out his *Life of Andrew Johnson*,* people would always have had the wrong impression of Andrew Johnson as a President of the United States. He's one of the great ones, because he was in a terrifically bad position. He was elected on the American Union ticket with Lincoln. He was a Democrat, and Lincoln was a Whig, a Republican of that day. When he took over, they had a bunch of radicals in the Congress headed by old Thad Stevens—"Old crippled moron" is what I call him—whose objective was to persecute the states who had attempted to leave the Union. Andrew Johnson wanted to carry out the policies of Abraham Lincoln, and he was a Constitutional President. He knew more about the Constitution of the United States, I think, than any other President up to his time.

Then you feel that there are still a lot of papers and documents and records which ought to be exhausted in telling the lives of the Presidents?

There isn't any doubt about that. The papers of the President ought to be thoroughly studied in the manner in which Stryker studied the background and history of Andrew Johnson. If every President had that sort of treatment, we'd know the facts completely. Mostly our facts come from newspaper reports, a great many of them hostile to the President who was in the office. It's going to take a long time to get the proper approach to the history of the Presidents of the United States. That's the reason we set up this institution here, in the hope that that can be done.

Actually, the history of the United States evolved and revolved around the personalities in the lives of Presidents from the beginning?

Yes. There isn't any question about that. It also evolved from the leaders of the Congress. Some of them are great leaders, and some of them weren't worth being in the Congress, but they got into positions of responsibility. It also was a part of the history of the country when you get the history of the courts that we were talking about a while ago. I think you'll find that when you have all the knowledge in connection with the various Presidential administrations and the Congresses with which they had to deal and the decisions of the courts in their time, we'll have a much better view of what the government of the United States means. It has survived all these things, and that's the reason I think it's a great government.

*Lloyd Paul Stryker, *Andrew Johnson: A Study in Courage* (New York: Macmillan, 1929).

To get back to the United States in terms of the peace role: The United States is perhaps the only nation in history, as you recall it, that had not during its greatest period of strength resorted to expansion of territory, the invasion of neighbors, and the colonization of anybody. As far as it is evident now, it has been the greatest evolved force for peace that history has known.

That's right.

This has happened during the administrations of Franklin Roosevelt and yourself. Don't you feel that its role in that sense is unique as perhaps the first really important power that has grown on this globe that may check a tendency of the warmakers to use war for aggression and expansion? You've done it in Korea as a move. How do you feel about America's future role in terms of the peacemaker of the world?

I think it can be if executives always kept in mind that the strength of the peacemaker must be such as to enforce the peace, if necessary. That's the only way in the world that an organization or government can operate, especially when you have people in the world whose objective is to follow through on the same program that Tamerlane, Genghis Khan, and Napoleon [Bonaparte] and all the rest of them followed when they were expanding their countries into territory with the objective of making themselves the greatest control in the political setup of the world. Now, we haven't had that ambition since ... well, I'd say ... since the Spanish-American War. Our objectives in taking over some of the colonies of Spain were to make them free and independent governments, which we did. You'll find that in the final windup of that war, every single one of the Spanish colonies were made free and independent republics. Even that's true in Puerto Rico, where we've given them self-government in a manner in which the people themselves can decide what they want. I'm of the opinion that this great country of ours can be the source of general peace in the world if we don't forget the objective which we have in view.

And how do you account for the change in our going from a set of colonies ... and have become a nation that was looking after little nations and giving them their freedom?

I think that came about as a result of the First World War. It was emphasized by the Second World War, when we ended that war as the strongest free nation in the world. I think we made good use of that period as the strongest free nation in the world in an effort to rehabilitate the other free nations and to rehabilitate even our enemies in that war—something that had never been done before in the history of the world.

Of course, may I suggest in that connection of our previous expansion ... that was expansion on a geographic entity. I mean, unless we held both sides of our continent, we would have been in difficulty.

That's true. The people who negotiated the treaty that ended the possibility of a fight on the 54°–40°* in the Northwest. [They] took a ruler at the
end of Lake Superior and drew a straight line on the Forty-Ninth Parallel to
the Pacific Ocean. Had we have maintained our claims, 54°–40°, we would
not be landlocked from Alaska.

*How do you see our relations with our neighbors? We're having a little
difficulty now in the Panama Canal, and we're having difficulty in Cuba,
which we have more or less watched over and delivered to independence, and
we're having some little strains with the Philippines.*

Well, that happens. That happens in the history of the world. Some youngster over here at Liberty at the William Jewell College asked me why strong
Presidents were followed by those who were rather indifferent to their powers and duties. I told him that after people go through an emergency, they begin
to think that that emergency was not necessary, no matter what it accomplished, and they'd like to have it changed to an easier-going period. All these
efforts of a strong President to keep the government of the United States in
the groove where it ought to be, . . . these efforts have been followed by men
who wanted to make the people believe that life was easy and that they didn't
have to do anything to keep what they'd attained.

Are we about due for a strong one, Mr. President?
(Laughter)

I can only quote to you a statement by Wayne Morse, a Republican Senator from Oregon who finally decided that he couldn't stomach what was
going on. In one of these *Meet the Press* conferences, somebody asked him
what he thought was the greatest accomplishment of the present occupant of
the White House. His statement and comeback was that he'd made a statesman out of General Grant, our worst President. . . .

*Mr. President, what great Americans outside of Presidents and Con-
gressmen do you recall as having had influence?*

Oh, there are a great, great number of great Americans who have made
contributions to the welfare of this republic who had no military or political
connection with the government of the United States. You take those men who
were responsible for the opening of the West. Their great transportation sys-
tems were headed by some of our great, really great, statesmen, and that is
also true of the organization of some of our states outside the original thirteen colonies. You'll find in the history of the organization of those states . . .

---

*The Convention of 1818 and the Oregon Territory Settlement in 1846 with Great
Britain established the Forty-Ninth Parallel from the Lake of the Woods to the channel
between Vancouver Island and the mainland. Some Americans argued that the 54°–40°
Parallel from the Rockies to the Pacific Ocean should be the northern U.S. boundary.

Ohio, Indiana, and Kentucky; Arkansas and Missouri . . . I'll put Missouri first because that was the second state in the Louisiana Purchase. Louisiana was the first one. The organization and the setup of those states was brought about by men of vision who had the opinion that the country's growth was a continuing affair, and it still is. It still is. We have plenty of men who are not in any way connected with politics or government who can see far enough ahead to understand that the continuing growth is necessary for the welfare of this country and for the welfare of a free world.

But we seem to have reached a point . . . and Dick Bolling was having a little trouble with that on Meet the Press *on Sunday, because they asked him, "How do you intend to improve our situation by insisting on more productivity and more production when we are suffering from overproduction due to automation on the farm and industry? What would you do with more if you produced it?"*

I think that that matter can be very easily answered. When a proper distribution of the income of the country is such that every person can obtain what he thinks makes life easier on a basis that he can afford to pay for, so that he has a position that will give him a chance to pay for it, then you never come to an end of increased production. Now, the only reason that the farm production has been increased is due to the fact that, by science and good sense, they've discovered how to make corn and wheat and oats and those products and cotton increase in yield per acre. In the old days, if you got forty-five or fifty bushels of corn to the acre on newly opened up land, you had a tremendous production. It's nothing unusual for this hybrid corn to produce 160 bushels of corn to the acre. While it's not as good as the old dent corn [Indian corn with kernels containing soft and hard starch] was, in my opinion, it still furnishes the same food value that the old dent corn did. Wheat . . . the average yield of wheat in the United States back in the early part of this century was about thirteen bushels to the acre. It's nothing unusual now to have thirty to fifty bushels to the acre in the production of wheat. That means that we've found a way to make the land produce anywhere from three to five times what it did in the old days. We've got to learn how to utilize that, and there are plenty of people starving to death in the world who could use that surplus without a bit of trouble if they had a man—and a way to make a trade, if necessary—to *put that food in circulation!*

Of course, you had Henry Wallace who was trying to think in those terms, and they laughed him off the stage by saying that he wanted to give a bottle of milk to every Hottentot.

He was on the right track. Every Hottentot ought to have a bottle of milk.

We have this problem now of definitions and names—communism, socialism, Marxism, and all the various shades. For some peculiar reason, they have a lot of variations on communism and socialism. We don't seem to have too many on capitalism; we seem to be stuck, and it's being used against us all over the world that we're a capitalist nation. Are we really a capitalist nation?

No. No. The capitalist nation—the so-called capitalist nation—is a nation that's made up of people who are in a position to help themselves better their standard of living under that system than under any other system. There isn't any communism in the world at all. The communist state is nothing but a totalitarian state modeled on Hitler and Mussolini and those dictators who were so terrible for the welfare and benefit of the world. There is a difference in the government in Russia and the government in Germany previous to the downfall of Germany, and it's my opinion that eventually we'll come to the point where we can understand what the distribution of the good things of life mean—that a man has to work for what he gets, and that if he can himself show that he has the ability to get a little better situation than the other fellow, that's capitalism. In communism, they regiment them. And if they don't do exactly what the dictator wants, they send them off to a labor camp and make them work for nothing. Now, which is better?

Are we really a capitalist society in the sense that money—capital— comes ahead of every other consideration? The capitalism control of all of our processes of industry . . .

I don't think that's true at all. You take the greatest of the great industries in this country: They are owned by small stock certificates in the hands of nearly all the people. It's an entirely different situation than it was when the old tycoons used to exploit the country, like old [Andrew] Carnegie and John D. Rockefeller, Sr., and these great railroad fellows . . .

[Edward H.] Harriman?

Old man Harriman, he's one of them. That's right. But that is gone forever, because they themselves brought about a reform which put them in a situation where they could not any longer exploit the fellow who couldn't afford to be exploited. That's all there was to it.

What kind of a system are we? How would you define our system? What would you call it?

It's just a first-class capitalist system that's in the hands of the people, that's all.

Then it's a people's capitalism?

That's right.

And when it does get out of hand and the people are being hurt, why, government always moves in?

They're in a position to control the government and straighten things out, just as I said last night when some of these union fellows who've gone wrong, . . . it's too much power and too much money. . . . The railroads now are begging for help, but there was a time when they controlled the country, and the operation of the Interstate Commerce Commission, which was set up in 1888,* cured that situation. Maybe it did too much to cure, I don't know. The transportation and communication system of the country has been set up practically by the assessment of taxes of the people. They've been willing to do it, because they want some form of communication. They want roads and things of that sort. Those things have been constructed and built at the expense of the taxpayers, and every railroad in the country was built the same way.

Now, we have had an enormous accumulation of agencies in your administration and that of FDR. I guess it started with Wilson, where we began to set up these regulatory bodies, which have become permanent parts of the government that regulate everything.

Those regulatory bodies are all right as long as they are serviced by men who are working in the public interest, but when those regulatory bodies are padded by the special-interests boys, then you're going to have to have a reorganization and find out what's the matter with them. And that's what's coming.

You now have controls built into the economy, or the system, where nothing really radical can take place insofar as anyone taking over anything on any important scale?

I think that's true. I think that's true, but here's the situation you want to take into consideration. Whenever these regulatory bodies become tyrannical in their attitudes, in the long run they'll be upset, and we'll get maybe a change in the operations, administratively, that will be for the welfare and benefit of the people. That's always happened. And that's the reason we've got a government such as we have. No outfit can ever take control of the people in the United States and get away with it, because they have a freedom of action that no other country has. . . . What I want to know, and I've been studying about the matter for some time, [is], What would have happened in the development of the sources of power that are necessary to make this a great republic if nothing had been done in the construction of these tremendous dams that create power, like Grand Coulee and Bonneville and TVA? Where would we have been if we had sat still and let the cutthroat people who had control of the distribution of power at that time? There wouldn't have been a

*The Interstate Commerce Act of 1887 established the first regulatory commission in U.S. history. Authorized to investigate railroad management, the commission could summon witnesses together with company books; however, commission orders did not have the power of a court decree. Difficulties in applying and interpreting the act weakened it after 1890.

single electric refrigerator, there would be no electric lights in the rural section of the country if we had sat still and let that happen. Eventually, the people would have got tired of that, and something radical might have happened. As it was, we had enough sense to go ahead and develop the thing in a way that brought the situation to a stop. The same thing happened in the control of the transportation system, and the only reason the railroads are in a bad fix [is that] they were so durned arbitrary in their approach to this thing that they didn't make any new improvements or anything else until the roads parallel to them forced them to do it.

Every time there is a question raised about federal aid to education, federal aid to housing, federal aid to power, federal aid to radio and communications, the hue and cry comes up to keep the government out of the people's trough.

Why, sure. The reason for that is these aids to institutions that you're talking about are easier to control locally than they are nationally, and when they get out of control locally, which they are slowly and gradually doing, eventually we'll come to an educational system that will make it just as fair for schools in Nevada as they are in New York City.

Would you be for having the government actually sponsor educational series via some of the television and the radio bands? Nationally?

Britain seems to be rather successful in doing that, and so has Canada.

But we haven't done it here?

No. We've given free enterprise a chance to cut its own throat, and that's what it's doing. And I'm for free enterprise! I've got an income-tax system which would be just as simple as it is possible to make it that would do away with all these bookkeepers and people of that kind. I'd start out on an income-tax basis of a simple 1 percent of total income and increase it so that when we got to the top bracket, we'd be in the same fix as we are now, but any man then could sit down and make out his income tax on what he got.

How does that work? Would you explain that a little bit more in detail?

Suppose now that you were making $1,000 a year, and that the first start of the income tax would be 1 percent of $1,000. You see what that would be? That would be $10.

Ten dollars.

And suppose you were making $100,000 a year and you got up to the point where the simple tax cost was 59 percent. You'd know exactly what you had and what to do with it. The whole thing would bring in the same income that's brought in now, without all these damn complications, and I wouldn't have any sort of deduction for things that really don't need to be deducted.

Deductions which also allow loopholes for people to get . . . without reporting.

Why, certainly. It's been fixed up that way. They had the Finance Committee in the Senate make all these complicated things so the fellows who knew how to keep books could get away with . . . almost get away with murder. One of the oil setups was one of the things that's absolutely out of line. Well, you couldn't do that if you had a straight income-tax assessment on the basis of total income.

That means you pay out of the gross, and the gross is whatever you took in?

That's correct. That's absolutely correct.

Less what you paid out?

It gives the corporations and everybody else the same way and be careful to arrange the thing so there wouldn't be a double tax, so the same money couldn't be taxed twice. . . . In the long run, it would be a simple matter. Of course, it would put a lot of bookkeepers and advertising fellows out of business, but then that . . .

That would be a good thing for the country. (Laughter) But if you take a power company on the one side and you take a mining company on the other, what [the mining company] takes in and what it gets to keep is much bigger than what a power company gets, so that, let's say, if the Edison Company takes in $100 million: If it got taxed on the same basis as a mining company that took in $100 million dollars, it would be paying out a great deal more. That's the problem.

In all those details, things could be worked out on a common-sense basis and make it simple so every fellow would know just what his tax was and he could sit down and figure in fifteen minutes, just like an assessment of property. I made a survey of the assessment of property of personal and real estate and business property in the cities, and I found out a simple method of assessments in Hamilton County, Ohio, and Hennepin County, Minnesota, where any man could sit down and figure what the value of his property ought to be. They had it classified so it was just as simple as it could be, and I tried to get it installed in Jackson County but couldn't get it done, because there were so many people where they'd have a property . . . we'd say its actual value on a square-foot basis and on a cubic-foot basis for buildings would be assessed for $100,000 when it was worth $2.5 million dollars. Well, you know that's wrong. Then I wouldn't let any of these religious organizations have business property that's not assessed. When they have business property, then they cease to be a church. Their church property is all right free from taxes, and that's done without any consideration of whether it's a Catholic, or a

Protestant, or a Jew. But when they begin to own property like the Washington University in St. Louis does in all the cities around and pay no taxes on it, then that's going just a little too far.

What about taxation for so-called cooperatives? That's been a moot question for a long time.

The cooperatives eventually are going to have to pay their part for the support of the government of the United States. They don't have real freedom from taxation. The income of these cooperatives is allocated to the people who really do pay taxes. They really pay taxes on all of it.

Then you think that the whole tax structure of the United States will have to undergo a major change?

It ought to have a scientific survey made by people who have no personal interest in how the thing is figured after they get through. And it can be done. It has been done, as I say, in Hamilton County, Ohio, and in Hennepin County, Minnesota, as far as taxable property is concerned. Then I'd make a division on this basis: I would confine the federal government's taxation to income. I would confine the state tax situation to sales tax. I would confine the local government's taxation to property and real-estate taxes in the home communities. It would work out then so there wouldn't be any three-times by the time you got state income tax, you got federal income tax; you've got sales taxes in some of these states that charge 7 and 8 cents a gallon on gasoline and use it for state operations. That tax on the operation of the roads should go entirely to the operation of transportation and not go into the state treasury when the state wants a sales tax. Mississippi was the first state in the country that had a sales tax, and they paid themselves out of debt with it on a reasonable basis—two cents. Missouri had the lowest sales tax in the United States until just a few years ago. I think now it's still the lowest—three cents. And those things can be worked out on a basis so that the governments do not infringe on each other's territory and make double taxes absolutely essential. That's when a fellow commences to starve. That's the reason he has to have these smart bookkeepers to keep him out of jail.

You're opposed to a federal sales tax?

Yes. I don't believe in federal sales tax.

Labor is fighting all kinds of sales taxes.

Of course. When you have a sales tax, the little fellow pays a vast amount on a loaf of bread, a pair of shoes, and things of that kind, and that's the reason for labor's opposition to it. But there isn't any reason in the world why they shouldn't pay their fair share, and the sales tax can be adjusted so that nobody will be hurt. Every state in the Union is using it.

That's right. Where do you see the most important cut in federal spending that could take place in order to cut federal tax?

I don't know where to start on that. I had a survey made on it, and we had an extreme amount of difficulty in finding out just exactly what the tax of the federal government . . . what effect it had on the exchange of goods and services. That's what makes the country run—the exchange of goods and services—and I don't know where you're going to end this thing unless you allocate the various supports of these things in the same way that you allocate the taxes. There are certain things the federal government ought not to stick its nose into, and there are certain things the state ought not to do with regard to counties and cities. And there are certain things that these cities ought not to do that will interfere with the federal and state governments. But it's going to take a tremendous amount of effort, and it's going to take a situation where the people are interested in having a reasonable tax system that can work. Eventually, when these things get so far up in the air, that's what's going to happen. For instance, right here in this city of Independence, they're thinking about putting on $5 per $100 on school taxes. Now, you know that a fellow who has property that's worth $100,000 is going to try to have that property set up on a $10,000 basis and you can see what the difference is. And if it is set up on the right basis, you wouldn't have to have but $1.50 [per $100].

This is kind of a runaway thing . . . the interest rates, inflation, and all the other things that are beginning to overtake municipalities. What happens, Mr. President, when a sudden cessation of the armaments race begins to shape up? There are all kinds of attitudes on that point.

I don't think that there will be any serious harm done, because it won't be done suddenly, you see. It should be done gradually, and eventually it will have to be done for the simple reason that that's almost as tremendous a burden as the schools. It's sacrilege for a fellow to say that, but they've got the school situation now in the shape that the burden of it is almost too great to carry. They say that they're going to have to work that out. Here's what really happens in the long run. If this thing keeps on—this climb and things of that kind—you have a wringing-out process, just like you did in [18]73 and [18]93, 1907, and 1929. And then, that's not good for anybody, and that can be prevented if the situation is developed so that the exchange of goods and services between people is on a fair and equitable basis. That's all there is to it.

The teachers have had a pretty good organization nationally. I know we had them out in California, and they've got this thing called "tenure" for a teacher. Once they're established, they're in forever.

I wouldn't be for that.

That poses quite a problem.

I wouldn't be for that. I think the teachers ought to be kept in their positions as long as they're able and capable of carrying on the necessary things that give the youngsters the proper idea of what an education is. But if you go ahead and make a tenure, the first thing you know, you're going to have a lot of featherbedding, just like you have on the railroads.

Then you think any general welfare ought to stem from an overall insurance program by the people, but not occupationally? They ought not to be permanently employed where they can't perform?

That's right. That's the point exactly. You have to have efficiency in all these things. . . .

In other words, Mr. President, you're certainly for welfare, but not welfare on a basis in which there is no return?

That's the point. You oughtn't to have welfare on a basis where a fellow will think more of welfare than he does of the work that he ought to be doing. That's kind of sacrilegious to me, Dave.

The communists have made a great deal of headway by proving that under capitalism, or under our system, there is always a certain number of people that are unemployed, and there always is a certain number of people that are starving, and always a certain number of people that simply cannot get into any kind of coverage under the system. How do you answer that challenge from the communists?

I don't think it's a challenge, because when the communists come to that point, they put them in slave labor camps and let them work for nothing.

But there are no unemployed.

But they're working for nothing.

But they feed them.

They're working for nothing at the behest of the government, and sometimes they feed them and sometimes they don't. They kill more of them than they cure.

In other words, it's better to be without a job than to be without freedom.

That's correct.

Everyone who has gone to Russia has come back with kind of a song and dance about how vastly improved they are as compared to what they were just a short time back.

Well, they couldn't do anything but improve, because they were at the bottom of the scale when they started.

Is it something that Russia created from within or something that Russia borrowed from the outside? Where does this industrial impetus really begin to spurt?

I don't know. I'm not familiar enough with the thing to make a sane answer on the subject, because I never was in Russia and never want to be. Sometime or other, I hope to have a chance to see what the country looks like. But I don't think we'll ever get the facts from the Russians.

You don't want to go to Russia yet? Would you like to go to Russia?

Oh, yes. Of course I would. I'd like to go to every country in the world if I could.

Do you think that they'll let you into Russia?

I think they would. I think they'd be courteous and cordial, just as we were to Khrushchev, who has the same standing over here as I would have in Russia.

Biographical Directory

L ISTED BELOW are biographical data for the persons noted in *Talking with Harry*.

Acheson, Dean G. (1893–1971). United States. Lawyer. Undersecretary of the Treasury, 1933; Undersecretary of State, 1945–47; Secretary of State, 1949–53. Supported U.S. hydrogen-bomb development.

Adams, John (1735–1826). United States. Lawyer and author. Vice President, 1789–97; President, 1797–1801.

Adams, John Quincy (1767–1848). United States. Lawyer and author. Secretary of State, 1817–25; President, 1825–29. Son of President John (and Abigail) Adams.

Adenauer, Konrad (1876–1967). Germany. Lawyer. Chairman, Christian Democratic Union, British Zone, 1945; Chairman, Christian Democratic Union, Federal Republic of Germany, 1950; Chancellor, 1949; Minister of Foreign Affairs, 1951–55.

Alemán Valdes, Miguel (1902–83). Mexico. Government official, Vera Cruz, 1930–40; Minister of the Interior, 1940–45; President of Mexico, 1946–52.

Allen, George Edward (1896–1973). United States. Lawyer and businessman. First lieutenant in machine-gun battalion in France in 1918. Gregarious friend and adviser of President Franklin Roosevelt and member of President Truman's informal cabinet. Member of the Reconstruction Finance Corporation, 1946–47. Supported Truman in 1948 election. Personal supporter also of President Eisenhower. Sat on thirty-two corporate boards of directors during the 1960s.

Anderson, Robert B. (1910–89). United States. Lawyer. Secretary, Department of the Navy, 1953–54; Secretary, Department of Defense, 1954–55; Secretary, Department of the Treasury, 1957–61.

Arthur, Chester A. (1829–86). United States. Lawyer. Vice President, 1881; President, 1881–85. Arthur took office following the assassination of President James Garfield in September 1881.

Attlee, Clement (1883–1967). Great Britain. Barrister. Leader, Labour Party, 1935–55; Deputy Prime Minister, 1942; Prime Minister, 1945–51.

Auriol, Vincent (1884–1966). France. Lawyer. Finance Minister, 1936; President, National Assembly, 1946; President of France, 1947–54.

Baldwin, Stanley (1867–1947). Great Britain. Engineer. Prime Minister, 1923–24, 1924–29, 1935–37.

Balfour, Arthur James (1848–1930). Great Britain. Statesman and philosopher. Secretary of Scotland, 1886; Chief Secretary, Ireland, 1887; Prime Minister, Great Britain, 1902–05; Chief British Representative to the League of Nations Assembly, 1920.

Barkley, Alben W. (1877–1956). United States. Lawyer. Representative (Ky.), 1912; Senator (Ky.), 1926, 1954; Vice President, 1949–53.

Beard, Charles Austin (1874–1948). United States. Political scientist, historian, and author. Professor, Columbia University, 1904–17; Co-founder, New School for Social Research, 1919. Beard wrote numerous American history books with truly significant economic interpretations. He was also a notable isolationist.

Beard, Mary Ritter (1876–1958). United States. Historian and author. Co-author with her husband, Charles A. Beard, of *The Rise of American Civilization*.

Beaverbrook, Lord (1879–1964). Great Britain. Lawyer. Cabinet Member (Chancellor of the Duchy of Lancaster) and Minister of Information, 1918–19; Minister of Aircraft Production, 1940–41; Minister of State, 1941; Minister of Supply, 1941–42.

Beck, David (1894–1993). United States. Served in the U.S. Navy during World War I. President, International Teamsters Union, 1952–57; Vice President, Executive Committee, American Federation of Labor, 1953–57.

Beethoven, Ludwig von (1770–1827). Germany. Composer.

Beneš, Edvard (1884–1948). Czechoslovakia. Diplomat and university professor. Minister of Foreign Affairs, 1918–35; Prime Minister, 1921–22; President of Czechoslovakia, 1935–38, reelected 1946. In 1939 he was a professor at the University of Chicago.

Benson, Ezra Taft (1899–1994). United States. Farmer and church executive. Executive Secretary, National Council of Farmer Cooperatives, 1939–44; Secretary of Agriculture, 1953–61.

Beveridge, Albert (1862–1927). United States. Railroad laborer, logger, teamster, historian, and lawyer. Senator (Ind.), 1899–1910.

Biddle, Nicholas (1786–1844). United States. Banker and local politician. Member of Pennsylvania State House of Representatives, 1810–11; President, Second Bank of the United States, 1822–36.

Bismarck, Otto von (1815–98). Prussia. Statesman. Minister to Russia, 1859; President, Council of Ministers, and Foreign Minister, 1862. When the German Empire was declared, Bismarck was given the title of prince; he was also the first Chancellor of the German Empire, 1871–90.

Blaine, James G. (1830–93). United States. Editor and author. Representative (Maine), 1862–76; Speaker of the House, 1869–75; Senator, 1876–81; Secretary of State, March–December 1881; Secretary of State, 1889–92.

Bland, Richard Parks (1835–99). United States. Lawyer. Representative (Mo.), 1873–94, 1896–99.

Bodet, Jaime Torres (1902–74). Mexico. Poet, educator, and statesman. Foreign Minister, 1946–48; Director General, United Nations Educational, Scientific, and Cultural Organization (UNESCO), 1948–52.

Bohr, Niels (1885–1962). Denmark. Ph.D. in Physics from the University of Copenhagen, 1911, and professor of theoretical physics. Awarded Nobel Prize in Physics, 1922. Lectured in the United States, 1938–39, on splitting the uranium atom. Rescued from Nazi-dominated Denmark in 1943 and assisted atomic-bomb research at Los Alamos, New Mexico. Returned to Denmark in 1945.

Bolling, Richard Walker (1916–91). United States. Lawyer. Representative (Mo.), 1949–83; Chairman, Committee on Rules, 1978–82.

Bonaparte, Napoleon (1769–1821). France. First Consul, 1800–04; Emperor of the French, 1804–14.

Bowers, Claude (1878–1958). United States. Historian, diplomat, and author. U.S. Ambassador to Spain, 1933–39; U.S. Ambassador to Chile, 1939–53.

Bradley, Omar (1893–1981). United States. Army officer. Coordinator, Operation Overlord (the invasion of Normandy), 1944; General, U.S. Army, 1950; Chief of Staff, U.S. Army, 1948–49; Chairman, Joint Chiefs of Staff, 1949–53.

Bragg, Braxton (1817–76). United States. Army officer. Commander in Chief, Confederate Army, 1864; Military Adviser to Confederate President Jefferson Davis, 1864.

Brandeis, Louis (1856–1941). United States. Lawyer. Associate Justice, U.S. Supreme Court, 1916–39.

Brannan, Charles F. (1903–92). United States. Government official. Secretary of Agriculture, 1948–53; General Counsel, National Farmers Union, 1953–90.

Bridges, Alfred Benton (Harry) (1901–90). United States. Union official. In 1934, Bridges led the strike against Pacific Coast shipowners; he also served as president of the Pacific Coast District CIO International.

Brooks, Ralph G. (1898–1960). United States. Lawyer. Governor of Nebraska, 1959–60.

Brown, Edmund Gerald (Pat) (1905–96). United States. Lawyer and author. Delegate to Democratic National Conventions, 1940–60; Governor of California, 1959–67.

Brownell, Herbert (1934–96). United States. Lawyer and federal official. U.S. Attorney General, 1953–57.

Bryan, William Jennings (1860–1925). United States. Lawyer. Representative (Neb.), 1891–95; Secretary of State, 1913–15. Bryan was nominated for the U.S. Presidency three times, in 1896, 1900, and 1908.

Buchanan, James (1791–1868). United States. Lawyer. Representative (Penn.), 1821–31; U.S. Minister to Russia, 1832–33; Senator (Penn.), 1834–45; Secretary of State, 1845–49; U.S. Minister to Great Britain, 1853–56; President, 1857–61.

Bunche, Ralph (1904–71). United States. Professor of political science at Howard and Harvard universities. Served as an adviser to the U.S. State Department in World War II; held a number of United Nations assignments from 1946 to 1971 in Palestine, Congo, Cyprus, and Yemen.

Burr, Aaron (1756–1836). United States. Lawyer. Served in the American Revolutionary War, 1777–79. Senator (N.Y.), 1791–97; Vice President, 1801–05. Burr mortally wounded Alexander Hamilton in a duel. He was tried for treason and acquitted in 1807.

Butler, Nicholas Murray (1862–1947). United States. Philosopher, educator, and author. President, Columbia University, 1901–45.

Butler, Paul (1905–61). United States. Lawyer and officer in the Indiana Democratic Party. President, Catholic Charities, South Bend, Indiana, 1946; Chairman, National Democratic Party, 1955–60.

Byrnes, James F. (1879–1972). United States. Court reporter and lawyer. Representative (S.C.), 1911–24; Senator (S.C.), 1931–41; Associate Justice, U.S. Supreme Court, 1941–42; Director, Office of War Mobilization, 1943–45; Secretary of State, 1945–47; Governor of South Carolina, 1951–55.

Caesar, Julius (100–44 B.C.). Roman general, statesman, and historian. Dictator of Rome, 45–44 B.C.

Carey, James B. (1911–73). United States. Labor executive and lawyer. National Secretary, Congress of Industrial Organizations, 1938–73. In 1949, Carey served as a member of the delegation to the founding meeting of the International Confederation of Free Trade Unions in London.

Carnegie, Andrew (1835–1919). United States. Industrialist. Born in Scotland, Carnegie came to the United States with his poverty-stricken parents in 1848. He trained as a telegrapher; established the Union Iron Mills in 1868; acquired Homestead Steel Works in 1888; and sold the steel company in 1901. He devoted his remaining years to philanthropic enterprises.

Casey, Lawrence B. (1905–77). United States. Catholic church official and author. Bishop, Rochester, N.Y., 1953–66; Bishop, Paterson, N.J., 1966–77.

Cato, Marcus Porcius, the Elder (234–149 B.C.). Roman statesman. Plebeian aedile, 199 B.C.; Praetor, 198 B.C.; Consul, 195 B.C.; Censor, 184 B.C.

Caudle, T. Lamar (1905–69). United States. Assistant Attorney General in Charge of the Criminal Division, 1945–47; Director, Tax Division, Justice Department, 1947–51. Caudle was convicted in 1960 of income-tax evasion and served six months in prison. He was pardoned by President Lyndon B. Johnson in 1965.

Chandler, Harry (1864–1944). United States. Publisher of the *Los Angeles Times*.

Charles I, King of England, Scotland, and Ireland (1600–49; r. 1625–49).

Charles XII, King of Sweden (1682–1718; r. 1697–1718).

Charles Martel (688–741). Frankish ruler; grandfather of Charlemagne.

Chiang Kai-shek (Chiang Chung-cheng) (1887–1975). China. Army general and statesman. Chiang led the southern Revolutionary movement from 1925; he was a member of the Kuomintang Party, serving as director from 1945 to his death.

Churchill, Sir Winston (1874–1965). Great Britain. Statesman. Member of Parliament, 1924–29; Prime Minister, 1940–45, 1951–55. Churchill received the Nobel Prize for Literature in 1953.

Cicero, Marcus Tullius (106–43 B.C.). Roman statesman, orator, and author. Praetor, 66 B.C.; Consul, 63 B.C.

Clark, John D. (1884–1961). United States. Economist. Adviser, Senate Commission on Government Reorganization, 1937–39; Dean, Business

School, University of Nebraska, 1941–46; President, American Finance Association, 1943.

Clark, Mark (1896–1984). United States. U.S. Army officer. General, 1945; Commander-in-Chief, U.S. Occupation Forces in Austria, 1945; U.S. High Commissioner, 1945; Deputy Secretary of State, 1947; Commander-in-Chief, United Nations Forces in Korea.

Clay, Henry (1777–1852). United States. Senator (Ky.), 1806–07, 1810–11, 1831–42, 1849–52; Representative (Ky.), 1811–21, 1823–25; Speaker of the House, 1811–20, 1823–25; Secretary of State, 1825–29.

Clemenceau, Georges (1841–1929). France. Statesman. Member, Chamber of Deputies, 1876–93; Senator, 1902; Minister of the Interior, 1906; Prime Minister, 1906–09; Prime Minister and War Minister, 1917–20.

Cleveland, Grover (1837–1908). United States. Lawyer. President, 1885–89, 1893–97.

Cody, John P. (1907–82). United States. Catholic church official. Bishop, Kansas City and St. Joseph, Missouri, 1956–61; Coadjutor and Archbishop, New Orleans, 1961–65; Archbishop and Cardinal of Chicago, 1965–82.

Conant, James B. (1893–1978). United States. Educator and scientist. Served in the Chemical Warfare Service of the U.S. Army in World War I. Professor of Chemistry, Harvard University, 1919–33; President, Harvard University, 1933–53. As chairman of the National Defense Research Council, Conant authorized atomic-weapon development in December 1940 and witnessed test firing of the atomic bomb in 1945.

Confucius (551–479 B.C.). China. Philosopher and teacher.

Constantine I, the Great (273–337). Emperor of Rome, 306–37. Constantine I legally sanctioned Christianity.

Coolidge, Calvin (1872–1933). United States. Lawyer. Governor of Massachusetts, 1916–18, 1919–20; Vice President, 1921–25; President, 1925–29. Took office following the death of President Harding in 1923.

Dalai Lama (Tenzin Gyatso) (1935–). Tibet. Religious and secular ruler. He was enthroned as Dalai Lama XIV in 1940; assumed full political power in 1950; went into exile in 1959.

Daniel, E. Clifton (1912–2000). United States. Newspaperman and author. Foreign and War Correspondent, Editor, *New York Times,* 1955–77. Daniel married Margaret Truman in 1956.

Davis, Richard Harding (1864–1916). United States. Novelist, playwright, and newspaperman. As a war correspondent, Davis covered the Greco-Turkish War, the Boer War, the revolution in Honduras, and World War I.

De Gaulle, Charles (1890–1970). France. Statesman. Undersecretary, National Defense, 1940; Chief, Free French, and President, French National Committee, 1940–42; President, French Committee of National Liberation, 1943; Head of the Provisional Government of the Republic, 1944–46; Chief of the Armies, 1944–46; Prime Minister, 1958; President of France, 1958–69.

Dewey, George (1837–1917). United States. Admiral. Served in the U.S. Civil War, 1861–65, and the Spanish-American War, 1898.

Dewey, Thomas E. (1902–71). United States. Lawyer. U.S. Attorney, 1933; Governor of New York, 1942–54; Republican candidate for President, 1944, 1948.

Dexter, Samuel (1761–1816). United States. Lawyer. Representative (Mass.), 1793–95; Senator (Mass.), 1799–1800; Secretary of War, 1800; Secretary of the Treasury, 1801–02.

Dibelius, Otto (1880–1967). Germany. Bishop of the Evangelical Church in Berlin–Brandenburg, 1945–66.

Douglas, Helen Gahagan (1900–80). United States. Author and lecturer. Representative (Calif.), 1945–51; Member, U.S. Delegation to the United Nations General Assembly, 1946.

Dulles, Allen (1893–1969). United States. Lawyer and diplomat. Served during World War II with the Office of Strategic Services. Legal Adviser to the American Delegation to the General Disarmament Conference, 1932–33; Director, Central Intelligence Agency, 1953–61.

Dulles, John Foster (1888–1959). United States. Lawyer. Served as a captain and a major in the U.S. Army during World War I. Secretary, Hague Peace Conference, 1907; American representative at the Berlin debt conferences, 1933; United Nations General Assembly, 1946, 1947, 1950; Acting Chairman, U.S. Delegation to the United Nations General Assembly, 1948; Consultant to the Secretary of State, 1950; Secretary of State, 1953–59.

Einstein, Albert (1879–1955). Germany and United States. Theoretical physicist. Einstein became a U.S. citizen in 1941; he developed the Theory of Relativity.

Eisenhower, Dwight David (1890–1969). United States. Army general. Allied Commander in Chief in North Africa, 1942; Commanding General of the Allied Powers, European Theater of Operations, 1943; Commander of U.S. Occupation Forces in Germany, 1945; Chief of Staff, U.S. Army, 1945–48; Supreme Commander of Allied Powers in Europe, 1950; President, 1953–61.

Eisenhower, John D. (1922–). United States. Army officer (1944–63) and author. U.S. Ambassador to Belgium, 1969–71.

Elizabeth II, Queen of Great Britain and Northern Ireland (1926– ; r. 1952–).

Farley, James (1888–1976). United States. Business executive. Chairman, Democratic National Committee, 1932–40; Postmaster General, 1933–40.

Faubus, Orval (1910–94). United States. Teacher, government official (Ark.), postmaster, and publisher. Governor of Arkansas, 1955–67.

Fermi, Enrico (1901–54). Italy/United States. Scientist. Fermi was awarded the Nobel Peace Prize for Physics in 1938. After emigrating to the United States, Fermi designed the manmade nuclear reactor for the Manhattan Project in 1942. He opposed U.S. hydrogen-bomb development.

Fillmore, Millard (1800–74). United States. Lawyer, Representative (N.Y.), 1833–35, 1837–41; Chairman, Ways and Means Committee, 1840–42; Vice President, 1849; President, 1850–53. Fillmore took office following the death of President Zachary Taylor.

Flemming, Arthur S. (1905–96). United States. Member of the U.S. Civil Service Commission and the Hoover Commission; President of three universities.

Franco, Francisco (1892–1975). Spain. Leader of the Fascist Party, 1937; Chief of State, Prime Minister, and Supreme Chief of Spain, 1939–75.

Frankfurter, Felix (1882–1965). Austria/United States. Lawyer. Harvard Law School Professor, 1914–39; Assistant to the Secretary of War, 1917–19; Associate Justice, U.S. Supreme Court, 1939–62.

Freeman, Douglas Southall (1886–1953). United States. Historian and newspaper editor.

Fuchs, Klaus (1911–88). Great Britain. Atomic scientist who worked on the Manhattan Project and passed valuable secrets to the Soviet Union.

Gallatin, Albert (1761–1849). Switzerland/United States. Member, Harrisburg Conference to Revise the U.S. Constitution, 1788; Member, Pennsylvania Constitutional Convention, 1789; Representative (Penn.), 1795–1801; Secretary of the Treasury, 1801–14; U.S. Minister to France, 1815–23, U.S. Minister to England, 1826–27.

Gallup, George Horace (1901–84). United States. Journalist and public-opinion statistician.

Gandhi, Mohandas (Mahatma) (1869–1948). India. Nationalist and religious leader who advocated nonviolent resistance to British imperial rule.

Gardner, Erle Stanley (1889–1970). United States. Lawyer and author of travel and mystery books.

Garfield, James A. (1831–81). United States. Lawyer. Served in the Union Army during the U.S. Civil War, 1861–63. Representative (Ohio), 1863–80; Member, Electoral Commission, 1876. Garfield was elected to the Senate in 1880 but never took the seat. He was elected President in 1881 but was assassinated in that year by Charles Guiteau.

George VI, King of Great Britain and Northern Ireland (1895–1952; r. 1936–52).

Glass, Carter (1858–1946). United States. Lawyer. Representative (Va.), 1902–18; Secretary of the Treasury, 1918–20. Glass resigned to accept a U.S. Senatorship by appointment from the governor of Virginia. Senator (Va.), 1920–46.

Gore, Albert Arnold (1907–1998). United States. Business executive and author. Representative (Tenn.), 1938–52; Senator (Tenn.), 1953–71.

Graham, Wallace H. (1910–96). United States. Physician. Graham served as a reserve brigadier general in the U.S. Air Force during World War II and was a personal physician to President Harry Truman and his family.

Grant, Ulysses S. (1822–85). United States. Army officer. Commander-in-Chief, U.S. Army, 1864; promoted to Full General, 1866; Secretary of War, 1867; President, 1869–77.

Gronchi, Giovanni (1887–1978). Italy. Political leader. Helped found the Italian Popular Party, 1919; Head of the Confederation of Christian Workers, 1920; Minister of Industry and Commerce, 1944–46.

Gustav II (Gustavus Adolphus), King of Sweden (1594–1632; r. 1611–32).

Haile Selassie (1892–1975). Ethiopia. Statesman. Emperor of Ethiopia, 1930–36, 1941–74. He was deposed.

Halleck, Charles A. (1900–86). United States. Lawyer. Representative (Ind.), 1935–62.

Hamilton, Alexander (1755–1804). United States. Lawyer. Secretary, Aide-de-Camp to George Washington, 1777–81; Member, New York Delegation to the Continental Congress, 1782–83, and to the Constitutional Convention, 1787–88; Secretary of the Treasury, 1789–95. Served as spokesman for the Federalist Party.

Hammurabi (approx. 1792–50 B.C.). King of the first dynasty of Babylon. Prepared a law code. His humanitarian code of laws, carved on a diorite column in 3,600 lines of cuneiform, includes punishment of "an eye for an eye."

Hanna, Mark (1837–1904). United States. Merchant and financier. Representative (Ohio), 1897–1904. Supporter of Governor, and later President, William McKinley.

Hannibal (247–183/182 B.C.). Carthaginian general who waged war against the Romans during the Second Punic War.

Harding, Warren G. (1865–1923). United States. Newspaper editor and publisher of Marion (Ohio) *Star*. Lieutenant Governor of Ohio, 1904–1906; Senator (Ohio), 1915–20; President, 1921–23.

Harriman, Edward H. (1848–1909). United States. Businessman, railroad executive. Chairman of the Board of Directors, Union Pacific Railroad, 1898.

Harriman, W. Averell (1891–1986). Businessman, author, government official. Special Representative in Great Britain, with Rank of Minister, 1941; U.S. Ambassador to USSR, 1943–46; U.S. Ambassador to Great Britain, 1946; Secretary of Commerce, 1946–48; Special Assistant to the President, 1950–51; American Representative on the Commission to Study Western Defense Plans, NATO, 1951; Governor of New York, 1955–59; U.S. Ambassador at Large, 1961, 1965–68.

Harrison, Benjamin (1833–1901). United States. Lawyer, Served in the Union Army during the U.S. Civil War. Senator (Ind.), 1881–87; President, 1889–93.

Harrison, William Henry (1773–1841). United States. Served in the military campaigns against Indians in the Northwest Territory. First Governor of Indiana Territory, 1801–12; Major General, War of 1812; Senator (Ohio), 1825–28; U.S. Minister to Colombia, 1828–29; President, 1841. Died after one month in office.

Hartke, Rupert Vance (1919–). United States. Lawyer. Served in the Coast Guard and the U.S. Navy during World War II. Senator (Ind.), 1959–77.

Hayes, Carlton J. H. (1882–1964). United States. Served as a U.S. Army captain in World War I. Historian, Columbia University, 1907–50; U.S. Ambassador to Spain, 1942–45.

Hayes, Rutherford B. (1822–93). United States. Lawyer. Representative (Ohio), 1865–67; Governor of Ohio, 1868–72, 1875–77; President, 1877–81.

Hearst, George Randolph, Sr. (1904–72). United States. Publisher of the *Los Angeles Examiner*, 1929–53.

Helen, Queen of Romania (1896–1982). Regent, 1927–30; Adviser to King Michael of Romania, 1940–47.

Henry IV, King of France (1553–1610; r. 1589–1610).

Heuss, Theodor (1884–1963). Germany. Politician. Deputy to the Reichstag, 1924–28, 1930–33; First President of the Federal Republic of Germany, 1949–59.

Hillman, Sidney (1887–1946). United States. Labor leader. Appointed labor member of the National Defense Advisory Commission, 1940; Associate Director General, Office of Production Management, 1940–42; Director, Labor Division, War Production Board, 1942.

Hillman, William (1895–1962). United States. Newsman and author. Correspondent, Universal Service and Hearst newspapers, Paris, Berlin, and London, 1926–31; Chief of Staff of Foreign Correspondents, Hearst newspapers, 1934–39; Foreign Editor, *Collier's,* 1939–40; Washington commentator, NBC, 1941–42; speechwriter for President Harry Truman; author of *Mr. President,* 1952.

Hitler, Adolf (1889–1945). Germany. Chancellor, 1933–45. As leader of the National Socialist (Nazi) Party, Hitler directed Germany's invasion of Poland in 1939, beginning World War II.

Hoffa, James R. (1913–75?). United States. Union leader. Organizer, International Brotherhood of Teamsters, 1937. Hoffa served as president of the Teamsters Union from 1947 until his official resignation in 1971.

Holmes, Oliver Wendell (1841–1935). United States. Jurist. Associate Justice, Supreme Judicial Court of Massachusetts, 1882–99; Chief Justice of Massachusetts, 1899–1902; Associate Justice, U.S. Supreme Court, 1902–32.

Hoover, Herbert (1874–1964). United States. Engineer. Secretary of Commerce, 1921; President, 1929–33. At the request of President Truman, Hoover undertook the coordination of the world food supplies of thirty-eight countries in 1946, and undertook a study of the economic situation in Germany and Austria in 1947.

Hopkins, Harry L. (1890–1946). United States. Government official. Federal Administrator of Emergency Relief, 1933; Works Progress Administrator, 1935–38; Secretary of Commerce, 1938–40; Head of the Lend-Lease Program, 1941–45. Hopkins traveled to Moscow for President Truman in 1945 to negotiate the status of Poland; retired July 1945.

Howard, Robert Mayburn (1878–1963). United States. Surgeon.

Hughes, Charles Evans (1862–1948). United States. Lawyer. Governor of New York, 1907–08, 1909–10; Associate Justice, U.S. Supreme Court, 1910–16; Republican candidate for President, 1916; Secretary of State, 1921–25; Chief Justice, U.S. Supreme Court, 1930–41.

Humphrey, George M. (1890–1970). United States. Steel corporation executive. Secretary of the Treasury, 1953–57.

Humphrey, Hubert H. (1911–78). United States. Politician. State Campaign Manager, Roosevelt–Truman Commission, 1944; Senator (Minn.), 1948–64, 1971–78; Vice President, 1965–69.

Hutcheson, William L. (1874–1953). United States. Labor leader. Member, War Labor Board, 1917–19. In 1932 and 1936, Hutcheson took charge of the Labor Division of the National Republican Party.

Ivan IV (Ivan the Terrible) (1530–84). Grand Prince of Moscow, Vladimir, and all Russia. Czar of Russia, 1547–84.

Jackson, Andrew (1767–1845). United States. Army officer. Served in several Indian wars and in the War of 1812. Representative (Tenn.), 1796–97; Senator (Tenn.), 1797–98, 1823–25; Judge, Tennessee Supreme Court, 1798–1804; President, 1829–37.

Jackson, Thomas (Stonewall) (1824–63). United States. West Point graduate. Served as a Confederate Army general in the Civil War.

Jacobson, Edward (1881–1955). United States. Retail merchant in Kansas City and partner with Truman in a men's accessories store. Jacobson was also a comrade of Truman's in the 129th Field Artillery during World War I.

James II, King of England, Scotland, and Ireland (1633–1701; r. 1685–88).

Jefferson, Thomas (1743–1826). United States. Lawyer and author of the Declaration of Independence. Member, Continental Congress, 1775–76; U.S. Minister to France, 1784–90; first Secretary of State under the new Constitution, 1790–93; Vice President, 1797–1801; President, 1801–09.

Jenner, William Ezra (1908–85). United States. Lawyer. State Senator (Ind.), 1935–42; Captain, Army Air Corps, 1944; Representative (Ind.), 1944–45, 1947–59. Vocal Republican anti-communist.

John, King of England (1164–1216; r. 1199–1216). King John signed the Magna Carta in 1215.

Johnson, Andrew (1808–75). United States. Tailor. Representative (Tenn.), 1843–53; Governor of Tennessee, 1853–57; Senator (Tenn.), 1857–62, 1875; Vice President, 1865; President, 1865–69. Johnson took office following the assassination of President Abraham Lincoln.

Johnson, Louis Arthur (1891–1966). United States. Lawyer. Served as a captain in the U.S. Army during World War I. Chairman, Democratic National Finance Committee, 1948; Secretary of Defense, 1949–50. Johnson, who was controversial as Secretary of Defense, was replaced by General George Marshall. Johnson supported U.S. hydrogen-bomb development.

Johnson, Lyndon Baines (1908–73). United States. Lawyer. Representative (Tex.), 1938–48; Senator (Tex.), 1949–61; Vice President, 1961–63; President, 1963–69. Johnson took office following the assassination of President John F. Kennedy.

Joy, Charles Turner (1895–1956). United States. Naval officer during World War II and the Korean War.

Juliana, Queen of the Netherlands (1909– ; r. 1948–80).

Kefauver, Estes (1903–63). United States. Lawyer. Representative (Tenn.), 1939–49; Senator (Tenn.), 1948–63.

Keller, Kaufman (1885–1966). United States. Executive at General Motors Corporation, and later vice president and president of the Chrysler Corporation. Secretary of Defense George Marshall appointed Keller as Guided-Missile Director in 1950, a post he held for three years while also serving as chairman of Chrysler.

Kennedy, John Fitzgerald (1917–63). United States. Lawyer. Served as an officer in the U.S. Navy during World War II. Representative (Mass.), 1947–53; Senator (Mass.), 1953–61; President, 1961–63. Kennedy was assassinated in Dallas in November 1963.

Keyserling, Leon H. (1908–88). United States. Economist and lawyer. Vice Chairman, President's Council of Economic Advisers, 1946–50.

Khrushchev, Nikita (1894–1971). USSR. Political figure. Member, Communist Party of the Soviet Union, 1934–64; Member, Supreme Soviet Presidium, 1939–64; Chairman, Council of Ministers, 1958–64.

King, Ernest J. (1878–1956). United States. Naval officer. Commander-in-Chief, Atlantic Fleet, 1941; Commander-in-Chief, United States Fleet, 1941–44; Admiral of the Fleet ("five-star admiral"), 1944–45.

Klein, Julius (1887–1961). United States. Economist. Assistant Secretary of Commerce under President Herbert Hoover.

Knox, Frank (1874–1944). United States. Publisher of the *Chicago Daily News*. Secretary of the Navy, 1940–44.

Kublai Khan (1215–94). China. Grandson of Genghis Khan; ruler of the Mongol Empire as Khagan, 1260–94; founder of China's Yuan Dynasty.

La Follette, Robert M. (1855–1925). United States. Lawyer. Representative (Wisc.), 1885–91; Governor of Wisconsin, 1901–07; Senator (Wisc.), 1905–25.

Laurence, William L. (1888–1977). United States. Journalist. In 1946, Laurence was awarded a Pulitzer Prize for his eyewitness account of the atomic bombing of Nagasaki.

Leahy, William D. (1875–1959). United States. Naval officer. Chief, Bureau of Ordnance, 1927; Chief, Bureau of Navigation, 1933; Chief of Naval

Operations, 1937; Governor of Puerto Rico, 1939; U.S. Ambassador to Vichy France, 1941; Chief of Staff, Chairman of the Joint Chiefs of Staff, 1942; Adviser to Presidents Franklin Roosevelt and Harry Truman.

Lee, Robert E. (1807–70). Commander-in-Chief of the Confederate Army during the U.S. Civil War. He was placed in command of the Army of Northern Virginia in 1862, and was defeated at the Battle of Gettysburg in 1863. After the Civil War, Lee became the president of Washington College.

Lenin, Vladimir I. (1870–1924). USSR. Russian revolutionary leader and writer. Lenin worked for the Social Democratic Party in 1895; in 1900, he began, with other Marxist leaders, to publish a newspaper called *Iskra*. He lived abroad from 1907 to 1917; in 1917, he organized the overthrow of the provisional Russian government. Soviet Premier, 1917–24.

Lewis, John L. (1880–1969). United States. Labor leader, President, Congress of Industrial Organizations, 1935–40; President, United Mine Workers of America, 1920–60.

Lilienthal, David E. (1899–1981). United States. Lawyer. Director, Tennessee Valley Authority (TVA), 1933–41; Chairman, TVA, 1941–46; first chairman of the Atomic Energy Commission, 1947–50. Lilienthal supported U.S. hydrogen-bomb development.

Lincoln, Abraham (1809–65). United States. Lawyer. Representative (Ill.), 1847–49; President, 1861–65. Lincoln led the nation through the Civil War and issued the Emancipation Proclamation in 1863. He was assassinated by John Wilkes Booth in 1865.

Lincoln, Mary Todd (1818–82). United States. Wife of Abraham Lincoln.

Lincoln, Robert Todd (1843–1926). United States. Lawyer. Secretary of War, 1881–85; U.S. Minister to Great Britain, 1889–93. Son of Abraham Lincoln.

Lippmann, Walter (1889–1974). United States. Journalist. Served as a captain of U.S. Army Military Intelligence. Editor, *New York World,* 1931; Assistant to the Secretary of War, 1917; Secretary, Organization to Prepare Data for the Peace Conference Board Overseers, 1933–39. Lippman won a Pulitzer Prize in 1962.

Lodge, Henry Cabot, Jr. (1902–85). United States. Lawyer. Senator (Mass.), 1936–42, 1946–53. Lodge left the Senate to serve in the U.S. Army during World War II. U.S. Representative to the United Nations, 1953–60, U.S. Ambassador to South Vietnam, 1963–64, 1965–67; U.S. Ambassador at Large, 1967–68; U.S. Ambassador to Germany, 1968–69.

Long, Huey (1893–1935). United States. Lawyer and politician. Senator (La.), 1931–35.

López Mateos, Adolfo (1910–69). Mexico. President of Mexico, 1958–64.

Louis XIV, King of France (1638–1715; r. 1643–1715). Louis XIV, known as the Sun King, set up court at Versailles. In 1685, he revoked the Edict of Nantes, which had given religious rights to French Protestants.

Louis XVI, King of France (1754–93; r. 1774–92). In 1770, Louis XVI married Marie Antoinette. In 1789, revolutionary forces stormed the Bastille, and the King was removed from Versailles to the Tuileries. He attempted to flee France in 1791. The monarchy was abolished in 1792, and the King was guillotined in Paris in 1793.

Loveless, Herschel C. (1911–89). United States. Corporate executive. Mayor, Ottumwa, Iowa, 1949–53; Governor of Iowa, 1957–61; appointed to the Federal Renegotiation Board, 1961–69.

Lovett, Robert A. (1895–1986). United States. Banker. Special Assistant to the Secretary of War, 1940–41; Assistant Secretary of War for Air, 1941–45; Undersecretary of State, 1947–49; Secretary of Defense, 1951–53.

Luther, Martin (1483–1546). Germany. Augustinian friar who inaugurated the Protestant Reformation movement. In 1517, Luther posted the Ninety-five Theses; in 1521, he was excommunicated from the Roman Catholic church. He opposed indulgences and the worship of icons, and was a proponent of justification by faith.

MacArthur, Douglas (1880–1964). United States. Army officer. Served in World War II and Korea; became a general in 1944. Chief of Staff, 42nd Rainbow Division, 1917; served with the Army of Occupation, Germany, 1918–19; Military Adviser to the Commonwealth Government of the Philippines, 1935; Field Marshal, Philippine Army, 1936–37; Commander-in-Chief, U.S. and Filipino Forces, during the invasion of the Philippines by the Japanese, 1941–42; Commander, U.S. Armed Forces in the Far East, 1941–51; Supreme Commander, Allied Forces in Southwest Pacific, 1942; Commander, Occupation Forces in Japan, 1945–51; Commander-in-Chief, UN Forces in Korea, 1950–51.

Macmillan, Harold (1894–1986). Great Britain. Politician. Member, House of Commons, 1924–29, 1931–63; Prime Minister, 1957–63.

Madison, James (1751–1836). United States. Lawyer. Chief Recorder, Constitutional Convention, 1787. In 1788, Madison participated in the writing of the Federalist Papers. Representative (Va.), 1789–97; Secretary of State, 1801–09; President, 1809–17.

Marshall, George C. (1880–1959). United States. Soldier and statesman. Served in the Philippines; Chief of Operations under Liggett, 1918; served under General John Pershing, 1919–24; Executive Officer, 15th Infantry Regiment, Tientsin, China, 1924–27; Assistant Commandant in Charge of Instruction, Infantry School, Fort Benning, Georgia, 1927–32; worked with the Civilian Conservation Corps; Chief, War Plans Division, 1938; Head of the Army, 1939; General of the Army, 1945. Marshall went to China in 1947–49, at the request of President Harry Truman. Secretary of State, 1947–49; President, American Red Cross; Secretary of Defense, 1950–51.

Marshall, John (1755–1835). United States. Lawyer. Representative (Va.), 1799; Secretary of State, 1800; Chief Justice, U.S. Supreme Court, 1801–35.

Marshall, Thomas Riley (1854–1925). United States. Lawyer. Governor of Indiana, 1909–13; Vice President, 1913–21.

Martin, William McChesney (1874–1955). United States. Banker and lawyer. Chairman and Federal Reserve Agent, Federal Reserve Bank, 1914–29; President, Federal Reserve Bank, 1936–41.

Marx, Karl (1818–83). Germany. Social philosopher and political economist. Editor, *Rheinische Zeitung* (a radical newspaper), 1842–43. Marx wrote the Communist Manifesto with Friedrich Engels in 1848; he resided in London after 1850.

Masaryk, Jan (1886–1948). Czechoslovakia. Statesman, diplomat. Minister of Foreign Affairs in Exile, 1940; postwar Foreign Minister, 1945, 1948. Masaryk was the son of the first President of the Czechoslovak nation. He favored a federal Europe. In 1948, he was found dead below a window at Cernin Palace; the exact cause of his death is unknown.

McCabe, Thomas B. (1893–1982). United States. Banker, Chairman, Board of Governors, Federal Reserve System, 1948–51; Member, Business Advisers Council, Department of Commerce, 1940; Chairman, Business Advisers Council, Department of Commerce, 1944–45; served on Council of National Defense, 1940; served with Office of Production Management, 1941; served with Department of the Lend-Lease Administration, 1941–42.

McCarran, Patrick A. (1876–1954). United States. Lawyer. Justice, Nevada Supreme Court, 1913–18; Senator (Nev.), 1932–56.

McCarthy, Joseph R. (1908–57). United States. Lawyer. Served in the Marine Corps during World War II. Senator (Wisc.), 1946–57.

McClellan, George B. (1826–85). United States. Army officer. Served in the Mexican War. Appointed Major General of the U.S. Army, 1861;

became Commander-in-Chief, 1861. In the U.S. Civil War, McClellan defeated Robert E. Lee at the Battle of Antietam. Democratic candidate for President, 1864.

McCormick, Robert Rutherford (1880–1955). United States. Editor and lawyer. Served in World War I. Editor and publisher of the *Chicago Tribune*.

McKinley, William, Jr. (1843–1901). United States. Lawyer. Served in the Union Army during the U.S. Civil War. Representative (Ohio), 1876–91; Governor of Ohio, 1891–95; President, 1897–1901.

McKinney, Frank E. (1904–74). United States. Banker. President, Fidelity Bank and Trust Company, 1935–59; Chairman, Democratic National Committee, 1951–53.

Meany, George (1898–1980). United States. Labor leader and plumber. President, New York State Federation of Labor, 1934–39; Secretary–Treasurer of the AFL, 1945–52; first President of combined AFL–CIO, 1955–79.

Mellon, Andrew (1855–37). United States. Banker. Secretary of the Treasury, 1921–32; U.S. Ambassador to Great Britain, 1933.

Mollet, Guy (1905–75). France. Socialist politician. Prime Minister, 1956–57.

Molotov, Vyacheslav M. (1896–1986). USSR. Communist Party leader. Secretary, Central Committee of the Communist Party, 1921; made full member of the Politburo, 1926; Premier, 1930–41; Commissar of Foreign Affairs, 1939; Deputy Prime Minister, 1941–49; Foreign Minister, 1953–56. In 1912, he helped establish the Communist Party newspaper *Pravda*.

Monroe, James (1758–1831). United States. Lawyer. Served in the Continental Army during the Revolutionary War. Member from Virginia, Continental Congress, 1783–86; U.S. Senator (Va.), 1790–94; Governor of Virginia, 1799–1802; U.S. Minister to France, 1803; U.S. Minister to England, 1803–1807; U.S. Secretary of State, 1811–17; U.S. Secretary of War, 1814–15; U.S. President, 1817–25.

Montgomery, Bernard Law (1887–1976). Great Britain. Field marshal and one of the leading Allied commanders of World War II.

Morgan, J. Pierpont (1837–1913). United States. Financier and lawyer who founded the United States Steel Corporation.

Morgenthau, Henry, Jr. (1891–1967). United States. Politician and agriculturalist. Undersecretary of the Treasury, 1933–34; Secretary of the Treasury, 1934–45.

Moro, Aldo (1916–78). Italy. Law professor at Bari University. Minister of Justice, 1955–57; later Foreign Minister and Prime Minister. Captured in March and executed in May 1978 by the Red Brigade terrorists after the government refused to exchange communist prisoners.

Morse, Wayne (1900–74). United States. Lawyer. Assistant to the Attorney General, 1936–39; Chairman, President's Emergency Board, 1941; Senator (Ore.), 1945–69.

Mossadegh, Mohammed (1880–1967). Iran. Prime Minister, 1951–53.

Mountbatten, Philip, Duke of Edinburgh (1921–). Great Britain. Naval officer. Married to Queen Elizabeth II of Great Britain.

Murphy, Paul, S.J. (1908–90). United States. U.S. Navy chaplain in World War II; professor at Holy Cross and Boston Colleges; director of St. Joseph's Retreat League for Workingmen; president of Morality in Media.

Murray, Philip (1886–1952). United States. Labor leader. President, CIO, 1940; President, United Steelworkers of America, 1942; Co-chairman, United Labor Policy Commission, 1950–51.

Murrow, Edward R. (1908–65). United States. Newsman. Murrow is famous for his broadcasts from Europe during World War II, and later during the Korean War, for CBS. Appointed director of the U.S. Information Agency in 1961.

Mussolini, Benito (1883–1945). Italy. Statesman. Organized the Fascist Party, 1921; Prime Minister, 1922; first Marshal of the Empire, 1938; Prime Minister, Minister of War, Minister of the Navy, Minister of the Air Force, Minister of Foreign Affairs, and Commander-in-Chief of the Armed Forces, 1939–43. Allied with Hitler in World War II.

Nasser, Gamal Abdel (1918–70). Egypt. President, United Arab Republic, 1958–70.

Nehru, Jawaharlal (1889–1964). India. Prime Minister, 1929, 1936, 1937, 1946, 1951–54. Nehru was imprisoned several times for political activities.

Nevins, Allan (1890–1971). United States. Professor of American History, Columbia University, 1931–58; Special Representative of the Office of War Information in Australia and New Zealand, 1943–44; Chief Public Affairs Officer, American Embassy in London, 1945–46.

Nimitz, Chester W. (1885–1966). United States. Naval officer. Commander-in-Chief, Pacific Fleet, 1941–45; Chief of Naval Operations, 1945–47.

Nitze, Paul (1907–). United States. Vice President, U.S. Strategic Bombing Survey, 1944; Assistant Secretary of Defense, 1961–63.

Nixon, Richard M. (1913–94). United States. Lawyer. Attorney, Office of Price Administration, 1942; Representative (Calif.), 1946–50; Senator (Calif.), 1950–53; Vice President, 1953–61; President, 1969–74. Resigned office in 1974.

Norris, George William (1861–1944). United States. Lawyer. Representative (Neb.), 1903–13; Senator (Neb.), 1913–43.

Nourse, Edwin G. (1883–1974). United States. Economist. Vice President, Brookings Institution, 1942–46; Chairman, Council of Economic Advisers, 1946–49.

Noyes, David M. (1898–1981). United States. Journalist, businessman, counselor to President Truman. Noyes helped organize the War Production Board. He served as assistant to Truman in the White House and at the Truman Library into the 1960s.

Oppenheimer, J. Robert (1904–67). United States. Physicist. Professor of Physics, University of California; Director, Los Alamos Science Laboratory, New Mexico, 1943–45.

Paderewski, Ignace Jan (1860–1941). Poland. Pianist and composer who organized concerts for the benefit of Polish war sufferers in World War I.

Parker, Alton B. (1852–1926). United States. Lawyer who served on several state courts in New York. Democratic candidate for President, 1904.

Patterson, Robert Porter (1891–1952). United States. Lawyer. Undersecretary of War, 1940; Secretary of War, 1945–47.

Perry, Oliver Hazard (1785–1819). United States. Naval officer. Perry served in the War of 1812 and commanded the American fleet on Lake Erie.

Pershing, John J. (1860–1948). United States. Army officer. General of the Armies of the United States, 1919–24. Pershing organized the Bureau of Insular Affairs; served in conflicts with the Sioux; headed the American Expeditionary Force in World War I; and fought the Mexican guerrillas.

Pierce, Franklin (1804–69). United States. Lawyer. Served in the U.S. Army during the Mexican War. Representative (N.H.), 1833–37; Senator (N.H.), 1837–42; President, 1853–57.

Pineau, Christian Paul (1904–95). France. Statesman. Minister of Foreign Affairs, 1956–57.

Pius XII (Eugenio Pacelli) (1876–1958). Member of the Vatican diplomatic corps. Vatican Secretary of State, 1930–39; Pope, 1939–58.

Pizzaro, Francisco (1475–1541). Spain. Conquistador. Conquered Peru, 1531–33.

Plutarch (46–120). Greek moralist and author, especially of biographies.

Polk, James K. (1795–1849). United States. Politician. Representative (Tenn.), 1825–39; Speaker of the House, 1835–39; Governor of Tennessee, 1838–41; President, 1845–49.

Polo, Marco (1254–1324). Italy. Traveler. Polo was the first European to cross the continent of Asia.

Pompey the Great (106–48 B.C.). Roman political and military leader.

Proxmire, William A. (1915–). United States. Businessman. U.S. Senator (Wisc.), 1957–89.

Quirino, Elpidio (1890–1956). Philippines. President of the Philippines, 1948–53.

Rayburn, Sam (1882–1961). United States. Lawyer. Representative (Tenn.), 1912–61; Speaker of the House, 1940–47, 1949–53, 1955–61.

Reed, James A. (1861–1944). United States. Lawyer. Senator (Mo.), 1911–29.

Reuther, Walter (1907–70). United States. Labor leader. Director, General Motors Department of UAW, 1939; President, CIO, 1952; President, AFL-CIO, 1955–70. Reuther also worked in the labor-policy commission of the Labor Productions Division of the War Production Board.

Ridgway, Matthew B. (1895–1993). United States. Army officer. Army Operations Officer, 1937–39; War Plans Division, War Department General Staff, 1939–42; Commanding General, 82nd Airborne Division, Sicily, Italy, Normandy, 1942–44; Commander, 18th Airborne Corps, Belgium, France, Germany, 1944–45; Chairman, Military Staff Commission, United Nations, 1946–48, 1949–50; Commander-in-Chief, Caribbean Commander, 1948–49; Commander-in-Chief, Far East Command, United Nations Command and Supreme Commander for Allied Powers, 1951–52; Supreme Commander, Allied Powers in Europe, 1952–53; Chief of Staff, U.S. Army, 1953–55.

Rockefeller, John D. (1839–1937). United States. Capitalist and philanthropist. Organized Standard Oil.

Rogers, William P. (1913–). United States. Lawyer. U.S. Attorney General, 1958–61; Secretary of State, 1969–73.

Roosevelt, Eleanor (1884–1962). United States. Author and delegate to the United Nations. Wife of Franklin D. Roosevelt.

Roosevelt, Franklin Delano (1882–1945). United States. Lawyer. Assistant Secretary of the Navy, 1913–20; Governor of New York, 1929–33;

President, 1933–45. Led the nation through the Great Depression, the New Deal, and World War II.

Roosevelt, James (1907–). United States. Business consultant. Worked in the motion-picture industry, 1938–40; Representative (Calif.), 1955–67. Son of Franklin D. Roosevelt.

Roosevelt, Theodore (1858–1919). United States. Army officer and statesman. Assistant Secretary of the Navy, 1897–98. Roosevelt organized the Rough Riders, who fought in Cuba. Governor of New York, 1899–1900; Vice President, 1901; President, 1901–09. Took office following the death of President William McKinley in 1901 and was reelected to a second term. Awarded the Nobel Peace Prize, 1906.

Ross, Charles Griffith (1885–1950). United States. Journalist. Chief Washington correspondent, *St. Louis Post–Dispatch,* 1918–34; appointed secretary to President Truman in charge of press relations, 1945.

Russell, Lord John (1792–1878). Great Britain. Statesman. Entered House of Commons, 1813; Home Secretary and Colonial Secretary, 1836–41; Prime Minister, 1846–52; Foreign Secretary, then Minister, in Lord Aberdeen's coalition prime ministry, 1852–55; Foreign Secretary, 1859–61; Prime Minister, 1865–66.

Sampson, William T. (1840–1902). United States. Admiral who served in the Spanish-American War.

Saud, Ibn al-Rahman al-Faisal Al- (1902–69). Saudi Arabia. Named crown prince, 1933; King, 1953–64. Opposed Israel.

Schley, Winfield Scott (1839–1909). United States. Naval Officer in the U.S. Civil War and Spanish-American War.

Schoeppel, Andrew F. (1894–1962). United States. Lawyer. Governor of Kansas, 1943–47.

Schwellenbach, Lewis Baxter (1894–1948). United States. Lawyer. Senator (Wash.), 1935–40; Secretary of Labor, 1945.

Scott, Winfield (1786–1866). United States. Army officer. Served in the War of 1812. General-in-Chief of the Army, 1841–61; fought in the Mexican War, 1847; Whig candidate for President, 1852.

Segni, Antonio (1891–1972). Italy. Statesman. Undersecretary of the Ministry of Agriculture, 1944–45; Minister of Agriculture, 1946–51; Prime Minister, 1955–57, 1959–60; Foreign Minister, 1960–62; President of the Italian Republic, 1962–64.

Sherman, William Tecumseh (1820–91). United States. Army officer. Served in the Mexican War. Sherman was promoted to brigadier general of the U.S. Army in 1863; was made Supreme Commander in the West; and was promoted to major general of the Army.

Smith, Alfred E. (1873–1944). United States. Politician. Governor of New York, 1919–20, 1923–28; Democratic candidate for President, 1928.

Snyder, John Wesley (1895–1985). United States. Business executive. National Bank Receiver, Office of the Comptroller of Currency, 1931–37; appointed Federal Loan Administrator, 1944; appointed Director, Office of War Mobilization and Reconversion, 1945; Secretary of the Treasury, 1946–53.

Souers, Sidney W. (1892–1973). United States. Business executive who worked for the General American Life Insurance Company. Admiral, U.S. Navy, 1945; Executive Secretary, National Security Council, 1947–50; Special Consultant to the President, 1950–53; first Director, Central Intelligence Group.

Spaak, Paul-Henri (1899–1972). Belgium. Government official. Prime Minister, 1938–39; Minister of Foreign Affairs, 1939 (continued as Minister of Foreign Affairs and Foreign Trade until 1957); Secretary-General. NATO, 1957–61; Vice Prime Minister, Minister of Foreign Affairs, 1961–66.

Spanier, John W. (1930–). United States. Political scientist and author. Professor, University of Florida, Gainesville, 1957– .

Sparkman, John J. (1899–1985). United States. Lawyer. Representative (Ala.), 1937–47; Senator (Ala.), 1956–79; unsuccessful Vice Presidential nominee, 1952.

Stalin, Joseph (1879–1953). USSR. Russian revolutionary and statesman. Founded the Communist Party newspaper *Pravda,* 1912; General Secretary, Central Committee of the Communist Party, 1922–53; Premier, 1941–53.

Stassen, Harold E. (1907–). United States. Lawyer and politician. Served in World War II. Governor of Minnesota, 1938–42; President, University of Pennsylvania, 1943–45, 1948–53; Director, Foreign Operations Administration, 1953–55; Special Assistant to the President on Disarmament Problems, 1955–58.

Stettinius, Edward R., Jr. (1900–49). United States. Businessman. Lend-Lease Administrator; Special Assistant to the President, 1941–43; Undersecretary of State, 1943–44; Secretary of State, 1944–45; Personal Representative of the President, 1945; Representative to the UN General Assembly, 1945.

Stevens, Thaddeus (1792–1868). United States. Lawyer. Representative (Penn.), 1849–53, 1859–68.

Stevenson, Adlai E. (1900–65). United States. Lawyer. Assistant to the Secretary of the U.S. Navy, 1941–44; Assistant to the Secretary of State, 1945; Governor of Illinois, 1948–52; Democratic candidate for President, 1952, 1956; Assistant to the Secretary of State, 1957; U.S. Ambassador to the United Nations, 1961–65.

Stimson, Henry L. (1867–1950). United States. Lawyer. Secretary of War, 1911–13; Special Representative of the President to Nicaragua, 1927; Governor General of the Philippine Islands, 1927–29; Secretary of State, 1929–33; Secretary of War, 1940–45.

Strauss, Lewis L. (1896–1974). United States. Government official. Member, U.S. Atomic Energy Commission, 1946–50; Special Assistant to the President on Atomic Energy Matters, 1953; Chairman, Atomic Energy Commission, 1953–58.

Stryker, Lloyd Paul (1885–1955). United States. Lawyer, author. District Court judge in New York.

Symington, Stuart (1901–88). United States. Banker. Surplus Property Administrator, Washington, 1945–46; Assistant Secretary of War for Air, 1946–47; Secretary of the Air Force, 1947–50; Chairman, National Security Resources Board, 1950–51; Senator (Mo.), 1952–77.

Taft, Robert A. (1889–1953). United States. Lawyer. Senator (Ohio), 1939–53. Co-sponsor with Representative Fred A. Hartley of labor legislation that modified the National Labor Relations (Wagner) Act of 1935 by tighter control of labor disputes. Truman vetoed the act; however, it was passed over his veto. Opponent of Franklin D. Roosevelt's New Deal and Lend-Lease programs. Lost Republican nomination for President to Dwight D. Eisenhower in 1952. Son of William Howard Taft.

Taft, William Howard (1857–1930). United States. Lawyer, Solicitor General of the U.S., 1890–1892; first civil Governor of the Philippine Islands, 1901–04; Secretary of War, 1904–08; President, 1909–1913.

Tamerlane (1336–1405). Turkish conqueror.

Taylor, Myron Charles (1874–1959). United States. Lawyer, industrialist, diplomat. Personal Representative of Presidents Roosevelt and Truman to Pope Pius XII, 1939–50.

Taylor, Zachary (1784–1850). United States. Army officer who was involved in the Indian wars. Commander, Army of Occupation on the Mexican border, 1845–46. Defeated the Mexicans at the Battle of Buena Vista in 1847. President, 1849–50.

Thurmond, J. Strom (1902–). United States. Lawyer. Governor of South Carolina, 1947–51; Senator (S.C.), 1955– .

Tito (Josip Broz) (1892–1980). Yugoslavia. Statesman. Private in the Austro-Hungarian Army, 1914; imprisoned in the Russian camps, 1915–17; fought with the Red Army, 1917–21; Premier, 1944–53; Minister of National Defense and President of Yugoslavia, 1953–80.

Toynbee, Arnold J. (1889–1975). Great Britain. Author and historian. Served with the Foreign Office, 1939–46; Member, British Delegation to the Peace Conference at Paris, 1946.

Trujillo Molina, Rafael Leónidas (1891–1961). Dominican Republic. Army chief during the Presidency of Horacio Vasquez. Elected President of the Dominican Republic, 1930–38, 1942–60. Powerful autocrat with a firm grip on the nation; assassinated in 1961.

Truman, Bess Wallace (1885–1982). United States. Wife of President Harry Truman.

Truman, Margaret (1924–). United States. Author, concert singer, actress, and editor. Daughter of Harry S. and Bess Truman; she married E. Clifton Daniel, Jr., in 1956 and is the mother of four sons. Her books *Harry S. Truman; Letters from my Father; Bess Truman;* and *Where the Buck Stops: The Personal and Private Writings of Harry S. Truman,* together with more than a dozen murder-mystery novels set in the Washington, D.C., area, highlight a remarkable career.

Tubby, Roger Wellington (1910–91). United States. Journalist. Press Officer, Department of State, 1945–49; Executive Assistant for Press Relations, 1950; Assistant to the White House Press Secretary, 1950–52; Acting Press Secretary to the President, 1952.

Tyler, John (1790–1862). United States. Lawyer. Served in the War of 1812. Representative (Va.), 1817–21; Governor of Virginia, 1827–36; President, 1841–45. Elected Vice President in 1840 and became President after William Harrison died.

Van Buren, Martin (1782–1862). United States. Lawyer. Senator (N.Y.), 1821–28; Secretary of State, 1829–31; Vice President, 1833–37; President, 1837–41.

Vandenberg, Arthur H. (1884–1951). United States. Newspaper editor. Senator (Mich.), 1928–53; U.S. Representative to the Council of Foreign Ministers and Peace Conference, Paris, 1946.

Vandenberg, Hoyt S. (1923–54). United States. U.S. Army Air Corps officer in World War II. Director, Central Intelligence Group, 1946–47; Chief of Staff, U.S. Air Force, 1948–53.

Van Fleet, James A. (1892–1992). United States. Army officer. Served in World War I; Commanding Officer, 8th Infantry, 4th Division, 1941–44;

Commanding General, 90th Infantry Division, 1944–45, and III Corps, 1945–46; Director, U.S. Army Group for Aid to Greece, 1948–50; Commanding General, Second Army, 1950–53.

Vaughan, Harry H. (1888–1964). United States. Engineer. Major General; military aide to President Harry Truman.

Velde, Harold Himmel (1910–85). United States. Lawyer and politician. Special Agent, FBI, 1943–46; Representative (Ill.), 1949–57; Chairman, House Un-American Activities Committee, 1953.

Vinson, Fred (1890–1953). United States. Lawyer. Director, Office of Economic Stabilization, 1943; Director, Office of War Mobilization and Reconversion, 1945; Secretary of the Treasury, 1945; Chief Justice, U.S. Supreme Court, 1946–53.

Voorhis, Horace Jeremiah (Jerry) (1901–84). United States. Executive director of the Cooperative League of the U.S.A., politician. U.S. Representative (Calif.), 1937–47.

Wallace, Henry Agard (1888–1965). United States. Editor and author. Secretary of Agriculture, 1933–41; Vice President, 1941–45; Secretary of Commerce, 1945–46; Progressive Party candidate for President, 1948.

Wallenstein, Albrecht von (1583–1634). Austrian general in the Thirty Years' War.

Warren, Earl (1891–1974). United States. Lawyer. Governor of California, 1943–46; Chief Justice, U.S. Supreme Court, 1953–69.

Washington, George (1732–1799). United States. Surveyor. Lieutenant Colonel in the French and Indian War, 1754–58; Member, Virginia House of Burgesses; Commander, Continental Army, 1775–83; presided over the Constitutional Convention, 1787; first President of the United States, 1789–97.

Watson, Thomas (1914–93). United States. Business executive. President, IBM, 1952–61; Chairman, IBM, 1961–79; U.S. Ambassador to the Soviet Union, 1979–81.

Wellington, Duke of (Arthur Wellesley) (1769–1852). Great Britain. Soldier and statesman. Served in the war against Napoleon. Prime Minister, 1828–30.

Whitney, Alexander F. (1873–1949). United States. Labor leader. Worked with the Brotherhood of Railroad Trainmen.

Whittier, John Greenleaf (1807–92). Poet and abolitionist. Editor of the *Pennsylvania Freeman*, 1838–40.

Williams, G. Mennen (1911–). United States. Lawyer. Governor of Michigan, 1949–61; Justice, Michigan State Supreme Court, 1971– .

Wilson, Woodrow (1856–1924). United States. Lawyer and educator. Professor, Bryn Mawr and Wesleyan colleges, 1885–90; Professor of Political Economics, Princeton University, 1890–1902; President, Princeton University, 1902–10; Governor of New Jersey, 1911–12; President, 1913–21. Designed the League of Nations.

Woodin, William H. (1868–1934). United States. Manufacturer with the American Car & Foundry Company. Director, Federal Reserve Bank of New York; Secretary of the Treasury, 1933.

Woodward, Stanley (1899–1951). United States. Diplomat who held posts in the Netherlands, Switzerland, Belgium, and Haiti. Assistant Chief of Protocol, 1937–44; Chief of Protocol, 1944–50; U.S. Ambassador to Canada, 1950–53.

Young, E. Merl (1913–1981). United States. Business executive and travel agent. Young served as an official with the federal Reconstruction Finance Corporation and was convicted of perjury in 1953 regarding a $10 million RFC loan. He served four months in federal prison in Florida.

Zhukov, Georgi (1896–1974). USSR. Military officer and Soviet government official. Commander-in-Chief, Western Front, 1941–42; Member, Allied Control Commission, 1945–46; Commander-in-Chief, Soviet Ground Forces, and Member, Supreme Soviet Presidium, 1946; Head, Soviet Military Mission in Poland, 1948; first Soviet Deputy Minister of Defense, 1953–55; Minister of Defense, 1955–57.

Bibliography

Acheson, Dean. *Present at the Creation: My Years in the State Department.* New York: Norton, 1969.

Alperovitz, Gar. *Atomic Diplomacy: Hiroshima and Potsdam.* New York: Simon and Schuster, 1965.

Ambrose, Stephen E. *Eisenhower, 1890–1952: Soldier of the Army and President Elect.* New York: Simon and Schuster, 1983.

———. *Nixon: The Education of a Politician 1913–1962.* New York: Simon and Schuster, 1987.

———. *Eisenhower: Soldier and President.* New York: Simon and Schuster, 1990.

American National Biography. 24 vols. New York: Oxford University Press, 1999.

Ayes, Alex. *The Wit and Wisdom of Harry S. Truman.* New York: Meridian Books, 1998.

Barkley, Alben W. *That Reminds Me: The Autobiography of the Veep.* Garden City, N.Y.: Doubleday, 1954.

Bernstein, Barton J. "Truman and the A-Bomb: Targeting Noncombatants, Using the Bomb, and His Defending the Decision." *Journal of Military History* 62 (July 1998): 547–51.

Bowers, Claude. *My Mission to Spain: Watching the Rehearsal for World War II.* New York: Simon and Schuster, 1954.

Boyd, Julian, Lyman Butterfield et al., eds. *Papers of Thomas Jefferson.* 27 vols. Princeton, N.J.: Princeton University Press, 1950–[97].

Bundy, McGeorge. *Danger and Survival: Choices about the Bomb in the First Years.* New York: Random House, 1988.

Burns, James MacGregor. *Roosevelt: The Lion and the Fox.* New York: Harcourt, Brace, 1956.

———. *Roosevelt: The Soldier of Freedom 1940–1945.* New York: Harcourt, Brace, 1970.

Burns, Richard Dean. *Harry S. Truman: A Bibliography of His Times and Presidency.* Wilmington, Del.: Scholarly Resources, 1984.

Byrnes, James F. *Speaking Frankly.* New York: Harper's, 1947.

———. *All in One Lifetime.* New York: Harper's, 1958.

Clifford, Clark, with Richard Holbrooke. *Counsel to the President: A Memoir*. New York: Random House, 1991.

Cochran, Hamilton. *Blockade Runners of the Confederacy*. Indianapolis: Bobbs-Merrill, 1958.

Current, Richard N. *Secretary Stimson*. New Brunswick, N.J.: Rutgers University Press, 1954.

Daniels, Jonathan. *The Man of Independence*. Philadelphia: J. B. Lippincott, 1950.

Donovan, Robert J. *Conflict and Crisis: The Presidency of Harry S. Truman, 1945–1948*. New York: Norton, 1977.

———. *Tumultuous Years: The Presidency of Harry S. Truman, 1949–1953*. New York: Norton, 1977.

———. *Nemesis: Truman and Johnson in the Coils of War in Asia*. New York: St. Martin's Press, 1984.

———. *The Words of Harry S. Truman*. New York: Newmarket Press, 1984.

Eisenhower, Dwight D. *The White House Years: Mandate for a Change, 1953–1956*. Garden City, N.Y.: Doubleday, 1963.

Feis, Herbert. *The Atomic Bomb and the End of World War II*. Princeton, N.J.: Princeton University Press, 1966.

Ferrell, Robert H. *American Diplomacy: The Twentieth Century*. New York: Norton, 1988.

———. *Harry S. Truman: A Life*. Columbia: University of Missouri Press, 1994.

———. *Harry S. Truman and the Bomb: A Documentary History*. Worland, Wyo.: High Plains Publishing, 1996.

Ferrell, Robert H., ed. *The Autobiography of Harry S. Truman*. Boulder: Colorado Associated University Press, 1980.

———, ed. *Off the Record: The Private Papers of Harry S. Truman*. New York: Harper and Row, 1980.

———, ed. *Dear Bess: The Letters from Harry to Bess Truman, 1910–1959*. New York: Norton, 1983.

Frank, Richard. *Downfall: The End of the Imperial Japanese Empire*. New York: Random House, 1999.

Freeman, Douglas S. *R. E. Lee: A Biography*. 4 vols. New York: Scribner's, 1934–35.

———. *Lee's Lieutenants: A Study in Command*. 3 vols. New York: Scribner's, 1942–44.

Gallen, David., ed. *The Quotable Truman*. New York: Carroll and Graf, 1994.

Grose, Peter. *Gentleman Spy: The Life of Allen Dulles*. Boston: Houghton Mifflin, 1994.

Groves, Leslie R. *Now It Can Be Told*. New York: Harper's, 1962.

Hamby, Alonzo L. *Man of the People*. New York: Oxford University Press, 1995.

Helm, William P. *Harry Truman: A Political Biography*. New York: Duell, Sloane and Pearce, 1947.

Hillman, William. *Mr. President*. New York: Farrar, Straus and Young, 1952.

———. *Harry S. Truman in His Own Words*. New York: Bonanza Books, 1984.

Hoff, Joan. *Nixon Reconsidered*. New York: Basic Books, 1994.

Jenkins, Roy. *Truman*. London: Collins, 1986.

Johnson, Neil M. *Power, Money, and Women: Words to the Wise from Harry S. Truman*. Olathe, Kan.: Burns Publishing, 1999.

Johnson, Paul. *Modern Times: The World from the Twenties to the Eighties*. New York: Harper and Row, 1983.

Johnson, Walter, ed. *The Papers of Adlai E. Stevenson*. 8 vols. Boston: Little, Brown, 1972–76.

Kane, Joseph Nathan. *Facts about Presidents: A Compilation of Biography and Historical Information*, 6th ed. New York: H. W. Wilson, 1993.

Keegan, John. *The First World War*. New York: Alfred A. Knopf, 1999.

Kennan, George F. *Memoirs: 1925–1950*. Boston: Little, Brown, 1967.

Kirkendall, Richard S. *The Harry S. Truman Encyclopedia*. Boston: G. K. Hall, 1989.

Keyes, Ralph, ed. *The Wit and Wisdom of Harry Truman: A Treasury of Quotations, Anecdotes, and Observations*. New York: Gramercy Books, 1999.

LaFeber, Walter. *America, Russia, and the Cold War, 1946–1971*. New York: Wiley, 1972.

Laurence, William L. *Men and Atoms: The Discovery, the Uses, and the Future of Atomic Energy*. New York: Simon and Schuster, 1959.

Lavender, David. *Climax at Buena Vista*. Philadelphia: J. B. Lippincott, 1966.

Leahy, William D. *I Was There: The Personal Story of the Chief of Staff of Presidents Roosevelt and Truman Based on His Notes and Diaries Made at the Time*. New York: Whittlesey House, 1950.

Leech, Margaret. *In the Days of McKinley*. New York: Harper, 1959.

Leuchtenburg, William E. *In the Shadow of FDR: From Harry Truman to Ronald Reagan*. Ithaca, N.Y.: Cornell University Press, 1983.

Lowitt, Richard. *The Truman and MacArthur Controversy*. Skokie, Ill.: Rand McNally, 1967.

MacArthur, Douglas. *Reminiscences*. New York: McGraw-Hill, 1964.

Manchester, William. *American Caesar: Douglas MacArthur, 1880–1964*. Boston: Little, Brown, 1978.

Marshall, George. *Memoirs of My Service in the World Wars*. Boston: Houghton Mifflin, 1974.

Martin, John Bartlow. *Adlai Stevenson of Illinois*. New York: Doubleday, 1976.

McCullough, David. *Truman*. New York. Simon and Schuster, 1992.

McNeil, William Hardy. *America, Britain, and Russia: Their Co-operation and Conflict, 1941–1946*. London: Oxford University Press, 1953.

McKeever, Porter. *Adlai Stevenson: His Life and Legacy*. New York: William Morrow, 1989.

McLellan, David S. *Dean Acheson: The State Department Years*. New York: Dodd, Mead, 1976.

Miller, Merle. *Plain Speaking: An Oral Biography of Harry S. Truman*. New York: Berkley Publishing Group, 1984.

Moore, Ruth. *Niels Bohr, the Man, His Science, and the World They Changed*. New York: Alfred A. Knopf, 1966.

Mosley, Leonard. *Marshall: Hero for Our Times*. New York: Hearst, 1982.

Nevins, Allan. *The War for the Union*. 4 vols. New York: Scribner's, 1959–71.

Newstadt, Richard E. *Presidential Power: The Politics of Leadership from FDR to Carter*. New York: John Wiley, 1980.

Nixon, Richard. *In the Arena: A Memoir of Victory, Defeat and Renewal*. New York: Simon and Schuster, 1990.

Parmet, Herbert S. *Richard Nixon and His America*. Boston: Little, Brown, 1990.

Phillips, Cabell. *The Truman Presidency: The History of a Triumphant Successor*. New York: Macmillan, 1966.

Poen, Monte M., ed. *Strictly Personal and Confidential: The Letters Harry Truman Never Mailed*. Boston: Little, Brown, 1982.

———, ed. *Letters Home by Harry Truman*. New York: Putnam, 1984.

Pogue, Forrest C. *George C. Marshall: Statesman, 1945–1959*. New York: Viking, 1987.

Rayback, Robert J. *Millard Fillmore: Biography of a President*. Buffalo, N.Y.: Buffalo Historical Society, 1959.

Robbins, Charles. *Last of His Kind: An Informal Portrait of Harry S. Truman*. New York: William Morrow, 1979.

Roosevelt, James, and Sidney Shalett. *Affectionately, FDR: A Son's Story of a Lonely Man*. New York: Harcourt, Brace, 1959.

Schachner, Nathan. *Alexander Hamilton*. New York: T. Yoseloff, 1957.

Schaller, Michael. *Douglas MacArthur: The Far Eastern General*. New York: Oxford University Press, 1989.

Schlesinger, Arthur M., Jr. *The Imperial Presidency*. Boston: Houghton Mifflin, 1973.

Sherwin, Martin J. *A World Destroyed: Hiroshima and the Origins of the Arms Race*. New York: Vintage, 1987.

Spanier, John W. *The Truman–MacArthur Controversy and the Korean War*. Cambridge, Mass.: Belknap Press, 1959.

Spector, Ronald H. *Eagle against the Sun: The American War with Japan*. New York: Free Press, 1989.

Stapleton, Margaret L. *The Truman and Eisenhower Years, 1945–1960*. Metuchen, N.J.: Scarecrow Press, 1973.

Sternberg, Alfred. *The Man from Missouri: The Life and Times of Harry S. Truman*. New York: Putnam, 1962.

Stone, Ralph. *The Irreconcilables*. Lexington: University Press of Kentucky, 1970.

Stryker, Lloyd Paul. *Andrew Johnson: A Study in Courage*. New York: Macmillan, 1929.

Taylor, Myron, ed. *Wartime Correspondence between President Roosevelt and Pope Pius XII*. New York: Macmillan, 1947.

Teller, Edward, and Allen Brown. *The Legacy of Hiroshima*. Garden City, N.Y.: Doubleday, 1962.

Toland, John. *The Last 100 Days*. New York: Random House, 1966.

Truman, Harry S. *Correspondence between President Truman and Pope Pius XII*, with an introduction by Myron C. Taylor. (privately printed, New York[?] 1953[?])

———. *Memoirs*. 2 vols. Garden City, N.Y.: Doubleday, 1955–56.

———. *Mr. Citizen*. New York: Bernard Geis Associates, 1960.

———. *Truman Speaks*. New York: Columbia University Press, 1960.

Truman, Margaret. *Harry S. Truman*. New York: William Morrow, 1973.

———. *Bess W. Truman*. New York: Macmillan, 1986.

Truman, Margaret, ed. *Letters from Father: The Truman Family's Personal Correspondence*. New York: Arbor House, 1981.

———, ed. *Where the Buck Stops: The Personal and Private Writings of Harry S. Truman*. New York: Warner Books, 1989.

Voorhis, Jerry. *Confessions of a Congressman*. Garden City, N.Y.: Doubleday, 1947.

———. *The Strange Case of Richard Milhous Nixon*. New York: Paul Eriksson, 1972.

Walton, Richard J. *Henry Wallace, Harry Truman and the Cold War*. New York: Viking, 1976.

Warner, Michael, ed. *The CIA under Harry Truman*. Washington, D.C.: Central Intelligence Agency, 1994.

Warren, Earl. *Current Constitutional Issues*. New York: Da Capo Press, 1971.

———. *The Republic, If You Can Keep It*. New York: Quadrangle Books, 1972.

———. *Memoirs*. Garden City, N.Y.: Doubleday, 1977.

Weber, Ralph E. *Spymasters: Ten CIA Officers in Their Own Words*. Wilmington, Del.: Scholarly Resources, 1999.

Weinstein, Allen. *Perjury: The Hiss–Chambers Case*. New York: Alfred A. Knopf, 1978.

Whitney, Courtney (Major General). *MacArthur: His Rendezvous with History*. New York: Alfred A. Knopf, 1964.

Willoughby, Charles A., and John Chamberlain. *MacArthur, 1941–1951*. New York: McGraw-Hill, 1954.

Wright, Gordon. *The Ordeal of Total War*. New York: Harper and Row, 1968.

Wyden, Peter. *Day One: Before Hiroshima and After*. New York: Simon and Schuster, 1984.

Index

Acheson, Dean G.: and atomic-bomb development, 6*n;* biographical data, 341; and Korea question, 321; on spy flights, 24*n;* and Truman's memoirs, xvii

Adams, John, 258; biographical data, 341; career of, 147; and Jefferson, 135

Adams, John Quincy, 124, 145, 147, 225, 257*n;* biographical data, 341

Adenauer, Konrad, 26, 248; biographical data, 341

administration(s): continuity of, importance of, 14–15; Republican, and Democratic Congress, 18–20. *See also* specific administrations

adult education, 113

advertising business, 96; BBD&O agency, 135

advice: listening to, 260; overruling of, 99

Africa, undeveloped areas in, 63

African Americans (Negroes), 109, 122, 315

agriculture. see farming

aid: federal, 335; foreign, 73–76, 87

Alaska, 318

Alemán Valdes, Miguel, 88, 200; biographical data, 341

"Alexander the Great" story, xvi

Allen, George Edward, 135; biographical data, 341

altruism, 286, 287; material success and, 278; U.S., 313

American Medical Association, 156–57, 286

American Revolution: generals of, 323; history of, Truman's plan to write, 96–97

Americans: defined, 313–15; great, 331–32

Americans for Democratic Action, 132*n*

Americas: communism in, 202. *See also* South America; specific countries

Anderson, Robert B., 46; biographical data, 341

antitrust laws, 60

Antoninus, Marcus Aurelius, 103–4

Antoninus, Pius, 103

Arabia: communism in, 253; undeveloped areas in, 63

Arabs: difficulty with, 252; and Jews, 317

arbitration: government and, 55; in strikes, 247–48

arbitration program, 235

Aristotle, 95

arms race, sudden cessation of, 338

Arthur, Chester A., 259, 259*n;* biographical data, 341

Arthur, William B., 23*n*

Atlantic and Pacific (A&P) stores, 61

atomic bomb: 1956 trip to Europe and topic of, 28; as campaign issue, 265–66; criticism of Truman's decision to use, 4*n;* decision-making regarding, 206–7; discussions at Potsdam Conference, 2–4; French development of, 160–61, 161*n;* further testing of, 265–66; and Japan's surrender, 71; Soviet development of, 3, 3*n,* 5–6, 269; Adlai Stevenson on, 179, 179*n*–80*n,* 206–7, 265; Truman's decision to use, 1–2, 4–5; unauthorized use of, risk of, 7–8; U.S. development of, 5–6, 8–9, 326

atomic energy, 270–71; development of, 206–7, 209; vs. oil, dependence on, 254; peacetime use of, 9–10, 266

Atomic Energy Commission: discussion of atomic bomb, 6*n;* Truman's historic order to, 5, 6

Attlee, Clement, 252*n;* biographical data, 342; relations with Truman, 23; visit to White House, 137

Auriol, Vincent, 136; biographical data, 342

autobiography, Truman's, xvii

Aztecs, history of, 97

Baldwin, Stanley, 314; biographical data, 342

Balfour, Arthur James, 252; biographical data, 342

Bankruptcy Law, 46

banks: position of, 51; unions compared with, 53

Baptists, 109, 122

Baring Brothers, 128*n*

Barkley, Alben W., 34*n,* 149, 204; biographical data, 342

Battle of Buena Vista, 258

Beard, Charles Austin, 94, 94*n;* biographical data, 342

Beard, Mary Ritter, 94, 94*n;* biographical data, 342

Beaverbrook, Lord, 25; biographical data, 342

Beck, David, 57; biographical data, 342

Belgium: 1956 visit to, 25; people of, 252

Belmont, August, 128*n*

Beneš, Edvard, 67, 67*n;* biographical data, 342

Berlin Airlift, 99

Bernstein, Barton, 1–2

Bernstein, Philip S., 252*n*

Beveridge, Albert, 327; biographical data, 342

Bible, 319

Biddle, Nicholas, 126; biographical data, 343

Bill of Rights, 105

bipartisanship, 138, 261–62

Bismarck, Otto von, 249; biographical data, 343

Blaine, James G., 230; biographical data, 343

Bland, Richard Parks ("Silver" Dick), 182; biographical data, 343

Bodet, Jaime Torres, 200; biographical data, 343

Bohr, Niels, 7*n;* biographical data, 343

Bolling, Richard Walker, 332; biographical data, 343

Bonaparte, Napoleon, 330; biographical data, 343

books, read by Truman, 93, 166–67

Bowers, Claude, 250; biographical data, 343

Bowles, Chester, 132*n*

Bradley, Omar, 69; biographical data, 343

Bragg, Braxton, 258; biographical data, 343

Brandeis, Louis D., 327; biographical data, 343

Brannan, Charles F., 87*n;* biographical data, 344

Brannan Plan, 87, 87*n,* 242–43, 243*n*

Brazil: undeveloped areas in, 63; undeveloped resources in, 201–2

Bridges, Alfred Benton (Harry), 243, 244; biographical data, 344

Britain: 1956 visit to, 25, 26; education in, 335; and gold, 77; government of, 151; natural scenery in, 314; polls in, 212–13; Privy Council of, 137; and trade, 160; traditional strategy of, 272

Brooks, Ralph G., 220; biographical data, 344

Brown, Edmund Gerald (Pat), 306; biographical data, 344

Brownell, Herbert, 35, 135; biographical data, 344

Bryan, William Jennings, 77, 125, 162, 181–82; biographical data, 344

Buchanan, James, 136, 259; biographical data, 344

Buddhists, 315

Bulgaria: possibility to save, 68; Soviet control of, 67

Bunche, Ralph, 232, 232*n,* 315; biographical data, 344

Burr, Aaron, 225; biographical data, 344

business: big vs. small, 60–62; mergers, 60; and politics, 227; and Republican Party, 226; Truman's relations with, 22; and unions, balance between, 53–54

Butler, Nicholas Murray, 309; biographical data, 344

Butler, Paul, 17; biographical data, 344

Byrnes, James F., 326; biographical data, 344

cabinet, Truman's, 326–27

Caesar, Augustus, 103

Caesar, Julius, 95, 103, 323; biographical data, 345

campaigns, political: attacks in, Truman's reputation for, 220; character assassination in, 198; money and, 223–24; personal matters in, avoiding, 137–38; Presidential. *See* Presidential campaign(s); television and, 219; Truman's participation in, 218–20, 298–99; union contributions to, 55, 244

Campbell, James, 146*n*

Canada: education in, 335; oil in, 253; U.S. relations with, 74, 75

capitalism, 333

Carey, James B., 55; biographical data, 345

Carlisle, John G., 128*n*

Carnegie, Andrew, 333; biographical data, 345

Casey, Lawrence B., 316*n;* biographical data, 345

Catholic church, 210; concerns of, in 1956, 28; and Democratic Party, 154; and government, control of, 153–54; Presidential candidate from, 153, 210–12, 316; suppression of historical writings by, 96–97

Cato the Elder, 102; biographical data, 345

Cato the Younger, 102–4

Caudle, T. Lamar, 217*n;* biographical data, 345

Central Intelligence Agency (CIA), 23–24, 218, 260

change, people's desire for, 229

Charles XII (King of Sweden), 73; biographical data, 345

checks and balances: farmers and, 91; in republic, 106

Chiang Kai-shek, 241; biographical data, 345

Chief Justice: position of, 110; and President, 111

children, of President, difficulties faced by, 274–76, 308–10. *See also* grandchildren

China: aid to, 87; dictatorship in, 73; division of, 241; evaluation of, 240–42; General Marshall in, 325; people of, 315; and Soviet Union, 73, 318

Christianity, moral code of, 289

church: business property of, 336–37; and state, separation of, 153–54, 210–11, 316. *See also* Catholic church

Churchill, Sir Winston: biographical data, 345; discussions about atomic bomb, 2–3; and post-World War II agreements, 68; relations with Truman, 23, 25; on Russians, 70, 272; visit to White House, 136; on World War II, 98

Cicero, Marcus Tullius, 95; biographical data, 345

Civilian Conservation Corps (CCC), 127

civil rights, 108–10, 231–32

Civil War, U.S., 25, 292; attempts to prevent, 136; causes of, 146; generals in, 323; period after, 66; and two-party system, 152; writings on, 94–95

Clark, John D., 128; biographical data, 345–46

Clark, Mark, 252*n,* 290*n;* biographical data, 346

Clark, Tom, 4*n*

Clausewitz, Karl von, 196

Clay, Henry, 142, 225; biographical data, 346

Cleveland, Grover, 125; abuse of, 44; biographical data, 346; children of, 309; fiscal policies of, 83, 128*n;* second administration of, 162

Cody, John P., 316*n;* biographical data, 346

Cold War: accommodation in, suggestion for, 267–68; cause of, 68, 91, 273; education as weapon in, 73; Institute on the Strategy of, 227; race in, 209–10

colonialism, 250

Columbus, Christopher, 314

common man. *See* little fellow

communications problem, in foreign relations, 75–76

communism, 67, 210, 333; in Americas, 202; in Arab world, 253; vs. capitalism, 333; challenge from, 339; Nixon and, 198; vs. religion, 291; as right, 232; vs. totalitarianism, 67

Comstock Lode, 105

Conant, James B., 6*n;* biographical data, 346

Confucius, 315; biographical data, 346

Congress, 106; and courts, 328; Eightieth, 273, 298; and Federal Reserve,

49; and former Presidents, relations between, 14–15; and labor movement, 106; leaders of, 329; opposition, 18–20, 281, 297, 302; Presidency compared with, 110; and President, relations between, 92, 111; Presidential candidates from, 142; Presidential vetoes and, 19–20; President's recommendations to, 297; seniority in, 106–7. *See also* House of Representatives; Senate

Congressional Record, 78

Constitution, 328; First Amendment of, 154

Constitutional Convention, 312

consumer, unorganized, 58

Continental Congress, 104

convention(s), Democratic Party, 221–23; 1948, 132; 1952, 39; 1956, 37–39

Convention of 1818, 331*n*

Coolidge, Calvin, 146, 146*n,* 259; biographical data, 346

cooperatives, 85; taxation of, 337

correspondence, Truman's, 21–22, 174–75, 214, 256–57, 262

cost of living, 61

courts, 234–35; Congress and, 328; two-party system and, 327–28

cultural exchanges, 285

currency, contraction and expansion of, 80

Czechoslovakia: history of, 73; possibility to save, 68; Soviet control of, 67, 69

daily routine, Truman's, 164

dams, 334

Daniel, Clifton Truman, 275*n*

Daniel, E. Clifton, 307*n,* 308; biographical data, 346

Daniel, Harrison Gates, 275*n*

Daniel, Thomas Washington, 275*n*

Daniel, William Wallace, 275*n*

Daughters of the American Revolution (DAR), 285, 314

Davis, Richard Harding, 284, 284*n;* biographical data, 346

Dead Sea Scrolls, 96–97

debt(s): national. *See* national debt; political, 224; private, 82

decision-making: on atomic bomb, 206–7; knowledge of history and, 321; popularity vs. correctness in, 100; Presidential, 98–100, 177, 218, 262–63; Truman's approach to, 320–21

Declaration of Independence, 105

Defense Department, 208; and U.S. economy, 60

De Gaulle, Charles: biographical data, 347; domestic policies of, 252; and nuclear program of France, 160, 161*n;* post-retirement relations with, 23

democracy: adversity and, 279; first major experiment in, 103; meaning of word, 124; and New England town meeting, 105; vs. republic, 105–6; Truman on, 105; two-party system and, 227

Democratic Party: 1948 convention, 132; 1952 convention, 39; 1956 convention, 37–39; and Catholic church, 154; chairmen of, 154–55; characteristics of, 152, 155; conventions of, 222–23; current state of, 17–18; and farmers, 86; and foreign policy, 160; and former President, 17; leader of, 16–17; liberalism in, shades of, 124; liberals and, 224–25; next Presidential nominee of, speculation about, 13–14; nomination of Adlai Stevenson, 31–32, 32*n,* 35; policy-making in, 154; presidential candidates from, 162, 181–82, 305–7; recommendation for, 231; vs. Republican Party, ideological differences between, 104; South and, 226; viewpoint of, 158

Democratic Republican Party, 225

Democrats of the South (Dixiecrats; Shivercrats), 19, 153, 246

Department of Agriculture, 242–43

Department of Justice, 59

Dewey, Thomas E., 135; biographical data, 347

Dibelius, Otto, 290; biographical data, 347

dictatorship, 53, 55–56, 250; in China, 73; in labor, preventing, 58; precautions against, 111

diet, Truman's, 118, 164–65

diplomatic language, 75

dislikes, Truman's, xix

Dixiecrats, 19, 246

doctors: public attitudes toward, 156; shortage of, 235–36; Truman on, 119–20

dollar diplomacy, 252

Dominican Republic, dictator of, 10*n*

Douglas, Helen Gahagan, 197, 245, 245*n;* biographical data, 347
Dulles, Allen, 23*n,* 24; biographical data, 347
Dulles, John Foster, 135; biographical data, 347
Dutch, evaluation of, 252

East Asia. *See* Orient
Eastern Europe: prospects for liberation of, 68, 72–73; Soviet control of, 67, 69; U.S. offers of aid to, 75–76. *See also* specific countries
East Germany, 248, 269
economic development: and peace, 74; preserving, 233
economy: controls built into, 334; defense and, 60
education: adult, 113; as Cold War weapon, 73; federal aid to, 335; fundamental, 277, 319; higher, 234; tenure for teachers, 338–39
educational background, Truman's, 112–13
Edwards, Willard, xviii
Egypt, 251–52
Einstein, Albert, 7*n,* 8; biographical data, 347
Eisenhower, Dwight David: advantage in presidential campaign, 33, 39; biographical data, 347; career of, 130*n;* and civil rights, 108*n;* criticism of, 131*n;* Democratic overtures toward, 34*n,* 130*n,* 130–32, 131*n,* 132*n;* discourteous attitude toward Truman, 134; and European situation, 69; friendship with Truman, 132–33; greatest accomplishment of, 331; on inauguration day, 134, 134*n,* 239–40; at Marshall funeral services, 168–70; as minority president, 159; praise for, 130*n;* and press conferences, 300; reconciliation with Truman, 134*n;* reelection of, 40–41, 302; religious affiliation of, 292*n;* as soldier, 324; as tool of Republicans, 133, 135; Truman's campaign against, 133–34, 183, 220–21; vetoes by, 297, 298. *See also* Eisenhower administration
Eisenhower, John D., 310; biographical data, 347
Eisenhower administration: and discrediting of previous administration, 14;

disregard for scientists, 209; drive for peace, 160; and fiscal policies, 128; policies in opposition to Truman's, 138–39
elder statesmen: consulting with, 182; work done by, 142. *See also* former President(s)
Elizabeth II (Queen of Great Britain), 25–26, 137, 294–96; biographical data, 348
employment, 339
espionage, Truman on, 23*n*–24*n*
Ethiopia, U.N. role in, 274, 274*n,* 321
Europe: 1956 trip to, 25–30. *See also* specific countries
exercise, Truman and, 117–18, 123

family: President's, difficulties faced by, 308–10; raising of, 114
Farley, James, 154; biographical data, 348
farmers: as checks and balances, 91; paying not to produce, 90–91; voting patterns of, 86
farming, 85–91, 242–43; ever-normal granary, 86–87; family farm, 85–86, 90, 242; horses vs. mules, 168; migrant labor and, 87–89; overproduction in, 86–87, 332; protection of, 91; in Soviet Union, 85; subsidies in, 90–91, 242; Truman's experience in, 166, 167*n*
farm organizations, 243
Faubus, Orval, 108*n;* biographical data, 348
Federal Deposit Insurance Corporation, 51
Federal Housing Administration, objective of, 47, 51
Federalists, 225
Federal Labor Relations Board, 55
Federal Reserve Act, purpose of, 45–46
Federal Reserve Bank of New York, 46–47, 128
Federal Reserve Board: Congress and, 49; money issued by, 80; President and, 48; Truman and, 48–50, 296; Woodrow Wilson and, 45–46, 77, 292
Federal Trade Commission, 59
Fender, Leonard, 130*n*
Fermi, Enrico, 6*n;* biographical data, 348
Ferrell, Robert, 2, 4*n*

Fillmore, Millard, 136, 147, 258; biographical data, 348; son of, 309
financial policy. See monetary policy
First Amendment, 154
Flemming, Arthur S., 118; biographical data, 348
foods, Truman's favorite, 164–65
food surplus, 86–87, 118, 332
foreign affairs: communications problem in, 75–76; President and, 34; Truman's evaluation of, 201–2, 240–42, 248–54
foreign aid, 73–74; to communist countries, 87; to Soviet satellites, 75–76
foreign policy: bipartisanship in, 138; Democrats and, 160; domestic interests and, 63–64
former President(s): and Congress, relations between, 14–15; consultations with, 136, 182; and continuity in government, 136; influence of, 14; ingratitude toward, 204; letters to, 21–22; neglect of, 203; pension for, xv. See also retirement, Truman's
Former Presidents' Act, xv
Formosa (Taiwan), 241
France: 1956 visit to, 25, 27; and gold, 77; government of, 151–52; as great nation, 162; as nuclear power, 160–61, 161n; work ethic in, 252
Franco, Francisco, 10, 56, 250–51; biographical data, 348
Frank, Richard, 2
Frankfurter, Felix, 247; biographical data, 348
freedom: vs. full employment, 339; vs. peace, 114, 160
free enterprise, 60, 62, 335
Freeman, Douglas Southall, 95; biographical data, 348
Fuchs, Klaus, 3; biographical data, 348

Gallatin, Albert, 293; biographical data, 348
Gallup, George Horace, 213; biographical data, 348
Gandhi, Mahatma, 141; biographical data, 348
Gardner, Erle Stanley, 93; biographical data, 348
Garfield, James, 259; biographical data, 349

general(s): ability to plan, 324–25; battle of, 323–24; vs. President, 194
Genghis Khan, 65–66, 242, 330; Russians compared with, 69
George VI (King of Great Britain), 295; biographical data, 349
Germany: 1956 visit to, 26; division after World War II, 68, 271; East, 248, 269; future of, 248–49, 314; people of, 252, 314
Glass, Carter, 83; biographical data, 349
gold, 76–78; Soviet mining of, 79–80
Gore, Albert Arnold, 49; biographical data, 349
government: as arbiter, 55; branches of, relations among, 110–11; British, 151; checks and balances in, 106; and church, separation of, 153–54; continuity in, 14–15, 136, 312; cost of, 293; financial policy of, 45–51, 77, 80–81; French, 151–52; ideals of, 105; liberals in, history of, 124–25; as monitor, 53–54; most powerful men in, 101, 110; regulation by, vs. self-regulation, 62; regulatory bodies in, 334; U.S., 313, 328, 334; taxation, 337; young people's interest in, 112
government contracts, 60
governors, as presidential candidates, 142, 147
Graham, Wallace H., 118, 120n, 120–21; biographical data, 349
grandchildren, Truman's, 275–79, 283, 308; advice to, 318; and public service, 319
Grandview farm, 166, 167n
Grant, Ulysses S., 39–40, 131, 259, 302, 331; biographical data, 349; children of, 309
Gronchi, Giovanni, 25; biographical data, 349
guided-missile technology, 208
Gustav II (Gustavus Adolphus), 211; biographical data, 349

Haile Selassie, 274; biographical data, 349
Hamilton, Alexander: biographical data, 349; vs. Jefferson, 124; theory of government, 104
Hanna, Mark, 100; biographical data, 349

Harding, Warren G., 46, 146, 259; biographical data, 350
Harriman, Edward H., 333; biographical data, 350
Harriman, W. Averell, 279–80; biographical data, 350; Truman's backing of, 37–38
Harrison, Benjamin, 44; biographical data, 350
Harrison, William Henry, 258; biographical data, 350
Hartke, Rupert Vance, 220; biographical data, 350
Hawaii, 318
Hayes, Rutherford B., 145, 259; biographical data, 350
health, Truman's, 118–19
health policies, 156–57, 233–34, 286
Hebrews, 315. *See also* Jews
hero worship, 302
Heuss, Theodor, 26; biographical data, 350
Hillman, Sidney, 55; biographical data, 351
Hillman, William, xv–xviii, 2; biographical data, 351
Hindus, 315
history: cycles in, 255, 280; education in, 319; evaluation of writings, 94–98; knowledge of, and decision-making, 321; propaganda in, 94–96, 98; of Roman Empire, 102–4; source material in, 96; Truman's interest in, 94–95; Truman's knowledge of, 143; verdict of, 258; viewpoint of, 98
Hitler, Adolf, 10, 249; biographical data, 351; invasion of Russia, Truman's suggestion after, xix, xvi
hobbies, Truman's, 78–79
Hoffa, James R., 55, 57, 243–44; biographical data, 351
Holmes, Oliver Wendell, 327; biographical data, 351
Hoover, Herbert: biographical data, 351; cause of troubles of, 176; evaluation of, 177; first meeting with, 172–74; as presidential candidate, 147; Truman's relations with, 136, 172–74, 176
Hopkins, Harry L., 72; biographical data, 351
hospital(s): shortage of, 235–36; Truman's stay in, 121–22

house, Truman's, in Independence, 166
House of Representatives, 106; members of, as presidential candidates, 142, 147
housing, 62, 233
Hughes, Charles Evans, 36; biographical data, 351
Hughes, Emmet, 133*n*
Humphrey, George M., 47; biographical data, 351
Humphrey, Hubert H., 132*n;* biographical data, 351; evaluation of, 305
Hungary, Soviet control of, 67, 69
Huntington, Collis P., 105
Hutcheson, William L., 55; biographical data, 352
hydrogen bomb. *See* atomic bomb

IBM Corporation, 22–23
Ickes, Harold, 132*n*
idealists, 266
illnesses, Truman's, 118–19
impeachment: Lincoln's, risk for, 43; right of, 7
imperialism, 250
Incas, history of, 97
income-tax system, Truman's proposal for, 335–36
inequalities, social, 104–5
inflation, 274; interest rates and, 50
information: Central Intelligence Agency as source of, 23–24; post-retirement sources of, 24, 78–79, 92–93; Presidential access to, 23–24, 92, 218, 260
Institute on the Strategy of the Cold War, 227
interest rates: and inflation, 50; Presidential control of, 51; on road bonds, cutting, 83
Interstate Commerce Commission, 334
investments, protection of, 252–53
investors, and workers, balance between, 54–55
Irreconcilables, 41, 44–45, 125
isolationism, 256
Israel, 252; future of, 317
Italy: 1956 visit to, 25; and Yugoslavia, division between, 69

Jackson, Andrew, 124, 126, 225, 259, 292; biographical data, 352; and Chief Justice, 111; and Democratic convention, 221; successor of, 258, 311;

successor of, difficulty in finding, 41; and United States Bank, 49
Jackson, Thomas (Stonewall), 323; biographical data, 352
Jacobson, Edward, 316; biographical data, 352
Japan: decision to use atomic bomb against, 1–2, 4–5; future of, 317–18; MacArthur's administration of, 194; Soviet Union and, 271; surrender of, atomic bomb and, 71
Japanese Americans, 318
Jefferson, Thomas, 105, 292; and John Adams, 135; biographical data, 352; career of, 147, 225; interest in weather, 79; papers of, 203; philosophy of, 124; successor of, 258; theory of government, 104
Jenner, William Ezra, 133; biographical data, 352
Jews: and Arabs, 317; resettlement in Palestine, 252, 252n
Johnson, Andrew, 329; biographical data, 352
Johnson, Louis Arthur, 6n; biographical data, 352
Johnson, Lyndon Baines, 200; biographical data, 352; defeated by Kennedy, 13n; as Senate leader, 16
Juliana (Queen of the Netherlands), 25–26; biographical data, 353
justice, administration of, 234–35
justices: great, 327; two-party system and, 327–28

Kefauver, Estes, 35n, 222; biographical data, 353
Keller, Kaufman T., 208, 208n; biographical data, 353
Kennedy, John Fitzgerald, 211–12; biographical data, 353; evaluation of, 305; funeral of, 134n; political maneuvers of, 153n; as Presidential nominee, 13n
Kennedy, Joseph, 245n
Keyserling, Leon H., 128; biographical data, 353
Khan, Liaquat Ali, 290
Khrushchev, Nikita, 227n, 318, 340; biographical data, 353
King, Ernest J., 69, 324; biographical data, 353
Know-Nothing Party, 146n

Knox, Frank, 261; biographical data, 353
Korean War, 160; conflicting advice on, 99; decision-making in, 321; United Nations and, 273–74, 321

labor movement, 52–58, 243–44; and Congress, 106; democratization of, 58; leaders of, 55; and sales taxes, opposition to, 337; and standard of living, concern for, 54; strikes, 247–48. See also unions
labor party, possibility for, 56, 228
La Follette, Robert M., 124, 229; biographical data, 353
Landrum-Griffin Act, 53n
Laurence, William L., 2, 2n, 5–6, 207; biographical data, 353
laws: antitrust, 60; interpreting, 52; labor, states and, 58; origin of, 297–98
lawsuit, against Truman, by steel companies, 111n, 248
leader(s): of business, 280; great, 145; ingratitude toward, 204; moral, 291; pre-testing of, 144; program of, 224
leadership: elite class and, 104; labor, 55; and public service, 62; in U.S., 142; world, 141–42, 255–56, 311–12, 317
League of Nations: and Ethiopia, 274n; opposition to, 45n; upset of, 273
Leahy, William D., 23; biographical data, 353–54
Lee, Robert E., 95, 323; biographical data, 354
legislation. See laws
Legislative branch: President as part of, 297; and Supreme Court, 110. See also Congress
Lend-Lease program, 270
Lenin, Vladimir I., 66; biographical data, 354
Leninism, vs. Marxism, 67
León, Pedro de Creza de, 97n
letters, 21–22; vilifying, 257
Lewis, John L., 54, 244; biographical data, 354
liberal(s): among Republicans, 152; and Democratic Party, 224–25; in government, history of, 124–25; meaning of word, 124; synthetic, 1, 4, 123–24
liberalism: in Constitution, 328; in Democratic Party, shades of, 124; Truman and, 128–29, 129n

Liberty Bonds, 46–47
Lilienthal, David E., 6*n;* biographical
 data, 354
Lincoln, Abraham, 292; assassination of,
 41; biographical data, 354; generals of,
 323; impeachment of, risk for, 43; as
 Jefferson Democrat, 105; philosophy of,
 125; on slavery, 292; son of, 309; Southern attitude toward, 226; wife of, 310
Lincoln, Robert Todd, 309; biographical
 data, 354
Lippmann, Walter, 138, 266–68, 270,
 270*n;* biographical data, 354
litigation, 234–35
little fellow, concern for, 51–52, 54, 62,
 129, 155; Democratic Party and, 231;
 personal experiences and, 167–68;
 President's responsibility and, 91
Lodge, Henry Cabot, 45, 130*n;* biographical data, 354
Long, Huey: biographical data, 355; and
 character assassination, 198
López Mateos, Adolfo, 199–200; biographical data, 355
Loveless, Herschel C., 220; biographical
 data, 355
Lovett, Robert A., 261; biographical data,
 355
loyalty, Truman's, xix
Luther, Martin, 153; biographical data,
 355

MacArthur, Douglas, 193–97; and administration of Japan, 194; biographical
 data, 355; China policy of, 255; defiant
 position of, 196, 211; dismissal of,
 opposition to, 197–98; McClellan compared with, 8; superiority complex of,
 194
Macmillan, Harold, 160; biographical
 data, 355
MacVeagh, Franklin, 83*n*
Madison, James, 147, 203, 258; biographical data, 355
magazines, 93
Manhattan Project, 3, 326
Marshall, George C., 325–26; accused as
 traitor, 35, 133, 183; biographical data,
 356; funeral services for, 168–70;
 papers of, 326; on Soviet satellites, 75;
 and Truman's memoirs, xvii; in World
 War II, 324

Marshall, John, 111*n;* biographical data,
 356
Marshall, Thomas R., 148; biographical
 data, 356
Marshall Plan, 270, 288, 313; offered to
 Czechoslovakia, 67
Martin, William McChesney, 48, 50, 296;
 biographical data, 356
Marx, Karl, 66–67; biographical data, 356
Marxist program, 66–67
Masaryk, Jan, 67*n;* biographical data,
 356
materialism, 284; material success, and
 altruism, 278
Mays, John, 172
McAdoo, William Gibbs, 83*n*
McCabe, Thomas B., 48–49; biographical
 data, 356
McCarran, Patrick A., 77; biographical
 data, 356
McCarthy, Joseph R., 133, 229; biographical data, 356; and character assassination, 198; slander of Truman, 197
McClellan, George B., 8, 194, 197; biographical data, 356–57
McKinley, William, 100; biographical
 data, 357; biography of, 96
McKinney, Frank E., 35; biographical
 data, 357
McNarney, Joseph T., 252*n*
Meany, George, 55; biographical data,
 357
medicine, developments in, 286
Mediterranean Sea, and power-generation
 program, 317
Mellon, Andrew, 46, 84; biographical
 data, 357
melting pot, 285, 313–15
memoirs, Truman's, xvii
memoranda, Truman's use of, 262–63
Mesopotamian valley, development of,
 317
Mexican War, 323
Mexico: 1947 visit to, 200; as asset to
 U.S., 76; civilization of, 314; migrant
 farm workers from, 87–89; President
 of, visit with, 199–200; relations with,
 74–75
middle class, health care for, 233
Middle East: evaluation of situation in,
 251; future of, 317; oil in, 253. *See
 also* Arabia

Middle West, philosophy of, 287
migrant farm labor, 87–89
military forces, 208
military personalities: role in emergencies, 194. *See also* general(s)
military service, 319
minority groups, Truman's relations with, 21–22, 167
Mississippi, sales tax in, 337
Missouri: sales tax in, 337; and settlement of West, 287–88, 332
Missourians, 294
Missouri Compromise, repeal of, 259
Mohammedans (Muslims), 315
Mollet, Guy, 25; biographical data, 357
Molotov, Vyacheslav M., 72; biographical data, 357
monarchy, 55; republic compared with, 144
monetary policy, 45–51, 77; Eisenhower administration and, 128; gold and, 76–80; national debt and, 80–81; Presidential interest in, 82–84; Franklin Roosevelt and, 126–29, 292; Theodore Roosevelt and, 83, 128; Truman and, 274, 296. *See also* dollar diplomacy
money: issuing, 80; and political campaigns, 223–24; as root of all evil, 53
Monroe, James, 147, 203, 257; biographical data, 357
Monticello, 79
Moody Bible Institute, 288
moral code, 277–78; in Americas, 202, 316; religion and, 289, 291
Morgan, J. Pierpont, 128, 128*n;* biographical data, 357
Morgan Oil and Refining Company, 253*n*
Morgenthau, Henry, 128; biographical data, 357
Moro, Aldo, 25; biographical data, 358
Morse, Wayne, 331; biographical data, 358
Mossadegh, Mohammed, 251; biographical data, 358
Mountbatten, Philip, Duke of Edinburgh: biographical data, 358; visit with, 25–26
Mr. Citizen (book), xvii–xviii; interview process for, xviii
Mr. President (book), xv–xvi
Murphy, Paul, 87*n;* biographical data, 358
Murray, Philip, 55; biographical data, 358

Murrow, Edward R., 135; biographical data, 358
Mussolini, Benito, 10, 274*n;* biographical data, 358
mystery novels, 93, 167

Nasser, Gamal Abdel, 251; biographical data, 358
National Baptist Convention, 109; Truman's speech to, 122
national debt: vs. assets, 81; components of, 82; cost of servicing, 47; increase in, 293; management of, 82; reduction of, 47, 80–81
National Farmers Union, 242
National Labor Relations Act (Wagner Act), 243
Native Americans (Indians), 66, 314
natural resources, 74; vs. gold, 77; of U.S., 232–33
nature, Truman and, 166
negotiations, vs. litigation, 234–35
Nehru, Jawaharlal, 29, 29*n,* 69, 141, 160; biographical data, 358
neighbors, willingness to help, 278, 288
Nevins, Allan, 95, 95*n;* biographical data, 358
newspapers, critique of, 98
Nile, development of, 317
Nimitz, Chester W., 324; biographical data, 358
Nitze, Paul, 267; biographical data, 358
Nixon, Richard M.: biographical data, 359; campaign tactics of, 197*n,* 198*n,* 220, 245*n;* and communism, 198; on MacArthur's dismissal, 198; misgivings for, 197, 199; relations with Truman, 244–45; slander of Truman, 35; as Vice President, 149
Nobel Peace Prizes, 9*n*
nonpartisanship, 138
normalcy, 229
Norris, George William, 229; biographical data, 359
North Atlantic Treaty Organization (NATO): objective of, 28, 160; in Spain, 251; U.S. Congress and, 270
Nourse, Edwin G., 128; biographical data, 359
Noyes, David M., xv, xvii–xviii, 2; advice to Truman, 177*n;* biographical data, 359
nuclear bomb. *See* atomic bomb

oil market, 253
Old Testament, 319
Oppenheimer, J. Robert, 6, 6*n;* biographical data, 359; disregard for, 209
optimism, 256, 316
Oregon Territory Settlement, 331*n*
Orient: evaluation of, 240–42; future of, 317–18. *See also* China; Japan
Owen-Glass Act, 45*n*

Paderewski, Ignace Jan, 73; biographical data, 359
Paine, Thomas, 154*n*
Pakistan, 290
Palestine, Jewish resettlement in, 252, 252*n*
Panic of 1837, 226
Panic of 1892–93, 127–28, 128*n*
Panic of 1929, cause of, 84
Parker, Alton B., 181; biographical data, 359
partisanship, avoiding, 138
patrician class, 104
Patterson, Robert Porter, 8, 261, 327; biographical data, 359
peace, 65–66; at any price, 160; associations important for, 136–37; Eisenhower administration's drive for, 160; factors for, 74; fighting for, 114–15; vs. freedom, 114, 160; issue of, in 1956, 33; prospects for, 114–15; U.S. role in, 330
pension, for former Presidents, xv
Pepper, Claude, 132*n*
Perry, Matthew C., 317
Pershing, John J., 169, 324; biographical data, 359
personal information, on Truman, 117–23, 163–68, 213–14, 319–20
personal philosophy, Truman's, 256
Peru, 314
Philippines, 318
Phoenicians, 209
physical fitness: Truman and, 117–18, 123; young people and, 156–57
Pierce, Franklin, 136, 146, 146*n,* 259; biographical data, 359
Pineau, Christian Paul, 25; biographical data, 359
Pius XII (Pope), 25, 28, 290–91; biographical data, 359
Pizarro, Francisco, 97; biographical data, 359

Plutarch, 96; biographical data, 360
Point IV Program, 65, 75, 234, 286–88, 313
Poland: history of, 73; possibility to save, 68; Soviet control of, 67, 69
politician(s): adversity and, 279–80; definition of, 131. *See also* leader(s)
politics: personal bitterness in, 137; Truman's pride in, 94*n*
Polk, James K., 145–46; biographical data, 360
polls, 212–13
Pompey the Great, 323; biographical data, 360
population growth: and economic expansion, 233; issues related to, 62–63, 74
postwar message, Truman's first, 129, 129*n*
Potsdam Conference, 70, 271; discussions of atomic bomb at, 2–4
Powers, Francis Gary, 23*n*
prayer, written by Truman, 122, 122*n*
President(s): abuses of, 43–44; aimless, 258–59; burden of duties of, 175–76; candidates for, 142–43, 146–48, 153, 181–82, 305–7; Catholic candidate for, 153, 210–12, 316; character of, 150–51; and Chief Justice, 111; choice of, 149–50; and Congress, relations between, 92, 111, 297; contemplation periods of, 91–92; cycles of, 280; decision-making by, 98–100, 177, 218, 262–63; descendents of, difficulties faced by, 274–76, 308–10; duties of, 297; eligibility for, 171; expectations from, 149; and Federal Reserve, 48; and foreign affairs, 34. *See former* President(s); former governors as, 142; vs. generals, 194; great, threats to, 43; impact on people's thinking, 172; information sources of, 23–24, 92, 218, 260; listening to people, 100, 260; and little fellow, responsibility for protecting, 91; and monetary policy, 51, 82–84; and opposition Congress, 18–20, 281, 302; and party, 226; popular, difficulty in finding successor for, 41; popularity of, 257; position of, 110; private papers of, 203; qualifications of, 143–44; recordings of lives of, 329; religion of, 291–92; security of, 214–15; statements of, full quotation of, 299–300,

301–2; strong, weak successors of, 331; successors of, difficulties in finding, 311; symbol of, 320; taking a chance in, 145; training for, 148; two-term limitation of, 246; understanding of, after retirement, 258; unfortunate choice of, 182; veto power of, 19–20, 158–59, 297–98; willful, protection against, 7; wives of, 310; as world leader, 255–56, 311–13
Presidential campaign(s): of 1948, 86, 219; of 1952 and 1956, 31–41, 179, 265–66
press, influence of, 230–31
press conferences, 214, 230–31, 299–301; full quotations in, 299–302; indirect quotations in, 300; radio and television in, 301
pressures, Truman's dealing with, 123
primaries: Presidential, 219, 222; state, 221–22
privacy, Truman and, 165, 320
propaganda: in history, 94–96, 98; Republican, 35, 159; Soviet, 71
property taxes, 336–37
Protestants, opposition to universal religion, 290
Proxmire, William A., 229; biographical data, 360
public service, 204; best example of, 261; Cato the Younger and, 102–3; educating young people about, 204–5; grandchildren and, 319; leadership and, 62
Puerto Ricans, 284–85
Puerto Rico, 330

Quirino, Elpidio, 173; biographical data, 360

race issues, 108–10, 315
radio: educational series on, 335; fireside chats, 301; as press-conference vehicle, 301
railroads, 334; strike, 248
Rayburn, Sam, 143; biographical data, 360; relations with Truman, 15–16, 38
Reader's Digest, 93
reading, Truman and, 93, 166–67, 319
Reconstruction, 43, 153, 226
Reconstruction Finance Corporation, objective of, 47
"red herring" incident, 300–1

Reed, James A., 45; biographical data, 360
Reformation, 210–11
religion(s), 320; vs. communism, 291; and moral code, 289, 291; of Presidents, 291–92; universal, 290–91. See also church
religious missions, 288–89; need for, 291
religious tolerance, in U.S., 289–90
republic, 105; checks and balances in, 106; vs. democracy, 105–6; ingratitude toward leaders in, 204; misrepresentation of rulers in, 44; monarchy compared with, 144; politics of government in, 53; Roman, 103
Republican Party: chairmen of, 154–55; characteristics of, 152; vs. Democratic Party, ideological differences between, 104; farmers voting for, 86; future of, 226; policy-making in, 154; present leader of, 225; propaganda of, 35, 159
Republicans: Eisenhower as tool of, 133, 135; and free enterprise, 60; liberals among, 152; in Franklin Roosevelt administration, 261; Truman's relations with, 22; viewpoint of, 158
retirement, Truman's, 13, 14, 17, 101–2, 174–75, 213–14, 316–17; correspondence in, 21–22, 174–75, 214, 256–57; decision regarding, 34–35, 41; information sources in, 24, 78–79, 92–93; neglect in, 203–4; readjustment in, 102; role in, 101–2; speaking engagements in, 262, 298–99, 316; visits in, 22–23
Reuther, Walter, 55; biographical data, 360
Revolutionary War: generals of, 323; history of, Truman's plan to write, 96–97
Ridgway, Matthew B., 195; biographical data, 360
Riga River, 80
right-to-work laws, 58
road bonds, cutting interest rates on, 83
Rockefeller, John D., 105, 333; biographical data, 360
Rogers, William P., 135, 285; biographical data, 360
Roman Empire, 66; downfall of, 281; history of, 102, 103–4; and Pax Romana, 255; Soviet Union compared with, 69

Romania, 73; possibility to save, 68;
Soviet control of, 67, 69
Roosevelt, Eleanor: biographical data,
360; on James Roosevelt's book, 206;
relations with Truman, 38*n*, 177*n*
Roosevelt, Elliott, 132*n*
Roosevelt, Franklin, Jr., 132*n*
Roosevelt, Franklin Delano, 41; abuse of,
44; achievements of, 125–27; admiration for, 125, 206; and atomic-bomb
development, 7–9; biographical data,
360–61; courtesy of, 136; erudition of,
94; European fondness for, 29–30;
family of, 309–10; fireside chats of,
301; fiscal policies of, 126–9, 292; and
Hoover, 174, 174*n;* on inauguration
day, 240; as leader of free world, 256;
as liberal, 124–25; and mystery novels,
93; and opposition Congress, 281;
relations with Truman, 94; Republicans in administration of, 261
Roosevelt, James, 132*n,* 205–6, 309;
biographical data, 361
Roosevelt, Theodore: biographical data,
361; children of, 309; election of, 181;
and fiscal policies, 83, 128; posing as
liberal, 124; posthumous understanding of, 258; successor of, 311
Ross, Charles Griffith, 93; biographical
data, 361
ruling class, attempt to make, 292
Rural Electrification Administration
(REA), 237
Russell, Lord John, 312; biographical
data, 361
Russians: Churchill's opinion of, 70, 272;
education of, 113; prospects for, 73,
249; Truman's opinion of, 33, 69, 315.
See also Soviet Union

Sahara Desert, development of, 63
sales tax, 337
Sampson, William T., 323–24; biographi-
cal data, 361
Saud, Ibn, 251; biographical data, 361
Sawyer, Charles, 111*n*
Schley, Winfield Scott, 324; biographical
data, 361
Schoeppel, Andrew F., 246; biographical
data, 361
Schwellenbach, Lewis Baxter, 149; bio-
graphical data, 361

Scott, Winfield, 131, 146*n,* 200, 323;
biographical data, 361; superiority
complex of, 194
sea water, program to change into fresh
water, 63
Secretary of Defense, 208; General Marshall as, 325
Secretary of State, as presidential candidate, 147*n*
Secretary of War, 208
Securities and Exchange Commission,
58–59, 247
Segni, Antonio, 25; biographical data, 361
Senate, 106; evolution of, 107; lack of
important voice in, 228–29; members
of, as presidential candidates, 142,
147; Truman's relations with, 92;
Truman's return to, 245–46
servants, Truman's, 163, 320
Sevilla-Sacasa, Don Guillermo, 170
Sherman, William Tecumseh, 323; biographical data, 361–62
Sherman Anti-Trust Act, 60
Shivercrats, 19
Siberia, 73, 80, 318
slavery, Lincoln on, 292
small town, Truman's preference for,
319–20
Smith, Alfred E., 136; biographical data,
362
snobbery, 171
Snyder, John Wesley, 48; biographical
data, 362
Souers, Sidney W., 23; biographical data,
362
South, and Democratic Party, 226
South America, 200–2; oil in, 253; undeveloped areas in, 63; United States of,
idea of, 202
Soviet Union: accommodation with, suggestion for, 267–68; aid to, 87; and
atomic bomb, 3, 3*n,* 5–6, 269; and
China, 73, 318; and Cold War, 91;
dealing with, Truman's recommendation for, 33, 69; education in, 113;
exploitation of neighbors, 66–67, 69;
farming in, 85; and Germany, 248–49,
269; gold mining in, 79–80; Hitler's
invasion of, Truman's suggestion after,
xix, xvi; improvement in, 339–40;
and Japan, 271; and Marxist program,
66–67; missionaries in, 289, 291;

propaganda against U.S., 71; prospects for, 73, 249, 315; race with, 209–10; satellite states of, 68–69, 72–73, 75–76; and Spain, 251; totalitarian state in, 67, 69, 315; and United Nations, 72; after World War II, 273; post-World War II agreements and, 68, 91, 271

Spaak, Paul-Henri: biographical data, 362; relations with Truman, 23, 25

Spain: future of, 250–51; U.S. relations with, 250

Spanier, John W., 195; biographical data, 362

Spanish-American War, 323–24; objectives in, 330

Speaker of the House, position of, 110

speaking engagements, Truman's, 262, 298–99, 316

special interests, 162; and Presidential vetoes, 19

speech, Truman's first, 299

staff, Truman's: choosing, 215–16; improving, 217

Stalin, Joseph: biographical data, 362; discussions about atomic bomb with, 2–3; and Hitler, 249; propaganda against U.S., 71; and United Nations, 72

standard of living: capitalism and, 333; helping people help themselves, 65; labor's concern for, 54; radical change in, 283–84

Standard Oil Company of New Jersey, 60–61

starvation, world, dealing with, 173

steel industry case, 111, 111n, 247–48

Stettinius, Edward R., 326; biographical data, 362

Stevens, Thaddeus, 43, 153, 329; biographical data, 362

Stevenson, Adlai E.: on atomic bomb, 179, 179n–80n, 206–7, 265; biographical data, 363; as Democratic nominee, 16; disassociation from Truman, 179; evaluation of, 177–78, 305; as governor of Illinois, 177; grandfather of, 36; grasp of domestic affairs, 34; meeting at Blackstone Hotel, 32–33, 180; meeting at Blair House, 35; nomination of, 31–32, 32n, 35; questioning Truman's honesty, 178, 178n; relations with Truman, 37; reluctance

about, 33–34, 39–40; Republican propaganda and, 35; in state primaries, 222; Truman's advice to, 33, 180–81

Stimson, Henry L., 3, 261, 326–27; and atomic bomb development, 8, 326; biographical data, 363

stock market, 58

Strauss, Lewis L., 6, 6n; biographical data, 363

strikes, 247; arbitration in, 247–48

Stryker, Lloyd Paul, 329; biographical data, 363

subsidies, farming, 90–91, 242

Suez Canal, 251

supermarkets, 61

superstitions, Truman and, 320

Supreme Court, and Legislative branch, 110

Symington, Stuart, 306–7; biographical data, 363

Taft, Robert A., 34, 246–47; biographical data, 363

Taft, William Howard, 181, 311; biographical data, 363

Taft-Hartley Act, 52–53, 57, 243–44

Taiwan (Formosa), 241

Tamerlane, 66, 330; biographical data, 363; Russians compared with, 69

tax(es): cooperatives and, 337; duplication of, 236–37; expanding, 236; income, 335–36; local, 337; for medical purposes, 236; property, 336–37; reduction of, cut in federal spending and, 338; reduction of, vs. payment of national debt, 81; sales, 337; state, 337; Truman's proposal for reform, 335–37

Taylor, Myron Charles, 290; biographical data, 363

Taylor, Zachary, 18, 258, 281, 302, 323; biographical data, 363

teachers, tenure for, 338–39

Teamsters' Union, 243

television: educational series on, 335; and political campaigns, 219; as press-conference vehicle, 301

Teller, Edward, 6n

Tennessee Valley Authority (TVA), 9, 237

Thucydides, 96

Thurmond, J. Strom, 137; biographical data, 363
time management, Truman's, 123
Tito (Josip Broz), 69; biographical data, 364
"To Secure These Rights" (report), 232, 232*n*
totalitarianism, 333; vs. communism, 67; in Soviet Union, 67, 69, 315
Toynbee, Arnold J., 97–98, 98*n;* biographical data, 364
transportation system, 334–35
Treasury report, 78, 81
Trujillo Molina, Rafael Leónidas, 10*n;* biographical data, 364
Truman, Anderson, 278*n*
Truman, Bess: biographical data, 364; cooking skills of, 164; discussions with, 320
Truman, Margaret, 172, 296; biographical data, 364; marriage of, 307–8; sons of, 275*n*
Truman Library, 214; contributions to, 316
Tubby, Roger Wellington, 180; biographical data, 364
two-party system, 152; and courts, 327–28; and democracy, 227; future of, 224–25; importance of, 228; success of, 15. *See also* Democratic Party; Republican Party
Tyler, John, 136, 258; biographical data, 364; children of, 309

U-2 reconnaissance plane, downing of, 23*n*–24*n*
underprivileged persons. *See* little fellow
unemployment, 339
unions, 52–58, 243–44; banks compared with, 53; and business, balance between, 53–54; contributions to political campaigns, 244; control over, 247–48; dues, use for political purposes, 55, 244; regulation of, 57. *See also* labor movement
United Nations: China and, 241; continuity of, 302; founding of, 72; future of, 249; Korean War and, 273–74, 321; role of, 74–75; Soviet Union and, 72; and world leadership, 255
United States: and atomic bomb, development of, 5–6, 8–9, 326; cultural

development of, 285; European feelings toward (in 1956), 29, 30; expansion of, 330–31; future of, 232–37, 276, 312–13; government of, 313, 328, 334. *See also* government; history of, leadership personalities and, 329; leaders in, 142; main task of, 75; neighbors of, relations with, 74–75, 331; oil production in, 253, 253*n;* opinions about government of, 28; peace role of, 330; people of, 284–85, 313–15; religious tolerance in, 289–90; resources of, 232–33; responsibility of, 286; settlement of, 283–84, 287–88; Soviet propaganda against, 71; withdrawal after World War II, mistake of, 68–71; and world leadership, 255–56, 317
United States of North and South America, idea of, 202
university, head of, Truman on requirements for, 112–13

Van Buren, Martin, 41, 136, 225–26, 258, 311; biographical data, 364
Vandenberg, Arthur H., 261; biographical data, 364
Vandenberg, Hoyt S., 69; biographical data, 364
Vaughan, Harry, 168; biographical data, 365
Velde, Harold Himmel, 35; biographical data, 365
Venezuela, 253
vetoes, Presidential, 19–20, 158–59, 297–98
Vice President(s): candidates for, 149; exposure of, 148; as presidential candidates, 147–48, 147*n;* Truman as, 148
Vinson, Fred, 34*n,* 36, 247, 261; biographical data, 365; funeral of, 135
Voorhis, Horace Jeremiah (Jerry), 198, 245; biographical data, 365

Wagner Act, 243
walks, Truman's, 117–18, 123, 165
Wallace, Henry Agard, 86, 128, 176, 332; biographical data, 365
Wallenstein, Albrecht von, 211; biographical data, 365
war(s): avoiding, problem of, 255; Democratic administrations and, 159–60; horrors of, inability to learn from,

10–11; origins of, 10, 66; prevention of, 66; progress related to, 9–10; rehabilitation of defeated after, 65–66; religious, 289; response to, 277. *See also* specific wars

War Between the States. *See* Civil War, U.S.

Warren, Earl, 36, 327; biographical data, 365

Washington, George, 292; abuse of, 44, 323; biographical data, 365; interest in weather, 79; papers of, 203; religiosity of, 292

Washington, D.C., 167

water, policies regarding, 63, 317, 334

Watson, Thomas, 22–23; biographical data, 365

weapons, abolition of, 10

welfare, 339

Wellington, Duke of (Arthur Wellesley), 312; biographical data, 365

West: opening of, men responsible for, 331–32; settlement of, 283–84, 287–88

Western civilization, survival of, concern about, 27–28

Whistle Stop Campaign, 36, 205

White House: facilities of, 217–18; heads of state visiting, 136–37

Whitney, Alexander F., 54; biographical data, 365

Whittier, John Greenleaf, 70; biographical data, 365

Wilhelm II (Kaiser), 249

William Jewell College, speech at, 316, 331

Williams, G. Mennen, 306; biographical data, 365

Wilson, Woodrow, 125, 162, 292; abuse of, 44; administration following, 280; biographical data, 366; children of, 309; and decision-making, 99; election of, 181, 311; and Federal Reserve, 45–46, 77, 292; and fiscal policies, 83–84; and Irreconcilables, 41, 44–45, 125; and opposition Congress, 18

wives, of Presidents, 310

Woodin, William H., 83*n*, 84; biographical data, 366

Woodward, Sara, 26

Woodward, Stanley, 26; biographical data, 366

Worchester v. Georgia, 111*n*

workers: and investors, balance between, 54–55. *See also* labor movement

working conditions, predictions regarding, 276–77

Works Progress Administration, 127

world leadership, 141–42, 255–56, 311–12, 317

world peace. *See* peace

World War I: casualties in, 161*n;* generals in, 324

World War II: agreements after, 68, 70, 91, 271; Berlin Airlift, 99; Churchill on, 98; decision to use atomic bomb in, 1–2, 4–5; draft in, reports on registration for, 156; generals in, 324; Irreconcilables and, 44–45; objective in, 325; Pacific front, 71; Truman's postwar message, 129, 129*n;* U.S. after, 330; U.S. withdrawal after, mistake of, 68, 69–71, 273; victors in, altruism by, 313

Yalta agreement, 68

Year of Decision (book), xvii

Years of Trial and Hope (book), xvii

Young, E. Merl, 217*n;* biographical data, 366

Young, Solomon, 278*n*

young people: educating about public service, 204–5; physical fitness of, 156–57; talking to, 111–12, 114, 313; upbringing of, 114

Yugoslavia: and Italy, division between, 69; Soviet control of, 69

Zhukov, Georgi, 70; biographical data, 366

ISBN 0-8420-2920-6

9 780842 029209

90000 >